W9-BJV-163

Child Language—
An International Perspective

401.9
In8c

118833

DATE DUE			

CARL A. RUDISILL LIBRARY
LENOIR RHYNE COLLEGE

Child Language— An International Perspective

Selected Papers from the First International Congress for the Study of Child Language

Edited by
Philip S. Dale, Ph.D.
University of Washington
and
David Ingram, Ph.D.
University of British Columbia

WITHDRAWN
R. COLLEGE LIBRARY

CARL A. RUDISILL LIBRARY
LENOIR RHYNE COLLEGE

University Park Press
Baltimore

401.9
In 8c
118833
July 1980

The International Association for the Study of Child Language has now held four conferences: in Brno, Czechoslovakia, 1970; Florence, Italy, 1972; London, England, 1975; and Tokyo, Japan, 1978. The first three meetings were Symposia. The most recent was a Congress, reflecting the rapidly expanding interest in the field of child language development. This volume, which contains some of the papers from the Congress, is representative of many of the different aspects of language acquisition that are currently the focus of interest.

The first International Congress for the Study of Child Language was chaired by Fred C. C. Peng at the Ikenohata Bunka Center in Tokyo, August 7–12, 1978. The International Association for the Study of Child Language has much pleasure in acknowledging Fred Peng's contribution to the success of the Congress, the first gathering of the Association to be held in the Far East.

Natalie Waterson
President, International Association
for the Study of Child Language

UNIVERSITY PARK PRESS
International Publishers in Science, Medicine, and Education
300 North Charles Street
Baltimore, Maryland 21201

Copyright © 1981 by University Park Press

Typeset by University Park Press, Typesetting Division
Manufactured in the United States of America by The Maple Press Company.

All rights, including that of translation into other languages, reserved. Photomechanical reproduction (photocopy, microcopy) of this book or parts thereof without special permission of the publisher is prohibited.

Library of Congress Cataloging in Publication Data
International Congress for the Study of Child Language, 1st, Tokyo, 1978.
Child language, an international perspective.
Includes bibliographies and index. 1. Language acquisition—Congresses. I.
Dale, Philip S. II. Ingram, David, 1944– III. Title.
P118.I57   1978   401.9   80-24801
ISBN 0-8391-1608-X

Contents

Contributors

Lawrence Bartak, Ph.D.
Faculty of Education
Monash University
Clayton, Victoria 3168
Australia

Ben G. Blount, Ph.D.
Department of Anthropology
University of Georgia
Athens, Georgia 30602
U.S.A.

Katharine G. Butler, Ph.D.
Director, Division of Special Educa-
  tion and Rehabilitation
Syracuse University
805 South Crouse Avenue
Syracuse, New York 13210
U.S.A.

Nancy L. Cook, Ph.D.
Department of Curriculum and
  Instruction
University of Washington
Seattle, Washington, 98195
U.S.A.

Richard F. Cromer, Ph.D.
Medical Research Council Develop-
  mental Psychology Unit
Drayton House, Gordon Street
London WC1
England

Toni G. Cross, Ph.D.
Institute of Early Childhood
  Development
4 Madden Grove
Kew, Victoria 3101
Australia

Philip S. Dale, Ph.D.
Psychology Department
University of Washington
Seattle, Washington 98195
U.S.A.

Patrice French, Ph.D.
Department of Psychology
University of California
  at Los Angeles
405 Hilgard Avenue
Los Angeles, California
U.S.A.

Howard Goldstein, Ph.D.
Department of Psychology
  and Human Development
George Peabody College for Teachers
Vanderbilt University
Nashville, Tennessee 37203
U.S.A.

Marged Goode, B.Sc.
Faculty of Education
Monash University
Clayton, Victoria 3168
Australia

Alison Gopnik, Ph.D.
Department of Psychology
Oxford University
Oxford
England

Lyn R. Haber, Ph.D.
College of Education
University of Illinois
  at Chicago Circle
Chicago, Illinois 60680
U.S.A.

Camille Hanlon, Ph.D.
Department of Child Development
Connecticut College, Box 1488
New London, Connecticut 06320
U.S.A.

David Ingram, Ph.D.
Department of Linguistics
University of British Columbia
Vancouver, B.C. VGT 1W5
Canada

Katsutoshi Ito, M.A.
Foreign Language Department
Kanagawa University
3-27-1, Rokkakubashi, Kanagawa-ku
Yokohama, 246
Japan

Chieko Kobayashi, Ph.D.
Tezukayama Gakuin Junior College
Tezukayama, Osaka
Japan

Takeshi Koizumi, M.D.
Department of Psychiatry
Niigata University School of Medicine
1-757 Asahimachi, Niigata City, 951
Japan

Dong Jae Lee, M.A.
Department of East Asian Languages
University of Hawaii at Manoa
Honolulu, Hawaii 96822
U.S.A.

Barbara Lust, Ph.D.
College of Human Ecology
Cornell University
Ithaca, New York 14853
U.S.A.

Keith E. Nelson, Ph.D.
Department of Psychology
The Pennsylvania State University
University Park, Pennsylvania
U.S.A.

Els Oksaar, Prof. Dr. phil., Fil. dr.
General Linguistics
Hamburg University
Von Melle Park 6
2000 Hamburg 13
West Germany

Kenneth Reeder, Ph.D.
Faculty of Education
University of British Columbia
Vancouver, B. C. V6T 1W5
Canada

Karen L. Rembold
Department of Educational
   Psychology
University of Wisconsin—Madison
1025 West Johnson Street
Madison, Wisconsin
U.S.A.

Velta Rūķe-Draviņa, Fil. dr.
Department of Slavic and Baltic
   Languages
University of Stockholm
Institutionen för slaviska och
   baltiska språk
S-106 91 Stockholm
Sweden

Catherine E. Snow, Ph.D.
Graduate School of Education
Harvard University
Larsen Hall
Cambridge, Massachusetts 02138
U.S.A.

Ragnhild Söderbergh, Ph.D.
Child Language Research Institute
University of Stockholm, Box 6404
S-113 82 Stockholm
Sweden

Ursula Stephany, Ph.D.
Department of Linguistics
University of Cologne
5000 Cologne 41
West Germany

Midori Tanaka, Ph.D.
Ochanomizu University
1-1 Otsuka 1 chōme, Bunkyōku
Tokyo 112
Japan

Sagako Usuda, M.D.
Department of Psychiatry
Niigata University School of Medicine
1-757 Asahimachi, Niigata City, 951
Japan

Tatsuko Wakayama, Ph.D.
Department of Human Development
  and Family Studies
Cornell University
Ithaca, New York 14853
U.S.A.

Louise Cherry Wilkinson, Ed.D.
Department of Educational
  Psychology
University of Wisconsin—Madison
1025 West Johnson Street
Madison, Wisconsin
U.S.A.

Preface

On August 7, 1978, scholars from over 20 countries gathered in Tokyo, Japan, for the First International Congress for the Study of Child Language. The chapters in this book were selected from the papers delivered at the Congress and were revised for publication here. The Congress was sponsored by the International Association for the Study of Child Language and co-sponsored by the International Christian University Language Sciences Summer Institute. The Association, which initiated the *Journal of Child Language* (David Crystal, editor, published by Cambridge University Press) and the *Child Language Newsletter* (Patrice French, editor, published at the University of California, Los Angeles), serves to bring together scholars from fields as diverse as linguistics, psychology, speech and hearing, pediatrics, neurology, early childhood education, special education, sociology, and others. The Association previously has sponsored three primarily invitational symposia. The Tokyo meeting was the first International Congress to which scholars in all fields and countries were invited to submit papers. The Tokyo meeting was also the first meeting of the Association in the Orient.

The Organizing Committee for the Congress was chaired by Sei Nakazima, and the Steering Committee by Fred C. Peng, who also served as conference organizer. At the Congress the following officers were elected: President, Natalie Waterson, University of London, England; Vice-President, Sei Nakazima, University of Kyoto, Japan; Secretary, David Ingram, University of British Columbia, Canada; Treasurer, Terry Myers, University of Edinburgh, Scotland.

Selected for this volume were papers that represent the international and multidisciplinary nature of the study of child language. Selection of papers was a difficult task, and we wish to express our appreciation to the following individuals who helped select and edit papers: Katharine Butler, Patrick Griffiths, Barbara Lust, Jean Rondal, Maureen Shields, Natalie Waterson, Lynn Waterhouse, and Thelma Weeks. An additional volume of proceedings is being published by the Association itself, under the editorship of David Ingram, Fred C. Peng, and Philip Dale.

For many of the participants, the Congress provided an opportunity to experience what it must be like to be a young child surrounded by a linguistic community whose language is not yet known! The justly renowned hospitality of the Japanese people, and the superb organizational efforts of the conference organizer, Fred C. Peng, made possible the occurrence of personal and professional communication which is the goal of an international Congress. We are also grateful to the International Christian University for their administrative and other assistance, and to the Japan Foundation for a grant which made the keynote lectures possible.

Science, like music, is often supposed to be a universal language. The claim is not quite valid in either case. The long dominance of the German-Italian tradition in Western music obscured the possibility of other forms, although variations on this form existed in Russia, Spain, and other countries. But it was only in the twentieth century that we have come to recognize the richness of the world's musical traditions, and the very different musical "languages" of India, Bali, China, Southern Africa, etc. As outsiders, we often fail to understand or appreciate other musical traditions; it is only with patient study that we come to appreciate each system from within. Indeed, the different musical traditions have enriched each other, for example, Indian influences on Western classical and popular music. Something similar happens in science as well. A particular scientific community (which may be defined either by discipline or by country) shares an extensive network of assumptions about the nature of science, the selection of topics for research, the kinds of evidence considered most persuasive. Often these "pretheoretical notions," to use Kuhn's term, are implicit, not expressly stated, and this fact may make communication very difficult at first. The effort of communication, however, often makes assumptions explicit, in a process parallel to what the Swiss psychologist Jean Piaget has referred to as overcoming egocentrism. Such was the nature of this conference, and the source of its most enduring effects.

The next International Congress will be held in Vancouver, B.C., Canada, in 1981, hosted by the University of British Columbia.

SECTION I

Basic Processes of Development

Phonological and Syntactic Development

It is always a concern of careful scientists that the significance of new findings and theoretical advances be considered in relation to the historical and cultural setting in which they occur. A new point of view that provides fresh insights into an area may represent an accepted perspective at another time or in another culture. Similarly, intensive research within a closed community may produce sustained, cumulative progress, or it may be the result of narrow-mindedness and a general resistance to change.

The field of first language acquisition probably is as susceptible as any field to these pitfalls. It is easy to get caught up in the latest issue in one's own scholarly community, and to over-emphasize the developmental quality of the acquisition of one's own native language. This collection of papers on different aspects of phonology and grammar provides an excellent example of the richness and diversity of information that can be obtained from research that is conducted from an international perspective. Three points stand out in particular.

First, it is clear that the structural features of individual languages lend themselves to particular research questions. Rūķe-Draviņa, for instance, reports on the acquisition of lexical tone in Latvian, which is an important characteristic of a variety of languages, but not of English. Any significant theory of phonological development, of course, will need to account for lexical tone. Stephany's investigation of the development of verb morphology by Greek children shows that more specific findings can be obtained on the development of mood and aspect in a language in which mood and aspect are more directly marked in the grammar. Insight into the development of word order, and the child's awareness of constituent structure in general, is gained in the Lust and Wakayama paper on Japanese, a language that is left-embedding instead of right-embedding, as is English.

Second, these papers reflect some major research issues in language acquisition, particularly the need to place the development of language structure into a broader context. For example, the role of the input language is the central topic of two of the papers. Kobayashi provides a pioneering study of the child's acquisition of the standard and nonstandard dialects. Selecting Japanese tonal patterns as the particular feature to follow, she describes the differences between standard and nonstandard Japanese and then traces their acquisition by children who are exposed to both. Stephany, in her paper on the acquisition of verb morphology, also deals directly with the effects of how aspect is used in the mother's language. Additional papers on the influence of parental speech are found in Section IV. Another important issue is the psychological reality of grammatical structure, which is evaluated in the papers by Tanaka, and Lust and Wakayama. Tanaka examined, in a series of experiments, the ability of Japanese children to imitate and produce sentences that vary in length and semantic complexity. Lust and Wakayama used in their research sentences of similar length, but of varied constituent structure.

The third point concerns the methodology involved in studying first language acquisition. If there is any single feature that characterizes the field of child language, it is the diversity of research methods used (and also the feeling that even more methods are needed). Stephany and Tanaka, for example, both are interested in the development of the semantic features of verbs, but they approach the topic with separate methodologies. Stephany bases her observations on spontaneous language samples, whereas Tanaka uses an experimental task applied to cross-sectional samples of children. It is becoming increasingly clear in the field of language acquisition (as it is in child development in general, and indeed in the physical sciences in the form of the "uncertainty principle") that any one observation cannot be regarded as conclusive. The means by which we estimate the child's knowledge are so indirect and require so many assumptions about the collection of data, the analytic categories, the appropriate form for generalizations, etc., that the results may be attributable more to those methods and assumptions than to anything else. The only way we can increase our confidence in our conclusions is to support them with many different kinds of evidence. This is yet another reason why interdisciplinary research is needed.

Earlier, it was mentioned that the field of first language acquisition is one that easily could become narrow and nonproductive if it did not maintain an international perspective. The existence of diverse research of the kind exemplified in these papers, however, portends well for the current and future states of the field.

Dialectal Variation in Child Language

Chieko Kobayashi

Language acquisition, for many Japanese children, does not take place in a homogeneous linguistic environment, but in a heterogeneous one in which children develop grammars of their own as well as the ability to communicate competently with speakers who have different grammars. A heterogeneous linguistic environment for language acquisition is typically produced when the parents' dialect differs from the local dialect. Although the parents' model is considered to be normative at an early stage of a child's development, current studies show that each child continually restructures his grammar through his contact with other models including the model of his peer group. It is generally assumed that a child normally acquires his dialect pattern, including recent changes, from children slightly older than himself.[1]

Although Japan is a small country, Japanese dialects show considerable differences in phonology, particularly within systems of accentuation. The Tokyo dialect, which is the standard dialect of Japan, and the Kyoto dialect represent the two major accentual systems of Japanese. They differ markedly in basic accentual patterns as well as in accentual rules. The study of phonological development in a child who is exposed to both of these regional dialects through his parents' model and the local dialect will provide much information on the role of the linguistic environment and the effect of the speech of parents and peers in the construction of the child's grammar. Furthermore, children in the nonstandard language region, whose parents are native speakers of the local

---

[1]See, for example, Weinreich, Labov, and Herzog (1968, p. 145) and also Labov (1972, p. 102), in which Labov states that "preadolescent children restructure the grammar learned from their parents to match that of their peers."

5

dialect, are still exposed to the standard dialect through television, education, and probably through their parents and other adults whose speech may show various degrees of standardization; thus, the children are exposed to a linguistically somewhat heterogeneous environment.

AIM OF THE STUDY

The primary purpose of this chapter is to investigate the phonological development of one child who has been exposed to two regional dialects since birth. This is done through analysis of dialectal variation observed in the child's speech, especially variation in the system of accentuation. It is not intended to be a longitudinal study of evolution of accentuation, but rather it treats two stages in the language development of this child. After a brief analysis of an early stage of development to show the acquisition of accentuation based on the mother's model is presented, the interaction of linguistic variation and the child's competence in using socially appropriate speech forms (which, it is assumed, children have acquired by the age of 7 or 8) are examined.

The girl, referred to as child C, is the only child of parents who speak only the Tokyo dialect of Japanese. The mother is a native of Tokyo and the father is from Shizuoka. Neither of them speak the local Kyoto dialect. The child spends every summer in Tokyo with her grandmother and keeps in contact with her during the rest of the year. The child lives in the western region of Otsu City, a rapidly changing—though still not completely urbanized—suburban community.

The data used for the analysis of the child's early stage to show the acquisition of accentuation are based on dialogue that had been recorded when the child was 2 years, 11 months (2;11). The primary data used for analysis of the child's later stage of development are based on her spontaneous and nonspontaneous speech (that had been recorded over a 2-month period just after the child turned 8 years old) in various social contexts including family interaction, mother-child interaction, and child-child interaction. This broad variety of speech situations was sampled so that both stylistic and dialectal variation could be observed.

This paper also presents a brief description of accentual variation observed in the speech of one local girl, called child U, who is the same age as child C. The purpose of this analysis is to examine the effect of the standard dialect on the language development of children in the nonstandard language region. Further analysis of variation, based on data collected from 20 local children, ages 8 to 14, explores the nature of variation and illustrates the complicated processes that Japanese children experience in linguistically heterogeneous communities.

ACCENTUATION

The accentual systems of the two dialects, Tokyo and Kyoto, are described below very briefly in terms of basic patterns and some accentual rules.[2]

Basic Accentual Patterns

Tokyo-type accentuation can be described as having only one marked accent that indicates the location of a pitch fall in a word, as in ka／mina′＼ri, which means 'thunder.' Phonetically, the initial mora[3] is low pitched in both accented and unaccented words, unless that initial mora itself is accented ('m' stands for a mora; '#' indicates a word boundary).

1. Accented: # ‾m′＼mm...#, # m／m′＼m...#,

            # m／mm′＼...#, # m／m m′ #

   Unaccented: # m／m m...#

In Kyoto-type accentuation, two marked accents, high and low, indicate the location of a pitch fall within a word and the low-initialness of a word that is distinct, producing contrast with a high starting word, as in ′gakko／o 'school' and ‾kamina′＼ri 'thunder.' The accent mark placed before the initial mora indicates low accent, whereas the accent mark placed after a mora indicates high accent.

2. Accented:

High: #‾m′＼ m m...#, #‾m m′＼ m...#

Low-high: # ′m ／m′ # / #_′m ／m＼′   #, # ′m／m′＼m...#,

            # ′m m／m′＼ m...#

Low: # ′m／‾m#, # ′m...m／‾m #

Unaccented: # ‾m m m...#

In both dialects, nouns may consist of one, two, three, or more moras and they may occur in any of the patterns described above.

---

[2]Here we do not intend to analyze accentuation in any depth. For detailed analysis, see McCawley (1968), Okuda (1975), Haraguchi (1977), and Kobayashi (1975).

[3]A brief explanation of the term *mora* is needed. Two units of accent, syllable and mora, are used in Japanese accentuation. A mora indicates the location of pitch fall in a word, whereas a syllable is considered to be the basic prosodic unit on which accentual rules operate. A mora may consist of a vowel, a consonant plus a vowel, a consonant plus [y] plus a vowel, or a single postvocalic consonant. A syllable, on the other hand, consists of a vowel, a consonant plus a vowel, a consonant plus [y] plus a vowel, which may or may not be followed by a vowel of a geminate cluster or the vowel [i], or a postvocalic consonant. Thus, a word like *ippai* 'full' consists of four moras, i-p-pa-i, but two syllables, ip-pai.

One- and two-mora nouns show the correspondences of the following sort quite regularly between the two dialects:

3.

	One-mora nouns	Two-mora nouns
Tokyo	m m m'	mm mm' m'm m'm
Kyoto	m m' 'm	mm m'm 'mm 'mm'

Notice that initially accented two-mora nouns in Tokyo correspond to two Kyoto patterns. On the other hand, in adjectives, the distinction between accented and unaccented bases is lost in Kyoto, where a one-mora base is low accented and longer bases receive a base penultimate accent. In both dialects, verbs are divided into two classes accentually: in Tokyo, accented and unaccented, and in Kyoto, low accented and unaccented classes in the present tense.

Accentual Rules

Accentual rules refer to alternations that result when one word forms an accentual phrase when used with another word.[4] For example, the sequence of the final accented noun *uma'* 'horse' plus the particle *no,* which becomes uma no in Tokyo with the elimination of the final accent of the noun, caused regularly by this particle, whereas sequences such as *uma'* plus other particle *wa,* which produces no accent loss, or a noun of another class *a'me* 'rain' plus *no* are phonetically uma wa and ame no with no accentual change, to which the accent elimination rule of the particle *no* does not apply. Although this rule is observed in both dialects in different formulations, some rules typically differ in the two dialects. For example, the negative and the desiderative endings, *-nai* and *-tai,* the polite past morpheme *-mašita* and the particle *'mo,* along with particles such as *'made* 'even, until,' *'yori* 'than,' etc., cause a pitch fall in Kyoto when preceded by unaccented or low accented bases or words. Kyoto also has a series of copulas that are morphologically and accentually distinct from the standard series.[5] Furthermore, Kyoto has a rather complex system for constructing negative forms of verbs, which are used along with the standard *-nai* ending.[6]

---

[4]An accentual phrase is a word or a group of words governed by one pitch pattern and it may therefore contain at most only one marked accent. In this chapter, only some accentual alternations in minor phrases are covered. See Kobayashi (1975) for further discussion of alternation.

[5]Kyoto copula forms consist of the present *'ya,* the past *'yatta,* the conditional *'yatta'ra,* the alternative *'yatta'ri,* the presumptive *'yaro(:),* and the gerund *de.*

[6]The negative of a verb in Kyoto is formed by adding either *-n* or *-'hen* ending to a verb stem, which then forms separate negative paradigms. Furthermore, the past, the conditional, and the alternative occur with two sets of endings: 1) *-'katta, -'katta'ra,* and *-'katta'ri,* and 2) *-'nanda, -'nanda'ra,* and *-'nanda'ri,* although the latter series does not occur in children's speech, indicating generational variation. Generational variation is also observed in accentuation of the polite past morpheme, as noted by Inoguchi and Horii (1975, p. 131).

ACQUISITION OF ACCENTUATION

The analysis of spontaneous dialogue between child C and her mother, recorded at 2;11, indicates that by this age the child had basically acquired Tokyo-type accentuation on the basis of the mother's model. Before describing accent, however, a brief description of segmental phonology is needed to show the phonological development of this child.

The transcribed data show frequent substitution of [s] by [š], [š] and [c] by [č], and [z] by [j], as in šuru for *suru* 'do,' ø̄u:šen for *øu:sen* 'balloon,' ošato: for *osato:* 'sugar,' ošoto for *osoto* 'outside'; čita:i for *šitai* 'want to do,' mōču for *mocu* 'have,' ø̄uta:ččū or ø̄uta:ču for *øutacu* 'two'; and re:jo:ko for *re:zo:ko* 'refrigerator,' mujukaši: for *muzukaši:* 'difficult.' Other replacements are observed in examples such as akabumi for *akagumi* 'the class of Red' (in the kindergarten) and kowaraši for *kobayaši* 'a family name.' The flap [r], although it is fairly stable, may drop with or without the following vowel, or be replaced by other sounds such as [b] or [y], as in koē or koī for *kore* 'this,' yukida:ma for *yukidaruma* 'snow man,' koma:ša for *koma:šaru* 'commercial,' beko:do for *reko:do* 'record,' and debeyon for *deberon* 'Deberon' (name of a character in a TV program). [ç], [y], and [w] may also drop in some words, as in itoi for *çitori* 'one person,' oyabiçime for *oyayubiçime* 'Tiny Princess,' and ma:tte for *mawatte* 'around.' Other processes such as metathesis, assimilation, or dissimilation are observed in some examples: takašiyama for *Takašimaya* 'Takashimaya Department Store,' dekka for *desu ka* 'is it?', i:matta for *i:mašita* 'said,' takkete for *tasukete* 'help,' and kamone for *kamome* 'seagull.'

Vowels are generally pronounced with distinct quality, and length often accompanies accented vowels, as observed in the examples described above. The loss of vowels is observed in examples such as waru: no for *warui no* 'it is bad,' čiga: no for *čigau no* 'it is not so,' and agera: wa yo for *agerareru wa yo* 'I can give,' as well as in longer words and phrases. Also, the devoicing of high vowels [i] and [u] may take place in environments in which Tokyo speakers may produce voiceless vowels.

As for the accentuation the child shows at 2;11, first examine the following passages from the transcribed data:

4. kobuta no hanaši šuru yo. o:kamišan otete o ø̄uta:ču konna yatten
    no. o:kamišan wa ne, entoču kara hairo: to šita: no yo. aččičči:tte
    itta no. datte ne, kobutašan ga, o:kami waru:i koto šita kara, oyu ga

aču: no. kore wa waru: no. o:kamišan, kobutašan tabečau. These
passages mean roughly: 'I'll tell a story of pigs. The wolf had two
hands and did like this. He tried to enter the pigs' house through the
chimney, but fell down in the hot water prepared by them. The wolf
did a bad thing, so the water was hot. He was bad trying to eat pigs.'

5. pandačan to inu: ga bo:ru paka:nte yatten no, aši de. čiga: wa yo.
    ča:čan wa otete de bo:ru pa:pa ni pante yarun da ze. aši wa aru wa
    yo. bo:ru akai no yo. kore wa ne, kakučan te yobu no yo. ča:čan no
    hon ni dete kun no, terebi de wa nani: mo dete konai wa yo. 'The
    panda and the dog tossed a ball with foot. Not so. I throw a ball with
    hands to my father. Of course, I have feet. My ball is red, which I
    call "Kakuchan," the name I found in a book, not on television.'

The initial mora, unless it is accented, is generally realized as low
pitched both in accented and unaccented words, although it may vary
when the following mora consists of a vowel length or a geminate consonant.

The basic accentual patterns of the child at 2;11 are:

6. Unaccented: kani 'crab,' hane 'wing,' kobuta 'piglet,' ušagi ga
                 'rabbit' (Subject), bo:ru 'ball,' honto 'true'

    Accented: te' de 'with hands,' kī' wa 'tree' (Topic), jī' o 'letter'
                 (Object), ma'do 'window,' a'sa 'morning,' yo'ru
                 'night,' ma'e 'before,' a'to de 'after,' do'ko 'where,'
                 i'ma 'now,' na'ni 'what,' aši' de 'with foot,' heya' de
                 'in the room,' mači' e 'to town,' oto' ga' 'sound'
                 (Subject), inu' mo 'dog, too,' nacu' ni wa 'in sum-
                 mer'

                 ko'ndo 'this time,' te'rebi 'television,' mi'ruku
                 'milk,' cito'ču 'one,' ode'ko 'forehead,' oba'ke
                 'ghost,' šuke':to 'skate,' ro:šo':ku 'candle,' mašši'ro
                 'pure white,' atama' ga 'head' (Subject), ašita' wa
                 'tomorrow' (Topic), hašami' de 'with scissors'

Variant accent is observed in nouns such as nani 'what,' øųta:ču
'two' and mičču 'three,' as well as the local word akan (or, akan) 'not
good,' and arigato: 'thank you.'

Accent in inflected words is very consistent with Tokyo patterns both in citation and inflected forms, as observed in the following adverbials and the past tense forms:

7. Adjectives: -i: i'i 'good,' na'i / na':i 'not,' waru':i 'bad,' aču':i 'hot,' kawai':i 'cute,' akai 'red,' amai 'sweet'

               -ku: na'kute, wa'ruku, i'taku/ita':ku 'painful,' ko':waku 'fearful,' attaka':ku 'hot,' akaku, amaku

    Verbs: -(r)u: a'ru 'exist,' ku'ru 'come,' ou'ru 'fall,' tabe'ru 'eat,' deki'ru 'be able,' iku 'go,' yobu 'call,' ageru 'give'

               -ta: a'tta, ki'ta, ou'tta, ta'beta, de'kita, nao'tta 'mended'; itta, yonda, ageta, šuwatta 'sat'

In the transcribed data, negatives occur only with *-nai* ending, with no occurrence of Kyoto forms. Accented and unaccented forms of negatives are generally kept distinct, whereas a single occurrence of the desiderative form is accented čita':i 'want to do.'

8. Negatives: Unaccented: inai 'not exist,' iwanai 'not say,' šinai 'not do'

                 Accented: noma'nai 'not drink,' ko'nai 'not come,' tabe'nai 'not eat,' deki':nai 'unable to do,' wakara'nai 'not understand'

The copula appears regularly in the standard series of *da, desu,* and *dešo(:),* as in yarun da ze: 'I would do,' ošuši desu 'it is *sushi,*' kobuta deš 'it is a piglet,' and inu dešo 'it would be a dog.' Kyoto copula forms are observed in four examples in the data, three of the examples are in the form of *ya de(:)* with the particle *de(:),* as in miččʊ ya de 'I am three,' irun ya de: 'I need it,' and šurun ya de: 'I'll do.'' The other example is či:ča:i yaro 'it would be small.'

Other accentual rules observed in the data are: The particle *no* regularly causes de-accentuation of a preceding final accented noun, as in heya no naka 'in the room,' inu no mimi 'dog's ear,' and atama no ue 'on the head,' from heya' + no + na'ka, inu' + no + mimi', and atama' + no + ue, respectively. Regular accentual alternation between the present tense and past tense forms of the accented vowel verbs, as in taberu 'eat' versus tabeta 'ate,' yomeru 'can read' versus yometa, and šimeru 'close' versus šimeta, shows the child's acquisition of shift rules in this type of verbs, which also apply regularly to extended bases, as in alternation haireru 'can enter' versus haireta. The accentual dominance of the polite morpheme is quite regular in the past tense form with -masita, as in kimašįta 'came,' arimašįta or arimatta 'was,' hairimatta 'entered,' and ikimatta 'went,' as well as in other forms, such as the present arima:šu 'exist' or the negative kimasen 'not come.' The pre-accentuation of the particles no, ši, wa, mon, de(:), etc., and of the copula presumptive is observed regularly, as in iku no 'do,' itta no 'went,' iku wa, ikanai wa 'not go,' yaru mon 'do,' šuru ši 'do,' čiga: wa 'it is not so,' ikana: de 'without going,' iku dešo 'I would go,' and yuwanai dešo 'I would not say.' Here unaccented words become accented.

Observations based on the data taken at 2;11 show that the child has developed Tokyo-type accentuation on the basis of her mother's model, which constitutes the primary linguistic input for the construction of the child's system, even when the child is raised in a different locality. The child's communication with parents in the home still constitutes the center of her social life, with interaction with peers still very limited, socially and linguistically, as reflected in a very limited occurrence of the variant accent and the local copula forms. The results also indicate that the acquisition of accentuation takes place at a fairly early stage of development, prior to completion of the acquisition of segmental phonology.

ACCENTUAL VARIATION

It was observed above that the child has developed Tokyo-type accentuation by age 3, due to the fact that the mother's speech provides primary linguistic input for the earlier stages of language development. At this stage, influence of other models is negligible as evidenced by the very limited variation. Since then the child has acquired local accent through increasingly active interaction, both social and linguistic, with her peers. This results in dialectal variation in her speech. Analysis of accentual variation in the data taken at 8;0 examines the nature of variation and investigates how the child has restructured her system of accentuation.

The following samples from the transcribed data may illustrate the variety of speech child C produced at age 8.

9. māma: kīno: no yōru āme ǿuttetá. kaminari natta děšo. āme ǿutta
yo ne. hōra āme no šizuku. konogoro wa yoku ōuru ne:. mo: gohan
tabenai yo. onaka ippai da mon. papa māda taberu no. ǿu:n, yap-
pāri debuččo da ne. mo: jikanwari yatta yo:. kyo: wa, sansu: to
kokugo to šakai. taiku wa nai no. Dialogue at breakfast table, which
roughly means: 'Mother, it rained last night, didn't it? There was
thunder, wasn't there? It sure rained; look at these raindrops. It
rains often these days. I won't eat any more, because I am full.
Father, are you still eating? You are fatty after all, aren't you? I
already did preparation for school. Today, we'll study mathematics,
Japanese and social studies, but no gymnastics.

10. kīno:, anta nanto: yatta. pu:ru de, are yatta yaro. watāši, e:. anta
wa. aši nankai cuketa. aši cukehenkattara yokattan ya. a? očita.
nande kasa irun ya. kyo:, āme ourahen de:. [Asked by another girl
whether she returns a library book], n kyo: kaešite māta kariru.
kīno: yomahenkatta ši na. osoi na:. dančo:. icukate osoi nen.
Dialogue while waiting at the roadside before going to school, which
 means: 'What grade did you get yesterday at the pool? I got an
"A." How about you? How many times did you touch the bottom
with your foot? You should not have touched it. Look! You
dropped your umbrella. Why are you taking it? It won't rain today.
Yes, I'm going to return it (the book) today and take it out again,
because I didn't finish it yesterday. The leader is late, isn't she? She
is always late.'

11. [To a question on a friend who is good at writing funny cartoons]
širakedori. torikago ni me: kaite, torikago kara te: dašite na:,
širakedori cukamaeyoru. e: mo kaite na:. ji: kaiten no mi:çinkattara
wakarahen. 'A "shirake" bird. She writes eyes on the bird cage,
hands pushed out of the cage. She catches the bird. She also draws
pictures. If you didn't watch her writing letters, you wouldn't be
able to read them.'

Notice that the first passage in family interaction is dominated by the
Tokyo accent, with the noticeable exception of kokugo and šakai, names
of subjects in school, which are kokugo and šakai in Tokyo. On the other
hand, the second and the third passages, taken from the child-child interaction, show the dominance of the Kyoto dialect both in accent and

negative morphology. The third passage is very characteristic of Kyoto speech and shows the vowel lengthening of monosyllabic nouns. These passages clearly indicate that the child has developed a Kyoto-type accent that she can use effectively in socially appropriate situations, according to the place and person. The range and types of variation in word accent are illustrated in Table 1, which also presents the frequency of occurrence of variant accents in three different contexts, reading and two dialogues, each representing the mother-child interaction (Dialogue I) and the child-child interaction (Dialogue II).[7]

In this table, which is based on the frequency of occurrence of the variant accent, noticeable differences can be observed and the correlation between linguistic features and stylistic difference is apparent. Reading, which is assumed to be a conscious, nonspontaneous speech style, is dominated by the Tokyo accent with only a very sporadic occurrence of the Kyoto accent. On the other hand, in Dialogue II, which is based on interaction with a peer, the Kyoto accent occurs with high frequency in both nouns and inflected words. Note that the class of low-high accented nouns is rather stable with the Tokyo accent, whereas high and low accented nouns show considerable variation. For example, high accented nouns, such as ko̅to̅ 'matter,' mo̅no̅ 'thing,' ya̅cu 'thing,' çi̅to 'person,' to̅ki 'time,' and to̅ko 'place,' occur along with koto̅, mono̅, toki̅, etc., which have accents on the final mora, as in Tokyo. Likewise, in low accented nouns, both the Tokyo and Kyoto accents alternate in words such as *ima* 'now,' *ato* 'later,' *icu mo* 'always,' *nani* 'what,' *doko* 'where,' and *naka* 'inside.' Also note that low accented two-mora nouns show another type of variation, and that out of 30 occurrences of the Kyoto accent in this class of nouns, 10 occurrences are with the variant accent. Thus, variant accents such as i̅ma̅ wa or ho̅ka̅ no 'other,' with pitch fall after the noun, are observed, as opposed to regular accents ima̅ wa or hoka̅ no in which no pitch fall takes place. As for the accent of inflected words in Dialogue

---

[7]In this chapter only a limited number of word classes and accentual rules are treated. The reading data in this chapter are based on a short story in a second grade reader, which both child C and child U studied at school prior to this reading. The data for Dialogue I are from a dialogue of about 30 minutes between child C and her mother, who talked about the child's favorite books and related topics on animals and insects. The data for Dialogue II come from a 1-hour dialogue between child C and child U, and are presented later. This dialogue was recorded with no adults present.

Table 1.   Accentual variation: Frequency scale

	Word Class	Nonspontaneous Reading	Spontaneous Dialogue I	Dialogue II
Nouns:[a]	'm	0/4[b]	0/9	7/10
	m'	2/5		
	'mm	1/23	4/20	30/48
	'mm'	0/8	0/18	2/13
	m'm	2/45	15/53	35/47
Adjectives:[a]	-i	0/23	0/34	28/48
	-ku	4/14	2/9	2/5
Verbs:[a]	-(r)u	1/12	1/45	33/39
	-ta	3/37	1/48	33/46

[a]Noun accent is classified by Kyoto patterns. Adjectives are listed in the citation forms ending in -i and the adverbials ending in -ku, whereas forms listed in -ta ending of verbs include the past -ta, the gerund -te, the conditional -tara, and the alternative -tari.

[b]Frequency indicates the ratio of the frequency of occurrence of the Kyoto accent to the total frequency of the word class: thus, 3/7 means that Kyoto patterns occur three times and Tokyo four times, constituting the total of seven.

II, in adjectives, 28 occurrences of the Kyoto accent include words such as c̅ume̅tai 'cold,' a̅mai 'sweet,' and e̅rai 'great,' although the total frequency is very high because of repetitive occurrences of i̲i̲ or e̲e̲ 'good' and na̲i̲ 'not.'[8] In citation forms of verbs, yo̅mu̅ 'read,' a̲ru̅ 'exist,' hairu̅ 'enter,' wa̅karu̅ 'understand,' etc., occur repetitively, whereas verbs such as d̅asu̲ 'put out,' ta̲be̲ru̅ 'eat,' and yo̅me̲ru 'can read' occur regularly with the Tokyo accent. Similarly, accentual variation occurs in inflected forms. Thus, the Kyoto accent is observed in yo̅nd̅a 'read,' kaite̅ 'wrote,' o̲čita 'fell,' ko̅bo̅šita 'spilled,' and yu̲:ta 'said,' along with Tokyo-accented y̅onda, k̅aita, t̅otta 'took,' o̅toši̲te 'drop,' and itt̅ara 'if one went.' Dialogue I, the mother-child interaction, shows that the child uses styles accentually quite close to reading style in interaction with her mother, although this particular closeness seems to reflect that the topics of the dialogue centered on books and related academic issues.

[8]Here we address the problem of interference. In adjectives ending in -i, the distinction between accented and unaccented classes in Tokyo generally seems to be kept when those adjectives are produced with the Tokyo accent. However, the occurrence of such accents as in a̲kai tokoro 'red place,' although it is very sporadic, indicates interference by Kyoto accentuation in which disyllabic and longer adjectives are all accented.

The same data show variation of the following sort in accentual rules:

12.

	Accentual rules[a]	Reading	Dialogue I	Dialogue II
Endings:	-'nai	0/5	0/25	1/5
	-'tai			4/6
	-'hen / -n		1/1	36/36
	-'mašita	0/27		
Particle:	'mo		0/4	10/13
Copula:	'da	0/3(28)	0/5(34)	—(4)
	'ya		3/3(7)	11/11(30)

[a]Accentual rules are classified by Kyoto rules. Figures in parentheses indicate the total occurrence of that morpheme class, including those in environments in which accentual difference does not show up.

The use of accentual rules shows a similar relationship between linguistic features and style. Dialogue II, the child-child interaction, is characterized by Kyoto rules, both in accent and morphology, as reflected in 30 occurrences of the local copula forms with regular low accent in expected environments versus only 4 occurrences of the standard form of the copula. In Dialogue I, the mother-child interaction, the ratio is 7 versus 34, showing the dominance of the standard forms. Likewise, local negative forms are dominant in the dialogue between the children with regular accent. It is also noted that only the child-child interaction contains examples of pitch fall caused by the particle *mo,* although this is limited to fixed phrases such as i̲c̲u̲ mo 'always' or n̲a̲n̲i̲ mo 'nothing.' In other environments, only two occurrences, e̲ː mo 'picture, too' and s̲o̲r̲e̲ mo 'that, too,' are observed against examples that show no pitch fall.

Table 2 indicates the interaction of variation in accentual rules with speech styles on implicational scales.[9] The increasing use of Kyoto rules correlates well with the process of language socialization, observed in interactions with peers. The strength of the influence of the topic is evident in Dialogue Ib. When talking about school events, the speech style used with peers, that is, "peers' code," shows up even in the dialogue with the mother. Note the strongest resistance of the copula *da* to low accent.

[9]For the use of implicational scales in language variation and related issues, see, for example, Fasold, 1970.

Table 2. Accentual variation: Implicational scale[10]

Rules	Nonspontaneous	Spontaneous		
	Reading	Dialogue Ia	Dialogue Ib	Dialogue II
'ya	*[a]	+	+	+
-'hen / -n	*	(+)	+	+
'mo	—	—	(×)	×
-'tai	—	—	—	×
-'nai	—	—	—	(×)
'da	—	—	—	—
-'mašita	—	(—)	(—)	*

[a]* = non-occurrence of that word class; + = systematic occurrence with regular accent; — = systematic occurrence with minus accent; × = variable occurrence (both regular low accent and variant accent occur); ( ) = very low frequency of occurrence

Here, correlation of accent and morpheme is quite consistent, as in pairs such as $\overline{\text{honto da}}$ versus $\underline{\text{hon}}\overline{\text{ma}}$ $\underline{\text{ya}}$ 'it is true.' Local form 'ya always causes pitch fall, whereas no fall takes place with the standard series. The child must have acquired both series of the copula with distinct accent. A similar correlation of accent with morphemes holds in local negative forms; thus, the negative ending -'hen regularly causes pitch fall, as in $\underline{\text{ara}}\overline{\text{hen}}$ 'not exist,' $\underline{\text{tab}}\overline{\text{ehen}}$ 'not eat,' and $\underline{\text{kaite}}$ $\underline{\text{ara}}\overline{\text{hen}}$ 'be not written' from 'ar-a- + -'hen, 'tabe- + -'hen, and 'kaite + 'ar-a-'hen. In the particle mo and endings -nai and -tai, variation is observed, although the occurrence of the local accent is still limited.[11]

[10]This table is based on the data reported in Table 1 and also on the following recorded data: Reading style is examined on the basis of a few other story readings of the school reader and others. The mother-child interaction (Dialogue I) is subdivided into two categories according to the topics of conversation: Dialogue Ia includes a dialogue on a visit to a locomotive exhibition plus the data analyzed for Table 1. Dialogue Ib is based on dialogues on school events such as a farewell party, a ball game, and a class meeting. Dialogue II consists of spontaneous conversations with local children.

[11]In the case of the negative, only a single occurrence of the Kyoto accent is noted with the standard ending in $\overline{\text{šira}}\underline{\text{nai}}$ 'not know.' In the desiderative, accented -tai is observed regardless of environment, as in yarita'i 'want to do,' ikita'i 'want to go,' etc., with the standard accent, along with 'nari'tai 'want to be,' or 'hairi'tai 'want to enter' with the local low accent. The distinction between accented and unaccented forms of negatives is well observed: inai 'not exist,' agenai 'not give,' sinanai 'not die,' cukamaranai 'cannot catch,' etc., are unaccented against accented kore'nai 'cannot come,' uta'nai 'not shoot,' abunakuna'i 'not be in danger.' Unaccented negatives become accented regularly when followed by pre-accenting particles, no, si, de, etc., or the copula deso(:), as in $\overline{\text{šira}}\underline{\text{nai}}$ $\underline{\text{ši}}$ 'I don't know, but,' or ikanai $\underline{\text{dešo}}$: 'I wouldn't go.'

The transcribed data contain examples of code switching, which provide further evidence for the child's strategy in the social use of language:

13. [Talking to child U about books she owns] are wa iči ya de, are ga ni: de, mo: yonda yaro. daibu koko ni mo aru ke do na, motto šita ni aru yo. mo: minna, yondešimota. kore yomahen no. [When the child's mother joined the children and asked them to read a poem] mite yomu no. wataši wa minai de yomeru yo. mo: zenbu oboečatta mon. yomanakute mo i: yo. [To child U beside her] annan mi:çin kate yomeru, na:. English equivalents are: 'That is volume one. That is the second volume which you read already. Though there are many books here, there are still more downstairs, all of which I had read. Don't you read this one? Do you have to read it (the poem)? I can recite it without looking, because I've already memorized all of it. I don't need to read it. We can recite a poem like that, can't we?'

14. [Talking to mother] mo: sakano no namae širanai yo. [To child U] tonbo ga sakana ya te, na:. kumo ya nanka ga sakana ya te. iriomo-teyamaneko tte neko to čau no. [To which child U responded with] homma ya, okaši: na:. This exchange means 'I know no other fish names. A dragonfly is a fish? A spider is a fish? "Iriomoteyaman-eko" is a cat, isn't it?' and took place when the children, having been left alone, expressed their comments after reading prepared cards of fish names in which, by mistake, some names of insects and animals were included.

Switching takes place regularly when quoting friends or local adults, as observed below:

15. onna no ko no naka de gakku:iin ni natta. jibun de naritai kara ne, gakku:iin no toko ni te: agetara, ju:nana haitta no. [To a question whether there is someone who did not get many votes] so:yu: çito de mo iru yo. ageta kedo, iči niço: šika hairanenkatta tte yuwahatta mon. 'I was elected as class chairman for the girls. Because I wanted to be, I raised my hand as a candidate and I got 17 votes. Of course, some didn't get many votes. A friend of mine said, "Though I raised my hand, I got only one or two votes."'

16. uenosan no obačan ga ne, çiromi to zenzen hanasu ma: ga arahen ya te. gakko: kara kaeru to, sugu čiharučan no uči e ittešimote, zenzen çiruma wa kao mo mi:çin ya te. 'Ueno's mother said to me, "I don't have time to talk with my daughter, because she goes to your house

right after coming home from school. I don't even see her face during the daytime.''' '

The above observations reveal that the child has developed competence in using speech styles that are appropriate to the particular social situations and in conducting interactions with or about peers in local dialect forms. These speech styles have been acquired through the restructuring of her system of accentuation and morphology on the basis of the model with which she is now in contact in daily social transactions. The development of "parents' code" and "peers' code," with separate domains, is obvious.

A short analysis of the variation shown in the speech of local girl U, a native of Kyoto, follows. Table 3 presents the frequency of occurrences of accentual variation in spontaneous and nonspontaneous speech. The reading data for this table are based on a reading of the same story read by child C. The dialogue (between child U and child C) is the same dialogue analyzed for Table 1.

It is evident that the standardized accent occurs with higher frequency in reading, both in nouns and in verbs and adjectives in citation forms. For example, in two-mora nouns in reading style, the Tokyo accent is observed in low accented and low-high accented words quite frequently. Thus, the Tokyo accent is noted in a̅r̲u̲ 'certain,' d̅o̲k̲o̲ 'where,' s̅o̲b̲a 'besides,' etc., in low accented class of nouns, and in h̅a̲r̲u 'spring,' w̅a̲k̲e 'reason,' a̅s̲e̲ 'sweat,' etc., in low-high accented class. In dialogue, the occurrence of the Tokyo accent is observed in nouns such as n̅a̲n̲i 'what,' k̅yo̲: 'today,' m̅a̲e̲ 'before,' t̲o̲k̅i 'time,' c̲u̲g̅i 'next,' etc., with

Table 3. Accentual variation: Frequency scale

	Word class	Nonspontaneous Reading	Spontaneous Dialogue
Nouns:	'm	1/4[a]	7/7
	m'	5/5	
	'mm	15/23	47/50
	'mm'	4/8	16/18
	m'm	35/45	46/51
Adjectives:	-i	16/23	23/27
	-ku	14/14	7/7
Verbs:	-(r)u	17/12	32/34
	-ta	32/37	52/55

[a]The ratio of the frequency of occurrence of the Kyoto accent is presented to the total frequency of the word class.

the frequency of occurrences of 11% in 'mm', 6% in 'mm, and 10% in m'm nouns, compared with corresponding figures of 50%, 35%, and 20% in reading.

In low accented two-mora nouns, the same type of variation observed in child C's speech appears in this child's data. Thus, in addition to the standardized accent sōba ni 'besides,' alternating pairs such as soba nī and sobā ni are observed in reading. In the dialogue, 11 out of 47 occurrences of this noun class show this variant accent, including repetitive occurrences of *naka* 'inside,' *koko* 'here,' *hoka* 'other,' *ima* 'now,' *kyo:* 'today,' etc., and a single occurrence of *umi* 'sea' in the phrase umi no sakana 'fish of the sea,' thus generating a ratio of 3/36/11 in the occurrences of the Tokyo accent versus the Kyoto accent versus the Kyoto variant accent, respectively.

Inflected words are consistently produced with the local accent with very limited occurrences of the Tokyo accent. One- or two-mora adjectives ending in *-i* forms, īi 'good,' šīrōi 'white,' çīrōi 'wide,' etc., are most likely to be produced with Tokyo accent, [12] longer adjectives being consistent with the Kyoto accent which occur with a regular base penultimate accent. In the citation form of verbs, the Tokyo accent is observed in words such as mīru 'see,' okīru 'get up,' and kūru 'come' in reading and in only two verbs, mieru 'be visible' and okīru 'get up,' in dialogue, whereas okite motte 'hold,' notta 'rode,' and hanašita 'spoke' and yonda 'read' are noted to occur with the Tokyo accent in inflected forms, in reading and dialogue, respectively. Likewise, Kyoto accentual rules are well observed both in reading and dialogue. Quite regularly, both the standard and local forms of the copula cause pitch fall in the expected environment. Thus, accentually, umī datta 'it was the sea' is equivalent to umī yatta, without any correlation between morpheme and accent. Even in reading examples with distinct pitch fall before the copula, such as širouma da 'it is the white horse,' are found. The standard negative ending *-nai* also occurs with the Kyoto low accent regularly, as in īnai 'not exist' and šīranai 'not know.'

The past polite morpheme occurs with the Kyoto accent four times out of 27 total occurrences, as in kimašita 'came' and ikimašita 'went,' against forms with accent on the initial mora of the morpheme kimašita

---

[12]Note the accent of the adjective akai 'red,' which may indicate that the child has not acquired the distinction between accented and unaccented adjectives in Tokyo, although she produces a Tokyo-type accent.

'came' and šimašita 'did.' Although the text analyzed contains no environment in which the particle *mo* causes pitch fall, another story reading supplies abundant examples, as in sore mo 'that, too,' wataši mo 'I, too,' etc. Also, the desiderative is produced with the local low accent, as in ikitai 'want to go' and šitai 'want to do.' The vowel lengthening of one-mora nouns takes place only in spontaneous dialogue, thus marking a regular stylistic difference as observed in adult speakers.

Table 4 shows a tabulation (based on available data) of the relationships between accentual rules and speech forms observed in child U.[13] The presence or absence of the local copula, negatives, and the polite morpheme distinguishes reading style from dialogue. Furthermore, the absence of the standard copula series seems to mark the casual speech style of this child, probably with the negative *-nai* ending, which is observed in a single example in the child-child interaction. It can be said that, in this child, stylistic difference is indicated morphologically rather than accentually.

Here reference may be made to the stylistic switching that this child showed when responding to child C's mother, reflected in the occurrence of the standard copula series, *da, desu,* and *dešo(:),* which are nonexistent in spontaneous exchange with children. The data contain utterances such as mada kodomo da mon 'I'm still a child,' mijime da mon 'I am very heartbroken,' morau dešo 'I would probably get it' or nan desŏ: ne: 'what would it be?' (all to child C's mother), and hairerun desu ka tte ki:tara 'why don't you ask if it is possible to join?' in reference to her teacher. These forms do not occur in the child's speech when, for example, she refers to her own mother, as in the utterance uči no oka:čan yattara, manga yonde mo nanni mo yuwarahen ke do na 'if it were my mother, she wouldn't say anything against comics.' Thus, it is assumed that child C's mother, who speaks the standard dialect, and her teacher, who represents formal education, require from the child a style distinct from that of other local adults.

The above observations reveal that in native children accentual variation is more or less limited to word accent, noticeably to two-mora nouns and to verbs and adjectives in citation forms. This constitutes a favorable environment for accentual standardization, which is most easily influ-

---

[13]Spontaneous speech is divided into two categories: Dialogue B is based on natural interaction between this child and child C, whereas Dialogue A is based on this child's response to child C's mother, although these data are quite limited.

enced by the high frequency of occurrence of these words as linguistic input through television, school education, etc. The fact that accentual
rules of the local dialect are well observed regardless of contexts shows a
marked difference between the basically monodialectal child and the bi-
dialectal child.

INTERDIALECTAL VARIATION AND INTRADIALECTAL VARIATION

In this chapter, two types of accentual variation, which we may refer to as
interdialectal variation versus intradialectal variation, were observed. In
this section, the hypothesis that the second type of variation is ultimately
caused by the first type is considered.

Interdialectal variation, dialectal borrowing, refers to the occurrence
of the standardized accent in local children's speech, which, it was observed, tends to increase in formal reading style. This variation takes
place widely in nouns and in verbs and adjectives in citation forms.
Another type of variation, intradialectal variation, on the other hand, is
the accentual variation, which is particularly observed in low accented
two-mora nouns and appears in such alternating accents as ima w̄a versus
ima wa 'as for now,' or hoka n̄o versus hoka no 'other,' the first accent
being regular whereas the second shows the variant accent. In child U, this
variant accent is observed in 11 out of 47 occurrences of this class of
nouns in dialogue, repetitively in such nouns as *naka* 'inside,' *koko*
'here,' *ima* 'now,' etc.

Before further discussing these two types of variation, the following
contrast in low accented and low-high accented classes of nouns in Kyoto
needs to be noted:

17.

	_____ #	_____ Particle	
Low accented:	umi	umi ga/ umi ga	'umi
Low-high accented:	ame ame⌐	ame ga/*ame ga	'ame'

The contrast between the two patterns shows up before a pause when a
low-high accented word is accompanied with a falling tone, which may or
may not occur,[14] as in ame⌐ 'rain' versus umi 'sea.' It also may appear in
the regular pattern when followed by a particle, as in ame ga versus umi
ga. The presence of high accent indicates a pitch fall after the marked
mora in a low-high accented word, whereas only the final mora of the par-

---

[14]A study by Sugifuji, Nakatsuka, and Takahashi (1973) reports that the falling tone is
observed in the 34% of Osaka adult speakers they checked in the pronunciation of the word
iki 'chic.' They also state that the falling tone is less frequent in the younger generation.

Table 4. Accentual variation: Implicational Scale

Rules	Nonspontaneous Reading	Spontaneous Dialogue A	Spontaneous Dialogue B
'ya	*[a]	+	+
-'hen/-n	*	+	+
'mo	+	+	+
-'tai	+	+	+
-'nai	+	+	(+)
'da	+	+	*
-'mašita	×	*	*

[a]Notation is the same as in Table 2.

ticle is high pitched in a low accented word when an unaccented particle is added, as in a̲m̲e̅ ka̲r̲a̲ 'from rain' versus u̲m̲i̲ ka̲r̅a̅ 'from the sea,' with distinct contrast. However, we observe in child U's data that this contrast was lost in examples such as u̲m̲i̲ no̲ na̲k̅a̅ 'in the rain' and a̲m̲e̅ no̲ na̲k̅a̅ 'in the sea.' Her speech also contained examples like i̲m̲a̅ no̲ h̅a̅naši 'the present tale,' ho̲k̅a̅ no̲ ç̲i̲t̲o̲ 'other person,' na̲k̅a̅ ni 'inside,' etc., with the variant accent, against regular i̲m̲a̲ no̲ j̅i̅kan 'the present time,' ho̲k̲a̲ no̲ to̲k̲o̲r̲o̲ 'other place,' and na̲k̲a̲ d̅e̅, which show no pitch fall before the particle. On the other hand, there is no occurrence of the variant accent in low-high accented nouns, such as *a̲m̲e̅ g̅a̅, which is not permitted.

Table 5 presents the frequency of occurrence of variation in the low accented 'mm and low-high accented 'mm' two-mora nouns on the basis of the data collected from 20 local children, with some background information: sex, age, and birthplace of parents.[15] Interdialectal variation,

---

[15]All the children belong to the same neighborhood, most of them quite familiar to the investigator. They were asked to read casually the list of short sentences, such as *haru ga kuru* 'spring comes,' in which low and low-high accented nouns are arranged at random with other classes of nouns. The class of low accented nouns tested includes: *sora* 'sky,' *umi* 'sea,' *naka* 'inside,' *soto* 'outside,' *soba* 'beside,' *koko* 'here,' *soko* 'there,' *doko* 'where,' *ato* 'later,' *hoka* 'other,' *ima* 'now,' *kazu* 'number,' *ito* 'thread,' *iki* 'breath,' *kata* 'shoulder,' *hada* 'skin,' *ine* 'rice plant,' *nae* 'plant,' *tane* 'seed,' *macu* 'pine tree,' *mugi* 'wheat,' *becu* 'other,' *icu* 'when,' *nani* 'what,' *suji* 'muscle,' *yane* 'roof,' *obi* 'belt,' *dai* 'step,' *uri* 'cucumber,' *oune* 'ship,' *kado* 'corner,' *yado* 'inn,' *kyo:* 'today,' *kasa* 'umbrella,' *cici* 'father,' *hasi* 'chopstick,' *ita* 'board,' *miso* 'bean paste,' *kara* 'empty,' *ban* 'number,' *sen* 'thousand,' and *hari* 'needle' (*umi, naka,* and *ato* are repeated to see environmental difference). The class of low-high accented nouns is: *yoru* 'night,' *ame* 'rain,' *haru* 'spring,' *mae* 'front,' *asa* 'morning,' *siro* 'white,' *aka* 'red,' *ao* 'blue,' *kuro* 'black,' *ase* 'sweat,' *koe* 'voice,' *wake* 'reason,' *uso* 'lie,' *aki* 'autumn,' *mado* 'window,' *saru* 'monkey,' *curu* 'crane,' *kame* 'turtle,' *kumo* 'spider,' *koi* 'carp,' *hebi* 'snake,' *hato* 'pigeon,' *hamo* 'sea eel,' *negi* 'onion,' *oke* 'bucket,' *abu* 'fly,' *ayu* 'sweetfish,' *ouna* 'carp,' *muko* 'son-in-law,' *kage* 'shadow,' *nabe* 'pan,' *sake* 'salmon,' *ago* 'chin,' mame 'bean,' and *hare* 'fine' (*yoru, ame, mae, aki,* and *mado* are repeated). The occurrence of the falling tone is examined on the basis of the low-high accented nouns listed above plus the imperative forms of the verbs *kaku* 'write' and *yomu* 'read,' which occur with this tone.

Table 5. Accentual variation in 'mm and 'mm'

Children	'mm' (Tōkyo/Kyoto/Kyoto variant)	'mm (Tōkyo/Kyoto/Kyoto variant)	'mm'/___# (Falling tone^b)(%)	Sex/Age	Parents (Male/Female)
1. MY	6/33/1*^a	7/33/5	39	G/8	N/N^c
2. IN	3/37/0	2/35/8	54	G/9	N/N
3. UH	2/38/0	4/34/7	59	G/8	N/N
4. SK	3/37/0	3/34/8	48	G/8	N/N
5. MR	0/40/0	3/32/10	54	G/8	N/N
6. MO	0/40/0	4/32/10	56	G/8	N/N
7. IY	4/36/0	3/32/10	54	G/8	N/N
8. UN	6/34/0	7/26/12	31	G/8	N/N
9. YM	4/35/1*	4/30/11	51	B/8	N/N
10. MI	3/37/0	6/32/7	59	B/9	N/N
11. SH	5/35/0	4/31/11	48	B/9	N/N
12. IZ	8/32/0	8/19/18	14	B/9	N/N
13. UD	5/34/1*	6/20/19	14	G/8	N/N
14. MU(K)	4/36/0	4/31/10	46	B/11	N/N
15. MU(M)	7/32/1*	6/30/9	40	G/14	N/N
16. MK	7/33/0	8/27/10	46	G/9	N/Hyogo
17. KM	10/28/2	11/18/16	14	G/9	N/Tokyo
18. WD	11/25/4	10/16/19	11	G/8	Shimane/ Shimane
19. HD	14/22/4	13/14/18	11	G/9	Shimane/ Shimane
20. YH	24/14/2	31/9/5	14	B/8	Hiroshima/ Hiroshima

^aFigures with * in the first column indicate the occurrence of such irregular accents as áme nò or mádo nò, misapplication of the de-accentuation rule of the particle no.

^bThe third column indicates the frequency of the occurrence of the falling tone before pause.

^c"N" in the fifth column means "native to Kyoto," and other names indicate the name of prefectures where parents were born and raised.

that is, the occurrence of the standardized accent, is observed in both classes of nouns in all children with some individual variation. Non-native children, that is, either or both parents being from other dialect areas, tend to show higher frequency of standard accent. Intradialectal variation, that is, variation in low accented two-mora nouns, is also observed in all the children, with considerable difference in frequency. In most native children, who tend to show lower frequency, the variant accent is frequent in words such as *naka* 'inside,' *ato* 'after,' *ima* 'now,' *soba* 'beside,' *kyo:* 'today,' *kado* 'corner,' and *soto* 'outside.' Individual variation is greater in words like *umi* 'sea,' *sora* 'sky,' *øune* 'ship,' *obi* 'belt,' *yane* 'roof,' *mugi* 'wheat,' and *miso* 'bean paste.' Non-native children tend to produce the variant accent with considerably higher frequency, as observed in children KM, WD, and HD, suggesting native dialect interference. Another characteristic of these non-native children is that they produced variation in low-high accented nouns, which is nonexistent in native children with the exception of the misapplication of the deaccentuation of the particle *no*. For example, child WD produced examples such as <u>curu</u> o 'crane' (Object), <u>hebi</u> ga 'snake' (Subject), mado no 'of the window,' and mado wa in one reading.

Two native children, IZ and UD, markedly differ from other native children, not only in higher frequency of variation but also in the considerable lexical variation they showed in their reading. For example, child UD produced 19 nouns, out of the 45 examined, with variant accents respectively in two readings at an interval of several days. In one reading she produced *ato*(2), *naka, soba, soto, ima, umi, mugi, kyo:, kado,* and *yado,* which were read with the same accent in the second reading, along with *obi, hada, ito, čiči, miso, kasa, macu,* and *sora,* with variant accents. Notice that, as illustrated in the third column of the table, these two children, along with non-native children, produce the falling tone in low-high accented nouns with noticeably lower frequency, suggesting a correlation between the relative non-occurrence of a distinct falling tone and the higher frequency of accentual variation. However, why these two children lack the falling tone, as well as why they show such a high frequency of variation, remained unanswered.

These observations present an intriguing question that is difficult to answer because of the limited data at hand and a lack of statistics on variation in adult speakers. One plausible explanation is that intradialectal variation, caused ultimately by interdialectal variation through language standardization, is taking place in the Kyoto dialect, perhaps causing a decomposition of the word class. In a dialect contact situation, in which interdialectal variation frequently takes place, people may develop a greater tolerance toward linguistic variation. Considering the standardized accent a̅to de 'later,' na̅ka de 'inside,' ka̅do de 'at the corner,' and ma̅e de 'in front' (the accent of the two classes of nouns is merged in Tokyo system), and the local accent ato d̅e̅, naka d̅e̅, kado d̅e̅, and mae̅ de (the accent of the two classes is distinct in Kyoto) on the other hand, both of which may be used by the same person interchangeably, the development of such variant accents as a̅to de, na̅ka de, and ka̅do̅ de, thus coalescing with mae̅ de, may not be inconceivable, in particular in speakers' attempts to use a standardized dialect. Children who hear these variations in their parents' speech and/or on radio and television may develop a greater tendency toward variation, the two native children representing cases of extreme overgeneralization of the variation rule. The effect of the standard dialect seems to be causing not just immediate interdialectal variation through borrowing, but deeper internal variation, which may ultimately result in language change.

SUMMARY

In summary, a child exposed to two regional dialects acquired accentuation by age 3 on the basis of her mother's model, which seemed to constitute primary linguistic input for constructing the child's system. Interaction with parents in the home still constituted the center of the child's social life at this age. The results reported here also indicate that acquisition of accentuation was complete around age 3, prior to completion of the acquisition of segmental phonology.

By age 8, the child developed competence in using socially appropriate speech forms through restructuring her system on the basis of the increasingly active interaction with peers. Implicational relationships were held in the interaction of linguistic features with speech styles, and were activated according to the requirements of the social situation. Furthermore, the switching observed seemed to indicate the development of a "parents' code" and a "peers' code" which had separate social domains. That reading, i.e., learning, was associated with the parents' code reflects the fact that it belongs to the standard dialect. The contact of two dialects gives children the opportunity to develop awareness of linguistic variation and effective verbal strategies in communication.

On the other hand, in the child of native parents, the immediate effect of the standard dialect seemed to be minor at age 8, with the occurrence of accentual variation still limited to word accent, which constituted a favorable environment for accentual standardization. Local accentual rules, more resistant to outside influence, were observed to prevail in any linguistic contexts.

However, the effect of standard dialect seems to produce more than interdialectal variation. The intradialectal variation observed in the speech of local children suggests a greater effect of contact phenomena on internal variation, illustrating the nature of variation that children experience in the nonstandard language region. The study of variation in child language is very useful in understanding the processes involved in language change, as well as in child language acquisition.

REFERENCES

Fasold, R. 1970. Two models of socially significant linguistic variation. Language 46:551–563.

Haraguchi, S. 1977. The Tone Pattern of Japanese: An Autosegmental Theory of Tonology. Kaitakusha, Tokyo.

Inoguchi, Y., and Horii, R. 1975. Kyotogo Jiten. [A Dictionary of Kyoto Words.] Tokyodo, Tokyo.

Kobayashi, C. 1975. Japanese dialects: Phonology and reconstruction of the proto-accentual systems. Unpublished doctoral dissertation, Cornell University, Ithaca, N.Y.

Labov, W. 1972. The internal evolution of linguistic rules. In: R. P. Stockwell and R. K. S. Macaulay (eds.), Linguistic Change and Generative Theory. Indiana University Press, Bloomington.

McCawley, J. D. 1968. The Phonological Component of a Grammar of Japanese. Mouton, The Hague.

Okuda, K. 1975. Accentual Systems in the Japanese Dialects. Bunka Hyoron Publishing Co., Hiroshima.

Sugifuji, M., Nakatsuka, Y., and Takahashi, E. 1973. Akusento no kata no yure to hatsuwa no yure. [Variation in accentual patterns.] Osaka Shoin Women's College Report 11.

Weinreich, W., Labov, W., and Herzog, M. I. 1968. Empirical foundations for a theory of language change. In: W. P. Lehmann and Y. Malkiel (eds.), Directions for Historical Linguistics. University of Texas Press, Austin.

The Acquisition of Syllable Intonations in "Tone Languages" A Longitudinal Study of Latvian Children

Velta Rūķe-Draviņa

There is a marked interest in the child's acquisition of phonemic structure in the so-called tone languages, but comparatively few studies have been conducted on tone acquisition. Usually the term *intonation* is used in connection with the difference between rise and fall within a sentence or clause. A frequent claim has been made that the acquisition of this sort of intonation in young children precedes other language-learning milestones. Syllable intonation, on the other hand, refers to the pitch contour of the syllable. The fact that this syllable intonation (or syllable tone) is phonemic is demonstrated by the existence of minimal word pairs that differ only in tone. In tone languages there are two or more prosodic distinctions of vowels or diphthongs in a syllable, for example, rising versus falling tone. This chapter presents the first systematic investigation of the learning of syllable intonations (or syllable tones) as they appear in the Baltic languages and in some of the southern Slavic languages.

LINGUISTIC STRUCTURE OF THE INPUT LANGUAGE

One characteristic of the Baltic languages (Latvian and Lithuanian) is the exploitation of tone differences in long (but not in short) syllables for purposes of meaningful contrast. The *length* of vowels, that is, short and long vowel contrasts, is of phonemic importance in Latvian. Compare, for example, such minimal word pairs as: *kaps* (with a short *a*) 'grave,' but *kāps* (with a long *a*) '(he) will climb,' and *lapa* (with a short *a*) 'leaf,' but *lāpa* (with a long *a*) 'torch.' This quantitative contrast does not depend on word stress which, as a rule, lies on the first syllable of the words; the same is true for compounds. Thus, several case endings can be differentiated only by the short or long vowel at the end of the word, e.g., *sirdi* (acc sg), but *sirdī* (loc sg) 'heart,' and *māja* (nom sg), but *mājā* (loc sg) 'house.' Long syllables (those containing a long vowel, a diphthong, or a short vowel combined with l, ļ, m, n, ņ, r) can be pronounced by modulating the voice in different ways, and these syllable intonations receive their optimal realization in stressed long syllables. The intonational contrast in short vowels is not phonemically relevant in Latvian and Lithuanian, but it is in Serbo-Croatian.

In modern Standard Latvian, a two-intonation system, namely, the contrast between 1) "level" intonation (˜) and 2) "non-level" intonation (ˆ), is being established (see examples 1 and 2 in Figure 1). The two-intonation system can be illustrated by the following examples:

1. *loks* /luõks/ 'onion bulb'
2. *logs* /luôks/ 'window,' *loks* /luôks/ 'curve, circle.'
1. tur ir liela *kãpa* 'there is a large *dune*'
2. viņi *kâpa* kalnā 'they *climbed* the hill'
1. skolas *zãlē* ir liela 'the school *hall* is large'
2. zem kokiem *zâle* ir rasa 'under the trees there is (some) dew on the *grass*'
1. ēd lēnām, nevajag tā *rĩt*! 'eat slowly, you don't need to *gulp* like that!'
2. *rît* sabrauks viesi 'the guests will come *tomorrow*'
1. *krêslā* grūti lasīt 'by *twilight* it is hard to read'
2. sēdi mierīgi *krêslā*! 'sit still in the *armchair*!'
1. gaļa sāk *pũt* 'meat starts to *rot*'
2. *pût* stabuli! '*blow* the pipe!'
1. vīri *sẽja* rudzus 'men were *sowing* rye'
2. viņš *sêja* maisu ciet 'he was *tying* up the sack'

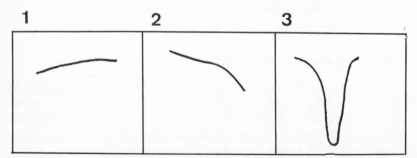

Figure 1. Latvian intonation curves. 1, level tone (˜); 2, falling tone (è); 3, broken tone (ê).

There are numerous words the lexical and grammatical meaning of which depend only on the type of intonation. Thus, these syllable intonations are valuable in the process of communication.

Within the area where Latvian is spoken, there are several other intonation systems in use that consist of three or two contrasting tone types. In a district in the central part of Latvia, three intonations, namely, the level, the falling, and the broken intonation, are distinguished (examples 1, 2, and 3 in Figure 1). Compare, for example:

Vili! 'William!' but *vīli* /vī:li/ 'file'
  vīli /vì:li/ 'seam'
  vīli /vî:li/ 'you deceived'

The first-mentioned form *Vili!* 'William!' has short vowels in both syllables. The form *vīli* contains a long vowel in the first syllable and a short vowel in the second syllable. If the long vowel /i:/ is pronounced with a level intonation, the word means 'file' (acc sg), with the falling tone it means 'seam' (acc sg), and with the broken tone it means 'deceived' (second person past tense form from *vilt*). Another example:

ka (with a short *a*) '(conjunction) that'
kā /kā:/ (level tone) '(the letter) K'
kā /kà/ (falling tone) 'whose'
kā /kâ:/ (broken tone) 'how'

In this study, the input language for the Latvian-speaking children belonged to the above-mentioned intonation systems with either three or two differing syllable intonations. The Eastern dialects of Latvian also have two intonations but of another character: either a contrast between the falling and the rising intonation, or a contrast between the falling and the broken intonation.

THE ACQUISITION OF TONE

There are two main questions concerning the development of these syllable intonations in early childhood. The first is the general belief that an adult basically cannot change his intonation system and re-learn intonational types that he acquired in childhood. If this is correct, an important question is: at what age does an individual form the intonation system that will remain the characteristic mark of his idiolect for the rest of his life? A second question concerns the observation that children adopt the intonation system of their environment (parents or grandparents). Nevertheless, linguists have found differences between the older and younger generations that show diachronic changes in intonation. For example, in modern Latvian there has been a change from the three-intonation system to the two-intonation system, but in some subdialects or linguistic communities there has even been a complete loss of phonemically different types in the pronunciation of young people. The second question is: when does this change happen, and under what conditions—in early childhood or later during the school years? A related question is: what happens if both parents do not come from the same intonation district?

In order to answer these questions, we wanted first to know the absolute age when the child has learned the intonations in accordance with the norms in the adult speech, and second, the relative age of acquisition, that is, the relationship of the mastery of syllable intonations to other phonetic developments. For example, does the child already correctly produce all phonemes and clusters of his mother tongue before he can master the intonation system? What basic elements of the phonemic system must be learned first to give the child the capacity to differentiate intonation types in a long syllable? Is the placement of the word accent easier to grasp than the total characteristics of a rising and a falling tone in long vowels?

A LONGITUDINAL INVESTIGATION

Insight into these problems is possible only by means of a longitudinal investigation. For this reason, the main focus of this chapter is the developmental process of dynamic language learning in early childhood. The intonation system acquired in the speech of 4-year-old children was compared with that of periods in their later life in order to determine the stability or instability of intonations learned in childhood and carried over into adulthood.

The language acquisition process in two Latvian-speaking children was studied by means of a diary consisting of annotations that were made practically every day, and longer observations written at least once a week. Everything that seemed to be of linguistic interest was recorded. Observations on other Latvian children, including sound recordings, were also used. The two Latvian-speaking children, a boy and a girl, came from the same family. The boy's language development was earlier and more rapid than the girl's. Both parents spoke the Central Latvian dialect: the mother with three differing intonations (level, falling, broken), the father, with two intonations (level and non-level).

There are two important things to notice in the process of learning intonations: first, the *manner* in which the syllable intonations are pronounced (i.e., whether the young child produces the level and the broken intonation in the same way as the adults do), and second, the distribution of the differing intonation types (i.e., does the child use the level and the non-level intonation in words in which adults use this intonation type?).

A Schematic Survey of Intonation Learning

Our results are shown in the form of longitudinal reports on a young boy and a young girl acquiring Latvian.

The Boy

Age 1;2   From the age of 14 months some words were noticed in active use, spoken with a long vowel or diphthong and with the same intonation as in the speech of adults, e.g., *aūto* (=aūto) 'car,' *mȩm̃mȩ* (=mem̃me) 'mommy,' *niñn* (=niñne) 'drink,' *aĩja* 'lullaby sound,' *am̃ma* (=ɳam̃ma) 'food,' and *Daĩ* (=Daĩnis) (previously, the last mentioned word was said with a falling tone).

On the other hand, some other words were pronounced with the correct long vowel, but with a syllable intonation different from that spoken in adult language (e.g., with a rising-falling tone instead of the broken intonation) *âb* (=âbols) 'apple,' and *â:c* (=acis) 'eyes' and acenes '(eye)-glasses,' with short vowels in the adults' speech); or (with level-falling tone instead of level tone) *kã̄:* (=kãja) 'foot' and *mã̄:* (=mãja) 'house.'

Sometimes the same word (*mȩm̃mȩ* 'mommy,' *tȩ̄tȩ* 'daddy') was said with the falling, sometimes with the level intonation. As a rule, the words in the child's speech that were in agreement with adult intonation had the level tone. The broken tone appeared in the form *vȩ̄* 'dirty,' but otherwise was very seldom used. A deviation from the adult pronunciation was noticed in *gailis* 'rooster,' spoken with the level (instead of broken) intonation, and in *ninne* 'drink,' and *panna* 'pan,' still at 1;5 spoken with a sort of falling intonation.

Age 1;6   The level intonation was still pronounced with a forceful expulsion so that it got a rising-falling tone because it was not possible to hold the tone to the end. This was also heard in the words *mȇ̄:* (=mērs) 'measure,' *śaũ:* (=slauka) '(he) wipes,' *tȇ:* (=tēja) 'tea,' and (instead of the falling intonation in the adult speech) *tâ̄u* or *taũ* (=tàure) 'horn.' Occasional confusion between the level, falling, and broken intonation often was found during this stage: the child pronounced the very same word one day with one intonation, another day with another type of intonation.

In place of the adults' broken intonation, sometimes the rising tone was used, e.g., *naũna* (=naûda) 'money.' However, the negation *nē* 'no' always was said with the broken tone: *nê̂!* or *dê̂!*

Age 1;8   During the later period, a closer coherence in length between the pronunciation of the child and the parents was reached; however, this was not observed for all words, and the long vowel was not always spoken in full length. Therefore, no definite intonations could be heard in such semi-long vowels. The former monosyllabic form *kã̄:* was now changed into *kã̃ja:* (= kājā) 'on the foot,' and *vã̃* was spoken as a bisyllabic form *vã̃źe:* (= vāze) 'in the vase.'

In some cases, the confusion could be explained as a result of variations in the language spoken in the home environment. Thus, the word *otrs* /uotrs/ 'another, second' usually was pronounced with the non-level intonation by the mother of the child whereas his father used the level tone.

Full agreement was recorded in the words *puĩka* (= puĩka) 'boy' and *puĩśi* (= puĩsītis) 'a little boy.'

Age 1;9 Even during the next months, the closest correspondence in intonations between child and adult was in words spoken with the level intonation. This was especially true for the words first learned at this time, e.g., *nã̃ka* (= nãk) '(he) comes.' In many other forms there was still disagreement: the expected broken intonation was replaced by a rising tone (as in *ogas* /uogas/ 'berries,' *ĩsa* 'short,' *lietus* 'rain'), or the expected level intonation was spoken as some kind of rising-falling tone (as in *balta* 'white,' *dūmi* 'smoke,' *spalva* 'feather').

Age 1;10 The same situation continued in the next month when agreement with adult form (in intonation) was found in the words: *kã̃śu* (= krãso) '(he) paints,' *kũ̃pã* (= kopā) 'together,' *kũ̃ka* (= kūka) 'cake,' *mẽ̃:s* (= mẽrs /mẽrs/) 'measure,' *jaũka* (= lauka) 'outside,' *Daĩ* (Dainis) (name), *puĩśi* (= puisītis) 'little boy,' but disagreement in: *ũzu* (= ozols /uôzuols/) 'oak,' *ũ̃c* (= ods) 'gnot,' *naũda* (= naûda) 'money,' *gũ̃zu* (= grozs /gruôzs/) 'basket.' In the word *aĩta* 'sheep' the level tone (instead of the falling intonation in the speech of adults) was heard.

At 1;10 the child had formed his first minimal contrasting pair on the basis of intonation type alone: *tã̃* 'that' (fem) and *tâ* 'that way.' The meaning of these two words was differentiated only by the level or the broken tone, in the same way as it is done in Standard Latvian. This month some vowels still varied between a short and long pronunciation, which hindered the development of a definite intonation for such forms, e.g., *sâp (= sâp)* 'it hurts' but sometimes also as *sap* (with a short vowel) or *sa:p* (with a semi-long vowel).

Greater agreement with adult intonations developed at the end of the second year, especially in words that were new for the child. The best agreement between the pronunciation of the child and his parents was in forms with the level intonation, e.g., in the words *aũka* (= aukla) 'string,' *aũk* (= auksts) 'cold,' *bã̃c* (= balts) 'white,' *bẽ̃:s* (= bẽrzs /bẽrzs/) 'birch tree,' *bũ̃ze* (= blūze) 'blouse,' *bũ̃da* (= bloda/bļuoda/) 'bowl,' *bũ̃dija* (= būdiņa) 'hut,' *buṁba* (= bumba) 'ball,' *caũvi* (= cauri) 'through.' Nevertheless, there were some actively used words with the broken tone although the child reproduced this intonation type in a somewhat different way from the adults, cf. *âźis* or *à:źiś* (= âzis) 'he-goat' and *gâbe*

(= grãbeklis) 'rake.' In some words an unexpected level or rising intonation was heard instead of the broken intonation, e.g., *ı̃si* (= ı̄si) 'short,'
gı̃du sęgu (= grı̄dsęgu /grı̃dsęgu/) 'rug.'

Age 1;11 At the end of the second year, correct intonations appeared also in the (unstressed) endings and suffixes, cf. *gaidı̂s* 'will wait,'
metı̂s 'will throw,' and *minẽs* 'will guess.'

At 1;11 the correspondence in intonations increased. In some words,
the former incorrect tone was replaced with the corresponding adult intonation; thus, *kāps* '(he) will climb' now was said with the broken (not
rising) intonation as at the beginning of this month. An important deviation from the norms still was observed in the usage of the broken intonation: some words in the child's active vocabulary were spoken with the
correct broken tone (*zābaki* 'boots,' *zāde* (= zāle) 'grass,' * ź̃ug* (= žogs
/žuoks/) 'fence'), but in other words the broken intonation (used in the
adults' pronunciation) was replaced by a rising tone: *ūzu* (= ozols
/uozuols/) 'oak,' *ūsa* (= osa /uosa/) 'handle (of a cup),' *ūga* (= oga
/uoga/) 'berry,' *zūbi,* dat pl *zūbim* (= zobi, dat pl zobiem) 'teeth,' and
vaiģe (= zvaigzne) 'star.'

Age 2;0 At 2 years of age, the most important new stage in linguistic development was that the child started to speak in longer forms and
with distinct final vowels. That, in turn, made for a distinct intonation of
the unstressed long syllables, cf. *visām pusēm* '(in) all directions,' *maš̄*
bukānı̄c (= mazs burkānı̄tis) 'a little carrot,' *ve dauʒāk* (= vēl daudzāk)
'even more,' and *fai:nı̄ti* (= spainı̄ti) 'a little pail.' A diphthong with the
corresponding intonation was noticed also in the word *pa·diẽs!*
(= paldies! /pal·diẽs!/) 'thank you' (with the stress on the second syllable).

Incorrect (i.e., not corresponding to adult) intonation was most
tenacious in words that were incorrectly pronounced from very early
childhood. Thus, at the age of 2 years *kāda* 'someone' and *gaijı̄ti*
(= gailı̄ti) 'little rooster' still were spoken with the level (instead of the
broken) tone.

Age 2;1-3;0 During the child's third year, the deviations were
minor. Most of them were of the same type, namely, the level intonation
dominated, and the child used the level tone even in words that had the
non-level intonation in the adults' speech. For example, *nauda* 'money'
was still heard with the level tone.

On the other hand, words that became active for the first time in the
child's vocabulary mostly had the correct intonation type. Cf. some illustrative examples: *Dañı̃c tã paśaı̃gã̂ gũtu viên uõtu pusi* (= Dainı̄tis tā
pastaigā /pa/ gultu /uz/ vienu otru pusi) 'the little boy is walking on the
bed that way, from one side to the other' (all words with correct corresponding adult intonation); and *màn i gaı̃jic* (= man ir gaı̃lı̄tis) 'I have a

little rooster' at age 2;5 (with an unexpected level tone instead of non-level); *es pasatîŝuôs juṁs uôgu* (= es paskatîŝos /uz/ jums /pa/ logu) 'I shall look at you through the window' ('logu /luôgu/' was spoken with an unexpected level tone instead of a non-level one).

At the end of the third year and the beginning of the fourth year of the child's life, the intonations generally corresponded to the types used in the child's family, although otherwise the child's speech was still phonetically incomplete and differed from the norms in the input language. For example, in the sentences recorded at 2;9,18 and 2;10,18 *sitūô âpstiju vȩl̂k fiñtijậs fîtas* (= /ar/ ŝito lāpstiņu /es/ velku smiltiņās svītras) 'with this shovel I'm making lines in the sand,' and *kâdậ kậsậ vinam bi buñgas?* (= kādā krāsā viņam bij bungas?) 'what color were his drums?' the usage of intonations (level and non-level) was correct but *f* was pronounced in place of *sv* and *sm,* the *r* sound was missing, *l* was missing, etc.

Age 4;0 Even at the age of 4, there were numerous imperfections in the child's phonemic structure, but the contrast between short and long vowels already had stabilized and there was a clear contrast between the level and the non-level intonation. Nevertheless, the way these two types of intonations were pronounced by the child differed somewhat: the broken tone was a little weaker, and the level intonation was mostly less long and continuous than in adult language. Up to the very end of this period, some words remained in variance to the adult form, e.g., *dzȩl̃tȩns* 'yellow' was said with the level (in place of the non-level) tone.

The Girl
Age 1;2 The girl was slower than the boy in linguistic development during the first years of life. At 1;2 the first actively used words with a long vowel (or a diphthong) appeared. Among these first words, no forms were noticed with the broken tone but some words were spoken with the level intonation (*aîju!* 'sleep!') and some other words sometimes with a falling tone (*ậ* (= ậrā) 'out,' *ũ:u* (= ur̃ru) 'baby carriage'). A rising-falling tone was fixed in the form *ũ* (= ũdens) 'water' and (= uguns) 'fire.'

Age 1;3 The first forms with a slight similarity to the broken intonation appeared at 1;3–1;4, e.g., *âba* (= âbols) 'apple,' and *âRā* (= ârā) 'out, outside.' It is interesting to note that in the next few months *ābols* 'apple' was no longer pronounced with the broken tone but with a tone similar to the level or the rising intonation (*ãbi!* or *a:bi*). Instability in vowel length still appeared, especially in the word *tete* or *tēte* 'daddy.' Because of the difficulty in lengthening the vowel, the form *lèlle* 'doll' also had a falling tone in place of the expected level intonation *(lel̃le)*.

Age 1;7 A similar situation continued during the next months: *l'aki:* (= lâcis) 'bear' was still pronounced at times with short *a,* at times with long *a;* even *abi* or *a:bi* or *ãbi* (= ābols) 'apple' was spoken with a short, a semi-long, and a normal long (rising intonated) vowel. But there were already some other words that the child pronounced with a level intonation in concurrence with the adult form, e.g., *ĩga* (= Rĩga).

Age 1;9 At age 1;9, there were still many words which, in the pronunciation of the child, were monosyllabic and thus shorter than the input form in the adults' language; the long vowel in this stem syllable was then often spoken with a rising falling intonation, of the same type as in the "Tamian" dialect of Latvian, e.g., *kâ* (= karote) 'spoon,' *mã:j* (= mãja) 'house'). In other words, the type of intonation corresponded to the model in the adult pronunciation: (with the level intonation) *paĩ* (= paĩ) 'nice, good,' *tẽte* (= tẽte) 'daddy,' *mem̃m* (= mem̃me) 'mommy,' (with the broken tone) *nê* (= nê) 'no,' *âbuo* (= ābols /âbuôls/) 'apple.'

Age 1;10 In the words first used actively during this month, the correct level intonation was imitated and learned in accordance with the norms in the adult language. Disagreements, when the non-level intonation was replaced by the level tone, sometimes could be explained by the use of homonym forms, i.e., by the girl's manner to exploit a former form in a new sense. Thus, *kãbī* (= kãrbiņa) 'satchel' (with the level tone), which corresponds to the adult form kārbiņa, at this time was used also to mean *zābaki* 'boots' (with the non-level intonation).

Age 1;11 Instability in the usage of intonations continued to the end of the second year and throughout the beginning of the third year. Nevertheless, correct word usage with the level intonation (= adult pronunciation) increased. The greatest difficulties were connected with the reproduction of the non-level (broken) tone. First, the intonation was not spoken with exactly the same broken character as in the parents' speech. Second, the broken tone often was replaced by an unexpected rising or level tone.

Age 2;2 At least in the minimal word pair *tã* 'that' and *tâ* 'that way,' the contrast of the two types of syllable intonations was clear and exact. But during this period the form *tãdu* 'such' was registered a few times with the level (instead of the broken) tone.

During the first months of the third year, the dominating intonation type in the girl's pronunciation was the level intonation. Sometimes it appeared also in place of the non-level intonation in the adults' language. Examples are: *âbula* (= âbols) 'apple,' *tã vãka* (= tas vãks) 'that cover,' *ũgu* (= oga /uôga/) 'berry,' *nàu t'ãpa* (= nesâp) 'doesn't hurt, *mãka mem̃me* (= memme mâk) 'mommy knows,' *pî lũga* (= pie loga /luôga/) 'by the window,' and *īd'i kâbẹ* (= ēdis skâbenes) '(he) shall eat sorrel' (in all long syllables the level or the rising intonation was spoken in place of the non-level). The broken tone was heard in *nê* 'no,' *pê* (= pẹ) 'dirty,' and (the new active form) *miêg* (= miêgs) 'sleep.'

Age 2;4 At age 2;4–2;5, the intonations had been stabilized both in pronunciation and distribution according to adult usage although there was still much to be learned about the correct pronunciation of Latvian phonemes and phoneme clusters. For example, in the child's pronunciation of *katā luôga pīliņa* (= skatās /pa/ logu pīlītes) '(she) is looking through the window at the ducks,' there were no consonant clusters or prepositions, nor was the diminutive suffix formed in accordance to norms, but the syllable intonations in the words "logu" and "pīlītes" were similar to those used by the parents. The same was true in another phrase recorded at that time: *gaîli diêd* (= gaîlis dziêd) 'the rooster crows.'

Age 2;6   In the middle of the third year, the correct distribution of the adult intonations (level and non-level) stabilized not only in stem syllables but also in suffixes and endings, cf. *nãkuôtã* (= nākošā) 'the next one' (with the level tone in the first and the third syllable but the non-level tone in the second syllable). At 2;6 the girl still spoke an incorrect diphthong instead of the long *ū* in the verb *būs* 'shall be' but, nevertheless, with the correct broken intonation: *tàmma miļa, guda buôt,' va nãk līdzu* (= /ja/ Saŕma miļa, gudra bûs, varês nãkt līdz) 'when Sarma will be sweet /and/ wise, she can come with us.'

Age 2;7   At age 2;7, the first actively used words appeared in which the second (not the first) syllable was stressed in the adult speech. At first, the unstressed first syllable in such words was dropped in the girl's pronunciation but the second stressed syllable had the same intonation as in the input language, cf. *nav kã* (= nav ne·kã) 'there is nothing.' At the same time even *âbuôli* (= āboli /âbuôli/) 'apples' was spoken with the correct non-level intonation (not level tone as it was said earlier). The same correction was noticed at 2;10 in the form *tâdi* 'such.'

Age 2;11–3;0   At age 3, the adult intonation types were generally acquired but much was still missing in the mastery of Latvian phonemes and phoneme groups, cf. the phrase a) in the parent's pronunciation, b) in the child's pronunciation:

a)   *divas mãsiņas kaĩsa graûdus saũjãm*
b)   *diva mãtiņa kaĩta gaûdu taũjã* 'two sisters are casting seeds by the handfuls'

In this example, the child's speech deviates widely from the correct pronunciation, but the syllable intonations are in complete agreement. The fourth year began with approximately the same situation. At times, in some words the adult long vowel or diphthong was replaced by a short vowel in the child's incomplete speech and thus no phonemically relevant intonations could appear, cf. *Lat' d'êja uôdeni pi kãna* (= Larss dzēra ūdeni pie krāna) 'Lars drank water at the water-tap,' where *pie* 'at' was changed into *pi* (with a short *i* instead of the diphthong *ie*). At 3;0 the following phrases were recorded: *et' g'ibu âbuôlu* (= es gribu ābolu) 'I want an apple' and *man nepatîk iêdî âbuolu* (= man nepatîk ēst ābolu) 'I don't like to eat the apple'), with wide deviations from the phonemic norms in Latvian but with intonations in full accordance with adult usage.

Common Features in the Intonation Learning in Latvian Children

By comparing these two longitudinal studies of the learning of Latvian syllable intonations, we see that, on the whole, the stages of intonation acquisition were parallel. Because the girl was slower in her linguistic development in general, her mastery of differing intonations during the first 2 years also came somewhat later. Nevertheless, at the age of about 3;6–4;0 the intonational system of their parents' speech was acquired by both children, but in both cases there were still some small deviations from the use of intonations in the input language. Table 1 summarizes the important stages in the development process and the correspondences between the boy's and the girl's language acquisition.

By comparing the results from the two longitudinal studies with many other observations and tape recordings of Latvian-speaking young children's speech, we can conclude that the mastery of syllable intonations seems to be arrived at in a similar way by all children and that there is a universal strategy in the acquisition of tones. The results of the investigation can be summarized as follows:

1. The mastery of differing syllable intonations is a gradual learning process that takes a long time—about 3 years. At this age, the child has learned to pronounce and to use the correct syllable intonations in the words of his active daily vocabulary but it takes a much longer period to learn all (or at least most) of the words in accordance with the intonational usage in the adult's speech.
2. The correct intonation type is not mastered in all words at the same time. In the speech of a 2- or 3-year-old child, words pronounced with the correct intonation appear side by side with words in which the intonation does not correspond to the adult's pronunciation.
3. At about age 3, the best correspondence between the child's pronunciation and the intonation type in the input language is in words that have been learned by the child at a later period.
4. By about age 3, the intonation system spoken in the child's environment basically has been acquired by the child. Individual variations are large, but the absolute age for normal children to master the syllable intonations seems to be about 3–4.
5. Even during the later preschool period, when the intonation system as a whole already corresponds to the input model, there are still a few words that have remained in the child's idiolect in an idiosyncratic form of pronunciation as a result of an early habit.

Table 1.   Summary of observations on tone acquisition in Latvian children

Age	Latvian-speaking boy	Latvian-speaking girl
1;2	*the first active words with correct intonation; a few words with long vowels but incorrect intonation; instability in intonation (the same word sometimes with a falling, sometimes with a rising or level tone)	instability in vowel length; very few words with the correct intonation
1;3		still mistakes in intonation types
1;6	occasional confusion of intonations; level tone in place of broken but ne! 'no!' with the correct broken tone	
1;7		still instability in vowel length
1;9	in new (latest learned) words, good correspondence with the parents' intonations	*the first words with the correct but still many other words with an incorrect intonation; instability in intonation
1;10	†first minimal contrast pair on basis of intonational type alone	numerous forms with correct level intonation
1;11	‡correct intonations also in endings and suffixes; still mistakes in the distribution of broken tone	still instability in the usage of intonations; increase of correct word usage with level intonation; broken intonation sometimes replaced by a rising tone, or the broken intonation somewhat different from the adult speech
2;0	words with long final vowels	
2;2	small deviations from the input language	†first minimal contrast pair on basis of intonational type
2;4–2;5		alone; still mistakes in the distribution of intonations as a whole, the intonational system already acquired
2;6		‡correct intonations also in endings and suffixes
3;0	level intonation dominates (also used instead of broken)	
3;0–4;0	still numerous imperfections in the phonemic structure but mastery of level and non-level intonation contrast	still numerous deviations from the input language but, in general, correct pronunciation and distribution of the level and non-level intonations

*, †, ‡ indicate ages at which comparable stages of intonation acquisition were attained by the boy and girl.

6. In all of these cases, the intonations acquired in early childhood stayed with the individual throughout the later period of his life (if a sudden transfer to another language or another dialect did not occur during the early school years).

7. Judging by this investigation, the intonation acquisition process during the first years of life is connected with two main difficulties: 1) learning how to reproduce correctly the specific type of intonation, and 2) learning to distribute the two (or three) different types of intonations in accordance with the adult usage, i.e., to choose the right type for each long syllable in the word (in the stem, in the suffix, and in the ending).

8. The observed Latvian-speaking children had greater difficulties with the broken intonation than with the pronunciation of the level intonation. At least during the first 2 years, the adult broken tone was sometimes replaced by a level or a rising tone.

9. The relative age when syllable intonations can be mastered depends on the general phonetic development of the child's speech. No syllable intonations can be acquired before the child has learned to differentiate between long vowels and diphthongs, on the one hand, and short vowels, on the other hand. During a certain period (about age 1;6) the child usually uses short, semi-long and long vowels indiscriminately (instead of short or instead of long vowels in the input language). But no contrast in intonation can be achieved while the length of the vowel is variable and random. In order for an intonation contrast to develop (for example, the minimal contrasting pair $k\hat{\bar{a}}$ 'how' and $k\tilde{\bar{a}}$ '(the letter) K, a necessary requirement is the phonemically relevant quantitative difference, i.e., the child's competence in pronouncing a short and a long vowel in distinct quantitative contrast (e.g., *ka* 'conj that' but *kā* 'how; (the letter) K; whose').

10. Because mastery of diphthongs occurs later than that of many monophthongal sounds, even the syllable intonations in such diphthongs belong to later appearances.

11. Concerning the relative age, the intonations, as used by the adults, are already stabilized in the speech of the child when 1) all consonant phonemes and clusters have not been learned yet, and 2) the quality of long vowels and diphthongs still deviates greatly from the adult norms, e.g., when the child still said *buot* instead of *būs* 'shall be' or *iedī* instead of *ēst* 'to eat.'

12. Because the forms used by children during the first speech phase tend to be monosyllabic (with the exception of frequently heard syllable repetitions), it is natural that the correct intonation type in unstressed endings and suffixes can appear only in a later phase, when the child begins to speak in bisyllabic or longer forms.

13. Thus, the relative age when the syllable intonations are mastered depends on the general phonetic development in which four developmental stages can be distinguished. Those stages are:

stage I   instead of short and long vowels in the input language, short, semi-long, and long vowels are used indiscriminately

stage II   phonemically relevant quantitative contrast: short vowels as opposed to long vowels have developed

stage III distinct intonative contrast and minimal contrasting pairs based on different syllable intonation types have been mastered

later stages   mastery of "difficult" phonemes, consonant clusters, and diphthongs

An illustrative example:

stage III   *Lat dḕja uôdeni pi kãna*
(about 3;0)

later stage   *Larss dzḗra ûdeni pie krãna* 'Lars was drinking water
(about 6;0)   from the tap.'

COMPARISON WITH OTHER "TONE LANGUAGES"

The Latvian material shows that a common strategy in the acquisition of tones exists. However, caution must be recommended in drawing any generalizations. Hitherto, there have been relatively few studies on tone acquisition, and more longitudinal studies are needed to find out the developmental stages and the relative order of mastering the various types of duration, tone height, and structure of the tones in the "tone languages." To make further generalizations, it would also be necessary to inspect comparative materials from other similar tone languages.

In this respect, the Lithuanian language would be of special interest because Lithuanian also has two types of syllable intonations (a rising and a falling) but, unlike the Latvian language, also has a free word accent. On the other hand, data from Serbo-Croatian also would be desirable because in that language, tonal contrasts appear not only in long syllables (as in Latvian and Lithuanian) but also in short vowels, and in long vowels the distribution of intonation types is governed by rules slightly different from those in the Baltic languages.

A somewhat parallel development is found in the speech acquisition process in Latvian-speaking and Czech-speaking children. Czech has no contrasting intonation types, but it has (as do Latvian and Lithuanian) short and long vowels. According to Pačesová (1972), the Czech-speaking children under observation (1;0–4;0) had not yet acquired the feature of length, and the long vowels represented a less mature stage of development as compared with their short counterparts. Instability was shown in the existence of the semi-long, long, short, and extra-long allophones that appeared in free variations and were not used contrastively. This phenomenon corresponds to the situation in the speech development in Latvian-speaking children (stage I). Nevertheless, the Czech children did perceive the *length* (this is seen especially in their replacing of the diphthongs with a long vowel, and vice vera). As is the case for Latvian-speaking children, the duration of the long vowels during the early periods did not exactly correspond to the length in Standard Czech, which is approximately twice as long as the corresponding short vowels.

An important study for comparison is the investigation of tone acquisition in Cantonese by Kwock-Ping Tse (1978). Both Latvian and Chinese are usually mentioned as "tone languages" even though the structure of these "tones" is quite different. In Chinese, the high or the low pitch-level in the word is important and phonemic because the meaning of the word depends on the degree of the pitch. In Latvian, the intonation contour (i.e., the modulation of rising and falling tones within the borders of a long syllable) is important.

Kwock-Ping Tse's study shows that tones were acquired earlier than the segmental system. By age 1;10, the child seldom made mistakes in tones but still had difficulties with many kinds of consonants (e.g., pronouncing the lateral *l* and the final stops *p, t, k*). Latvian syllable intonations also were mastered earlier than some "difficult" phonemes and clusters, but the absolute age for the mastery of syllable intonations was much later. According to Kwock-Ping Tse, the Chinese tones were acquired very early, and the duration of the process was 8 months.

There is another important difference in the tone acquisition process in Chinese and Latvian. In Kwock-Ping Tse's opinion, the stages of tone acquisition in Cantonese have some correspondences in the child's *syntactic* development, namely, "children start to acquire tones from their single-word stage and acquisition appears to be complete at the two- to three-word stage." In Latvian, the quantitative contrast in vowels and diphthongs is relevant for the syllable intonations, and the intonational system has connection not with the syntax but with the length of the actively used words, namely, the syllable intonations are mastered when two- and three-syllabic forms appear in the child's active speech and when long vowels and diphthongs are distinctly differentiated from short vowels.

REFERENCES

Ābele, A. 1932. Par neuzsvērto zilbju intonācijām. [On the intonation of unaccented syllables.] Filologu Biedrības Raksti 12:149–163.

Bendiks, H. 1978. Lai uz paraugu varētu paļauties. [One should be able to rely on a standard.] Literatūra un Māksla 27:5.

Blinkena, A., Cīrule, Dz., Cīrulis, K., Freidenfelds, I., and Moze, M. 1976. Latviešu valoda 7.-9.klasei. [The Latvian language for class 7-9.] Zvaigzne, Riga.

Ceplītis, L., and Katlape, N. 1960. Izteiksmīgas runas pamati. Latvijas PSR Zinātņu Akadēmijas izdevniecība, Riga.

Ekblom, R. 1933. Die lettischen Akzentarten. Uppsala.

Endzelīns, J. 1971 (1897). Diftongu un garo vokāļu izruna latviešu valodā. [Pronunciation of diphthongs and long vowels in Latvian.] In: H. Bendiks, A. Bergmane, R. Grabis, T. Jakubaite, M. Rudzīte, E. Šmite, and D. Zemzare (eds.), Jānis Endzelīns. Darbu izlase, Vol. 1, pp. 17-30. Zinātne, Riga.

Endzelīns, J. 1971 (1899). Über den lettischen Silbenakzent. [Concerning the Latvian syllable accent.] In: H. Bendiks, A. Bergame, R. Grabis, T. Jakubaite, M. Rudzīte, E. Šmite, and D. Zemzare (eds.), Jānis Endzelīns. Darbu izlase, Vol. 1, pp. 117-132. Zinatne, Riga.

Grīsle, R. 1970. Latviešu heterotoni. [Latvian heterotoners.] In: V. Rūķe-Draviņa (ed.), Donum Balticum. Almquist & Wiksell, Stockholm.

Kwock-Ping Tse, J. 1978. Tone acquisition in Cantonese: A longitudinal case study. J. Child Lang. 5:191-204.

Laua, A. 1969. Latviešu literārās valodas fonētika. [The phonetics of the Latvian literary language.] Zvaigzne, Riga.

Liepa, E. 1979. Vokālisma un zilbju kvantitāte latviešu literārajā valoda. [Vocalic and syllabic quantity in the Latvian literary language.] Zinātne, Riga.

Pacešová, J. 1972. The growth of phonemic repertory in Czech-speaking children. In: Colloquium Paedolinguisticum. Proceedings of the First International Symposium of Paedolinguists held at Brno, October 14-16, 1970, pp. 199-207. Mouton, The Hague.

Rudzīte, M. K. 1969. Latyšskaja dialektologija. [Latvian dialectology.] Avtoreferat. Akademija Nauk Latyšskoj SSR. Otdelenie obščestvennyx nauk, Riga.

Rūķe-Draviņa, V. 1963. Zur Sprachentwicklung bei Kleinkindern. [On the development of language in small children.] 1. Syntax. Slaviska institutionen vid Lunds universitet, Lund.

Rūķe-Draviņa, V. 1969. "Naturgesetze" in der Lautaneignung beim Sprechenlernen? [Natural laws in sound acquisition in learning to speak?] In: Actes du Xe Congrès International des linguistes, Vol. 3, pp. 170- 179. L'Acadèmie de la République Socialiste de Roumanie, Bucarest.

Rūķe-Draviņa, V. 1977. The Standardization Process in Latvian 16th Century to the Present. Almquist & Wiksell, Stockholm.

Rūķe-Draviņa, V. Zilbes stabilitāte divu paaudžu laikā. [The stability of the syllable in the course of two generations.] In press.

Verbal Grammar in Modern Greek Early Child Language

Ursula Stephany

Previous studies on first-language acquisition have concentrated on the propositional side of the sentence, that is, the occurrence and interplay of semantic roles, such as agent, benefactive, objective, and on syntax. The grammar of the verb, however, has received much less attention. This may be partly attributable to the impetus that more recent research in this field has received from studies of the acquisition of English, a language with limited verb morphology, as compared to synthetic languages. This chapter concerns an early stage of first-language acquisition of Modern Greek, a language with a particularly rich verb morphology. Because aspect, tense, and mood are obligatorily marked on the main verb in Modern Greek, this language offers an excellent opportunity for studying these fundamental categories of verbal grammar at an earlier stage of acquisition than is possible in most analytic languages.

The data come from the first phase of a longitudinal study of four monolingual, middle class children (three girls and a boy) in Athens, Greece. The data were tape-recorded in the children's homes during interactions of the children and their mothers in natural activities such as playing, eating, and dressing. The children were visited five to eight times during a 2-week period, and each session lasted 60–90 minutes. At the first session, the subjects' ages ranged from 20 months, 10 days (20;10) to 22 months, 25 days (22;25). Three of the four children had a mean length of utterance (MLU) of about 1.5. The fourth child (age 21;17) had an MLU of just above 2.00. Mean length of utterance has been computed in words, with clitics counted as separate words, because in highly inflecting languages such as Modern Greek, it is not possible to decide on morpheme segmentation unarbitrarily in the stage of language development that is studied in this chapter.

Because this study focuses on the semantic categories of verbal grammar (aspect, tense, and mood) as well as on their formal expression, only utterances containing a verb are considered. Also, only those utterances containing a main verb are included in this study. These utterances are divided into two classes; modal and non-modal. In modal expressions, the verb is either in the imperative mood, as in example 1 below, or in the subjunctive mood, as in example 2. Semantically, modal expressions are limited to volitive (example 3) and obligative expressions (1 and 2) at this stage of development.

1. *fije apo kí (go-away*-IMP.2S. *from there)*
2. *na kasísi i mamà (= na kaθísi i mamà)* (MODAL PART. *sit*-3S. *the mummy*) 'Mummy shall sit down'
3. *pìo vavási (= /o/ spìros /na/ ɖiavási) (/the/ spiros* /MOD.PART./ *read*-3S.) 'Spiros wants to read'

Although Calbert (1975) claims that there are no strictly non-modal expressions, affirmative and negative statements as well as questions not containing a modal verb are considered to be non-modal. As is explained below, modal and non-modal expressions are formally differentiated at the stage of language acquisition studied.

ASPECT, TENSE, AND MOOD IN MODERN GREEK CHILD LANGUAGE

The majority of verbs in Modern Greek have two formally differentiated stems: a present stem and an aorist stem. In simple tenses, the present stem is used in expressions with an imperfective aspect and the aorist stem is used in expressions with a perfective aspect. The distribution of the two stems in the simple tenses is represented in Table 1. The past tense is differentiated from the non-past tenses, present and future, by inflectional endings, and the imperfective and perfective aspects are indicated by the stem. The future is formed by preposing the future particle *θa* to the present or aorist stem with a present ending. The subjunctive mood is marked by modal particles, most often *na*.

The following combinations of stem and inflectional endings occur in the children's productions: present stem with present inflectional ending, aorist stem with past inflectional ending, and aorist stem with present inflectional ending. These three linguistic forms express the semantic categories non-modal imperfective, non-modal perfective, and modal perfective, respectively. Except for the imperative forms, which have not been considered here because the perfective and imperfective aspects very often are not differentiated in the imperative, even in the adult language, these categories account for about 98% of the children's utterances containing a main verb.

Table 1.   Modern Greek verb morphology

| Mood | Tense | Aspect | |
		Imperfective	Perfective
Indicative	Present	Present stem + present inflection *gráf-o* 'write' 1S.	
	Past	(Augment) + pres. st. + past infl. *é-graf-a*	(Augment) + aorist stem + past infl. *é-graps-a*
	Future	Future particle + pres. st. + pres. infl. *θa gráf-o*	Future part. + aor. st. + pres. infl. *θa gràps-o*
Subjunctive	Non-past real	Modal part. + pres. st. + pres. infl. *na gráf-o*	Modal part. + aor. st. + pres. infl. *na gràps-o*

Modal imperfectives, expressed by the combination of a present stem and present inflectional ending, occur only rarely even in the data on the child with the highest MLU. Modal imperfectives usually are not formally differentiated from non-modal imperfective expressions because modal particles are used very inconsistently in this stage of language acquisition. Examples of non-modal imperfective, non-modal perfective, modal perfective, and modal imperfective expressions are given below in examples 4, 5, 6, and 7, respectively.

4. (a) *bèni ató:* (= *bèn-i aftó) (go-in*-3S. *this-one)* 'this one goes in'
    (b) *ze vàzun to pódi* (= *de vàz-un to pódi) (not put*-3P. *the foot)* 'one doesn't put one's foot /there/'
5. (a) *bíke* (= *bík-e) (go-in*-3S.) 'it has gone in'
    (b) *itáki tàvala* (= /*sto/ spitáki tò-val-a) (/into the/ houslet it-put*-1S.) 'I have put it /into the/ little house'
6. (a) *a lí* (= *na bí)* (MOD.PART. *go-in*-3S.) 'it shall go in'
    (b) *do vàlo mésa* (= /*na/ to vàl-o mésa)* (/MOD.PART./ *it put*-/S. *into)* 'I am going to/ would like to put it into /it/'
7. (a) *i túla tài* (= *i xrisúla /na to/ kratà-i) (the xrisula* /MOD.PART. *it/ hold*-3S.) 'Chrisula shall hold it'
    (b) *na lépume* (= *na vlép-ume)* (MOD.PART. *see*-1P.) 'let's look /at it/'

Both 7(a) and 7(b) contrast with perfective modal expressions formed from the same verbs in the respective children's data. The imperfective modal expressions refer to actions that have a relatively long duration. Contrary to the adult language, in which modal use is only one of the functions of the subjunctive mood, the subjunctive is almost exclusively used modally by the children. Expressions in which the subjunctive is syntactically triggered by the presence of a second verb in the sentence are rarely used by the children because of the relative complexity of such expressions. Two examples from the child with the highest MLU are:

8. (a) *sèlo katíto* (= *θèl-o* /na/ *kaθís-o*) (*want*-1S.IND./MOD. PART./ *sit*-1S.SUBJ.) 'I want to sit down'
   (b) *èla kasísis* (= *èla* /na/ *kaθís-is*) (*come*-2S.IMP./MOD. PART./ *sit*-2S.SUBJ.) 'come and sit down'

By describing the non-modal expressions (4 and 5) as imperfective and perfective, respectively, the category tense has been disregarded and aspect alone is relied on for their differentiation. The children's imperfective non-modal expressions always describe either ongoing or habitual situations and not situations that occurred prior to the speech; therefore, there is no need for more than one category to differentiate between the kinds of non-modal expressions. This is quite different from adult language, in which imperfective expressions can be either present or past tense (*gráfo* 'I write,' versus *égrafa* 'I used to write'). The past imperfective or *paratatikos* does not appear in the data. Imperfective expressions are never past tense. As is discussed below, perfective non-modal expressions only occur with dynamic verbs, most of which describe situations with a clear end result. Forms such as 5(a) *bíke* and 5(b) *távala* refer to states of affairs resulting from a prior event or action rather than expressing the relation between these situations and the speech act deictically as one of priority. Thus, the description of situations in early child language is non-deictic, either imperfective or perfective. Evidence supporting this conclusion can be found in research on the acquisition of French (Ferreiro, 1971), of Italian (Bronckart and Sinclair, 1973), and of English (Antinucci and Miller, 1976), and from universal characteristics of language. In the languages of the world, aspect is more fundamental than tense. According to Lyons (1977), "there are many languages that do not have tense, but very few, if any, that do not have aspect." It should come as no surprise, then, that aspect occurs earlier than tense ontogenetically.

It seems natural that the forms used for the expression of the imperfective and perfective aspect in non-modal expressions are those of the adult present tense imperfective indicative and past tense perfective indicative, respectively. As Comrie (1976) states, the present tense is fundamentally imperfective and is used for the description of ongoing or habitual situations, but it is "most natural for a past tense verb to have perfective meaning." Thus, in early Greek child language, present and past tense forms are used exclusively for expressing their most characteristic aspect. This also explains why the past imperfective, *paratatikos,* does not occur at this stage of language acquisition.

Because particles are not consistently used at this stage, there is no formal category corresponding to the adult future that would differentiate it from the present tense or the subjunctive. The large class of expressions having a verb form consisting of an aorist stem with a present inflectional ending are almost always used modally. Instances of present stem plus present inflectional ending being used modally are rare; most modal expressions have a perfective aspect (compare, for example, 6(a) and 6(b)). If one agrees with those linguists who attribute a strong modal character to the so-called future tense, and takes into consideration the fact that modal expressions are always future or, more correctly *prospective* (Seiler, 1971), it should seem natural that children do not yet differentiate between a deictic category to express posteriority to the speech event and a modal category because what is expressed by the formal category aorist stem plus present inflectional ending are intentions, wishes, or obligations. The incidence of a prospective-temporal character predominating over the prospective-modal is minimal and occurs only with verbs having a meaning that makes the expression of a positive wish pragmatically unlikely. An example is:

9.   *a bési (= θa pés-i)* (FUT.PART. *fall*-3S). 'it's going to fall'

The categories of verbal grammar discussed are summarized in Table 2. The two categories most strongly represented in the children's data are non-modal imperfective and modal perfective.

Semantic Verb Classes

As mentioned above, there is an interdependence of the semantic class of a verb and the classes of expressions in which it is most characteristically used. By classing non-modal verbs into stative and dynamic ones and the latter into resultative and non-resultative ones, certain neat correlations

Table 2.   Categories of verbal grammar in early Greek child language

Mood	Aspect	
	Imperfective	Perfective
Non-modal	Present stem + present infl. (example 4)	Aorist stem + past infl. (example 5)
Modal	(Particle) + pres. st. + pres. infl. (example 7)	(Particle) + aorist stem + pres. infl. (example 6)

will appear among these three verb classes and the expression classes—non-modal imperfective, non-modal perfective, and modal perfective.

Stative verbs describe existing situations that are "homogeneous, continuous and unchanging throughout [their] duration" (Lyons, 1977). Typical examples of stative verbs are *kséro* 'to know' and *krióno* 'to be cold.' In contrast to stative verbs, dynamic verbs describe situations that are occurring. Resultative-dynamic verbs characteristically describe situations of short duration that end in a state different from the one before the situation occurred (*péfto* 'to fall,' *pérno* 'to take'), whereas non-resultative dynamic verbs more often describe durative situations not striving toward a natural end-point (*kléo* 'to cry,' *điavázo* 'to read'). Table 3 represents the relative and absolute use of verbs of these three semantic classes in the four expression classes set up for the children's data in Table 2.

The following observations concern the relation between semantic verb and expression classes in the children's data. Stative verbs are almost exclusively used in non-modal imperfective expressions. Three of the four children did not use stative verbs in any other category. Examples of non-modal imperfective use of stative verbs are 10(a) to 10(c), and of modal imperfective use, example 11. The latter example comes from the child with an MLU of just above 2.0.

10. (a) *ponái lìga (= poná-i lìgo) (hurt-*3S. *a little)* 'it hurts a little'
     (b) *mìízi (= mìríz-i) (smell-*3S.) 'it smells'
     (c) *ováte (= fováte) (fear-*3S.) 'he is scared'
11.   *i fováse, nini (= min fováse, nini)* (MOD.NEG.PART. *fear-*2S. *baby)* 'don't be afraid, baby'

As opposed to stative verbs, dynamic verbs occur more frequently in modal expressions than in non-modal ones. Because stative verbs generally are not suitable for forming imperatives, it is natural that dynamic verbs are used for this function. Dynamic verbs are used because of the

Table 3. Use of semantic verb classes in the children's data

| | | Verb Class | | |
| | | Stative (%) | Result. Dyn. (%) | Non-Result. Dyn. (%) |
Mood	Aspect			
Non-modal	Imperfective	93[a]	15	26
	Perfective		11	3
Modal	Perfective		73.7	64
	Imperfective	7	0.3	7

[a]The values refer to utterance tokens. Numbers of tokens are: stative verbs, 54; resultative dynamic verbs, 914; non-resultative dynamic verbs, 479.

general preponderance of expressions directing the communication partner's behavior in mother-child dialogue. As stated above, modal expressions are mostly perfective because most of them refer to a certain action or event that the speaker wishes would or would not occur. Of the few modal expressions in the imperfective aspect, most are formed from the non-resultative dynamic verb type (compare, for example, 7(a) and 7(b)).

In modal expressions the perfective aspect is most frequent, whereas in non-modal expressions the imperfective aspect predominates. The reason for this is that most of the children's statements and questions are about ongoing or habitual situations. Perfective non-modal expressions occur relatively frequently; however, they occur with resultative dynamic verbs when they express states resulting from prior actions or events.

Child-Directed Mother's Speech

The speech of the four mothers—that which is directed to their young children—is analyzed below so that the children's language can be interpreted in light of the language to which they are exposed.

If verb forms are classified according to standard grammatical categories, child-directed mother's speech contains the temporal categories present, past, and future, the aspectual categories perfective and imperfective, and the moods indicative and subjunctive. Except for the imperative forms, which are not studied in this chapter, these categories account for almost 100% of all the expressions containing a non-modal verb. Only one of the four mothers used a compound tense—the perfect—and only a few times (0.8% of all utterances containing a verb). On the whole, mothers limit themselves to the use of simple tenses in their child-directed speech.

As can be seen in Table 4, the verb forms are not evenly distributed among the categories listed. The verb forms most commonly used are the subjunctive used modally, and the indicative present. The past and future tenses with perfective aspect together occur almost as frequently as the present. Except for the present, which can only occur with an imperfective

Table 4. Distribution of verb forms in child-directed mothers' speech

Mood	Tense	Aspect	
		Imperfective (%)	Perfective (%)
Indicative	Present	26[a]	
	Past	0.6	11
	Future	0.4	13
Subjunctive	Non-past real	3	46

[a]The values refer to utterance tokens. $N = 2260$.

aspect, the verb forms with the perfective aspect outnumber those with the imperfective aspect. Before refining the analysis by taking the semantic classes of stative, resultative, and non-resultative dynamic verbs into account, it can be observed at this point that the distribution of the perfective and imperfective aspects closely resembles the one in the children's data. In the child-directed mothers' speech, 96% of all past forms are perfective, compared to 100% in the children's speech.

For the sake of comparison, when future and subjunctive forms are combined in the mothers' data, 95% of these forms occur with the perfective aspect, and the corresponding value for the children is 96%. Thus, the mothers' data show a strong connection between the two aspectual categories and the categories of tense and mood. In the mothers' speech, most future verb forms have a strong modal character; thus, 98% of all remaining non-modal imperfective forms are in the present tense and 100% of all perfective forms are in the past tense. For nearly all non-modal forms, tense is predictable from aspect and vice versa. In the children's data just one of the categories of aspect and tense was needed to differentiate between the types of non-modal verbal expressions. If Seiler's (1952) theory that in the verbal grammar of Modern Greek "l'expression des aspects domine nettement celle des temps," ('the expression of aspect clearly dominates that of tense') is accepted, the results of our analysis of child-directed mother's speech show that this general characteristic of Modern Greek is stressed in the special quality of "motherese."

Additional evidence supporting the preponderance of aspect over tense in child-directed mother's speech can be obtained by studying the distribution of verb forms in the three semantic verb classes set up for the

Table 5.   Distribution of semantic verb classes in child-directed mothers' speech

Mood	Tense	Aspect	Verb class		
			Stative (%)	Result. Dyn. (%)	Non-result. Dyn. (%)
Indicative	Present	Imperfective	93[a]	15	28
	Past	Perfective		15	8
		Imperfective	0.5		0.8
	Future	Perfective		21	7
		Imperfective	0.5	0.2	0.2
Subjunctive	Non-past real	Perfective		47	53
		Imperfective	6	1.8	3

[a]The values refer to utterance tokens. Numbers of tokens are: stative verbs, 139; resultative dynamic verbs, 1050; non-resultative dynamic verbs, 1071.

analysis of the children's data. Table 5 shows that past tense forms occur almost exclusively with the perfective aspect and nearly twice as often with resultative dynamic verbs than with non-resultative dynamic verbs. Thus, about two-thirds of all past forms express present results of prior situations rather than the priority of situations to the speech event.

By comparing the values presented in Tables 3 and 5 a surprising conformity of the distribution of semantic verb classes with respect to expression classes can be seen between child speech and child-directed mother's speech. With stative verbs, 93% of the occurring verb forms are indicative present imperfective forms in both kinds of data, and 6% versus 7% in the subjunctive imperfective in the mothers' and the children's data, respectively. If for the two categories of dynamic verbs, future and modally used subjunctive forms are subsumed under the heading *modal* in the mothers' data, the values for non-modal versus modal expressions quite closely correspond for both of these verb classes in the two kinds of data.

Finally, in the non-modal expression of dynamic verbs, the values of the imperfective present are almost identical. The same is true for the past perfective forms of resultative dynamic verbs. Although the value for the past perfective of non-resultative dynamic verbs is more than twice as high in the mothers' data as in the children's, it occupies the same rank in the scale of diminishing frequency from modal perfective to non-modal past perfective.

To summarize this comparison of child speech and child-directed mother's speech, it can be stated that in both kinds of data, modal expressions occur at least twice as frequently as non-modal ones with dynamic verbs. The preponderance of partner-directing speech events over information-transmitting or information-requiring ones holds for both communication partners in mother-child interaction. In both kinds of data, non-modal expressions also are used more frequently with the imperfective aspect, although most of the modal expressions are in the perfective aspect. Statements and questions are mainly about ongoing or habitual situations, whereas modal expressions are most often concerned with directing the communication partner's behavior in certain well-defined instances of interaction. Interestingly, situations described by resultative dynamic verbs are expressed as ongoing or habitual, and as resulting in a present state, with about equal frequency in both kinds of data. This is evidence of the preponderance of aspect over tense. While the children's non-modal imperfective expressions are exclusively present tense forms, the mothers' speech contains a few occurrences of past imperfective forms in the classes of stative and non-resultative dynamic verbs.

Child-Directed Versus Adult-Directed Mother's Speech

So far, important parallels between child speech and child-directed mother's speech have been pointed out. In order to understand the status of child-directed speech as a register of adult language, a comparison of child-directed and adult-directed mother's speech follows. The data are from natural dialogues between each of the four mothers and another native adult, either a relative or an acquaintance. The results of the analysis are presented in Table 6.

It must first be noted that although the categories of Table 5 cover 100% and 92.5% of stative and dynamic verb forms of child-directed speech, respectively, these same categories in Table 6 handle only about 96% of the forms of adult-directed speech containing a stative verb and 80% of those with a dynamic verb. Categories of adult-directed speech not covered in Table 6 are mainly the compound tenses and non-modal uses of the subjunctive. In comparing Tables 5 and 6, some interesting differences and parallelisms can be seen between the two registers of adult-directed and child-directed mother's speech. In child-directed speech, modal expressions occur at least twice as often as non-modal ones with dynamic verbs; in adult-directed speech, the relation is reversed. As expected, the dominant role of partner-directing speech is a particular feature of mother-child interaction. As in the children's and in child-directed mother's speech, the perfective aspect is used much more frequently than the imperfective aspect with dynamic verbs in those categories where both aspects are possible. With stative verbs, however, the imperfective aspect is preferred in all expression classes. Thus, semantic verb class and aspect are interdependent in all three kinds of data. For dynamic verbs, the perfective aspect is the normal or unmarked form, ex-

Table 6.   Distribution of semantic verb classes in adult-directed mothers' speech

Mood	Tense	Aspect	Verb class		
			Stative (%)	Result. Dyn. (%)	Non-result. Dyn. (%)
Indicative	Present	Imperfective	81[a]	35	47
	Past	Perfective	6.5	29	17
		Imperfective	8	4	8
	Future	Perfective	1	15	7
		Imperfective	2	1	1
Subjunctive	Non-past real	Perfective	0.5	15	18
		Imperfective	1	1	2

[a]The values refer to utterance tokens. Numbers of tokens are: stative verbs, 289; resultative dynamic verbs, 691; non-resultative dynamic verbs, 777.

cept for the description of ongoing or habitual situations, but for stative verbs, it is the imperfective aspect, although frequency is just one criterion for determining markedness (Comrie, 1976, Chapter 6). In child-directed mother's speech, only 3.5% of all past expressions in the three semantic verb classes are in the imperfective aspect but in adult-directed speech, the value is 24%, more than six times as high. Tense, therefore, plays a more important role in adult-directed speech than in child-directed speech. In the modal categories future and subjunctive, however, it is uncommon for the imperfective aspect to be used with dynamic verbs in adult-directed speech.

It can be noted that in talking to the very young child, mothers restrict the number of grammatical categories used as well as the frequency of certain of these categories. The frequency restriction is not at all accidental; it is just those combinations of semantic verb and expression categories that are most characteristic or natural that are represented with an especially high frequency in child-directed speech. Thus, in non-modal expressions, the two most natural combinations of tense and aspect, present-imperfective and past-perfective, almost always occur.

DISCUSSION

This study shows that children who acquire Modern Greek as their native language differentiate between modal and non-modal expressions semantically and formally at a rather early stage of language development. Modal and non-modal expressions differ inflectionally in Modern Greek; therefore, it is a case of early emergence of regular morphological means for the expression of a certain semantic category. This finding sharply contrasts with Brown's (1973) statement about the acquisition of English, in which Stage I sentences (MLU 1.75) do not have "tense, aspect, mood, number, or the like." However, English is a language in which, except for imperatives, modal expressions are formed by modal verbs or modal auxiliaries, and as Klima and Bellugi–Klima (1966) found, even at a stage of language development where the MLU is 2.5 to 2.75, modal auxiliaries are used only in combination with negation. According to Wall (1974), nine out of 12 modal verbs are only used in combination with negation—even when the MLU reaches 4.9. Assuming that cognitive development is fundamentally the same in all cultures, this difference in the sequence of language development must be attributable to differences in formal linguistic structure between languages such as Modern Greek, a language with a highly inflectionalized verbal grammar, and English, a language in which (at least in the spoken language) modality is expressed by analytic grammatical means, except for the imperative. It would be worthwhile to learn whether children acquiring English as their native language differentiate modal and non-modal expressions intonationally at the stage of language acquisition studied in this chapter. There is some evidence for such a formal device from the acquisition of German (Miller, 1976).

As far as the adult grammatical categories of aspect and tense are concerned, the evidence obtained from this study points in the same direction as the findings from other language studies. According to Antinucci and Miller (1976), the category of aspect seems to occur much earlier in English child language than was suspected by Brown (1973).

By studying the mother's child-directed speech and the child's speech at the same time, a surprisingly high degree of conformity between the two registers was detected. In order to appreciate the child's performance in language acquisition, it is important to study the language actually spoken to the child. Because child-directed speech differs from adult-directed speech in important ways, a comparison of child language to some ideal, standard adult language would not be very meaningful. It has been found that the language spoken to the child by his mother is "the product of carefully adjusted interactional processes" (Snow, 1977). Researchers are just beginning to address the effect of the input language in the process of language acquisition and they are studying the actual speech addressed to the child in more sophisticated ways. Rather than pointing out differences between child language and input language, similarities between the two registers have been stressed. Only an input language close enough to the child's own cognitive and linguistic abilities can conceivably play an important role in the process of language acquisition. Although the mother clearly confines herself to a subsystem of her linguistic possibilities when addressing the young child, her language is, of course, not identical to the child's. One important difference for the acquisition of aspect and its formal expression in Modern Greek is that the mothers' data include many more verbs that were used with both the present and aorist stem than were included in the children's data. It is the congeniality rather than the identity of the mother's language that makes it conceivable that the mother's language may be a constant source of "irritation" of the child's language system. It may well be that the instability resulting from this interaction and from other factors makes possible the gradual transformation of child language into adult language.

REFERENCES

Antinucci, F., and Miller, R. 1976. How children talk about what happened. J. Child Lang. 3:167–190.

Bronckart, J., and Sinclair, H. 1973. Time, tense, and aspect. Cognition 2:107–130.

Brown, R. 1973. A First Language: The Early Stages. Harvard University Press, Cambridge, Mass.

Calbert, J. 1975. Toward the semantics of modality. In: J. Calbert and H. Vater (eds.), Aspekte der Modalität [Aspects of Modality], pp. 1–70. Verlag Gunter Narr, Tübingen.

Comrie, B. 1976. Aspect: An Introduction to the Study of Verbal Aspect and Related Problems. Cambridge University Press, New York.

Ferreiro, E. 1971. Les relations temporelles dans le langage de l'enfant. [Temporal Relations in Child Language.] Droz, Geneva.

Klima, E. S., and Bellugi-Klima, U. 1966. Syntactic regularities in the speech of children. In: J. Lyons and R. J. Wales (eds.), Psycholinguistic Papers, pp. 183–208. Edinburgh University Press, Edinburgh.

Lyons, J. 1977. Semantics. Cambridge University Press, New York. Vol. 1 and 2.

Miller, M. 1976. Zur Logik der frühkindlichen Sprachentwicklung: Empirische Untersuchungen und Theoriediskussion. Ernst Klett Verlag, Stuttgart.

Seiler, H. 1952. L'aspect et le temps dans le verbe néo-grec. Société d'édition 'Les Belles Lettres', Paris.

Seiler, H. 1971. Abstract structures for moods in Greek. Language 47:79–89.

Snow, C. E. 1977. Mothers' speech research: From input to interaction. In: C. E. Snow and C. H. Ferguson (eds.), Talking to Children: Language Input and Acquisition, pp. 31–49. Cambridge University Press, New York.

Wall, C. 1974. Predication: A Study of Its Development. Mouton, The Hague.

Structural Development of the Simple Sentence in Japanese Children

Midori Tanaka

The main components of a simple sentence in Japanese are Bunsetsu—phrases that consist of one or more words, including a content word. In the sentences studied in this chapter, Bunsetsu consist of either a noun and a case particle (Kaku-Joshi), or a verb and auxiliary verb (Jodoshi). (For a more precise definition of Bunsetsu, see Hashimoto, 1948.) Verbs can be classified as monovalent, divalent, or trivalent, depending upon the number of arguments (nominal Bunsetsu) that the verb requires for constructing a sentence. These three verb categories roughly correspond to intransitive, transitive, and dative verbs, respectively. Each of them can be sub-categorized according to the categories suggested by Chafe (1970): state, process, action, experiential, and benefactive. Table 1 presents these distinctions and the kinds of semantic relations that nominal Bunsetsu may represent. The similarities of case particles and the semantic relations that they may represent are shown in Table 2. For example, Table 2 shows that *ga* connected with a noun can represent a patient, experiencer, agent, locative, or beneficiary, but not an instrument or complement.

The development of simple sentence structure in Japanese children can best be described in terms of the number of Bunsetsu within a sentence and the valences of the verbs. That is, the more Bunsetsu in the sentence and the more valences of the verb, the more difficult the sentences are for children to acquire. Tanaka (1979) points out that the number of Bunsetsu affects the way children process a simple sentence. This "span in sentence processing," which is expressed by the maximum number of Bunsetsu within a sentence that children can reproduce, increases parallel to short-term memory span for words as children grow older.

Table 1. The categorization of Japanese verbs according to the number of valences each verb may have and the semantic relations of each one[a]

No.	Category	Semantic relations						
		Patient	Experiencer	Agent	Locative	Beneficative	Instrument	Complement
1	State	+	−	−	±	−	−	−
	Process	+	−	−	±	−	−	−
	Action	−	−	+	±	−	±	±
2	Process, action	+	−	+	±	±	±	−
	State, experiential	+	+	−	±	−	±	−
	State, benefactive	+	−	−	±	+	±	−
3	Process, action, experiential	+	+	+	±	−	±	−
	Process, action, benefactive	+	−	+	±	+	±	−

[a] +, Verb always takes that semantic relation; −, verb never takes that semantic relation; ±, the semantic relation is optional.

Table 2. Semantic relations that may be represented by Japanese case particles (Kaku-Joshi), depending on the particular verb

Kaku-Joshi	Semantic relations						
	Patient	Experiencer	Agent	Locative	Beneficiary	Instrument	Complement
Ga	+	+	+	+	+	−	−
Wa	+	−	−	−	−	−	−
No	+	+	+	−	+	−	−
Ni	+	+	+	+	+	−	−
E	−	−	−	+	+	−	−
O	+	+	+	+	−	−	+
To	+	−	−	−	−	−	−
Kara	−	−	+	+	−	−	−
Yori	−	−	−	+	+	−	−
De	−	−	−	+	−	+	−
Made	−	−	−	+	−	−	−

Experiment 1 below shows that the span in sentence processing is virtually identical to the short-term memory span for digits. There also is a relationship between the span in sentence processing and the valences of the verbs that children can produce. Table 3 presents an analysis of the complexity of Japanese sentences based on the span of sentence processing and the number of valences on verbs. The following four experiments show that Table 3 is an accurate representation of the structural complexity of Japanese sentences for young children.

EXPERIMENT 1

Experiment 1 tested the hypothesis that the span in sentence processing increases with age and is closely related to short-term memory span.

Method

Subjects   The subjects, ages 2 to 5, were from a public nursery school in Tokyo. In each of the four age groups there were 20 children. About half of the subjects in each group were boys.

Materials   A set of five sentences in which the number of Bunsetsu within a sentence increased systematically from one to five was used (see Table 4). Except for sentence 1, which is a one-word sentence, every sentence is composed of a Bunsetsu with a verb and one or more Bunsetsu with a noun and a case particle.

Procedure   The subjects were tested individually. After the children were instructed to reproduce the five sentences orally, each of the sentences was read. A response was considered incorrect if one or more Bunsetsu were left out or if a case particle was misused. If the first response was incorrect or irrelevant, or if there was no response, the sentence was read again. The first response was not corrected before the subject responded a second (and final) time. If a subject failed to respond twice, no further presentations were made.

Results

The mean percentage of correctly reproduced sentences is shown as a function of age in Figure 1. From this figure, it can be seen that the shorter the sentence and the higher age, the easier it is for the children to reproduce the sentence. Most of the 3-year-olds could reproduce the three-Bunsetsu sentences; most of the 4-year-olds and all of the 5-year-olds could reproduce the four-Bunsetsu sentences. The correct use of *kara* 'from' and *made* 'to' is difficult for all young children, so the percentage for sentence 5 was especially low in all four age groups.

The maximum number of Bunsetsu within a sentence that children were able to reproduce was averaged for each age level. The values are

Table 3.   Analysis of Japanese sentence structures that vary according to number of Bunsetsu and the number of verb valences[a]

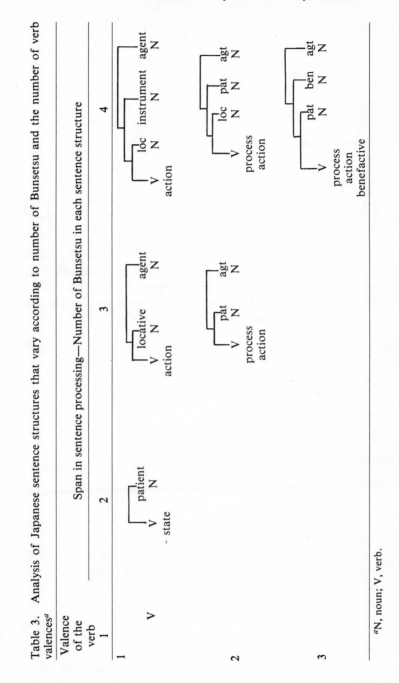

Valence of the verb	Span in sentence processing—Number of Bunsetsu in each sentence structure			
	1	2	3	4

[a]N, noun; V, verb.

Table 4.   Sentences used in Experiment 1.

1. Inu.
   Dog.

2. Usagi -ga   hashitta.
   (rabbit)   (ran)
   The rabbit ran.

3. Okāsan-ga   kōen-ni   itta.
   (Mother)   (park)   (went)
   Mother went to the park.

4. Otōsan-ga   isu-ni   futon-o   oita.
   (Father)   (chair)   (cushion)   (put)
   Father put the cushion on the chair.

5. Onīsan -ga   eki-kara   ie-mada   nimotsu-o   hakonda.
   (brother)   (station)   (home)   (luggage)   (carried)
   Brother carried the luggage home from the station.

1.1, 3.5, 3.7, 4.5., for 2-, 3-, 4-, and 5-year-olds, respectively. The values were found to be nearly the same as that for the short-term memory span for digits as given by Munn (1974) (see Figure 2).

Experiment 1 verified that in children's processing of a simple sentence, the span of processing may be defined in units of Bunsetsu. This

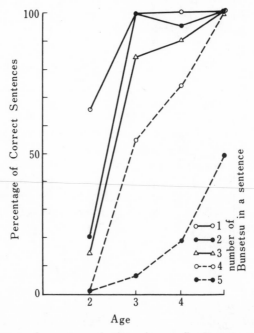

Figure 1.   Percentage of correct reproductions of one- to five-Bunsetsu sentences as a function of age.

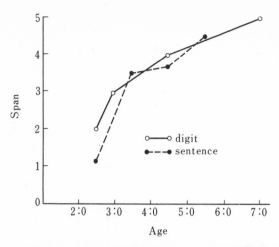

Figure 2.   Span in sentence processing and the short-term memory (STM) span for digits as a function of age. The values of the STM span for digits are taken from Munn (1974).

span increases as age increases, and is practically the same as the short-term memory span for digits.

EXPERIMENT 2

Experiment 2 examines the relationship between the sentence-processing span and the production of sentences that contain monovalent, divalent, or trivalent verbs.

Method

Subjects   The children who served as subjects in Experiment 1 were also the subjects for Experiment 2.

Materials   Pictures and scenes were presented with hand puppets to elicit four types of sentences: two-Bunsetsu sentences with monovalent verbs (Type 1); three-Bunsetsu sentences with monovalent verbs (Type 2); three-Bunsetsu sentences with divalent verbs (Type 3); and, four-Bunsetsu sentences with trivalent verbs (Type 4). Two examples of each type were prepared, as is shown in Table 5.

Procedure   The children were pre-tested individually on their knowledge of the relevant names for the materials to be used, and when necessary the names were taught. Then, they were instructed to look at and describe some actual scenes. If in their first response they missed one or more components, those materials corresponding to the omitted noun or nouns were presented again. If in their second response they missed one or more components, no further attempts were made.

Table 5. Descriptions of expected sentence structures for scenes presented in Experiment 2.

	Scenes presented	Structures

1.a. Bin (bottle) -ga taoreta. (fell)
A bottle fell.

Structure:
V process *taoreta* — N patient *Bin*

1.b. Oningyō-ga (doll) tobiorita. (jumped down)
A doll jumped down.

2.a. Oningyō-ga (doll) isu-ni (chair) suwatta (sat)
A doll sat on a chair.

Structure:
V action *suwatta* — N locative *isu* — N agent *oningyō*

2.b. Ōsama-ga (king) benchi-ni (bench) neta (lay)
The king lay on a bench.

3.a. Ōsama-ga (king) supūn-o (spoon) otoshita. (dropped)
The king dropped a spoon.

Structure:
V process action *otoshita* — N patient — N agent *supūnOoama*

3.b. Inu-ga (dog) usagi-o (rabbit) oikaketa. (chased)
A dog chased a rabbit.

4.a. Ōsama-ga (king) kodomo-ni (child) ame-o (candy) ageta. (gave)
The king gave a child a candy.

Structure:
V process action benefactive *ageta* — N patient *ame* — N benefactive *kodomo* — N agent *Ōsama*

4.b. Kodomo-ga (child) ōsama-ni (king) hana-o (flower) ageta. (gave)
A child gave the king a flower.

Results

The number of children at each span of sentence processing, as determined in Experiment 1, is 8, 7, 12, 33, and 13 for span one, two, three, four, and five, respectively.

In response to scene 1.a., about 15% of the children said *bin-ga taoreta* 'a bottle fell'; with children at longer spans, the proportion of the complete-sentence response increased, confirming the hypothesis that sentences with monovalent verbs can be produced at span two. Children at span two responded to scene 2.a. with one-word utterances at best. At span three, however, the required agent-locative-verb (monovalent) sentence appears and the proportion increases with increased span, confirming the hypothesis that three-Bunsetsu sentences with a monovalent verb can be produced at span three.

Figure 3 shows the results with 3.a. At span two, children used only monovalent verbs: *Supūn-ga okkochita* 'A spoon dropped.' At span three, children were able to produce divalent verbs, and the full sentence of agent-patient-verb (divalent) appeared. The proportion increases with the increase of the span. The results confirmed the hypothesis that the divalent verbs are acquired later than monovalent verbs, and also the hypothesis that well-formed sentences with divalent verbs are acquired at span three. However, the results did not support the hypothesis that a three-Bunsetsu sentence with a monovalent verb is acquired earlier than the same sentence with a divalent verb within the stage of span three.

Figure 4 shows the response to scene 4.a. As early as span three, the full sentence of agent-beneficiary-patient-verb (trivalent) begins to appear, although it was hypothesized that this is acquired at span four.

The most common sentence structures for each span and other important structures are shown in Table 6. The results generally support the hypotheses mentioned above except for two points. First, it has not been shown that three-Bunsetsu sentences with a monovalent verb will be acquired earlier than those with a divalent verb. (Experiment 3 further examines this point.) The second concerns the four-Bunsetsu sentences with trivalent verbs. Agent-beneficiary-patient-verb sentences, which were expected to appear at span four because they are hardest to acquire, appeared as early as span three, not later than the agent-patient-verb (divalent) structure. One possible explanation is that the trivalent verb used in the experiment *ageru* 'to give' is commonly used in daily communication. It might be assumed that sentences with trivalent predicate structure generally would be harder to process than those with divalent verb structure (agent-locative-patient-verb). Experiment 4 tests this assumption.

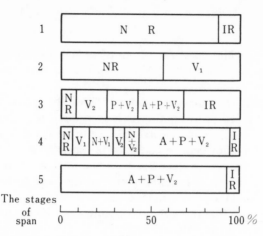

Figure 3.   Response types obtained in 3(a) (*Ōsama-ga supūn-o otoshita*) at each of the span stages. NR, no response; IR, irrelevant response; N, noun; V_2, expected divalent verbs; V_1, monovalent form of V_2; A, Agent; P, Patient.

EXPERIMENT 3

Method

Subjects   The subjects were 20 public nursery school children: 4 2-year-olds, 5 3-year-olds, 5 4-year-olds, and 6 5-year-olds.

Materials   Three types of sentences were constructed: three-Bunsetsu sentences with monovalent verbs (agent-locative-verb), three-Bunsetsu sentences with divalent verbs (agent-patient-verb), and four-Bunset-

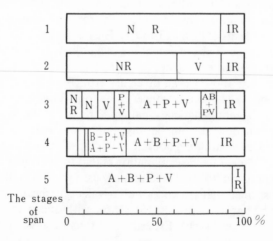

Figure 4.   Response types obtained in 4.a. (*Ōsama-ga kodomo-ni ame-o ageta*) at each span. NR, no response; IR, irrelevant response; N, noun; V, verb; A, agent; P, patient; B, benefactive.

Table 6. Most common sentence structures for each span of processing

Tasks	Span in sentence processing			
	1	2	3	4
1.a.	NR	V / process — [pat: V N] / process	[pat: V N] / process	[pat: V N] / process
2.a.	NR	agt / N — V / action	[loc agt: V N N] / action — [agt: V N] / action	[loc agt: V N N] / action
3.a.	NR	V / process	[pat agt: V N N] / process action	[pat agt: V N N] / process action
4.a.	NR	V / process action benefactive	[ben pat: V N N] / process action benefactive — [ben pat agt: V N N N] / process action benefactive	[ben pat agt: V N N N] / process action benefactive

setsu sentences. Five sentences of each type were formed. Examples of the three types are: *Okāsan-ga hoikuen-ni* 'Mother came to the nursery school' (Type A); *Okāsan-ga empitsu-o katta* 'Mother bought a pencil' (Type B); and *Onēsan-ga neko-gi miruku-o* 'Sister gave the cat some milk' (Type C).

Procedure Each sentence of each group was tape-recorded. The subjects were instructed to reproduce a sentence exactly as they heard it immediately after it was presented.

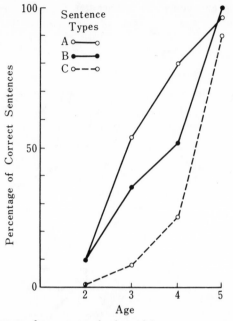

Figure 5.   Mean percentage of correct reproductions of three sentence types as a function of age. A, agent-locative-verb (monovalent); B, agent-patient-verb (divalent); C, agent-beneficiary-patient-verb (trivalent).

Results

Figure 5 shows the mean percentage of correctly reproduced sentences for the three sentence types as a function of age. Both of the three-Bunsetsu sentences were reproduced more accurately than the four-Bunsetsu sentences by 3- and 4-year-olds. Figure 5 also shows that three-Bunsetsu sentences with monovalent verbs (Type A) were reproduced earlier than those with divalent verbs (Type B).

EXPERIMENT 4

Method

Subjects   The subjects were 3-, 4-, and 5-year-olds from a nursery school. Ten children were in each age group.

Materials   Five sentences of the agent-locative-patient-verb (divalent) type and five of the agent-beneficiary-patient-verb (trivalent) type were constructed. Examples are: *Okasan-ga yuka-ni osara-o otosita* 'Mother dropped a dish on the floor' (Type A), and *Onisan-ga ojisan-ni hagaki-o okutta* 'Brother sent uncle a post-card' (Type B).

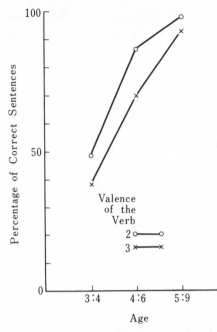

Figure 6.   Percentage of correctly reproduced sentences as a function of verb valence and age.

Procedure   Children were individually instructed to reproduce the sentence immediately after they heard it.

Results

The percentage of correctly reproduced sentences is shown in Figure 6. The percentage for sentences with divalent predicate verbs is significantly higher than that for trivalent predicate verbs for 4-year-olds.

DISCUSSION

The results of the four experiments confirm that Table 3 is an accurate representation of the structural complexity of Japanese sentences for young children.

Miller (1956) first proposed that the human information-processing capacity had the limit of "7 ± 2" chunks. Somewhat different characteristics have been observed in the case of sentence processing (Fodor, Bever, and Garrett, 1974; Mandler and Mandler, 1964; and Marks and Miller, 1964). Experiment 1 shows, however, that there is also a span with Bunsetsu as a unit in the processing of a simple sentence by children and that this span is practically the same as short-term memory span for digits. This implies that the ability to process serial information underlies the acquisition of syntax because there is little difference between immediate recall of sentence and that of digit series in terms of human information processing ability.

The results also demonstrate the importance of verb valence in determining the difficulty of sentences for children. It is interesting that the difference between transitive (divalent) and intransitive (monovalent) verbs also has been observed in adults. Asked to give the first word that comes to mind when presented with an intransitive and a transitive verbs, adult subjects reported a significantly greater number of nouns with less latency in the case of transitive verbs than in the case of intransitive verbs (Polzella and Rohrman, 1970). Bacharach, Kellas, and Mcfarland (1972) concluded from their experiments that the memory load of a transitive verb was greater because one memorized it by supplying the object nouns, which was not the case with the intransitive verb. This is why children used a transitive verb only after the memory span had grown to a certain point.

REFERENCES

Bacharach, V. R., Kellas, G., and Mcfarland, C. E. 1972. Structural properties of transitive and intransitive verb. J. Verb. Learn. Verb. Behav. 11:486–490.

Chafe, W. L. 1970. Meaning and the Structure of Language. University of Chicago Press, Chicago.

Fodor, J. A., Bever, T. G., and Garrett, M. F. 1974. The Psychology of Language: An Introduction to Psycholinguistics and Generative Grammar. McGraw-Hill Book Company, New York.

Hashimoto, S. 1948. Kokugohō Yōsetsu. [Theory of Japanese grammar] In: Hashimoto Shinkichi Chosakushyū, Vol. 2. Iwanami Shoten, Tokoyo.

Mandler, G., and Mandler, J. 1964. Serial position effects in sentences. J. Verb. Learn. Verb. Behav. 3:195–202.

Marks, L. E., and Miller, G. A. 1964. The role of semantic and syntactic constraints in the memorization of English sentences. J. Verb. Learn. Verb. Behav. 3:1–5.

Miller, G. A. 1956. The magical number seven plus or minus two: Some limits on our capacity for information processing. Psychol. Rev. 63:81–96.

Munn, N. L. 1974. The Growth of Human Behavior. Houghton Mifflin Company, Boston.

Polzella, D. J., and Rohrman, N. R. 1970. Psychological aspects of transitive verbs. J. Verb. Learn. Verb. Behav. 9:537–540.

Tanaka, M. 1979. The development of the simple-sentence processing in Japanese children. Jpn. J. Psychol. 50:183–190.

Word Order in First Language Acquisition of Japanese

Barbara Lust and Tatsuko Kaneda Wakayama

Whether young children are sensitive to word order during the early stages of language development is a critical question that must be addressed in any theory of first language acquisition. Linear order is one of the fundamental properties of natural language; therefore children learning a first language either must begin the language learning process with a sensitivity to linear order or they must learn to be sensitive to it. (See Bach, 1975; Li, 1975; Steele, 1978, for a precise explanation of the role of linear order in natural language.)

Because all languages make use of it to some degree, linear order is an issue for first language acquisition of any language. It therefore can be framed in terms of possible universals of first language acquisition. All children must learn the specific word order (or orders) of their language. Whether there is a universal sensitivity to order that allows and supports this learning process is discussed in this chapter.

Existing studies of word order in first language acquisition are inconsistent and inconclusive. This is true for studies of English, on which the most research has been done, as well as for those of other languages. See, for example, Brown's (1973) review of this issue. Brown concludes that "attention to the sequential order of words and morphemes is one of the earliest principles to operate in language acquisition"; however, the data reviewed by Brown are not entirely consistent with this conclusion. While some studies have argued that early use of word order by children occurs naturally in the acquisition of languages with relatively fixed word order such as English, (Bloom, 1970; Slobin, 1973; Brown, 1973), other studies have reported the opposite: the use of free word order by children has been noted not only in English, (Gruber, 1969; deVilliers and deVilliers, 1973; Braine, 1976) but also in German (Park, 1970a), and French, (Sinclair, 1972, 1973) and German, languages that also have a relatively fixed word order.

Similar inconsistencies can be found in studies of acquisition of languages that have free word order. For example, fixed orders have been observed in the early acquisition of Russian (Slobin, 1966, on Gvozdev's study) and Korean (Park 1970b), and free orders have been observed in Finnish (Bowerman, 1973).

WORD ORDER IN JAPANESE

This chapter addresses the issue of word order in first language acquisition through an analysis of first language acquisition of Japanese. Word order in Japanese (adult grammar) is considered to be relatively free. Although the verb has a fixed position, which is at the end of the sentence, the subject and object, for example, can occur in alternate orders in Japanese as in sentence 1 below.

1. (a)   Kazuko-san-ga Masayuki-san-o yonda
           (Kazuko-subject Masayuki-object call-past)
           Kazuko called Masayuki
    (b)   Masayuki-san-o Kazuko-san-ga yonda
           (Masayuki-object Kazuko-subject call-past)
           Kazuko called Masayuki

The indirect object in Japanese also can be rather freely permuted. Case-marking of terms often determines grammatical relations in Japanese and this may obviate word order in marking these relations. This distinguishes Japanese from English, in which the order of a term (either before or after the verb) in a subject-verb-object (SVO) sentence may determine whether it is a subject or an object, as can easily be seen in 2.

2. (a)   Kazuko called Masayuki
    (b)   Masayuki called Kazuko

Because word order is not critical in determining grammatical relations in Japanese, the model language for Japanese does not evidence word order distinctions for the language learner as the English model does. It might be expected therefore that in early Japanese child language a sensitivity to word order might not exist. Children learning Japanese as their first language might demonstrate free use of word order (as Bowerman, 1973, found in the acquisition of Finnish) or they might demonstrate an arbitrarily constrained word order (as Slobin, 1966, found in the acquisition of Russian).

The issue of word order is more complex than it often is considered to be. Perhaps previous studies of word order in first language acquisition appear inconsistent and inconclusive because these complexities have not been recognized.

Constituent Structure

Languages differ not only in their linear order of words, but also in their order of major constituents. Constituents may have complex structure, and may be embedded within each other. Japanese order, for example, differs from English order not only in the position of the verb and in the permutation of subject-object order, but in a whole host of complex structures that may seem to be "mirror images" of similar structures in English. See, for example, 3 below, which was taken from Smith's (1978) review of several such mirror image reversals between Japanese and English order.

3.   (a) Tōkyō eki   kara densha de ichijikan kurai nishi e
          (Tokyo station from train by one hour about west toward
            14   13 12   11 10   9   8
          itta tokoro ni Kamakura to   iu   machi ga   arimasu.
          go place at Kamakura quote called town) (subject exists)
          7 6 5   4   3 2   1
    (b) There is a town called Kamakura at a place (you can reach)
             1   2   3   4   5   6
          going west about one hour by train from Tokyo Station
           7   8   9   10 11   12   13   14

Such mirror image reversals of order result from systematic differences between Japanese and English in the direction of their embedding of major constituents, as shown in 4 (Kuno, 1973).

4.   [[[Kazuko-ga katte-iru] neko-ga korosita] nezumi-ga tabeta]
      (Kazuko-subj. keep cat-subj. killed   rat-subj.   ate
    tiizu-wa   kusatte-ita.
    cheese-topic rotten-was)
    [The cheese [that the rat [that the cat [that Kazuko keeps] killed] ate]
    was rotten].

Japanese embeds many different types of constituents leftward, that is, it is a left-branching language. English embeds them rightward and is a right-branching language. Japanese, for example, embeds relative clauses to the left of head nouns. English embeds them to the right, as can be seen in 4.

Order Permutation

All natural languages allow permutation of some basic or unmarked word order. The variation in Japanese is shown in 5(a) and 5(b).

5.   (a) Taroo-wa takusan-no bara-o daidaiteki-ni   saibai site iru
          (many   roses on a large scale grow be ing)
    (b) Taroo-wa daidaiteki-ni   saibai site iru, takusan-no bara-o
          (on a large scale grow be ing   many   roses)

Sentence 5(b) quite clearly is systematically related to 5(a) in Japanese. It is essentially synonymous with 5(b). Haraguchi (1973) treats sentences such as 5(b) as though they were derived from sentences like 5(a) by right dislocation, that is, by the movement of constituents in (a) to the right of the verb in (b). Jorden (1963) calls them inverted sentences. More recently, Jorden (personal communication) described such sentences as ones based on afterthought. Oshima (1978) also agrees with the afterthought theory and argues that sentences should be described by discourse grammar rather than by sentence grammar.[1] By any account, however, the linear order in 5(b) is not independent of the order in 5(a).

It may be said that children acquiring a first language essentially do not understand the role of order in language unless they understand that word order in natural language corresponds to profound order differences of constituent structure, and that variations of specific linear orders may be systematically related to each other within a language.

In this chapter, whether Japanese children are sensitive to linear order at early stages of learning the Japanese language is discussed in terms of the following two fundamental questions on ordering: 1) Are children sensitive to the order of major constituents in their language, for example the leftward direction of embedding of complex constituents? 2) Do children distinguish between marked and unmarked variation in word order, such as in 5, and do they appreciate the systematic relation between these variations? If children are sensitive to constitutent-structure embedding and do interpret surface linear order by reference to constituent structure (for example, map surface linear order onto constituent structure), then one might expect that they could interrelate a marked surface order (for example, the dislocation in 5(b)) with the constituent structure in its unmarked order (for example, that underlying 5(a)).

It is commonly observed that major constituents of sentences often are omitted in early Japanese child language and they are appended after

---

[1]Right-dislocated sentences such as 5(b) are marked by sentence-final intonation on the verb, and a pause (possibly a short one) after the verb. The structure of right-dislocated sentences in Japanese is still not well understood. Haraguchi (1973) shows the wide range of constituents that may occur to the right of the verb in such sentences, especially in informal speech. He argues that these sentences do not result from deletion of full conjoined sentences, and he demonstrates a number of selectional restrictions on these constituents that appear to be determined by the initial (matrix) sentences. Oshima (1978) argues that these ostensibly dislocated sentences should be described by rules of discourse grammar that generate the initial (matrix) sentences with an empty node for the constituent that appears to the right of the sentence-final verb. The constituent to the right of the verb results from a separate sentence that is reduced by rules of discourse grammar. As evidence for this position, Oshima notes that the rightmost constituent can take *yo*, a marker that is restricted to sentence-final position:

John-wa [empty] nagutta *yo*.   [empty] Mary-(w)o   [empty] *yo*.
NP   nagutta yo.   NP   V

sentence closure (Okubo, 1973). In a study of natural speech of 205 Tokyo kindergarten children between the ages of 3;3 and 6;6, Okubo noted frequent evidence of sentence types such as those in 6 and 7. These sentences may append either a subject or a part of the predicate complement after the sentence-final verb.

6. Subject
    (a) age 5;8
         Soide unto-ne necha-tta-no. Usagi-ga
         (And well   slept   . Rabbit)
    (b) age 4;8
         Soide nigi(ge)-te yuko-no. Simauma-ga.
         (And running   away   . Zebra)
    (c) age 3;10
         Soide nezumi taben(ru)-no. Kumasan-ga.
         (And mouse eat   . Mr. Bear)
7. Predicate complement constituent
    (a) age 5;7
         Konogoro-ne yoma-nai-de   miru-dake-ni suru-no. Gohon.
         (Lately   read not but look at - only do. Book.)
    (b) age 5;1
         Shiranai-yo.   Sore-mo
         (know-not.   It-also.)
    (c) age 3
         Usagi-ga kayui kayui-tte kai-teru. Hoppe.
         (rabbit itchy itchy   scratching. Cheek.)

Similar dislocated orders were noted for many other sentence constituents such as adverbs or prepositional phrases of place or time.

On the other hand, a number of recent studies have suggested that young Japanese children seem to prefer subject-object-verb order in simple sentences (Yoshida, 1963; Hayashibe, 1975; Hakuta, 1977, 1978). A preference for object-verb order has been noted as early as at age 2 by Murata (1961). The subject-object-verb order is the most common order in Japanese. (Kuno, 1973, observed a 17 to 1 ratio of that order to the object-subject-verb order.) As noted above, the final position of the verb is quite rigid. It is not known at what age or language level this preference first appears, nor how it is acquired.

On the surface, Okubo's (1973) data, such as those exemplified in 6 and 7, seem to be inconsistent with the observed preference for verb-final order in Japanese child language. However, Okubo's data also may reflect a sensitivity in children to verb-final basic word order, and to right dislocation of this order, because he implies that in all the dislocated sentences, children seem to know that the verb signals basic sentence closure.

It is not possible to evaluate this claim, however, without information on whether children can relate the order of constituents in sentences to their basic undislocated order.

No research has directly studied whether Japanese children are sensitive to the more fundamental notions of order: direction of constituent structure embedding, and permutation of basic order. Several studies, however, indirectly suggest that these sensitivities may exist even at early ages. Sanches (1968) observes that the Japanese child she studied appeared to discriminate order inversions by intonation at a very young age—24 months.

AN EXPERIMENTAL STUDY

In this research simple forms of right-dislocated sentences (such as 5, 6, and 7) were used to test these two fundamental notions of word order in Japanese language acquisition. A series of simple sentences, which are listed in Table 1, were used in an elicited imitation task with young Japanese children. (See Slobin and Welsh, 1973 for a description of this task.)

Rationale

In the analyses of children's imitation of these sentences, the following questions were asked: 1) Would children find right-dislocated (RD) sentences significantly more difficult to imitate than standard order (SO) sentences, which would show that they distinguished between these orders and that the SO pattern may represent a more basic pattern? 2) In their imitations, would children perhaps convert the RD sentences to SO, thus showing that they understood the relationship between these orders? 3) In their imitations, would children perhaps relocate to its SO position the whole complex constituent (even a coordinate phrase) that had been dislocated in an RD sentence, showing that they understood a relationship between constituent structure and linear order?

Method

The sentences used in this study varied according to whether they had inverted orders (resulting from right dislocation) as in sentences 1–4 (RD), or standard orders (SO) as in sentences 5–8, in Table 1. RD sentences had constituents moved to the right of the verb. SO sentences had standard verb-final order. The emphatic sentence marker *yo* 'I am telling you that...' was used in the dislocated sentences so that they seemed more natural for young children. The *yo* marker followed the verb and marked closure of the main sentence. Half the sentences had subjects and verbs (SV), and half had objects and verbs (OV).

Table 1. Comparison of standard order and right-dislocated coordination in Japanese[a]

Right-dislocated coordination	Standard order coordination
Nominal	*Nominal*
1. V (S + S) Hashiru-yo, usagi-to kame-ga (Run, rabbit and tortoise)	5. (S + S) V Raion-to tora-ga hashiru (Lion(s) and tiger(s) run)
2. V (O + O) Taberu-yo, ringo-to nashi-o (Eat, apple and pear)	6. (O + O) V Ringo-to banana-o taberu (Apple and banana eat)
Verbal	*Verbal*
3. (V + V) S Aruku-shi tobu-yo, kotori-wa (Walk and fly, bird)	7. S (V + V) Inu-wa hoeru-shi kamitsuku (Dog bark and bite)
4. (V + V) O Tsukeru-shi nameru-yo, jamu-o (Spread and lick, jam)	8. O (V + V) Okashi-o ageru-shi morau (Sweets give and receive)

[a]S, subject; O, object; V, verb; +, coordinate conjunction, either by *shi* or *to* in Japanese.

The sentences also varied in the type of constituent that was right-dislocated. In all cases, sentences included a complex constituent, namely, a coordination, either a nominal coordination (for example, *usagi-to kame-ga*, 'rabbit and tortoise') or a verbal coordination (for example, *aruku-shi tobu*, 'walk and fly'). (The connective *shi* was used in verbal coordinations and the connective *to* was used in nominal coordinations.)[2] The RD sentences reverse normal orders for embedding phrasal coordination in Japanese sentences. Although nominal coordinations are embedded left of the verb in SO form, they are embedded right of the verb in RD form and although verbal coordinations are embedded right of the noun in SO form, they are embedded left of the noun in RD form.[3]

Although sentences were systematically varied in grammatical structure, they were all nearly equivalent in syllable length (11–12 syllables) and in morpheme length (5–6 morphemes). There was one replication for

---

[2]Japanese does not allow the connective *to* to occur with VP or sentence. The connective *shi* also occurs between sentences.

[3]"Embedding" is used in a general sense here. In the tree structure of a simple sentence with nominal coordination in Japanese, for example, the conjoined nouns occur more deeply in the tree than the verb, and are referred to as "embedded."

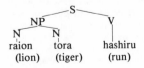

The reverse is true for verbal coordination.

each sentence type (with different lexical content), making a set of 16 sentences for each child.

Subjects

Eighty-one children, ages 2;5 to 5;10 (mean age 3;8), in the Tokyo-Yokohama area were asked to imitate a set of RD sentences and a set of comparable SO sentences. The imitations were part of a larger study of acquisition of coordination in Japanese (Lust and Wakayama, 1979). Almost half of the children were tested on RD 1 and 2 and SO 5 and 6; the others on RD 3 and 4 and SO 7 and 8. Mean age was 3;8 for both groups.

The children were divided into four age groups with mean ages 2;9, 3;2, 3;10, and 5;0 for groups with the following ranges: 2;5–2;11, 3;0–3;5, 3;6–4;3, and 4;4–5;10. Younger children were interviewed in their homes where their mothers administered the imitation task. Older children were interviewed in a Yokohama kindergarten where an experimenter (native speaker of Japanese) administered it. (A speech sample also was gathered for each child, although analysis of the samples is not reported here.) All sessions were tape-recorded. There were 648 sentences in all for analyses.

Results

As can be seen in Table 2, children found right-dislocated sentences to be significantly more difficult than standard order sentences.[4] Both types of RD sentences (either those with nominal coordination or those with verbal coordination) were significantly more difficult than their comparable SO sentence type.

Moreover, the RD sentences vary just as the SO sentences do. That is, just as SO sentences with nominal coordination are easier than those with verbal coordination, so RD sentences with nominal coordination are easier than those with verbal coordination.

As can be seen from Figure 1, this relation is consistent over development until the highest age group (mean 5;0), where RD and SO sentences become equivalent in difficulty, except for the RD sentences with verbal coordination, which remain extremely difficult for children (still only 50% correct at this age).

These results suggest that children distinguish inverted and standard orders quite early. They further suggest that RD sentences may be related

---

[4]Correct imitations (shown on Table 2) included all imitations that retained all of the basic constituents of the model sentence. Reduction or elaboration of redundant terms was considered incorrect, as was any change of order, for example, relocation of the dislocated noun, or any change of lexical items. Minor changes in imitation, such as tense changes, or particle change (omission, addition, or substitution) were disregarded in scoring, so sentences with these minor changes were scored correct if none of the major changes above was made also. Model sentences were administered once, unless the child did not respond, or echoed only a single word, in which case the sentence was administered again. Except for these latter cases, first responses were scored.

Table 2. Mean number of correct imitations of right-dislocated and standard order coordinations[a]

Right dislocation			Standard order			F Test of significant difference
Group I[b]						
1. V [S + S]	1.13	5.	[S + S] V	1.58		
2. V [O + O]	1.03	6.	[O + O] V	1.74		
	1.08			1.65		41.49 (1;34) $p < 0.001$
Group II[c]						
3. [V + V] S	0.42	7.	S [V + V]	1.30		
4. [V + V] O	0.40	8.	O [V + V]	1.12		
	0.41			1.21		54.99 (1;39) $p < 0.001$

[a]Each child was asked to imitate two sentences of each imitation type. Range was thus 0–2.

[b]N = 38 students.

[c]N = 43 students.

to (interpreted or processed with relation to) SO sentences because the RD sentences show the same pattern of difficulty as the SO sentences. This was confirmed by observation of children's errors on the RD sentences. Finally, these results also suggest that the difference between RD and SO sentences is overcome with development, except for sentences with verb coordination, which seem to pose a particular difficulty for Japanese children (compare, for example Lust and Wakayama, 1979).

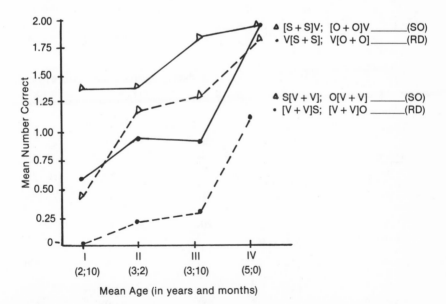

Figure 1. Successful imitation of right-dislocated sentences and standard order sentences over four age groups.

Errors

Fifty-one percent of errors on RD sentences consisted of inversions wherein the (possibly complex) right-dislocated constituent, or some portion of it, was moved back to its standard order position. Summaries of these relocations are shown in Table 3 and examples are shown in Table 4. As can be seen from Table 3, 13% of these relocations were successful, that is, SO was re-established completely. The remainder of these relocations reordered some constituents in standard order, for example, SV, or they contained all constituents with only some in SO, for example, V + SV (see Table 4 for examples). As can be seen from Tables 5 and 6, however, more relocations occurred in the RD sentences with nominal coordinations (57% of errors) (Table 5) than on those with verbal coordination (47% of errors) (Table 6). In particular, relocations on nominal coordinations were different in nature from those with verbal coordinations. When a nominal coordination had been dislocated (compare, for example, Table 5), children moved the whole coordinate constituent back to its standard order position. (See the first two examples on Table 4.) Thirty-eight percent of errors on the nominal coordinations were successful relocations. On the other hand, when a verbal coordination was involved, and a single noun had been dislocated, children never relocated the dislocated constituent to achieve a completely successful relocation (see Table 6). Rather, children's relocations of these sentences (RD with verbal coordination) consisted of forms of ungrammatical split coordinations, as is shown for model sentences II and IV in Table 4. Here the verbal coordination is split by the intercalated nominal. In these relocations with verb coordination, children again try to reconstitute SO, but when

Table 3. Total percent of relocation on right-dislocated sentences (V[S + S], V[O + O], [V + V]S, [V + V]O). Percent of Errors. (Percent of items in parentheses)

		Unsuccessful relocation		
Group	Successful relocation	With all segments	With partial segments	Total
I	15	3	26	44
(2;5–2;11)	(13)	(2)	(23)	(38)
II	11	18	29	58
(3–3;5)	(8)	(13)	(21)	(42)
III	12	20	18	50
(3;6–4;3)	(8)	(14)	(13)	(36)
IV	14	14	32	59
(4;4–5;10)	(4)	(4)	(9)	(16)
Total	13	13	25	51
(2;5–5;10)	(8)	(8)	(16)	(33)

Table 4. Examples of relocation of RD sentences by children

Group	Model sentences	Child's successful relocation	Child's unsuccessful relocation
I	V[S+S] Hashiru-yo, usagi-to kame-ga (Run rabbit and tortoise)	[S+S] Usagi-to kame-ga hashiru-yo (Rabbit and Tortoise run)	S[S+S] Kame usage-to kame-ga (Tortoise rabbit and tortoise)
II	[V+V]S Aruku-shi tobu-yo, kotori-wa (Walk and fly, bird)	None	V+SV Aruku-shi tori-wa tobu (Walk and bird fly) V+S Aruku-shi kotori-wa (Walk and bird) SV+ Kotori-wa tobu-shi (Bird fly-and)
III	V[O+O] Taberu-yo, ringo-to nashi-o (Eat apple and pear)	[O+O]V Ringo-to nashi-o taberu-yo (Apple and pear eat)	[O+O] Ringo-to nashi-o (Apple and pear) [O+O]O Ringo-to nashi-o nashi (Apple and pear, pear)
IV	[V+V]O Tsukeru-shi nameru-yo, jamu-o (Spread and lick, jam)	None	V+OV Tsukeru-shi jamu-o nameru-yo (Spread jam lick) OV+ Jamu-o nameru-shi (Jam lick-and) OV Jamu-o nameru (Jam lick)

Table 5. Percent of right-dislocated sentences that were relocated by Japanese children in each age group [Nominal Coordinations V[S+S], V[O+O]] Percent of Errors (Percent of items in parentheses)

Group	V[S+S] Successful	Unsuccessful With all segments	Unsuccessful With partial segments	Unsuccessful Total	V[O+O] Successful	Unsuccessful With all segments	Unsuccessful With partial segments	Total	TOTAL
I	29 (20)	0 (0)	21 (15)	50 (35)	50 (35)	0 (0)	21 (15)	71 (50)	61 (43)
II	40 (22)	0 (0)	30 (17)	70 (39)	22 (11)	0 (0)	44 (22)	67 (33)	68 (36)
III	25 (10)	0 (0)	0 (0)	25 (10)	31 (20)	0 (0)	8 (5)	38 (25)	36 (20)
IV	100 (11)	0 (0)	0 (0)	100 (11)	100 (6)	0 (0)	0 (0)	100 (6)	100 (8)
Total	37 (17)	0 (0)	17 (8)	54 (25)	38 (18)	0 (0)	23 (10)	59 (29)	57 (27)

Table 6.   Percent of right-dislocated sentences that were relocated by Japanese children in each age group [Verbal Coordinations [V + V]S, [V + V]O] Percent of Errors (Percent of items in parentheses)

Group	[V + V]S				[V + V]O				TOTAL
	Successful	Unsuccessful			Successful	Unsuccessful			
		With all segments	With partial segments	Total		With all segments	With partial segments	Total	
I	0 (0)	5 (5)	32 (32)	36 (36)	0 (0)	5 (5)	27 (27)	32 (32)	34 (34)
II	0 (0)	39 (35)	17 (15)	56 (50)	0 (0)	17 (14)	33 (30)	50 (45)	52 (48)
III	0 (0)	37 (32)	32 (27)	68 (59)	0 (0)	26 (23)	21 (18)	47 (41)	58 (50)
IV	0 (0)	22 (9)	11 (5)	33 (14)	0 (0)	10 (5)	50 (24)	60 (27)	47 (20)
Total	0 (0)	25 (20)	25 (20)	50 (40)	0 (0)	14 (12)	30 (24)	45 (36)	47 (38)

the individual dislocated nominals are moved to SO position, they are attached to a single verb, splitting the verbal coordination, and the second verb is left dangling, for example, *Aruku-shi tori-wa tobu* 'walk and bird fly' (V + SV). The same pattern of errors held both for sentences with subject and for those with object.

In contrast to the RD sentences, there was almost no dislocation of SO sentences. There was only 1% relocation of standard order sentences and they occurred in verbal coordination. For example, the child gave VSV (*Kamitsuku inu-wa hoeru-shi* 'Bite dog bark-and') when the child had been given S[V + V]).

In summary, in these errors on RD sentences, it seems that, when given RD sentences, children attempted to reconstitute SO, confirming that they distinguish standard and inverted orders and they interrelate them. They reconstitute SO by mapping constituent structure (even complex constituents such as coordinate phrases) into standard linear order. They differentiate constituent structure of dislocated (and nondislocated) constituents. It appears that conjoined nouns (*usagi-to kame-ga* 'rabbit and tortoise' as in example 1 in Table 1) are a single constituent in Japanese child language. They are moved as a whole to a new position. Conjoined verbs (*aruku-shi tobu* 'walk and fly' as in examples 3 and 4 in Table 1) are not a single complex constituent in Japanese child language; they are split in the process of relocation to SO.

Discussion

Japanese children in early stages of first language acquisition show a complex sensitivity to both linear order and to constituent structure and their interrelation. In early stages, children associate constituent structure with a basic word order (in this case, SOV or V-final order). Over development in the 2–5 year age period, children acquire a flexibility in the mapping from constituent structure to surface linear order, thus acquiring modulation of basic word order, as in the RD sentences studied here.

This chapter may further explain the differences that have been observed between coordination in Japanese and English child language. For example, it has been found in previous research that children learning English as a first language strongly prefer coordination types (such as in 8 below) with a forward reduction of redundancy over those (such as in 9) with a backward reduction of redundancy.

8. Forward reduction
   (a) *Dogs* bark and *dogs* bite   SV + $V
   (b) *Dogs* bark and Φ bite   SV + $V → S[V + V]

9. Backward reduction
   (a) Birds *sing* and crickets *sing*   S∜ + SV
   (b) Birds ∅ and crickets *sing*   S∜ + SV → [S + S]V

Japanese children, on the other hand, have been found (Lust and Wakayama, 1979) to strongly prefer coordination structures with a backward reduction of redundancy (for example, 11) over those with forward (for example, 10), which is the reverse of the preference in English.

10. Forward reduction
   (a) *Inu-wa* hoeru-shi *Inu-wa* kamitsuko   SV + ∯V
        (*Dog* bark - and *dog*   bite)
   (b) *Inu-wa* hoeru-shi ∅ kamitsuki   SV + ∯V → S[V + V]

11. Backward reduction
   (a) Tori-wa *naku*-shi mushi-wa *naku*   S∜ + SV
        (Bird   *sing* and cricket   *sing*)
   (b) Tori-to ∅ mushi-wa *naku*   S∜ + SV → [S + S]V

These results suggest that children learning English strongly favor ordering of anaphors (reduction sites) rightward of their governing expressions at early levels of language acquisition, while Japanese children favor leftward ordering of these anaphors. It has been theorized (Lust, in press) that this difference may relate to the differences in basic branching direction (embedding direction) between Japanese and English (Japanese is left-branching and English is right-branching; Kuno, 1973). The results reported here seem to support this explanation because they have shown that Japanese children both discriminate basic word order and attempt to map complex constituent structure onto this order.

More generally, the results may provide the basis for an explanation of the results of other Japanese researchers who have found evidence of Japanese children's discrimination of standard word orders (for example, Yoshida, 1963; Hayashibe, 1975; Hakuta, 1977, 1978.) If Japanese children are sensitive to the more fundamental notions of order isolated in this chapter, and they learn their values for their specific language at an early age, this may help to explain how they are able to learn the simpler notion of SOV word order.

Notably, the finding that even very young Japanese children discriminate between nominal and verbal coordination confirms that children are sensitive to even more subtle facts of Japanese than surface constituent structures. The *to* connective in nominal coordination is essentially phrasal, while the *shi* connective in verbal coordination is essentially sentential (Okubo and Takahasi, 1978, personal communication). Similar results on Japanese children's acquisition of coordination in Japanese are reported and discussed in Lust and Wakayama (1979).

In conclusion, the results suggest that Japanese children may proceed through the language learning process with a rather complex and abstract sensitivity to order. Other works in English first language acquisition have reported a similar conclusion.

These results cannot directly bear on the issue of whether such complex sensitivity to linear order is learned or predetermined by some cognitive competence for language. Children at very lowest levels of Japanese language acquisition (below 2 years) have not been studied. The fact that the basic pattern of the results was constant from the lowest age group, when children were at quite an early stage of acquisition of syntax, however, suggests that this complex sensitivity may be one of the earliest principles of language acquisition.

Moreover, while this early sensitivity would appear to be a function of grammatical competence, it does not disagree with more general cognitive-perceptual principles that have been discovered for early language processing. Sinclair (1972), for example, found that when young French-speaking Swiss children (ages 2–7) were tested on random orders of NNV or VVN combinations, they showed a series of processing strategies over development. While the strategy of grouping units by relative linear ordering was late developmentally, various other strategies of clustering units into "subconstituents" appeared early in development. Such early strategies may be related to the early constituent groupings observed in young Japanese children, particularly in the case of verbal coordinations.

Conclusion

The results from this experimental study suggest that Japanese children may go through the language learning process with a rather complex sensitivity to order. The fact that the results reported here are based on the Japanese language provides a stronger argument for the existence of a universal sensitivity to factors related to order in early child language because Japanese is more free than English in surface word order.

ACKNOWLEDGMENTS

We thank Professor Eleanor Jorden and Mrs. A. Okubo for their helpful comments on this chapter and Professors Shin Oshima, Sho Haraguchi, and Taroo Takahashi for their helpful discussion of the linguistic structures involved. We thank Miss Hiroko Kitamoto and Mrs. Fumiyo Yamazaki for their assistance in interviewing the young children of this study. In addition, we are indebted to the following persons in Japan: Professors Hikohito Hiraide and Emiko Inoue, Miss Tusune Hirano, Mrs. Matsaya Funada, Mrs. Noriko Terakawa, Mrs. Fumiko Kananda, and Mr. and Mrs. Hidetatsu Kaneda.

REFERENCES

Bach, E. 1967. Order in base structures. In: C. Li (ed.), Word Order and Word Order Change. University of Texas Press, Austin.

Bloom, L. 1970. Language Development. M.I.T. Press, Cambridge, Mass.

Bowerman, M. 1973. Early Syntactic Development. Cambridge University Press, New York.

Braine, C. 1976. Children's first word combinations. Monogr. Soc. Res. Child Dev. 41(1, Serial No. 164).

Brown, R. 1973. A First Language. Harvard University Press, Cambridge, Mass.

deVilliers, J., and deVilliers, P. 1973. Development of the use of word order in comprehension. J. Psycholinguist. Res. 2(4):331–341.

Gruber, J. 1969. Topicalization in child language. In: D. Reibel and S. Schane (eds.), Modern Studies in English. Prentice-Hall, Englewood Cliffs, N.J.

Hakuta, K. 1977. Word order and particles in the acquisition of Japanese. Paper presented at the Stanford Child Language Research Forum, March, Stanford, Cal.

Hakuta, K. 1978. A word on word order is in order: Constraints on Japanese children's comprehension of complex sentences. Unpublished manuscript, Harvard University, Department of Psychology.

Haraguchi, S. 1973. Remarks on dislocation in Japanese. Unpublished manuscript, M.I.T., Cambridge, Mass.

Hayashibe, H. 1975. Word order and particles: A developmental study in Japanese. In: Descriptive and Applied Linguistics, Vol. 7. pp. 1–18, International Christian University, Tokyo.

Jorden, E. 1963. Beginning Japanese. Yale University Press, New Haven, Conn.

Kuno, S. 1973. The Structure of the Japanese Language. M.I.T. Press, Cambridge, Mass.

Li, C. Word Order and Word Order Change. 1975. University of Texas Press, Austin.

Lust, B. 1977. Coordination reduction in child language. J. Child Lang. 4:257–287.

Lust, B. Constraint on anaphora in child language: A prediction for a universal. In: S. Tavakolian (ed.), Linguistic Theory and First Language Acquisition. M.I.T. Press, Cambridge, Mass. In press.

Lust, B., and Wakayama, T. 1979. The structure of coordination in first language acquisition of Japanese. In: F. Eckman and A. Hastings (eds.), First and Second Language Learning. Newbury House, Rawley, Mass.

Murata, K. 1961. The development of verbal behavior: III. Early developmental processes of the linguistic forms and functions of requests. Jpn. J. Educ. Psychol. 9:220–229.

Okubo, A. 1968. Yooji Gengo-no Hattatsu. [Development of Young Children's Language]. Tokyo-do-shoten.

Okubo, A. 1973. Yooji-no bunkoozoo-no hattatsu: Samsai-rokusai-ji-no baai. [Development of sentence structure in young children: In three to six year olds]. Kokuritsu Kokugo Kenkyuujo [National Language Research Institute], Tokyo. (Monograph.)

Park, Tschang-Lin. 1970a. The acquisition of German syntax. Unpublished manuscript, University of Bern, Bern, Switzerland. (Cited by Brown, 1975).

Park, Tschang-Zin. 1970b. Language acquisition in a Korean child. Unpublished manuscript, University of Bern, Bern, Switzerland. (Cited by Brown, 1973.)

Sanches, M. 1968. Features in the acquisition of Japanese grammar. Unpublished doctoral dissertation, Stanford University, Stanford, Cal.

Sinclair, H. 1972. SVO. A linguistic universal? J. Exp. Child Psychol. 14:329–348.

Sinclair, H. 1973. Language acquisition and cognitive development. In: T. Moore (ed.), Cognitive Development and the Acquisition of Language. Academic Press, Inc. New York.

Slobin, D. 1966. the acquisition of Russian as a native language. In: F. Smith and G. A. Miller (eds.), The Genesis of Language: A Psycholinguistic Approach. M.I.T. Press, Cambridge, Mass.

Slobin, D. 1973. Cognitive prerequisites for the development of grammar. In: C. Ferguson and D. Slobin (eds.), Studies of Child Language Development. Holt, Rinehart & Winston, Inc., New York.

Slobin, D., and Welsh, C. 1973. Elicited imitation as a research tool. In: C. Ferguson and D. Slobin (eds.), Studies of Child Language Development. Holt, Rinehart & Winston, Inc., New York.

Smith, D. 1978. Mirror-images in Japanese and English. Language, 54:78–122.

Steele, S. 1978. Word order variation: A typological study. In: J. Greenberg (ed.), Universals of Human Language. Vol. 4. Stanford University Press, Stanford, Cal.

Yoshida, M. 1963. A study on the order of verb modifiers. Summaries of papers and reports presented at the 4th Institute Descriptive and Applied Linguistics. International Christian University, Tokyo.

Semantic Development

The term semantic development refers to the acquisition of lexical items and the development of their meaning. The following three chapters all include an investigation of the child's use of negative words such as *no* and its Japanese equivalents. The centrality of negation in the language, as well as the social life of the 2-year-old is obvious to any parent. Because negation is simultaneously an expression of self and will, and a manifestation of the understanding of reality and possibility, it exemplifies many important issues in semantic development.

In recent years, much descriptive work in semantic development has been done, and the major challenge now is to formulate generalizations and explanations concerning semantic development. This is no easy task, as semantic development is an extremely rich field, undoubtedly because meaning is a very diverse phenomenon.

Among the major questions of this area of research are:

1. Which words are acquired first, and why? Among nominal (naming) words, there is considerable uniformity in the early appearance of names for common, modest-sized objects that are active (cars, animals) or can be acted upon by the child (cookies, shoes), or that play a role in the child's everyday routine (milk, blanket). To a certain extent, these are the words that parents frequently use in speaking to young children, but the direction of influence— parent to child or child to parent—is not clear. Most research on early vocabularies has focused on these nominals because of the possibility of applying various linguistic theories, such as semantic features. However, Gopnik, in Chapter 6, shows that non-nominals appear at least as early as nominals in young children's vocabularies.

2. How do word meanings change with time? It has long been noted that words do not have the same meaning for young children as they do for adults; phenomena such as overextension, underextension, and overlap are quite common. Is semantic development merely a matter

of adding additional semantic features, or are more substantial re-organizations necessary? Ito's description in Chapter 7 of the changing meaning of negatives that appear early, such as *nai* and *iya*, illustrates the complexity of the problem.

3. What is the relationship between the apparent meaning underlying the child's production of a lexical item and that governing the child's comprehension? The fact that the two are not always identical, for example overextension is far more common in production than it is in comprehension, implies that evidence from production alone gives a misleading estimate of the child's knowledge. It also raises important questions concerning the mechanism of acquisition.

4. What is the relationship of semantic categories to conceptual categories in general, that is, categories developed and utilized in nonlinguistic contexts? It has been proposed that, at least early in development, children are simply attaching labels to existing nonlinguistic categories. Such an account seems most plausible for nominals. Gopnik suggests that there is an interaction between linguistic and cognitive development in which non-nominal expressions are used to encode concepts that are still developing, for the further benefit of both. Her observations also reveal a considerable social-affective content in early word meanings, which is a useful reminder that the term *nonlinguistic* is not identical to the term *cognitive*.

Ito argues even more explicitly that there is an emotional basis to early language. His chapter on negation in the Japanese language is a good example of the value of cross-linguistic research. Because Japanese has a wider range of negative forms than English, aspects of meaning that are more difficult to investigate in English can be distinguished.

In Chapter 8, Hanlon demonstrates how much can be learned from a careful linguistic analysis of a set of related forms (a semantic field), and the extent to which internal factors of complexity determine order of acquisition within such a set. The relevant factors—specificity, transformation of suppositional set, and distributivity—are cognitively substantial. That they predict the order of acquisition might reflect the fact that the labels are learned just as each concept is mastered, although it also is possible that the nonlinguistic concepts all are present earlier and simply are lexicalized in this regular fashion. Research comparing children's performance on Hanlon's tasks with similar, but nonlinguistic tasks would help decide between these two possibilities.

Development of Non-nominal Expressions in 1-2-Year-Olds
Why the First Words Aren't About Things

Alison Gopnik

During the one-word period, children use a number of abstract, non-nominal expressions such as *that, gone, no, more, oh dear, there,* and *down,* as well as object names such as *Mommy* and *dog.* This study examines the way nine 1-2-year-old children used these expressions.

The sample consisted of three groups of three children. Children in the first group were visited every 2 weeks in their homes from the time they were 12 months old, when they did not produce any recognizable speech, until they reached the two-word stage (mean length of utterance (MLU) approximately 1.4). During each visit, 1 hour of the child's spontaneous speech was audiotaped. Notes were taken to describe the context of the speech.

Children in the second group were visited in their homes every month from the time they were 15 months old, when only one of them produced recognizable speech, until they were 21 months old. Children in the third group were visited in their homes every month from the time they were 18 months old, when all of them produced some speech, until they were 24 months old. The children in both of these groups were videotaped for 1 hour during each visit.

In order to discover the meaning of a particular expression, the researchers examined all the contexts in which the expression was uttered. It was assumed that there was a common factor present in each context. If this common factor was discovered, the reseachers could at least guess at the meaning of the expression. An expression was classified a nominal (name) if the common factor in all the contexts in which it was used was a specific type of object. All other expressions were classified as non-nominals.

All nine children used non-nominal expressions in their earliest recorded speech. (See Table 1.) In fact, some children used non-nominals before they used names. Furthermore, non-nominal expressions were used more frequently than names in the early recordings.

TYPES OF NON-NOMINAL EXPRESSIONS

Seven kinds of non-nominal expressions were used by almost all the children. These expressions were used very frequently, and they were used in the earliest recorded period. (See Table 2.) They occurred in contexts that involved notice, disappearance, refusal, repetition, success, failure, and movement. These contexts are described in more detail below.

Notice

All nine children used an expression, usually *that* or *whatsat*, when they noticed or focused attention on an object. *That* was produced when children pointed to an object, or when they looked at or listened to the object, or when they touched it, picked it up, or showed it to someone else.

That was used in contexts involving every conceivable object, including phenomena that adults would not call objects at all, such as sounds and other momentary perceptual configurations. For example, in a single session one child used *that* to refer to a small drop of milk that fell on the table, as well as to a Christmas tree and a cement mixer.

Things that the child might consider novel or unusual such as the recording equipment used were especially likely to be called *that*. However, *that* was also used in referring to familiar persons like "Daddy," or to a favorite toy and to phenomena that were not very interesting in themselves but were relevant to the child's immediate concerns. *That* was also applied to a jigsaw puzzle piece that the child tried to fit into place, or to a block that he tried to put on a tower.

Table 1.   Number of children using non-nominal expressions

Expressions used by nine children:
Down
Gone
That

Expressions used by eight children:
There
No
In

Expressions used by seven children:

Up	Bye bye
Yes	More
On	Oh dear (Oh no-oh)

Expressions used by six children:

Hereyare
Off
Fall

Expressions used by five children:

Hello	Again
Out	Look
Go	

Expressions used by four children:

Two	Wheres
Do it (do)	Drink
Get it	

Expressions used by three children:

Open	Come	Push
Find night-night	Now	Back
Read	See	Sit
Me	Kick	Eat done it (did it)
Jump	Mine	Top

Expressions used by two children:

Ah	Cuddle	Fit
Here	Want why	Burn
Crying	Please	Five
Wee Poo	Finish	Bang
Draw	Make (made)	Ready
Press	Wrong	One
Painting	Walk	This
		Eh

Expressions used by one child:

Dress	Tickle	Shut up	Heave	Broke
Bam	Stick	Lost it	Roll	Poor
Stop	Shut	Away	Round	Wa
Hold	Bite	Ironing	Beep	Ow
Close	Bump	Games	Woops	Hooray
Undone	Ride	Yee	Empty	Yere
Swimming	Show	Shh	Yucch	That way
Knock	Thank you	Right	Good	Good girl
Dull	Cough	Boom	Can't	Sing
Put away	Drop it	Yeh	Which way	Come off
End	Kiss	Quick	Room	
Build	Sleep	Inside	Called	
Another	Over	Eight	These	
Rub our	Tidied	Three	Stroking	
Up side down	Outside	Four	Stuck	
Ringing	Upsy daisy	Six	Thereyare	

Table 2.   Time of appearance and frequency of non-nominal expressions for Group I[a]

Session Number	Expressions		
	Jonathan		
1	Down 63		
3	There 549		
	Hello 32		
5	Hereyare 67		
11	Ah 4		
16	Up 69		
17	Oh dear 98		
18	No 149		
	Yes 60		
	Dress 2		
19	More 31		
	Bam 1		
20	Off 30		
22	Gone 20		
	Stop 19		
23	On 26		
	Fall 10		
	Open 22		
	Hold 1		
24	Bye 8		
	In 10		
25	Close 20		
	Undone 10		
26	Out 34		
	Go 8		
	Swimming 2		
	Two 15		
27	Again 2	Knock down 1	Read 4
	That 63	Pull 3	Crying 4
	Here 2	Put away 9	
	Do it 3	End 7	
	Find it 4	Night-night 2	
28	Build 1	Coming 6	
	Wee 1		
	Nother 17		
	Me 4		
	Jump 1		
29	Draw 16	Press 2	
	Rub out 4	Now 1	
	Upside down 4		
	Ringing 1		
	Get it 1		
	Henry		
4	No 114		
11	Gone 169		
	Hereyare 114		
	That (whats at) 178		

Session Number	Expressions		
13	Oh No 28		
	More		
16	Tickle 6		
17	Tosee 78		
18	Hello 5		
	Yes 10		
	Night-night 8		
	Wheres 63		
	Kick		
19	Down 16	Painting 25	
	On 35	There 54	
	Bye bye 8		
	In 35		
	Out 10		
20	Look 29		
	Jump 8		
	Cuddle 20		
	Want 28		
21	Go 6		
	Mine 74		
	Stick 3		
22	Fall 6		
	Shut 15		
	Bite 2		
	Bump 4		
	Push 7		
23	Up 12		
	Off 10		
	Why 6		
	Back 1		
	Here 23		
24	Sit 2	Come 3	Show 1
	Eat 1	Please 10	
	Again 4	Press 2	
	Open 1	Do it 2	
	Get it 6	Ride 1	

Rachel

Session Number	Expressions		
1	There 102		
3	Down 27		
	Bye 8		
4	No 33		
	Fall 18		
	Mine 45		
5	More 19		
6	On 25		
	Thank you 1		
7	Hereyare 22		
	Look 3		
8	In 9		
	Drink 10		

continued

Table 2—*continued*

Session Number	Expressions		
	Finish 5		
9	Gone 30		
	Find it 3		
10	Come off 27	Drop it 1	
	Off 14	Kiss 2	
	Get it 1	Done it 17	
	Made it 20		
	Cough 6		
11	Yes 1	Now 10	
	Night-night 3	See 3	
	Wheres 1		
	Eat 1		
	Sleep 2		
12	Up 2	Over 3	Walk 3
	Out 5	Tidied up 2	Read 3
	Go 4	Outside 6	Shut up 1
	Dat 3	Upsy daisy 1	Lost 1
	Come 2	Wrong 2	
13	Painting 1	Fit 1	
	Back 1	Games 7	
	Sit 1	Drawing 1	
	Away 1		
	Ironing 1		

[a]The expressions are listed in chronological order. All the expressions occurring first in each session are listed. Next to each expression is the number of times the expression was used in the entire corpus.

Disappearance

All nine children used *gone* when they could not see or hear an object. They said *gone* as they searched for a missing object, when an object disappeared from sight (or earshot), or when a stable configuration broke up, for example, when a tower of blocks fell, and when containers were emptied. Children were particularly likely to use *gone* in the last three contexts if they themselves caused the disappearance or destruction of the object, or the emptiness of the container.

Several children used *gone* when they turned away from an object, or placed an object behind them. Otherwise, the contexts in which *gone* occurred involved a wide variety of objects and actions. *Gone* was used when children searched for mother, when they turned over drawings, turned away from a disturbing sight, pushed blocks into boxes, emptied tins, opened empty paper bags, and when a generator noise suddenly stopped, or the TV went blank. The common factor in all these contexts was that an object that the child expected to see or hear was not in fact seen or heard by the child.

Refusal

No was used by eight children when a plan of action was not carried through. For example, children used *no* when they refused to perform an action suggested by someone else such as a request by a mother that the child put on shoes. They also used it when they protested the action of someone else, or when that action conflicted with their own plans, for example, when one child's sister tried to take a toy bear away from her. Children said *no* when they began to perform an action and then decided to perform some other action instead. For example, one child started to climb into her chair, said *no*, stopped and walked to the other side of the room. Finally, *no* was produced when the child tried to complete a task but failed. All these contexts involve a plan on the part of the child. The child said *no* when the plan did not go through either because the child refused to act, or because other people or objects hindered the action.

In a few later sessions, children used *no* to negate propositions. One child said "No John-john clothes on no" in a discussion of nude swimming.

Repetition

Seven of the nine children used *more*, or occasionally *again*, in contexts involving the repetition of an action on an object. *More* was used both in repeating an action on the same object, for example, shaking a box for a second time, and in repeating an action on a similar object, for example, inserting a second, slightly different block into a box. The expression was also used when children wanted to repeat an action on an object but were unable to do so, and when the child wanted someone else to repeat an action.

In the last sessions, *more* was occasionally used to comment on the presence of two similar objects.

Success

Seven children used a variety of expressions, most often *there*, but also *did it hooray*, and *good girl*, when they successfully completed a plan. For example, one child said *there* after she got a block into the correct hole of a puzzle box after several unsuccessful attempts. *There* was also used when children built a tower of blocks without knocking it down, stuck two pieces of Lego together, and climbed down from high chairs.

In all these contexts, the child tried to bring about certain consequences by acting in a particular way, and predicting that objects around him would also "act" in a particular way. When his actions and the "behavior" of objects brought about the desired consequence, he produced the expression. The children often seemed less interested in the result of the plan than in the process of conceiving and executing it. For example, a tower would be knocked down as soon as it was finished, and jigsaw puzzles were broken up as soon as they were completed. Sometimes children even intentionally complicated a task so that it would be more difficult for them to succeed.

Failure

Eight children used expressions like *oh dear* and *oh no* when they failed to complete a plan. *Oh dear* was produced in the same contexts as *there*, that is, when the child tried to complete a moderately difficult task, but *oh dear* marked unsuccessful attempts. It was used when a block would not fit into the hole of a puzzle box, when a tower of blocks fell before it was completed, or when the child was unable to climb down from a high chair. Often, a succession of *oh dears* accompanying unsuccessful attempts would be followed by a triumphant *there* when success was finally achieved.

Movement

All nine children used the expressions *there, down, up, off, on, in,* and *out* primarily when an object moved. The expressions were also used when the children moved, for example, when they climbed on and off chairs, and when they caused an object to move. One child said *up* when he placed a toy chair on a table. The expressions were very rarely used when someone else moved an object, or when an object moved accidentally.

There marked movement in any direction, while the other expressions were correctly used to indicate movement in a particular direction. Sometimes one expression marked movement in two directions. *Down*, for example, occasionally marked upward and downward movement.

In the last sessions the expressions were used to mark the location of stationary objects. One child, in his last session, said *up dare* pointing to a toy on a high shelf.

THE MEANING OF NON-NOMINALS

There are several interesting features of the concepts that seem to be encoded by these non-nominal expressions. By definition, these expressions do not refer to specific types of objects, nor are they used to express relationships between objects, at least not in the early period. Notice, disappearance, success, failure, refusal, and repetition are not concepts that involve relationships between objects. Objects are involved in success, failure, refusal, or repetition, only insofar as they play a role in the child's plans. Even in movement contexts, the object's movements are generally significant only if they are the result of an action.

On the other hand, the expressions do not encode particular actions or types of actions. They do not resemble simple concrete verbs in the adult language. Notice and disappearance contexts do not involve actions at all. Virtually any action may be repeated, may lead to success or failure, may cause movement, or may remain unperformed. The same action, for example knocking down a tower of blocks, might be marked by *no* if someone had just said *Oh leave the tower up; more,* if the tower had been knocked down previously; *oh dear* if the child was trying to build the tower; *there* if he was trying to push the tower over; or *down* if he was commenting on the downward movement of the blocks.

These non-nominal expressions also do not seem to be social, conversational, or expressive devices although they do occur in a wide variety of social and emotional contexts. Sometimes an expression served a particular social function, for instance, *no* was used to refuse a suggestion, and *more* was used to demand that someone else repeat an action. But at other times, the same expressions could serve a very different social function— *no* was also used to protest another person's actions, and *more* was used when the child was demanding that he be allowed to repeat an action. Furthermore, non-nominal expressions were often used in apparently non-conversational ways—children said *no* when they changed their minds about a course of action, or *more* when they repeated a previous action. In both of these instances, the children had no clear conversational intent.

Similarly, the conversational context of a particular expression varied, and sometimes expressions were used when there was no conversational context. The emotional context also varied. A particular expression such as *no* could be accompanied by fury, joy, malice, or despair, but generally, non-nominal expressions were produced when the children were playing contentedly.

The concepts encoded by these non-nominal expressions have a certain egocentric quality, particularly in the early period. Children seem to mark relationships between themselves and objects, or between themselves, their actions, and objects. For example, *that* marks the fact that the child notices or attends to an object, and *gone* marks the fact that the child does not see an object. *No, more, oh dear,* and *there* almost always referred to the child's decision not to perform an action, or to repeat an action, or to the success or failure of the child's plans. The earliest and most frequent uses of movement expressions marked the child's own movements or movements he caused.

Even when other persons were involved in the contexts in which these expressions were produced, the actions of those persons seemed to be significant only insofar as they were related to the child's plans or inten-

CARL A. RUDISILL LIBRARY
LENOIR RHYNE COLLEGE

tions such as when an action was desired by the child because it was necessary to bring about a certain result. The children used *no* to protest the actions of others when those actions interfered with their own plans. Thus, non-nominal expressions were not used only to comment on the fact that someone else repeated an action, or refused to perform an action, or succeeded or failed.

Another significant feature of the concepts encoded by some of these expressions, particularly *no, more, oh dear, there,* and movement expressions, was the importance of the consequences of actions. The expressions did not seem to encode actions or intentions as such; instead, the expressions were used when the child predicted that a certain consequence would ensue if he acted in a particular way, or if other actions occurred.

Concepts of success and failure only make sense in terms of this goal-oriented framework, because plans, rather than actions, succeed or fail, and plans involve actions and calculations of the consequences of actions. Movement expressions were used particularly for actions that had a consequence, namely the movement of an object. *More* was only used when the consequences of the original action and the repeated action were similar either because the objects involved were the same, or because they were similar. *More* was not used when the child repeated an action on a number of disparate objects with disparate results. *No* was used when the child refused to act, and when objects did not "cooperate." In both cases, the expected consequences of his action did not ensue.

Another interesting feature of the concepts encoded by these expressions is their abstractness and generality. It has already been noted that these expressions do not encode particular types of objects, or relationships between objects, or actions, but they also do not indicate particular, concrete relationships between the child and objects, or particular plans or types of plans. They do encode, however, the fact that an object is or is not perceived, and they encode the implementation or lack of implementation of a plan, the success or failure of a plan, or the fact that two plans are similar. Even movement expressions can be applied to a very wide variety of contexts, and one of them, *there,* does not even specify the direction of movement.

The semantic development of each of these non-nominal expressions is strikingly similar. Many of the expressions were first used in an egocentric action-oriented way, but toward the end of the one-word period they were used in a more objective way. *No,* which first was used to mark the fact that a plan was not carried through, began to be used to negate propositions in the last sessions. *More,* which initially marked the repetition of an action, came to be used as a comment on the similarity of objects. Movement expressions that were initially applied to the child's movements, or to movements he caused, were later applied to the spatial relationships of stationary objects.

In summary, for most of the one-word period, the seven kinds of non-nominal expressions described do not encode relationships between objects, or types of actions, nor are they social, conversational or expressive devices. The concepts encoded by these expressions seem to be both egocentric and abstract. Many of them seem to involve plans, that is, actions and a calculation of their consequences. Toward the end of the one-word period, the expressions begin to encode less egocentric and action-oriented concepts.

For most of the one-word period, then, some of the most common non-nominal expressions encode rather abstract relationships between the child and objects, or rather abstract features of the child's plans. In particular, *that* encodes the fact that the child perceives an object; and *gone* encodes the fact that the child does not perceive an object. Expressions such as *no* encode the fact that the child's plan is not carried through. *More* encodes the fact that a plan is to be repeated. *There* and *oh dear* encode that an attempted plan is successful or unsuccessful respectively. Expressions such as *up* and *down* encode the fact that a plan involves movement in a particular direction.

This account of the meaning of early non-nominal expressions has some interesting implications. One of them concerns a difference between the child's language and the adult's. Concepts of success, failure, disappearance, or refusal are much less important in the adult semantic system than concepts of agency, temporal concepts, or concepts of truth and falsity.

However, the concepts encoded by non-nominal expressions play an important role in the cognitive development of 1–2-year-olds. In particular, some evidence suggests that the type of plans described in this chapter develop at about age 1. At this age, children begin to appreciate the relationship between their actions, the objects they act on, and the consequences of their actions. Abstract concepts pertaining to plans (concepts such as success, failure, or repetition) might be developed in the 12–24-month period. There is also evidence that there are important changes in the child's understanding of the disappearance and reappearance of objects, and in his understanding of spatial concepts around the age of 18 months. Similarly, the development from egocentric concepts to more objective ones is typical of the 12–24-month period.

Some child language theorists have suggested that the child's early language reflects the structure of his cognition. This chapter suggests, in addition, that children use early expressions, at least early non-nominal expressions, to encode concepts they are in the course of developing rather than well-established or primitive concepts. The child begins to talk about abstract relationships between himself and objects, and about abstract features of plans at about the same time that he begins to understand those relationships and features.

This raises some interesting possibilities about the relationship between early language and cognitive development. In particular, children might actually use early language to solve cognitive problems. For example, a 12-month-old child who is on the brink of making certain generalizations about his plans, or about the disappearance and reappearance of objects will focus his attention on situations that involve plans or disappearances. The fact that adults say *there* in a variety of contexts involving successful plans, or that they use *gone* to describe a variety of disappearances, could help the child to generalize about these contexts. At the same time, the child would ignore adult utterances of *there* or *gone* when they occur in contexts that are not cognitively significant.

As the child grows older and his cognitive frontiers expand, he becomes capable of appreciating generalizations that were previously uncomprehensible. For example, once he understands his own plans, with the help of linguistic clues he can begin to apply that understanding to the plans of others, with the help of other linguistic clues. Eventually the child's semantic and cognitive structures match the adult's.

The adult language provides a series of signposts that help the child find his way around uncharted cognitive territory. However, the child can only make use of the signposts that he is able to comprehend. As the child covers more cognitive ground, he can take advantage of new linguistic signposts.

There is an interaction between linguistic and cognitive development. Children use language to make cognitive advances, and these advances allow them to develop new linguistic structures. This is in line with Vygotsky's hypothesis that children use language to make cognitive advances, and to regulate their intelligent action (Vygotsky, 1962). This chapter, however, suggests that language is used in this way from the very beginning of a child's language development. Some of the earliest words—*that, there, gone, no, more, oh dear,* and *in*—may help the child to develop abstract relational concepts.

REFERENCE

Vygotsky, L. S. 1962. Thought and Language. Tr. by E. Hanfmann and G. Vakar. M.I.T. Press, Cambridge, Mass.

Two Aspects of Negation
in Child Language

Katsutoshi Ito

Emphasis in the study of child language recently has shifted from syntactic to semantic and pragmatic aspects. The same tendency can be seen in studies of the development of negation in child language. In 1966, Edward Klima and Ursula Bellugi conducted an extensive study of the syntactic aspects of the development of negation in child language. Although they clarified the syntactic processes of the acquisition of negation, they almost totally ignored the semantic aspects, as was pointed out by Bloom (1970).

Bloom was one of the first authors in the field to describe the semantics of the development of negation in child language. On the basis of her observations and descriptions of the utterances of three children, she concluded that "the order of the acquisition for all three children was specified as nonexistence, rejection, denial." Bloom's (1970) findings are basically similar to those of McNeill and McNeill, as Bloom herself, referring to an earlier version of McNeill and McNeill (1973), noted: "McNeill and McNeill raised the issue of the semantic interpretation of negation in Japanese... The three dimensions described were "Existence-Truth, Internal-External, and Entailment-Non-entailment." From the descriptions provided, these three dimensions appear to correspond generally to the semantic categories of negation proposed for Kathryn, Eric and Gia: Nonexistence, rejection and denial."

It is the claim of this chapter that the developmental sequence of negation proposed by Bloom and by McNeill and McNeill does not really reflect the developmental stages of children's negation. Certain aspects of child's early negation such as rejection, which seem to be closely related to emotionality and egocentricity, appear in child's behavior well before the acquisition of negative linguistic expressions. The free alternation of negative forms in the early stage of linguistic development is attributable to those shared semantic features. Through an analysis of the misuse of negatives, it can clearly be seen that function precedes form in the development of negation.

The use of negation can be characterized as having two aspects: the emotional, and the rational or intellectual. The child's use of negation is emotional in the prelinguistic and early linguistic stages, and only gradually does its use become rational or intellectual. Gleason (1973), Raffler-Engel (1977), and Weeks (1979) also have noted the affective nature of young children's communication with other people. This chapter suggests that there are five rather than three categories of negation, and it describes six stages in the development of negation in Japanese children along the emotionality-rationality axis.

METHOD OF INVESTIGATION

The data for this study come mainly from a longitudinal analysis of the communicative behaviors of three sisters. The data were collected in the children's home in the form of written notes. In addition, an 18-month-old boy, who communicated by gestures but who was still in the prelinguistic stage, was carefully observed. Additional information came from the responses to questionnaires sent to 31 mothers, concerning the communicative behaviors of their children who ranged in age from 13 to 39 months.

NEGATION IN PRELINGUISTIC AND EARLY LINGUISTIC STAGES

Babies are emotional beings in that they communicate to demand, to protest, to reject, and to insist. For instance, they cry to protest, to refuse to obey, or to insist that they be allowed to stay outdoors. They also use different gestures such as turning their faces away to reject or to protest. Some of these forms of communication are common to children everywhere. On the other hand, the linguistic manifestations of children's negative intentions vary in different languages. In English, for example, the lexical item "no" is used to express different types of negation such as nonexistence, rejection, and prohibition. In Japanese, however, those three types are lexically differentiated. The word *iya* signifies rejection; *dame* expresses prohibition; and *nai* indicates nonexistence. Denial is expressed by different forms such as *chigau* and *zya nai*.

First Stage

The first negative uttered by 22 out of the 31 children who were the subjects of the questionnaires was *iya,* or simply *ya,* sometimes followed by self-assertive particles such as *da, yo,* or the combination of the two particles—*dayo*. In many cases, the utterance of *iya* was accompanied by whines or cries if their desires were not satisfied. *Iya* was uttered in a high emotional tone. This seems to support the view that *iya* is used by children to express a strong emotional reaction to their parents' commands or to other circumstances that are unfavorable to the child. An 18-month-old boy, for example, shook his head and said "iya" when his parents did not move in the direction that he wanted them to. There are cases, however, in which lexical items other than *iya* are used in similar contexts. A 20-month-old boy uttered "dame" when his mother told him to sit down in his seat on the train. *Dame*, which signals prohibition, is normally used to tell someone not to do something. It may be semantically equivalent to the English phrase 'don't' or 'don't do that.' The boy used *dame* in place of *iya* probably because his parents frequently used *dame* to scold him.

Another misused word is *nai*, which is generally used to denote non-existence but which is used in situations that require *iya*, which means 'I don't want to do so.' Megumi, one of the three sisters studied, used *nai* until she was 20 months old, at which time it was completely replaced by *iya*. When she was told to get down from a desk, for example, she responded "nai." Another time, her mother said, "Come over here" and she answered "here nai," by which she supposedly meant 'I don't want to go there.'

This practice is aptly explained by Slobin: "New forms first express old functions, and new functions are first expressed by old forms" (1973). McNeill and McNeill (1973) made a similar observation: ". . . if Izanami's mother said, "Let's give you some," Izanami would sometimes reply, "There is no giving" instead of "I don't want." 'Nai' (adj.) intruded into as many as 40 percent of the contexts appropriate for 'iya'."

At the age of 26 months, Megumi was still vacillating between *dame, iya* and *nai*, as is evident from the following examples:

Mother: Osuna asobi shinasai 'Play in the sandbox'
Megumi: Dame (repeated several times)
         Iya

Father: Bye bye
Megumi: Bye bye nai
         Bye bye iya (Corrected by herself)

These examples clearly show that Megumi used the three negatives, *iya, dame,* and *nai* almost interchangeably. That she was in the transitional stage is evident from the fact that she corrected her errors by herself. The interchanging of the three terms of negation in the early stages also can be found in the speech of other children. A tentative assumption is that the three negatives were in free variation for Megumi because the underlying meanings were virtually the same for all three terms.

The dominant underlying feature in the initial stage of the acquisition of negation is rejection. Greenfield and Smith (1976) state: "*No* was first used to accompany the performance of desired, but forbidden actions. However, its most common use in a volitional context was to reject objects or events."

However, judging from the contexts in which the three negatives were used, it seems incorrect to single out rejection as the only characterizing semantic feature. There is a bundle of semantic features that constitute a "semantic complex" or an "undifferentiated semantic whole." The uses of this semantic complex are: 1) to reject, demand, or command, 2) to prohibit someone from doing something, and 3) to insist upon carrying out the forbidden act.

Second Stage

In the second stage of the development of negation, the semantic complex begins to be differentiated and each meaning or semantic feature begins to be expressed by a different lexical item. Rejection, for example, is expressed by *iya* and prohibition by *dame*. As was noted above, in the transitional stage *iya* is liable to be substituted by *dame*.

At the second stage, *nai* begins to be used to signify disappearance. In the early developmental stage, children seem to be cognitively incapable of speaking about something that is not visible in their immediate surroundings. This may be partly attributable to the fact that the child's language is restricted to the here and now, that is , ongoing events in the situation, and partly because of children's limited memory span. Therefore, a careful distinction must be made between disappearance and nonexistence.

In many cases, children at this stage of development express disappearance not to report the disappearance of something, but to report their expectations of its reappearance. Bloom's (1970) observation of this is most interesting: "The absence of the syntactic process of negation in the Gia grammars may be attributed. . . to the fact that the syntactic operator *more*, signalling recurrence, was fully productive in both noun and predicate constructions. It is possible that this operated somehow to preclude the development of a similarly functioning syntactic operator to signal a contrastive notion (negation) at the same time."

Bloom's other subject, Eric, however, used *no more* and *more* in the same syntactic contexts. It may be said that *no more* and *more* are, so to speak, different sides of the same coin.

The following dialogue occurred during a game of *Inai inai ba*, a game like peek-a-boo, which is played very often by parents and their children.

Mother: Inai inai 'I am gone'
Megumi (18 months):   Nai ne 'You are gone, aren't you?'
Mother: Ba! 'Here I am!'
Megumi: Atta! 'I found you!'

When Megumi uttered "nai ne" in a high emotional tone, she was wondering where the mother had disappeared to and she was anxiously waiting for her to reappear.

The word *atta* actually has two meanings. In the sentence *Kinoo reezoko ni salami ga atta* 'There was salami in the refrigerator yesterday,' *atta* means 'was' or 'existed.' On the other hand, when someone is looking for something that he or she has misplaced and says, "atta!" it means 'I have found it'. If *nai* means 'not exist,' then, its corresponding affirmative should be *aru* 'exist.' However, the fact that the corresponding affirmative is *nai ne* in the above dialogue clearly indicates that *nai* was used to mean 'has disappeared,' not the state of nonexistence.

Aru and its past form *atta* refer to inanimate objects and *iru* and its past form *ita* refer to animate objects. It was not until Megumi was 21 months old that she was able to distinguish between the two. The following utterance by Megumi shows the transitional stage: Okaasan *aru* kore, *iru* koko 'Mommy is here.' She switched from *aru* to *iru* by herself.

The *nai* in the contrastive pair *nai–atta* seems to correspond in meaning and function to 'no more,' which Bloom (1970) found in such examples as "no more plane," "no more noise," "no more apple," because Bloom says "...*No more* was used in contexts where negation signalled nonexistence of objects that occurred previously—the negation of recurrence." If this is so, then the semantics of "no more" in the above examples would be more suitably characterized as disappearance than as nonexistence. "All gone," which is often used by English-speaking children, seems to signify disappearance, also.

Atta in the above peek-a-boo game was pronounced in a high emotional tone because the exact meaning of *atta* is not simply 'I have found it,' but 'To my great joy I have found it.' Thus, *nai*, whose corresponding affirmative is *atta*, has an emotional or an affective connotation. This reinforces the assumption that all the negatives, *iya, dame,* and *nai* are emotionally motivated up to the second stage.

Third Stage

In the third stage, the distinction between *iya* and *dame* is firmly established. The negative *nai*, however, is used as an "omnibus negative" (McNeill and McNeill, 1973). *Nai* is used to mean rejection, disappearance, nonexistence, and denial. The following utterances were produced by a 20-month-old boy:

When his mother tried to wipe his face with a towel, the boy said:	Nai (Rejection)
When his father went out of sight, the boy said:	Nai ne (Disappearance) + Animate
After eating one rice ball, the boy opened his mouth and said:	Nai ne (Disappearance) − Animate
When the boy saw no fruit on the tray, he said:	Nai ne (Nonexistence)

In the following dialogue, Megumi, at the age of 24 months, used *nai* to signal denial:

Megumi: Otoosan! 'Daddy!'
Mother: (Jokingly) Hai 'Yes'
Megumi: Okaasan otoosan nai 'Mommy, not daddy'

Fourth Stage

In the fourth stage, *nai* is no longer used for disappearance. An interesting sample from a 35-month-old girl shows that she distinguished between disappearance and nonexistence by means of the lexical items *naku* and *nai*, respectively:

Kami naku 'Paper has gone'
Otoosan naku 'Daddy has gone'
Mizu nai 'There is no water'

Naku may be interpreted as a shortened form of *nakunatta*, which means 'has gone' or disappeared.

Fifth Stage

In the fifth stage, a new lexical item *chigau* is used along with *nai* to signal denial. *Chigau* means 'that is not the case,' or 'that is different from what one has expected.' For example, someone called Megumi jokingly by her sister's name, Yurichan, and 27-month-old Megumi protested: "Chigau! Meguchan" 'No! Meguchan.' And, in response to her father's comment, "Meguchan nakimushi" 'Megumi is a crybaby,' Megumi replied: "Chigau!" 'No!'

Sixth Stage

In the sixth stage, another lexical item *zyanai* was used to signal denial. *Chigau* can occur both in the sentence-initial and sentence-final positions but *zyanai* can occur only in sentence-final position. *Zyanai* is a reduced form of *de wa nai*, but it seems to be used as a single unit. For example, at the age of 29 months, Megumi said, "Meguchan no seal *zyanai*" 'That is not Megumi's seal.' Table 1 summarizes the developmental sequence of negation in Japanese children.

DISCUSSION

The Danish linguist Otto Jespersen (1922) made the following comment on the development of negation: "Most children learn to say *no* before they can say *yes*...simply because negation is a stronger expression of feeling than affirmation." This keen observation points out implicitly the emotional nature of negation in the early developmental stage.

For infants in the early prelinguistic stage, whining and crying are the chief means of expression. They whine and cry when they want something, when they do not like an object or event, or when they do not want someone to do something. Thus, it would be quite natural for such semantic intentions as desire, rejection, and prohibition to be expressed first.

According to the statistical studies done by the Soviet psychologists Luria and Yudovich (1959), expressions that indicate desires and negation

Table 1.   Correlations between forms and meanings in the development of negation in Japanese children[a]

1	S. C.	Rejection			Prohibition		
	L. I.	Nai		Iya		Dame	
2	S. C.	Disappearance		Rejection		Prohibition	
	L. I.	Nai		Iya		Dame	
3	S. C.	Denial	Nonexistence	Disappearance	Rejection		Prohibition
	L. I.	Nai			Iya		Dame
4	S. C.	Denial	Nonexistence (± Animate)		Rejection		Prohibition
	L. I.	(I)Nai			Iya		Dame
5	S. C.	Denial	Nonexistence (± Animate)		Rejection		Prohibition
	L. I.	Chigau	(I)Nai		Iya		Dame
6	S. C.	Denial		Nonexistence − Anim.	Nonexistence + Anim.	Rejection	Prohibition
	L. I.	Chigau	Zyanai	Nai	Inai	Iya	Dame

[a]S. C. means semantic category and L. I. means linguistic item. The numbers in the left-hand column indicate the stages of development of negation.

are among the ten most frequently used ones. The developmental sequence of the expression of desires and negative intentions seems to give a natural explanation and convincing evidence for the claim that the first type of negation is rejection, which is typically expressed by the word *iya*. This is a highly emotional and egocentric word.

Greenfield and Smith (1976) made an insightful observation concerning rejection: "Rejection is expressed first with regard to actions that directly concern the child; later, the child expresses volition regarding the action of others." Both types of rejection are expressed by one lexical item, no, in English, but in Japanese, the first type is lexicalized as *iya* and the second type by *dame*. In this chapter, the distinction between the two types of rejection has been made by calling the first "rejection" and the second "prohibition."

What is significant about the shift from rejection to prohibition is that cognitive development seems to be involved in the transition. At the rejection stage, the child is egocentric. On the other hand, at the prohibition stage, he can perceive himself in relation to other people, in other words, the interrelationship between "ego" and the "outside world" has been established. Greenfield and Smith (1976) characterize this shift as a "decentration process." The shift marks the child's entrance into the world of rationalization and socialization.

As was pointed out by Cromer (1976), Bloom (1970) does not elaborate on the development of negation at the one word stage because of the indeterminacy of the meaning of the single-word use of *"no"* in many cases. This may be attributable to the fact that in English, *"no"* is used to express more than one negative semantic intention. In Japanese, however, single negatives like *iya* and *dame*, which have different negative meanings, are acquired rather early and the difficulty of interpretation can be avoided in most cases. A careful description of negative intentions not only in the one-word stage but also in the prelinguistic stage is needed for further studies of the semantic development of negation in child language.

McNeill and McNeill (1973) state that *chigau* is one of the last developments of negation because it denotes a denial which "requires a child to hold in mind two propositions at once." Although this observation is confirmed by the present study, their observation that *chigau* was used as an omnibus negative by their subject, Izanami, seems rather odd and unusual. They maintain that *chigau* is equivalent to 'un-uh' in English. In fact, they are only partially similar in function and meaning. *Chigau* cannot usually be used as a negative answer to such questions as "Do you want some?" or "Does she have a wart on her nose?"

As is clear from the description above, by the time *chigau* is acquired, the use of most of the other negative forms has already been mastered.

Therefore, it is unlikely that children use *chigau* for all other forms of negation. McNeill and McNeill (1973) did not give any examples nor did they specify the contexts in which *chigau* was used as an omnibus negative. None of the subjects in this study used *chigau* in that way. At an early stage, *nai* was used by many subjects as an omnibus form of negation, as has already been pointed out.

According to Tokizane (1962), the British neurologist Jackson argued—on the basis of his assumption about the developmental sequence of brain function—that language be divided into two main categories, emotional and rational. The former precedes the latter in development. If his argument is plausible, perhaps the developmental sequence of negation from emotional to rational is related to the developmental sequence of brain function.

ACKNOWLEDGMENTS

I wish to express my gratitude to Laurence Lau and M. Michael Akiyama for their helpful comments. My special thanks to Paula Menyuk for her suggestions and critical comments.

REFERENCES

Bloom, L. 1970. Language Development: Form and function in emerging grammar. M.I.T. Press, Cambridge, Mass.

Cromer, R. 1976. The cognitive hypothesis of language acquisition and its implications for child language deficiency. In: D. Morehead and A. Morehead (eds.), Normal and Deficient Child Language, pp. 283–334. University Park Press, Baltimore.

Gleason, J. B. 1973. Code switching in children's language. In: T. E. Moore (ed.), Cognitive Development and the Acquisition of Language, pp. 159–167. Academic Press, Inc., New York.

Greenfield, P. M., and Smith, J. H. 1976. The Structure of Communication in Early Language Development. Academic Press, Inc., New York.

Jespersen, O. 1922. Language: Its Nature, Development and Origin. Allen & Unwin Ltd., London.

Klima, E., and Bellugi, U. 1966. Syntactic regularities in the speech of children. In: J. L. Lyons and R. J. Wales (eds.), Psycholinguistic Papers, pp. 183–208. Edinburgh University Aldine Press, Edinburgh.

Lenneberg, E. H. 1967. Biological Foundation of Language. John Wiley & Sons, Inc., New York.

Luria, A. R., and Yudovich, F. 1959. Speech and Development of Mental Processes in the Children. Staples Press, London.

McNeill, D., and McNeill, N. 1973. What does a child mean when he says "No"? In: C. A. Ferguson and D. I. Slobin (eds.), Studies of Child Language Development, pp. 619–627. Holt, Rinehart & Winston, Inc., New York.

Menyuk, P. 1974. Early development of receptive language: From babbling to words. In: R. L. Schiefelbusch and L. L. Lloyd (eds.), Language Perspectives—Acquisition, Retardation, and Intervention, pp. 213–236. Macmillan Publishing Company, Inc., New York.

Raffler-Engel, W. V. 1977. A pluri-modal communicative approach to language acquisition. In: C. C. Peng (ed.), Development in Verbal and Nonverbal Behavior, pp. 1–29. Bunka Hyoron Publishing Company, Hiroshima.

Slobin, D. I. 1973. Cognitive prerequisites for the development of grammar. In: C. A. Ferguson and D. I. Slobin (eds.), Studies of Child Language Development, pp. 175–208. Holt, Rinehart & Winston, Inc., New York.

Tokizane, T. 1962. The Story of Brain. Iwanami Shoten Publishing Company, Tokyo.

Weeks, T. E. 1979. Born to Talk. Newbury House Pubs., Rowley, Mass.

The Emergence of Set-relational Quantifiers in Early Childhood

Camille Hanlon

It is commonplace that most children have acquired a good working knowledge of the basic lexicon of their first language by their sixth year. For example, native speakers of English typically show productive knowledge of the meanings of thousands of words before they reach the age of formal schooling; that is, they can use these words in appropriate circumstances, they can respond appropriately to sentences that contain these words but have no obvious contextual clues, and they can even provide simple definitions in many cases (McCarthy, 1954). However unremarkable this observation is, it seems likely that as more adequate descriptions of these early accomplishments become available, attempts to study the complexity of the requisite acquisition processes will parallel the efforts made in recent years in children's grammar. For example, some scholars will doubtlessly claim that the development of meanings and their relationships are too complicated to be learned, at least in such a short time, by small children. Thus, they will argue, the semantic structures must be innate, and uniquely human (compare for example, Chomsky, 1967). Then, someone else will discover that small chimpanzees can learn it, too (compare, for example, Fouts, 1974).

Others will try and then fail to program a computer to simulate the full range of lexical semantic information processing done by the ordinary adult speaker of a language, and then they will suggest that someone instead simulate the human acquisition process, believing that it is simpler to write the necessary developmental algorithms (compare, for example, Anderson and Bower, 1973).

This research was supported by U. S. National Institute of Mental Health Small Grant, MH-27638.

The purpose of this chapter is to assist future research efforts by broadening and deepening the understanding of the complex processes of lexical semantic development. This is done by exploring the acquisition of a particular semantic domain—set-relational quantification—by native speakers of American English. Despite the current scientific interest in the general topic of quantification in natural languages, little work has been done on the full range of lexical contrasts involved in set-relational reference, either for English alone, or comparatively. Thus, a model of the organization of lexical semantic knowledge associated with set-relational reference in English was constructed for this chapter to provide useful information for the study of developmental psycholinguistics.

Set-relational quantification is a particularly interesting semantic domain for developmental study, for several reasons. First, the processes of ordinary sentence quantification have so far eluded adequate linguistic description and recent efforts in this direction have led at least one major theorist (Chomsky, 1975) to reformulate his theoretical position. Yet, quantified sentences are found among the earliest sentences used by young children (Brown, 1973; Wepman and Hass, 1969). Second, neither of the prevailing notions of lexical semantic acquisition—feature theory (E. Clark, 1973) or prototype theory (Heider, 1971)—seems to be an entirely satisfactory account of quantification. Third, the child's understanding of sets and quantitative relationships is an important aspect of the language acquisition process, and it provides an ideal opportunity for the exploration of the complex patterning of linguistic and nonlinguistic cognitive activities in human development. (Compare, for example, Hanlon, 1976.)

This study focuses on a small group of high-frequency quantifiers that are used to characterize set relations in ordinary conversations. Those words are: *all, some, no, none, any, each, every, other, another, both, either,* and *neither.* (In some instances, the related forms *all the* and *another of the* occur in the model, and some uses of the lexical items in the list, such as the conjunctive use of *either,* are not considered.) These quantifiers, like other delimitative terms such as *the* and *few,* delimit the reference set associated with a nominal in an utterance.

The terms studied here take the general class of objects denoted by the predicative elements of a noun phrase and add information about both the size of the reference set and its role in the discourse. For example, in the sentence *The hiker found neither trail,* the term *neither* indicates that the reference set associated with the noun phrase *neither trail* is null, that it is drawn from a potential set of two, and that the writer assumes that the reader understands a unique pair of trails to be a potential reference set. (The writer's assumption is inappropriate in this case, of course, but it would not be incorrect if the above example had been preceded in discourse by a sentence like *Two trails lead down the side of the canyon.*)

The quantifying terms studied in this chapter are just those members of the larger set of English quantifiers and quantifier-specifiers for which adult knowledge can be described by the set-relational model of the semantic relations involved. For this set of terms, it is argued that there are rational bases for predictions about the order of acquisition for various aspects of the adult system, especially when particular aspects of the model are related to what is known about cognitive development. However, the set of terms for which the model is relevant is not precisely co-extensive with any traditional linguistic category. The study set includes some, but not all, of the English terms that linguists describe as having quantifying and specifying features (compare, for example, Bierwisch, 1971). The set also includes some terms that, because of their deviant grammatical function in more complex constructions, are not considered by some linguists (for example, Carden, 1970) to be true quantifiers.

The central idea of the model proposed here is that the sentence comprehender starts with a general class in mind as the potential reference set for a quantified sentence nominal and uses the information provided by the set-relational quantifier to: 1) define the reference set as a transformation of that general class, and 2) apply the relevant extra-nominal sentence predicates appropriately.

THE MODEL

The nature of the transformation defining the relation between the general predicative class of the nominal and its actual reference set is specific to the particular quantifier word used. For example, in the sentence *Some flowers are yellow*, the word '*some*' can be interpreted as an instruction to the reader to start with the general class referred to by the nominal *flowers,* and to take an indefinite portion of that set for the actual reference set. In contrast, the use of *all* in the sentence *All men are mortal,* indicates that the actual reference set for the quantified nominal *all men* is identical to the general class referred to by the noun *men*. More generally, the quantifier *some* instructs the reader to set the actual reference set of the quantified nominal as an indefinite portion of the potential set referred to by the predicates of the nominal, whereas *all* instructs the reader to make the actual reference set identical to the potential one.

The nature of the relationship between the members of the reference set and the syntactically related extra-nominal predicates is also specified by the lexemic value of the quantifier. That is, the predicates in the sentence that are outside the quantified nominal often must be applied to the reference set of the nominal, and the quantifier word used specifies, in some cases, that the predication must be distributive rather than collective. *Each* contrasts with *all* on this single characteristic—*each* is used only when predication is distributive. The following illustrates the general nature of the model with two sentences in which the different quantifiers provide a clear semantic contrast on both of the above-noted characteristics: 1) *Some of the children in the class sang a song,* and 2) *Each of the children in the class sang a song.* In sentence 1, the quantifier *some* contributes the information that the actual reference set of the nominal *some of the children in the class* is an indefinite portion of the total potential reference set, *the children in the class.* (Hereafter the potential reference set associated with a nominal will be called the suppositional set, because at least under some conditions of this model of quantifier usage, it is "supposed" by the sentence processor as a temporary condition for the comprehension of the sentence. (For a parallel usage of the term suppositional in models of sentence processing in negation see Clark, 1973.)

Some also permits (and indeed predisposes one toward) a *collective* rather than a distributive interpretation of the relationship between the members of the reference set *some of the children in the class* and the extra-nominal predicate *sang a song* in this sentence; that is, one clearly permissible interpretation is that the children involved sang a single song in chorus. The semantic import of *each* in Sentence 2 differs from that of *some* in Sentence 1 in both these general ways. For the nominal *each of the children in the class,* the reference set is equivalent to the suppositional set, and the relation between the members of the reference set and the related extra-nominal predicate must be distributive. It is understood that the entire set of children in the class sang, and their songs were sung separately, one song to a child. In summary, the suppositional set is transformed to the reference set in the case of *some* by selecting an indefinite portion of the suppositional set, and in the case of *each*, by setting the reference set to be equivalent to the suppositional set. The meaning of the two quantifiers is further distinguishable by the occurrence of *each* only in the context of distributive predication (presumably providing a signal for such predication). In contrast, *some* indicates collective predication with relational predicates, as in the example above.

One further contrast involved in the model concerns the definition of the suppositional set. The most abstract case is the use of the set-relational quantifiers in the general statements of formal logic, for example, the universal quantifier *all* in the sentence *All men are mortal,* and the particular or existential quantifier *some* in *Some roofs are flat.* For this generic quantifier use, the suppositional set is defined as the entire set that can be characterized by the predicates of the reference nominal. A contrasting use of these quantifiers involves a specific suppositional set associated with a particular reference nominal. Examples of this usage are: 1) *Each* of the dogs has its own house and 2) Take *any* apple in this basket. Here the suppositional set is specified in the sentence, or it is assumed to be specific, in a way that is parallel to the rules for specification involved in the use of the definite article in English (compare, for example, Karttunen, 1968; Brown, 1973). A third type of set-relational quantifier usage does not seem to be set-relational at all, although some of the same lexical items occur in this usage, and, at least theoretically, these instances can be related to the generic statements described above. This type of usage is called nonspecific suppositional set usage. Examples are: 1) May I have *some* milk? and 2) The store had *no* peanuts in stock. The model defines the reference set as a transformation of a nonspecific suppositional set. However, this category of set-relational quantifier usage makes the interpretation of the model as a performance model implausible.

There is a distinctive set of terms in English set-relational quantification for the case in which the suppositional set size is two. *Both, either,* and *neither* are used only in this case. For many English informants, the use of the parallel forms *all, any,* and *none* is restricted to suppositional set sizes of more than two. Thus, suppositional set size constraints constitute another aspect of meaning for these terms.

It is important to note that in this research project, the model is used only in the sense of an hypothesized form of organization of semantic knowledge, and is to be used for making predictions about the nature of the sequence of acquisition of the relevant semantic elements and contrasts involved in the adult use of these terms. (For a similar use of transformational grammar, see Brown and Hanlon, 1970.) A full list of the set-relational quantifiers used in the study and a summary of their respective semantic characterizations within the model are presented in Table 1. The notation used in the table is also used in the rest of this chapter.

In summary, the proposed model is based on contrasts among the terms of four qualitatively different types: 1) there are three levels of generality in reference i.e., generic, specific, and non-specific, 2) the meaning of each quantifier word also is described in terms of a characteristic transformation of a supposed (or suppositional) set to an actual reference set, 3) each quantifier word constrains the size of the suppositional set, for example, for *both*, the suppositional set equals two, and 4) the reference instruction may be to apply the extranominal predicate distributively only (as for *each*), or it may be unspecified.

In general, the predictions about order of acquisition are made on the basis of cumulative semantic complexity. Thus, forms for which the reference set is identical to the suppositional set are predicted to emerge earlier than corresponding forms that require a transformation of some type to derive the reference set from the suppositional set. That is, it is predicted that the specific form of *all* (all_{sp}) is mastered earlier than $some_{sp}$, $none_{sp}$, any_{sp}, $another_{sp}$, and $other_{sp}$. Similarly, *both* is predicted to emerge earlier

Table 1.   Summary of the model for adult semantic knowledge of the English set-relational quantifiers[a]

Term	Suppositional set definition	Reference set definition	Reference instructions
all_g	The entire set characterizable by the predicates of the reference nominal	$S_R = S_S$	Apply relevant sentence predicates collectively or distributively to S_R
no_g	,,	$S_R = 0$	,,
$some_g$	,,	S_R = indefinite portion of S_S	,,
any_g	,,	S_R = indefinite portion of S_S with equipotentiality for selection across all members (or portions) of S_S	,,
$each_g$	,,	$S_R = S_S$	Distributive predication
$every_g$	,,	$S_R = S_S$	Distributive predication with summation across series
no_{ns}	An unspecified set characterizable by the predicates of reference nominal	$S_R = 0$	Unrestricted predication
$some_{ns}$	,,	S_R = an indefinite portion of S_S	,,
$another_{ns}$	,,	S_R = indefinite new individual sharing predicate characteristics of S_S members	,,
any_{ns}	,,	S_R = indefinite portion of S_S with equipotentiality for selection across all members (or portions) of S_S	,,
all_{sp}	Specific; for count nouns $S_S = 2$	$S_R = S_S$	,,
no_{sp}	,,	$S_R = 0$	,,
$some_{sp}$	Specific; for count nouns $S_S = 2$	S_R = indefinite portion of S_S; for count nouns $S_R = 1$	Unrestricted predication

continued

Table 1.—*continued*

any$_{sp}$	”	S_R = indefinite portion of S_S with equipotentiality for selection across all members (or portions) of S_S	”
other$_{sp}$	Specific	S_R = portion of S_S remaining after specific subset has been subtracted	”
another$_{sp}$	Specific; with count nouns only	S_R = indefinite new member of S_S	”
each$_{sp}$	”	$S_R = S_S$	Distributive predication
every$_{sp}$	Specific; with count nouns only; $S_S = 2$	$S_R = S_S$	Distributive predication with summation across series
both	Specific; with count nouns only; $S_S = 2$	$S_R = S_S$	Unrestricted predication
neither	”	$S_R = 0$	Unrestricted predication
either	”	S_R = one member of S_S with equipotentiality for selection of both members (or portions) of S_S	”

[a]The quantifier forms are followed by a subscript when necessary to indicate which suppositional set level is intended. Subscript g is used for generic; ns for nonspecific; and sp for specific. The symbol S_S stands for suppositional set, and S_R for the reference set.

than *either* and *neither*. Forms used only when distributive predication is intended (*each, every*) are predicted to emerge later than their unrestricted equivalent, *all*.

Predictions concerning the developmental ordering of levels of generality in reference are based on different contrasts across levels. Thus, the prediction that nonspecific suppositional set forms are mastered earlier than specific forms is based upon that aspect of the model that requires cognizance of a specific suppositional set as well as a reference set for the specific forms but not for the nonspecific forms. The prediction that the generic suppositional set forms are acquired later than the specific forms is not strictly grounded in semantic complexity, but is based instead on the well-documented trend in language development during early childhood toward more remote (Cromer, 1968) and general (Brown, 1957) reference. That is, the generic forms, unlike the specific forms, require a cognizance of the entire set or class characterized by the predicates of the quantified nominal, and this level of conceptualization seems at least somewhat more advanced than that required for the specific forms. And, of course, grammatical complexity is not equivalent across the three levels of generality in reference, but it is greatest at the specific level. So, the prediction of nonspecific before specific forms also can be made on the basis of grammatical complexity, but for specific and generic forms, the semantic model and grammatical complexity make opposing predictions.

The major predictions, then, can be briefly summarized: 1) nonspecific forms will precede their specific equivalents, and specific forms will precede their generic equivalents, 2) forms for which suppositional and reference sets are identical will be acquired earlier than transformational forms that are their semantic equivalents in other ways, and 3) the distributive forms *each* and *every* will be mastered later than their unrestricted equivalent form *all*.

The primary manifestations of semantic knowledge—comprehension, and production in conversation—were selected for an initial study of the problem. The data were obtained and are being analyzed by a combination of specific hypothesis-testing and exploratory work. Practical considerations led to the use of comprehension and production data from different subjects, so the two sets of results are presented separately in the discussion that follows. There is no compelling rationale for predicting a different order of acquisition for these terms in comprehension and production, and whenever possible the hypotheses about the developmental sequence are tested for both indices of semantic knowledge.

A STUDY OF CONVERSATIONAL PRODUCTION

Method

Subjects   Three children, two girls and one boy, were observed at home, where their mother-child conversations were sampled systematically throughout most of their early childhood. These data were collected and transcribed by Dr. Roger Brown and his associates. Those transcripts are analyzed in this chapter. The children are identified in the research as Adam, Eve, and Sarah, and a full summary of the subject selection and data collection and transcription procedures may be found in Brown's own research monograph (1973). This chapter summarizes the data characteristics that are especially relevant to this study.

The observations began when all of the children had a mean length of utterance in morphemes (MLU) of 1.75 and extended until the MLU reached 4.00. For two of the children, the samples continued for more than a year after this time. The age span for each of the children was: Adam, 27 through 73 months; Eve, 18 through 27 months; and Sarah, 27 through 64 months.

Procedure All instances of set-relational quantifiers, numerical quantifiers, and generic nominals with articles or plurals in the children's speech were coded for computer analysis. Inter-rater reliabilities on all coding categories ranged from 90% to 100% for two independent judges. The frequencies of the same forms in the mother's speech were computed for each child.

Results

The children's production frequencies were used to test the study hypotheses about the order of emergence for the set-relational quantifier forms. The point of emergence was defined in each case as the time at which the form had occurred in three different phrase contexts, summing across samples.

Nonspecific Forms Precede Specific Forms For four quantifiers (*some, another, none,* and *any*) there are corresponding nonspecific and specific forms. Thus, the hypothesis that nonspecific forms precede specific forms can be tested for matched pairs of these quantifiers (e.g., nonspecific *some* before specific *some*) with the longitudinal data for each child. The hypothesis generated one prediction for each of the four quantifier words for each of the three children, for a total of 12 predictions that had to be checked. Eleven of the 12 were correct. The single exception was one prediction for Eve which was not disconfirmed, but is simply untestable because neither of the relevant forms (nonspecific and specific *any*) had reached criterion in the samples by the time she left the study. The results of this analysis are in Table 2, Part A.

Specific Forms Precede Generic Forms There are six quantifier words that occur in both specific and generic forms (*all, some, none* or *no, any, each,* and *every*). The hypothesis that specific forms become productive before generic forms can be tested in parallel fashion to the nonspecific to specific comparison. This time there were six predictions for each child, 18 in all. However, nine of these predictions were rendered untestable by the failure of both the specific and the generic forms for a given pair to achieve the productive criterion for a specific child. The remaining nine predictions were confirmed. The results of these tests are shown in Table 2, Part B.

Untransformed Forms Precede Transformed Forms The major hypothesis tested is that the terms denoting the identity of suppositional set and reference set (*all, both*) emerge productively before forms otherwise corresponding in semantic complexity. That is, at the specific and generic levels, *all* is productive before *some, none, any, another,* and *other;* and *both* is productive before *either* and *neither.* The paucity of generic quantification in the children's speech made it possible to test this hypothesis at the specific level only. There are nine of these predictions for each of the three children, and 26 predictions were confirmed. For Adam, specific

Table 2. Predictions confirmed for order of emergence in production of set-relational quantifiers based on semantic complexity (Brown longitudinal data)[a]

A. Nonspecific forms before specific forms e.g., *some hats* (with nonspecific reference) before *some of the hats:*

	Adam			Sarah			Eve		
	+	?	−	+	?	−	+	?	−
some	×			×			×		
another	×			×			×		
none	×			×			×		
any	×			×				×	

B. Specific forms before generic forms e.g., *some of the hats* before *some hats* (with generic reference):

	Adam			Sarah			Eve		
	+	?	−	+	?	−	+	?	−
all	×			×			×		
some	×			×			×		
none	×				×			×	
any		×			×			×	
each	×				×			×	
every	×				×			×	

C. Specific *all* and *both* before other equivalent specific forms:

	Adam			Sarah			Eve		
	+	?	−	+	?	−	+	?	−
all < some		×		×			×		
all < none	×			×			×		
all < any	×			×			×		
all < another	×			×			×		
all < other	×			×			×		
both < either	×			×			×		
both < neither	×			×			×		

D. Specific *all* before specific *each* and *every*:

	Adam			Sarah			Eve		
	+	?	−	+	?	−	+	?	−
all < each	×			×			×		
all < every	×			×			×		

[a]The symbol (+) means predictions confirmed; (−) means they were disconfirmed and (?) indicates they were untestable.

some was productive about 2 months before specific *all*, contrary to the predicted order. Table 2, Part C presents a summary of these results.

Forms Restricted to Distributive Predication Follow Unrestricted Forms This hypothesis also was testable only at the specific level, where *all* was found to precede *each* and *every* for all three children, as predicted. A summary of these results is presented in Table 2, Part D.

The fact that these longitudinal productive data were consistent with a set of predictions derived from considerations of semantic complexity is, of course, merely a first step toward demonstrating the usefulness of the model. The emergence of a form in conversational use is only one index of the acquisition of semantic knowledge. All such indices are subject to difficulties of interpretation that require investigators to seek alternative indicators of the phenomenon under study. In this case, an examination of elicited comprehension data provided independent information on the acquisition sequence for the specific level forms.

A STUDY OF ELICITED COMPREHENSION

Method

Subjects Seventy children, ages 3 to 7, and 10 college students served as subjects in this study. The children were enrolled in private nursery or elementary schools. Among the child subjects, there was an almost equal number of boys and girls at each age level. All 75 children in the classrooms visited participated in the study. The data obtained were complete, except for that from two 5-year-olds and three 3-year-olds, who withdrew without completing the tasks.

Procedure Two tasks were used to test the subject's discriminative comprehension of the specific set-relational quantifiers under study. The subjects were tested individually in two sessions, except for the adults, who performed both tasks in one session. In both tests, the subject was shown an array of identical objects on each trial with a quantifier word and was asked to select objects from the array and place them in a nearby container. One task (Letters) involved placing letters on a shelf with a series of six pigeonholes. The trials began on this task with the instruction, "Put (quantifier) of the letters in a box." The quantifiers $other_{sp}$ and $another_{sp}$ required a different instruction for an appropriate context. For the trials with these terms, the examiner picked up one letter at the end of the array and moved it slightly apart from the others, saying, "This is a special letter now put (*another of the, the other, all of the*) letters in a box." For the trials with *all, none, some, any, each,* and the special object trials described above, four objects were presented in the array. For *both, either,* and *neither,* the array contained two objects. The full set of specific quantifiers, including the two instructional versions for *all,* but omitting *every,* were presented three times to the subjects, for a series of 33 trials on each task. Two random quantifier word orders were used, each subject getting a different one on each of the two tasks.

The second task (Cookies) involved feeding plastic cookies to a "cookie monster" puppet by placing them in a small bowl and then handing the bowl to the puppet. The procedure was similar to that used for the Letters task, with the exception that the Letters task was designed to facilitate spatial distributivity; the Cookies task, temporal distributivity. The order in which the two tasks were administered was counterbalanced, with half of the subjects receiving each order. The 3-year-olds were tested with a shorter version of the task that involved three trials for each of the quantifiers *all, none, some, any,* and *both.* The subject's placement of objects was recorded by an observer, and verbal responses were tape-recorded. The results that follow are selected entirely from the object placement data.

Results

The finding of principal interest was the sequence of acquisition of these terms. A comment on the validity and reliability of these two tests as measures of comprehension follows. For all the quantifiers except *some, any,* and *each,* there is a unique adult-correct response on the tasks. For the latter terms, any of the range of responses elicited from our 10 adult subjects, who thus served as our native American-English informants, were scored correct. Their choices were, in fact, consistent with the model. *Some* led to placement of two or three objects, *any* to a range of one to four objects, and *each* was consistently four objects placed distributively. The greater number of correct response possibilities for *some* and *any* elevates the probability that a subject will score correctly on the basis of chance relative to that for the other quantifiers, a factor that complicates but does not obviate the interpretation of the results. Analyses of variance with each trial scored as 1 or 0 (correct or incorrect) indicated that there were no task-order effects or word-order effects. The single difference in response to the tasks was that the children tended to respond more distributively to *each* in Letters than in the Cookies task, suggesting that the variable of spatial versus temporal predicate distributivity in development might be worth studying with a wider range of tasks.

Furthermore, the overall pattern of responding was highly structured so that subjects showed great consistency in their response to a given quantifier across trials and tasks, and so that they differentiated consistently among quantifiers, even when responding erroneously. The errors and their accompanying verbalizations are highly indicative of the children's semantic formulations of this domain. This part of the analysis, however, is too lengthy to summarize here. These considerations suggest that these tasks can be considered a reasonable assessment of the children's comprehension.

To test the hypotheses about the developmental sequence for the quantifiers, it was necessary to look at the response patterns for individual children. The knowledge criterion chosen for this examination is the traditional test standard—at least two correct responses on three trials. The first question to be answered in this vein is whether any children failed to show knowledge of any of the quantifiers by this criterion. This question is easily answered in the affirmative from an inspection of the proportions of subjects, shown in Table 3, who passed the tests for each quantifier. (These proportions are from the 4- to 7-year-olds' samples, for whom data were obtained on the full range of terms.) This outcome supports the previous interpretation of the productive emergence data as reflecting a real sequence in the acquisition of knowledge and not just a false impression created by different production probabilities. More importantly, however, it tells that the developmental level at which this knowledge is being acquired (at least in this task context) has been found and the sequence can be checked in a cross-sectional analysis. The ideal case for proving the prediction will be the one in which some items are failed, but there is no subject in this sample who failed an item that was predicted to be relatively easy and who also passed one that was predicted to be hard. The descriptive statistic chosen to summarize this analysis is Loevinger's (1947) index of inter-item homogeneity (H_{ii}) for which 1.00 represents the ideal case.

Untransformed Forms Precede Transformed Forms   Mastery of *all* does indeed precede its transformed equivalents (*none, some, any, another,* and *other*) in these data. And, *both* precedes *either* and *neither*. For all the predictions the ideal case is found to hold, there is no subject ($N = 80$) who responded in a way that was contrary to the predictions. The predictions and the corresponding H_{ii} values are listed in Table 4.

Forms Restricted to Distributive Predication Follow Unrestricted Forms   Comprehension of *each* also follows that of its unrestricted equivalent *all* for these data. Again, no subject acted contrary to prediction. The H_{ii} value for this prediction is found in the last row of Table 4.

Table 3.   Percent of 4- to 7-year-old subjects passing each quantifier comprehension test in each task (Pass = 2 out of 3 trials correct, $N = 61$)

| | Task | |
Quantifier	Letters	Cookies
all	100	100
none	87	89
some	89	92
any	93	92
other	80	93
another	49	51
both	100	100
either	46	46
neither	31	43
each (4 objects)	54	56
each (4 objects placed distributively)	31	3

Table 4.   Predictions confirmed about order of emergence in comprehension of specific set-relational quantifiers based on semantic complexity[a]

Prediction	Letter task	Cookie task
all < some	1.00	1.00
all < none	1.00	1.00
all < any	1.00	1.00
all < another	1.00	1.00
all < other	1.00	1.00
both < either	1.00	1.00
both < neither	1.00	1.00
all < each	1.00	1.00

Source: Hanlon (1976) cross-sectional data: 70 3-to 7-year-olds and 10 adults.

[a]Tabled values are Loevinger's (1947) H_{ii} where 1.00 represents the absence of any subjects in the sample passing the harder and failing the easier term.

DISCUSSION

These results indicate that for this set of common English words, at least three aspects of meaning have developmental significance: 1) level of generality in reference, 2) re-definition (or transformation) of a supposed set into an actual reference set, and 3) distributive versus collective predication. Predications made on the basis of a model incorporating contrasts on these dimensions are consistently supported by the production and comprehension data from early childhood presented here.

As one might expect from what is generally known about cognitive development during this period, forms that require cognizance of a particular set, and then of its transformation, are mastered later than forms that do not require such cognition. And forms involving conceptualization of universal classes, for example, Adam's *Some animals wake up in the morning time,* come latest of all.

The set-relational model presented in the introduction is consistent with the knowledge tested at the specific level for the adult subjects. However, there is a residual question posed by the children's performance in this study. That is, why do the children respond with such ease and appropriateness to set-relational terms at an age that researchers (e.g., Inhelder and Piaget, 1959) say is a time when children's notions of set relations are extremely primitive? An analysis of error patterns in the comprehension test data strongly suggests that the younger children do not, in fact, respond to the specific transformed forms in a set-relative way; instead, they use notions of absolute quantity. For example, a very common error in response to instructions using *another of the* and *the other* was to place two objects in the containers. When one thinks of the common contexts for these forms, it is clear that an interpretation of these forms as "two" is not a bad guess. Furthermore, an examination of the productive emergence of the absolute or numeric quantifier forms reveals that these forms generally emerge earlier than their set-relative equivalents. This is especially true for the most frequent numeric form, *two*. Thus, the evidence at hand suggests that we have found another instance of the general tendency of young children to reduce the relational aspects of adult word meaning to a simpler system involving absolute values (compare, for example, Piaget, 1928; Clark, 1973; Haviland and Clark, 1974). However, in another sense, the puzzle remains because the observations indicate that some 4- and 5-year-olds did respond to the tests in a set-relative way.

Some aspects of the early childhood data described here also can be given feature and prototype interpretations in ways that are not really incompatible with the proposed model. The shift from absolute to set-relative meaning and the addition of the distributive predicative restriction fit well with Clark's (1973) ideas about the addition and modification of features in development. And what can *two* be but the prototypical quantity? And what can *all* be but the prototypical set relationship? However, the system, as it emerges toward the end of early childhood, makes these two tem, as it emerges toward the end of early childhood, makes these two theoretical accounts seem insufficient, taken either singly, or in combination. A model with more highly differentiated semantic components, including particular transformations, seems necessary to capture the complexity of the developmental phenomenon under study in this case.

ACKNOWLEDGMENTS

The author wishes to express her appreciation to Dr. Roger Brown for generously sharing his data; to the children, teachers, and administrators of the Connecticut College Children's School and Pine Point School of Stonington, Connecticut for their cheerful help; and to her research assistants, Ms. Theresa Carpino, Ms. Kathryn Tweedie Erslev, Mr. Harold Flagg, Mr. Wayne Ingersoll, Ms. Miriam Kalamian, Mr. James Kestenbaum, Ms. Nathalie Lowe, and Ms. Beverly Sweny for their competent and dedicated work on the project.

REFERENCES

Anderson, J., and Bower, G. 1973. Human Associative Memory. Winston, New York.

Bierwisch, M. 1971. On classifying semantic features. In: D. Steinberg and L. Jakobovits (eds.), Semantics: An Interdisciplinary Reader in Philosophy, Linguistics and Psychology, pp. 410–435. Cambridge University Press, England.

Brown, R. 1957. Linguistic determinism and the part of speech. J. Abnorm. Soc. Psychol. 55:1–5.

Brown, R. 1973. A First Language: The Early Stages. Harvard University Press, Cambridge, Mass.

Brown, R., and Hanlon, C. 1970. Derivational complexity and order of emergence in child speech. In: H. Hayes (ed.), Cognition and the Development of Language, pp. 155–207. John Wiley & Sons, Inc., New York.

Carden, G. 1970. Logical predicates and idiolect variation in English. Unpublished doctoral dissertation, Harvard University, Cambridge, Mass.

Chomsky, N. 1967. Recent contributions to the theory of innate ideas. Synthese. 17:2–11.

Chomsky, N. 1975. Syntactic structure and logical form. Paper presented at the Psychology Department Colloquium, M.I.T. February 7, Cambridge, Mass.

Clark, E. 1973. What's in a word? On the child's acquisition of semantics in his first language. In: T. Moore (ed.), Cognitive Development and the Acquisition of Language, pp. 65–110. Academic Press, Inc., New York.

Clark, H. 1973. Semantics and comprehension. In: T. Sebeok (ed.), Current Trends in Linguistics, pp. 1–251, Vol. 12. Mouton, The Hague.

Cromer, R. 1968. The development of temporal reference during the acquistion of language. Unpublished doctoral dissertation, Harvard University, Cambridge, Mass.

Fouts, R. 1974. Artifical and human language acquisition in the chimpanzees. Paper presented at the Burg Wartenstein Symposium on the Behavior of the Great Apes, July 20–28, Burg Wartenstein.

Hanlon, C. 1976. Lexical semantic development in early childhood. Paper presented at the Conference on the Nature and Principles of Formation of Categories, Social Science Research Council, May 29, Lake Arrowhead, Cal.

Haviland, S., and Clark, E. 1974. This man's father is my father's son: A study of the acquisition of English kin terms. J. Child Lang. 1:23–47.

Heider, E. 1971. "Focal" color areas and the development of color names. Dev. Psychol. 4:447–455.

Inhelder, B., and Piaget, J. 1959. La genése des structures logiques élémentaires: Classifications et seriations. [The Early Growth of Logic in the Child.] Delachaux et Niestle, Neuchatel.

Karttunen, L. 1968. What makes definite noun phrases definite? Rand Corporation, San Diego, Calif.

Loevinger, J. 1947. A Systematic Approach to the Construction and Evaluation of Tests of Ability. Psychological Monographs, Vol. 61, no. 4 (Whole No. 285).

McCarthy, D. 1954. Language development in children. In: L. Carmichael (ed.), A Manual of Child Psychology. 2nd Ed. John Wiley & Sons, Inc., New York.

Piaget, J. 1928. Judgment and Reasoning in the Child. Routledge & Kegan Paul, Ltd., London.

Wepman, J., and Hass, W. 1969. A Spoken Word Count (Children—Ages 5, 6, and 7). Language Research Associates, Chicago.

Pragmatic Development

One of the most fundamental aspects of language is that it is a social phenomenon. Human beings use language to communicate and their conversations are set in specific physical and social contexts. The most exquisitely structured sentences are ineffectual if they are not used in the proper context. (In fact, something like this does happen in the speech of some autistic children, and the result is extraordinarily bizarre.)

Pragmatics has been defined as the rules for using language in context. This is an area which is undergoing rapid development both in linguistic theory and in the study of child language. To date, there is no overall theory that unifies the several aspects of language use that have been labeled pragmatics. Perhaps the most intensively studied topic is functions of language, also referred to as speech acts. This work, stemming from the research of the British philosopher J. L. Austin and from other work in "ordinary language philosophy," has emphasized the many functions that utterances can have, and the fact that the surface form of utterances does not always correspond to the intended function (illocutionary force, in Austin's ,1962, terminology). In Chapter 9, Reeder opens with a charming example of an indirect speech act, in which an utterance that apparently is a declarative (reporting a fact) is, in fact, a request. Two other aspects of pragmatics follow from the fact that people ordinarily talk in conversations, rather than in single utterances. The first comprises rules for conversational interaction, for example, taking turns and providing clarification. The second concerns the relationship between sentences, and between propositions within a given sentence. Pragmatics also is often referred to as the study of presuppositions. For example, in the sentence *Was it John who was riding the bicycle?* the presupposition is that someone was riding the bicycle; and, from the use of the definite article *the* in *Then the car hit the stop sign,* it is presupposed that earlier in the conversation, the speaker and the listener had identified a specific car.

Because of the lack of an established theoretical framework, most research in language development to date has been descriptive, for example, a common topic is what children at various ages can do. In many areas of research on language development, children have proved to be more competent than might have been supposed. Dale, Cook, and Goldstein, for example, developed a coding system for the functions of utterances in the one- and early two-word periods, and observed a steady increase in the range of functions expressed. This is discussed in Chapter 10. Like most of the research to date, their work and that of Wilkinson and Rembold in Chapter 11 focuses on children's productions. Little is known about children's comprehension ability in the preschool years. Shatz (1974) and others have reported that 2-year-olds respond appropriately to certain indirect request forms but this is probably based on a strategy of responding to language with action. Reeder's paper shows that between the ages of 2½ and 4, children give clear evidence of interpreting utterances on the basis of context; that is, on the basis of deriving social inferences.

Many previous works have suggested that the role of gestures in the initial development of language is important. Bates (1976) proposed an explanation for the role of gesture. One of the most highly evolved human specializations is for tool-use, and this specialization is centered on the hands. Language, and communication more generally, can be seen as a tool, by means of which children can gain another person's attention, or cause another person to aid in obtaining a desired object or state of affairs. Thus, the hands are most likely to be used first for this function. The relationship of gestures to vocal speech is almost completely unexplored but Wilkinson and Rembold, in Chapter 11, break new ground with their research. Their results demonstrate, for example, that gestures clearly are not supplanted by verbal language, but that during a child's third year, the two modalities supplement each other.

Cross-linguistic research is very much needed in the area of pragmatic development. Many psycholinguists have hypothesized that pragmatics is that aspect of language which is most closely tied to cognition. The evidence for this is not yet conclusive, however. Dale, Cook, and Goldstein, in Chapter 10, provide one relatively negative piece of evidence that will have to be integrated into the final picture of the relationship between language and cognition, a picture that is almost certain to be far more complex than it is believed to be. In any case, the cognition hypothesis suggests that pragmatic development, like cognitive development, should be relatively universal. In contrast, the view of the average layperson is undoubtedly that the use of language is highly social and culture-dependent, and perhaps is based on stereotypes concerning use of gesture, flattery, deception, etc. Bates' (1976) work on the Italian language is the only substantial cross-linguistic research available.

REFERENCE

Bates, E. 1976. Language in Context. Academic Press, New York.

How Young Children Learn To Do Things with Words

Kenneth Reeder

Sheila, who is almost 3 years old, was visiting me late one warm Saturday afternoon while her parents were shopping. An ice cream van, loud-speaker jangling its promise of syrupy confections, stopped nearby. "Every night I get an ice cream," declared Sheila. Nonplussed, I used my stock response: "That's very nice, Sheila." "Yes, even when there's a baby-sitter, I get an ice cream," Sheila explained patiently. I had been backed into a corner by a 3-year-old's grasp of the use of language as a social tool.

EARLY INTERPRETATION OF ILLOCUTIONARY ACTS

Clearly, this youngster demonstrated skills that are associated not so much with syntactic or semantic conventions as with how linguistic expressions could be employed as illocutionary acts (Searle, 1969)—requests, assertions, offers, and so on. Moreover, she had systematically illustrated the very set of conditions—Austin's felicity conditions—necessary and sufficient to assign the illocutionary force of a request to her declarative sentence.

The few explanations of how this aspect of young children's communicative competence develops deal mainly with the production and comprehension of requests. Marilyn Shatz (1974), in a study of children's responses to adult's directive speech, discovered that there was a high proportion of accurate responses, even from 2-year-olds. When asked *Can you find me a truck?* or even the seemingly oblique question *Are there any more suitcases?* with a directive intent, the children would respond with

Some of the experimental data used in this study were gathered while the author was supported by a fellowship from the Canada Council; other data were gathered with support from a Humanities and Social Science Grant from the University of British Columbia, Canada.

whatever act had been specified in the utterance's lowest clause. Shatz's rule of conversation for this early interpretation of requests captures the phenomenon neatly: "Mommy says, child does." However, it cannot be concluded that 2-year-olds can discriminate a directive illocutionary intent behind the utterances. Their responses could have represented sensorimotor replies—doing or demonstrating an answer—to what perhaps had been interpreted as an enquiry, not as a request. Susan Ervin-Tripp (1974) proposed another account—the embedded imperative hypothesis—for similar phenomena. Probably because of developmental constraints upon information processing, younger children first interpret the perceptually salient final clause in polite requests that are structurally similar to imperative sentences, such as a command to *find me a truck* or to supply *more suitcases.*

Michael Halliday (1975) observed that his 2-year-old subject initially displayed an isomorphism between lexical and illocutionary act types. Thus, any *more + noun* construction invariably expressed a request, while any *two + noun* construction expressed an assertion. Only later—how much later is a question to explore—is the standard phenomenon of differential assignment of illocutionary force to a type of syntactic form observed. The developmental trend, then, appears to proceed from isomorphism to the capacity to differentiate many-to-one relations syntactically and pragmatically.

This study comprises two experiments designed to provide information on the early discrimination of the illocutionary force of so-called indirect speech acts (Searle, 1975). Among the questions addressed are:

1. What is the lower developmental bound of true discrimination of illocutionary force?
2. What features, linguistic or otherwise, are relevant cues for such discriminations?
3. If the ability to discriminate illocutionary force develops unevenly across various illocutionary acts, in what order is the emergence of mastery of the repertoire of such acts?

The various experimental treatments were selected from the range of illocutionary interpretations potentially assignable, given the right sets of extralinguistic felicity conditions, to the commonplace polite form *Would you like to do A?* where A represents some simple, concrete act. For this form, the range is conveniently broad and includes the illocutionary acts *request, offer,* the so-called literal reading of *enquiry* or question, and even *warning* in the right circumstances, for example, *Would you like to go to bed early?* uttered by an exasperated parent to a 5-year-old. If Searle's account of the structure of illocutionary acts is psychologically valid, native speakers should be expected to search for cues in addition to strictly propositional-linguistic ones in order to assign an illocutionary interpretation to such forms and thus respond appropriately in ongoing discourse.

Puppet-play was used to stage for young children just those cues that were expected to suffice as distinct illocutionary contexts for linguistically identical performances of the form *Would you like to do A?* The question to be answered first was whether subjects would discriminate the various illocutionary interpretations as is suggested in the theory of the structure of illocutionary acts. The measurement of such putative discriminations by very young children was a methodological challenge. The direct probing of subjects' intuitions about interpretation or illocutionary well-formedness was ruled out. It was decided that indirect judgments about paraphrase relations that would entail decisions about illocutionary force of utterances performed in the experimental contexts would be elicited. The set of privileges of occurrence from an illocutionary standpoint of various linguistically possible paraphrases of the form *Would you like to do A?* may be summarized:

		Enquiry	Request	Offer
(a)	Do you want to do A?	+	−	−
(b)	I want you to do A	−	+	−
(c)	I'll let you do A	−	−	+

Each of these phrases may be used to convey an illocutionary act equivalent in force to just one of the model form's possible illocutionary readings. What is termed a pragmatic hypothesis of paraphrase relations between the model form and each of (a), (b) and (c) predicts, to the extent that the model form is staged in a valid enquiry context, that it would be paraphrase (a), *Do you want to do A?* which comes closest to performing an enquiry about whether the hearer would like to do A. Similarly, for putative request and offer stagings of the model form, alternatives (b) and (c) are the preferred equivalents, respectively, again strictly from the standpoint of equivalence of illocutionary acts conveyed. Full details of the adaptation of an elicitation technique to young children appear below. Where these elicited judgments accord with the predictions for mature native speakers of English, and can be demonstrated to have emerged from the experimental treatment, a strong basis for the valid attribution to young children of knowledge about the use of the particular illocutionary acts staged is provided. In addition, a by-product of successful elicitation of illocutionary judgments is an empirical verification of speech act theory's formal proposals about what sorts of information were employed in order to assign illocutionary force to linguistic forms.

EXPERIMENT 1:   REQUESTS AND ENQUIRIES

Procedure

Subjects   Three girls and 3 boys were selected, on the basis of chronological age only, from a play center attached to a large complex of colleges in Birmingham, England. Approximately half the play center's children were students' children, and the other children were from the local community, which was judged to be middle-class. A mean age of 41.8 months was achieved in the sample, with a range of 38 to 46 months.

Design   Two contrasting situations were devised in which to present variants of the stimulus items in order to operationalize two levels, enquiry and request, of an independent variable, context. Each child was given eight trials of a discrimination task under each of the two contextual levels in a repeated-measures design, and the order of exposure to contextual level was counterbalanced.

The Constructed Contexts   The same physical setting was used in each condition: a Fisher-Price toy nursery school that opened on one side to reveal finger-puppets of teachers and pupils, five pieces of playground equipment, and a classroom zoo containing five typical school pets drawn in color. The speaker of the stimulus items, who was a distinctly identifiable teacher puppet, remained constant across each condition. The hearer, however, for reasons outlined below, had to be varied across contexts.

In the first of two forms of the enquiry condition, it was agreed with each subject that the teacher puppet would talk to a pupil puppet, Peter. The prefatory part of the stimulus material,

> Peter, off you go outside and play...you choose what you want to play on...

like all stimulus material, was actually presented by means of a nearby tape recorder, and proved quite convincing to the young audiences. At *go outside and play,* Peter was moved by the experimenter, or, in later trials, by the child, outside to the playground area. *You choose...* led Peter to approach and move on from each of four playthings in rapid succession. Peter then turned to face the teacher, who uttered the remainder of the stimulus item in one of four variants:

Would you like to play on the $\begin{cases} \text{slide?} \\ \text{seesaw?} \\ \text{roundabout?} \\ \text{climbing frame?} \end{cases}$

After a 2-second pause, the illocutionary discrimination task was administered.

A second indoor form of the enquiry contextual condition consisted of the teacher addressing Peter with:

> Peter, in you come and help me feed the animals...you choose which one you want to feed...

On *feed the animals,* Peter moved into the classroom zoo area, and on *you choose,* Peter approached, then left, each of four pets in rapid succession. Peter then turned, as before, to face the teacher, who uttered the stimulus item in one of these four variants:

$$
\text{Would you like to feed the} \quad \begin{cases} \text{rabbit?} \\ \text{tadpoles?} \\ \text{tortoise?} \\ \text{mice?} \end{cases}
$$

whereupon the discrimination task was administered after a short pause. The four variants of each of the two forms of the enquiry condition yielded a total of eight presentations per subject of this contextual level.

In the request condition, the first form of the context appeared as follows. A different pupil addressee, Simon, who, as each subject is told in practice sessions, has a marked preference for the sole swing in the playground, was moved toward "his" swing. The swing was, however, already occupied by one of four playmates. Simon was placed squarely before the swing, whereupon the teacher said

$$
\text{Simon, leave the swing,} \quad \begin{cases} \text{Susan's} \\ \text{Peter's} \\ \text{etc.} \end{cases} \quad \text{on it...}
$$

immediately followed by the stimulus item in one of the set of four variants,

$$
\text{Would you like to play on the} \quad \begin{cases} \text{slide?} \\ \text{seesaw?} \\ \text{roundabout?} \\ \text{climbing frame?} \end{cases}
$$

followed by administration of the discrimination task.

A second, indoor form of the request contextual condition required, as did the first, each subject's prior understanding that Simon had a marked preference in this case, for feeding one of the pets, the fish. Simon was first moved into the classroom zoo area and placed squarely before the fishbowl, whereupon the teacher addressed him with the tape-recorded utterance:

Simon, leave the fish, they've been fed today. . .

immediately followed by the stimulus item in one of its four variants,

Would you like to feed the $\begin{cases} \text{rabbit?} \\ \text{tadpoles?} \\ \text{tortoise?} \\ \text{mice?} \end{cases}$

Again, the four variants in each form yielded eight presentations.

In addition to the above features that distinguished one contextual level from the other on fairly explicit grounds, verbal and nonverbal, it was assumed that certain highly specific inferences concerning the teacher's, Peter's, and Simon's attitudes toward doing A would have to be drawn by subjects on the basis of evidence from each of the above, more explicit scenarios. Such inferences concerning implicit, socially constructed features of each contextual condition will provide crucially contrasting premises upon which the subject's decision about illocutionary force of the stimulus items will be based.

Accordingly, in a play session leading to acquisition of the enquiry context and familiarization with the discrimination task's format, two explicit features of this context were probed briefly.

1. The subject's comprehension of teacher's *you choose what you want to play on* and *you choose which one you want to feed* was probed, by direct questioning along the lines of *What must Peter play on?* and *Which pet must Peter feed?* to which satisfactory answers might be *anything, anything he wants,* or a short list of alternative playthings or pets.
2. The child's interpretation of the fact that the addressee, Peter, approached and moved on from each available plaything or pet was probed by asking the child why Peter might have done so. Satisfactory responses included *he likes them all, he doesn't know which he wants, he can't decide,* or some combination thereof.

Familiarization sessions for the request context began with demonstrations of the puppet, Simon's marked preference for playing on the swing, and feeding the fish by means of placing Simon on the swing and before the fishbowl and simply remarking on these preferences with discussion. Each subject's mastery of a single, attitudinal inference judged to be critical was then probed: the child was asked, when he was placed squarely before the swing or the fishbowl, *what does Simon want to do?* to which *play on the swing* and *feed the fish* would constitute the only sorts of acceptable responses, respectively. In addition, children's comprehension of the prefatory stimulus material, *leave the swing*... and *leave the fish*..., was probed informally to ensure plausibility of the teacher's proscriptions of each of Simon's favorite activities. All subjects interpreted these proscriptions in the expected fashion, in terms of waiting one's turn in the playground, and the ill consequences, invented with relish, of overfeeding fish.

The Discrimination Task   The required paraphrase judgments were elicited by indirect means, using a passive recall technique requiring discrimination of a pair of alternative forms, the appropriate variants of *Do you want to do A?* and *I want you to do A,* where A corresponded to the complement of its respective stimulus item. Thus a typical trial under the enquiry condition consisted of the following:

Contextual preface: Off you go outside and play...you choose what you want to play on.
Stimulus item: Would you like to play on the seesaw?
Response alternatives: Do you want to play on the seesaw?
I want you to play on the seesaw.

After exposure to a contextualized preface and stimulus item, subjects were asked to determine simply which one of the two response alternatives the teacher had "said." In pilot trials, subjects experienced no difficulty in coming to a decision despite the deliberate vagueness of criteria for identity, and literal impossibility of the task. All verbal material was recorded under studio conditions by a female teacher. Prefaces and stimulus items were edited in alternating indoor and outdoor order for playback on a tape recorder placed in the midst of the constructed contexts. Response alternatives, however, were edited onto pairs of tracks on tape loops played in modified cassettes. Playback for these was activated by the subject's pressing either of a pair of buttons on a selector switch. It was thus possible for a subject to hear either alternative form as often as he or she wished, in whatever order, prior to performing the discrimination and matching called for. Moreover, a simple pointing response to either button was sufficient to represent a successful discrimination.

The effect of terminal intonation contour upon the discrimination task was controlled by recording all stimulus items with a *rise* terminal contour and all response alternatives with a *mid-fall* terminal contour, thus affording subjects no prosodic basis upon which to prefer either response form.

The Elicited Imitation Task   This task was designed to test the embedded imperative hypothesis as an account of very young children's comprehension of such polite or indirect directives. Following the eighth trial of the discrimination task in each contextual condition, one stimulus item was replayed and became the model form for imitation.

Children were familiarized and tested in a quiet corner of their nursery school in a series of 15-minute sessions over a week, with the two contextual treatments separated by a 3- to 4-day gap to offset a possible serial effect.

Results

Discrimination Task   Theoretical predictions which were summarized in (a) through (c) led to the hypothesis that the response alternative *Do you want to do A?* would be selected as the paraphrase of the stimulus item *Would you like to do A?* when the latter was presented under the enquiry condition, and that the alternative *I want you to do A* would be selected as the paraphrase under the request condition. Mean scores for the eight trials per subject per context are summarized in Table 1. Scores for indoor and outdoor variants of each contextual condition have been pooled. The null hypothesis was tested by submitting the pairs of observed means for either response alternative to an analysis of variance. Scoring, for example, each instance of *I want you to do A* as 1 and each instance of *Do you want to do A?* as 0, a significant main effect of context was discovered, $F = 38.15$ $(1,5)$, $p < 0.01$. Moreover, the directions of the difference in means are exactly as was predicted by the pragmatic hypothesis of paraphrase relations among the test items.

In the request contextual condition, however, there are two possible linguistic bases for supposing that the discrimination task's means would have been higher for the *Do you want to do A?* form. First, this response alternative resembles the stimulus form in syntactic mood, interrogative in each case. Second, it resembles the stimulus form on the basis of the semantic relations of elements within each sentence, for it is the hearer (you) which serves as subject of the verbs *want* or *like* in each case. Although syntactic and semantic similarity have been confounded with illocutionary similarity in the enquiry condition, they must be rejected conclusively as accounts of the discrimination process in the request condition.

Finally, it is evident by virtue of experimental controls employed that similarity of intonation contour is not a necessary condition for discrimination of test items.

Table 1.   Discrimination task means

Response alternative	Context	
	Enquiry	Request
Do you want to do A?	5.50	2.16
I want you to do A	2.50	5.83

Elicited Imitation Task   The most striking feature of these data, which appear in Table 2, is the number of complete, accurate imitations—9 out of the 12 imitations. Five of the six children produced such full forms in at least one of their two imitation trials. Moreover, these full imitations were virtually equally distributed across contexts. These results are particularly important for understanding how the subjects comprehend requests. The data constitute evidence against the embedded imperative hypothesis, for five out of the six children in our sample provided counterexamples to a prediction derived from the embedded imperative hypothesis, that the verb phrase of the syntactically lowest complement would be more salient than its matrix clause(s) in an imitation task. It was the full form, in all its syntactic and semantic detail, which was being reproduced—and processed to that extent—in the imitation task.

Prior to considering an informal account of the discrimination of illocutionary force attributed to our 3½-year-olds, three questions may be raised. First, data on a task that entailed native-speaker paraphrase judgments from subjects who are rather young were obtained. The native-speaker judgments were treated implicitly as a developmental control, and the data found displayed a reasonably good fit to these theoretical predictions (a) through (c). Is it justified, then, to attribute native speaker competence for these illocutionary acts to the subjects? or is it more advisable to search for a developmental effect by way of gradual approximation to an idealized adult model? Second, how generally will the theoretical account of illocutionary paraphrase and of the experimental simulations hold up when tested with additional types of illocutionary acts? Third, it will have been noted that the discrimination task actually

Table 2.   Elicited imitation responses

| Subject | Context | |
	Enquiry	Request
1.	Will you like to play on the climbing frame	Would you like to play on the climbing frame
2.	Would you like to play on the climbing frame	Would you like to play on the climbing frame
3.	Play on the climbing frame	I want you to play on the climbing frame
4.	Would you like to play on the climbing frame	Would you like to play on the climbing frame...he wouldn't like to, would he
5.	Would you like to play on the climbing frame	Would you like to play on climbing frame
6.	Would you like to play on the climbing frame	Would you like to play on the climbing frame

consists not of 16 trials per subject, but rather, of one trial replicated eight times serially under context A, then another trial replicated eight times serially under context B. Could subjects discriminate illocutionary force of stimulus utterances randomly assigned to contexts A or B over a single test session of *n* trials? These three questions are addressed in the second experiment.

EXPERIMENT II: REQUESTS AND OFFERS

Procedure

Design   Two levels of the variable context were constructed to simulate felicity conditions proposed independently for the illocutionary acts request and offer. Tape-recorded variants of the stimulus form *Would you like to do A?* were presented in each contextual condition to subjects at two age levels who served as their own controls. Interpretation of illocutionary force for each contextualized performance was measured by means of a discrimination task similar to that employed in Experiment I. One response alternative was a variant of *I want you to do A,* and the other, a variant of *I'll let you do A.* The experimental hypothesis predicted that children would employ contextual cues differentially in order to discriminate a stimulus item's illocutionary force, and they would therefore select the form *I want you to do A* as the best paraphrase only when the stimulus items were represented under the request condition, and *I'll let you do A* only under the offer condition. A 2×2 factorial design employed repeated measures on the context variable, and results of multiple trials of the discrimination task were submitted to an analysis of variance.

Subjects   Seven children at each of two age levels, 2½ and 3 years, served as subjects. Four girls and three boys ranging in age from 26 to 32 months comprised the 2½-year-old age group, and two girls and five boys ranging in age from 31 to 44 months comprised the 3-year-old age group. All children attended day-care centers in lower-income neighborhoods of Vancouver, Canada.

The Constructed Contexts   The physical setting for both contextual treatments consisted of a low table top filled with six Fisher-Price toy playthings: a train, bicycle, horse, airplane, merry-go-round, wagon, and several "Little People" puppet figures designed to fit the toys. The speaker (S) of the stimulus items was represented by an adult puppet figure whose identity was established as the teacher. Hearer (H) puppets were assigned that role randomly across trials.

The sole feature of the context manipulated experimentally was the relative location of S and H in relation to each plaything (P) mentioned in the stimulus item. As indicated in Figure 1, in the request condition, S stood immediately before plaything P, while H stood 12 to 15 centimeters away from P, facing both S and P. Arrows indicate lines of visual regard. In the offer condition, (Figure 2), positions of S and H were simply reversed, and H faced P directly.

The Discrimination Task   The format was comparable to that employed in Experiment I, as was the preparation and playback of items. The stimulus items differed only according to the plaything mentioned, as did the corresponding response alternatives. A representative discrimination task trial consisted of the following elements:

> *Stimulus item:*   Would you like to play on the bike?
> *Response alternatives:*   I want you to play on the bike
> I'll let you play on the bike

Each of the six stimulus items employed appeared once under each contextual condition for a total of 12 trials per subject, but unlike our previous experiment, contextual conditions appeared in random order over a single test session. In order to control effects of intonation, all stimulus items were performed with a high-fall terminal contour, and all response alternatives with a mid-fall contour.

Children were tested in quiet areas of their day-care centers following familiarization with the experimental materials in which each group was given practice in same-different discriminations using colored blocks. Paraphrase judgments were elicited exactly as for Experiment I: the stimulus item was presented, and following a brief interval, the subject was asked to *find which button says what the teacher said* on the switched tape-loop system. Either pointing or a verbal indication counted as a response.

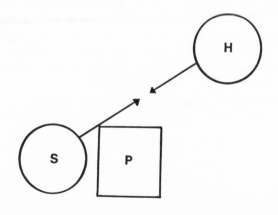

Figure 1.   Constructed context for request condition.

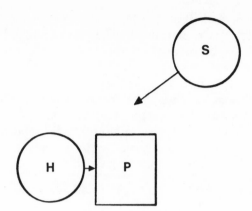

Figure 2.   Constructed context for offer condition.

Results

Mean discrimination scores for each age group in each contextual condition are summarized in Table 3. An analysis of variance on means for each response alternative detected a significant main effect of context, $F = 61.30$ (1;12), $p < 0.01$. While no main effect of age level emerged, a significant interaction between age and context was found, $F = 10.08$ (1;12), $p < 0.01$. While both age groups display illocutionary judgments in accord with those predicted for mature native speakers, it would appear that those skills develop unevenly across the two illocutionary acts: the 3-year-olds could discriminate the requests more reliably than could their 2½-year-old counterparts. One possible account for such a developmental effect might be that younger children tend to be exposed to relatively fewer requests than their older counterparts. The younger children could be regarded by caregivers as more dependent, thus in need of offers of help, while older children might be regarded as increasingly capable of carrying out requests made of them. Using a large corpus of spontaneous parent-child discourse, the author is investigating these possibilities.

Table 3.   Discrimination task means

Age	Response alternative	Context	
		Request	Offer
2½	I want you to do A	3.43	1.86
	I'll let you do A	2.57	4.14
3	I want you to do A	4.71	1.00
	I'll let you do A	1.29	5.00

DISCUSSION

The following conclusions may be drawn from the results of these experiments.

1. The reliable differential discrimination of requests from enquiries appears to be under control by 3½-year-olds, and the differentiation of requests from offers appears to be under control by 2½-year-olds.
2. The distribution of discriminating responses for the illocutionary acts studied was a function of the experimental treatments rather than of semantic, syntactic, or prosodic variables.
3. Of the three illocutionary acts studied, a developmental sequence may be inferred for two, in which mastery of offers precedes that of requests.

However, the second conclusion warrants at least informal discussion, for some analysis is needed of just how the various experimental treatments provided the set of cues necessary and sufficient for discrimination of illocutionary force.

In the first experiment, which contrasted hypothetical requesting and enquiring contexts, the following sets of felicity conditions must be satisfied in order for each performance of the stimulus item to convey one or the other illocutionary act:

Request	Enquiry
1. S wants H to do A	1. S wants to know p
2. H can do A	2. H can tell S p
3. H is willing to do A	3. H is willing to tell S p
4. A hasn't already been done	4. S doesn't already know p.

Rather than claiming that native speakers necessarily search for supporting evidence for such felicity conditions in the utterance's context, a more efficient approach to the assignment of illocutionary force is proposed: deductive falsification of each candidate act linguistically performable by an utterance. Given this experiment's enquiry context, one such candidate to be tested is a request interpretation. Here, the teacher's advice to Peter, *You choose what you want...*, contradicts the first condition necessary for well-formed requesting, which states that S wants H to do A. Similarly, given this experiment's request context, quite apart from the teacher's demonstrated interest in steering Simon away from the (occupied) swing and (overstuffed) fish, it had already been verified by probing that all actors involved knew the literal answer—no—to a simple enquiry about H's preferences. Here the fourth condition upon true (not pedagogical or otherwise rhetorical) enquirying is contradicted by the observed facts. (A fuller, formalized account of candidate illocutionary acts and conditions is in Reeder, 1975.)

Turning to the request-offer contrast studied in the second experiment, an additional set of felicity conditions enters the illocutionary picture:

<u>Offer</u>

1. H wants to do A
2. S can permit H to do A
3. S is willing for H to do A
4. H is not already doing A

However, it is again maintained that the more efficient approach to assignment of illocutionary interpretation will be falsification of those linguistically possible interpretations that cannot be supported by contextual evidence.

In the simulated request context (Figure 1), it was hoped that the teacher's location beside plaything P would support the conclusion that S wanted H to do A. By virtue of H's noncommittal location in this context, the subjects could conclude that there was no indication that H wanted to do act A in particular, nor was there any indication that H particularly objected to doing A; that is, no special interest, one way or another was indicated. Now the candidate interpretations that are linguistically performable by the stimulus form will be request, offer, enquiry and threat, or warning. First, an offer interpretation fails on the basis of H's noncommittal stance, which contradicts the first felicity condition upon well formed offering. A possible enquiry interpretation founders because of a similar lack of attitudinal evidence: for a sincere question to be asked, S must not know whether H wants to do A, but subjects can assume that H doesn't want to do A in particular. S has her answer, and the question quite literally fails to arise. Finally, the interpretation fails for lack of evidence that H will object to playing on P, the latter constituting a felicity condition upon any good threat. It is assumed that the absence of contextual evidence incompatible with well formed requesting, leaving that interpretation standing up to the deductive procedure.[1]

In the simulated offer context (Figure 2), it is assumed that H's physical location beside the designated plaything P this time will permit subjects to conclude that H wants to do A. Moreover, S's noncommittal location this time will permit subjects to draw two further inferences, and to

---

[1]It also can be shown that felicity conditions upon well formed requesting find positive support in the contrived request context. Here, it was possible to conclude that S wanted H to do A, that H could do A (H appears normal, healthy, etc.), that H was willing to do A, and finally, that A had not occurred or would have occurred in the absence of a request.

attribute these as shared assumptions to S and H: first, there is no indication that S wants H to do A, and second, there is no indication that S objects to H doing A. For the stimulus item to have been conveyed, first, an appropriate request that H do A, condition 1, which requires that S wants H to do A, must be supported. To the contrary, if anyone had indicated an interest in playing on P, it was the hearer. Next, the enquiry reading is ruled out, thus, for S to sincerely enquire whether H would like to do A, S must not know the answer (condition 4). By placing H immediately beside the plaything in question, a patent answer for S's benefit was staged, thus rendering the question irrelevant. Finally, playing on P cannot constitute a particularly good threat in light of H's demonstrated interest in playing on P, which calls to mind the familiar pragmatic report, "Was that a threat or a promise?" The only illocutionary act whose felicity conditions cannot be falsified by contextually-derived inferences is the offer reading.[2]

ON LINGUISTIC INTERSUBJECTIVITY

It is proposed here that even very young children quite capably and systematically derive inferences from social contexts about the attitudes, abilities, intentions, and knowledge or shared assumptions of conversational participants. This argument for the early development of linguistic intersubjectivity seems incompatible, however, with earlier conclusions (Flavell et al., 1968) that attribute only primitive levels of role-taking ability to children even well into their school years. But Flavell's work erred seriously on the conservative side concerning role-taking skills as applied to everyday conversation. This is evident in light of the reassessment of role-taking skills undertaken by Masangky et al. (1974) and some striking results from adaptations of Piagetian tasks reported by Donaldson (1978). In any case, studies of young children's adaptations of speech to the conversational needs of various types of listeners have, for some time, supported the early attribution of linguistic intersubjectivity (Garvey and Hogan, 1973; Keenan, 1974). Gelman and Shatz's account (1977) of 4-year-olds' adjustment of the use of verbs of cognition, among other features, to the perceived communicative capacities of 2-year-old listeners argues strongly for the reflexivity of young children's conversational skill,

---

[2]It may be demonstrated that conclusions derived from the contrived offer context, together with some elementary knowledge of the world, supports felicity conditions upon well formed offering. Specifically, evidence that H wants to do A, that S is willing for H to do A, that S can permit H to do A (from knowledge of S's role as adult and teacher), and that H is not already doing A, thereby rendering any offer irrelevant (evident by virtue of H's location) have all been found.

as does Bates' report (1976) of 2-year-old Italian children's developing grasp of the semantics of the counterfactual conditional inflection. Finally, studies of prelinguistic communication (Bruner, 1975) and of very early reference (Ninio and Bruner, 1978) continue to yield evidence for a position that underlies this study: that human linguistic communication emerges from a matrix of socially acquired schemata of personhood and of intimate human relationships.

REFERENCES

Austin, J. L. 1962. How To Do Things With Words. Oxford Univ. Press, Inc., New York.

Bates, E. 1976. Language and Context: The Acquisition of Pragmatics. Academic Press, Inc., New York.

Bruner, J. S. 1975. The ontogenesis of speech acts. J. Child Lang. 2:1–19.

Donaldson, M. 1978. Children's Minds. William Collins Sons, Glasgow.

Ervin-Tripp, S. 1974. The comprehension and production of requests by children. Papers and Reports on Child Lang. Dev. 8:188–195.

Flavell, J. H., Botkin, P. T., Fry, C. L., Wright, J. W., and Jarvis, P. E. 1968. The Development of Role-Taking and Communication Skills in Children. John Wiley & Sons, Inc., New York.

Garvey, C., and Hogan, R. 1973. Social speech and social interaction: Egocentrism revisited. Child Dev. 44:562–568.

Gelman, R., and Shatz, M. 1977. Appropriate speech adjustments: The operation of conversational constraints on talk to two-year-olds. In: M. Lewis and L. Rosenblum (eds.), Interaction, Conversation and the Development of Language. John Wiley & Sons, Inc., New York.

Halliday, M. A. K. 1975. Learning How to Mean: Explorations in the Development of Language. Edward Arnold, London.

Keenan, E. O. 1974. Conversational competence in children. J. Child Lang. 1: 163–183.

Masangky, Z. S., McClusky, C. A., McIntyre, C. W., Sims-Knight, J., Vaughn, B. E., and Flavell, J. H. 1974. The early development of inferences about visual percepts of others. Child Dev. 45:357–366.

Ninio, A., and Bruner, J. S. 1978. The achievement and antecedents of labeling. J. Child Lang. 5:1–16.

Reeder, K. F. 1975. Pre-school children's comprehension of illocutionary force: An experimental psycholinguistic study. Unpublished doctoral thesis, University of Birmingham, England.

Searle, J. R. 1969. Speech Acts: An Essay in the Philosophy of Language. Cambridge University Press, London.

Searle, J. R. 1975. Indirect speech acts. In: P. Cole and J. Morgan (eds.), Syntax and Semantics, pp. 59–82. Vol. 3. Seminar Press, New York.

Shatz, M. 1974. The Comprehension of Indirect Directives. Paper presented at the Summer Meeting of the Linguistic Society of America, August, Amherst, Mass.

Pragmatics and Symbolic Play
A Study in Language and
Cognitive Development

Philip S. Dale, Nancy L. Cook, and Howard Goldstein

An emerging subfield of research in child language is pragmatics: "the study of the rules for using language in context" (Bates, 1976). Of the various aspects of pragmatics, the most studied is the notion of speech act. In defining speech acts, J. L. Austin (1962) wrote, "To say something is to do something." People produce utterances to request, to demand, to promise, to call attention to, to reject, and to perform many other functions. Speech acts are not identical to linguistic forms; for example, interrogatives may be used to command *(Would you put your toys away now?)* as well as to request an answer *(Can you see her?)*. In fact, the learning of the complex relationships between form and pragmatic function is a lengthy task (Ervin-Tripp, 1974; Ervin-Tripp and Mitchell-Kernan, 1977).

The pragmatics of early language is of particular interest for several reasons. First, children may have command over a number of pragmatic functions at a time when their vocabulary and syntax are quite limited (Dore, 1974, 1975; Ingram, 1974; Greenfield and Smith, 1976). Second, there is some evidence that pragmatic development is, to some extent, statistically independent of other aspects of language development. Snyder (1976) compared language-delayed children with normal children who were matched for mean length of utterance (MLU) on their ability to produce declarative and imperative functions under structured elicitation conditions, and found that language-impaired children were even more

This research was supported by Research Contract HD-3-2793 from the National Institute of Child Health and Human Development entitled "An Investigation of Certain Relationships Between Hearing Impairment and Language Disability," and by the Child Development and Mental Retardation Center, University of Washington, Seattle, Wash.

delayed in pragmatics than in syntax (see also Blank, Gessner, and Esposito, 1979, for a striking case study). Third, it is often said that pragmatic development is the aspect of language most closely tied to cognitive development (for example, Bates, 1976), for it rests upon an understanding of both the social and inanimate worlds and their relationship.

It is unclear which aspects of cognitive development might be functionally related to language. Despite the plausibility of a connection between early language and a conception of the world as being composed of permanent and substantial objects arranged in a system of spatial relations, attempts to demonstrate a relationship between early language and the development of the object concept have not generally been successful (see Bowerman, 1978, for a review). Research comparing language development with the development of imitation and with the understanding of means-end relationships (causality) has had mixed success.

Surprisingly, little research has been done on symbolic play as an index of cognitive development, despite its coordinate importance with imitation and object permanence in Piaget's theory (1945, 1962), and the important fact that it is easily observable without structured testing. Furthermore, relatively consistent developmental sequencs of play development have been reported, although none of the reports cover the full developmental range of this study.

Despite the lack of empirical evidence, there is considerable speculation, and a modest amount of evidence that symbolic play is disrupted in language-disabled children (Weiner and Weiner, 1974; Lovell, Hoyle, and Sidall, 1968), and therapy directed at fostering symbolic play based on an assumption of an unidirectional causal relationship has been suggested (Morehead and Morehead, 1974; Jeffree and McConkey, 1974). On the other hand, Lovell et al. (1968) have argued that language transforms play, rather than the reverse. This is an issue of clear clinical as well as theoretical importance.

A major goal of this research is to translate some current theoretical notions about pragmatic development, based on case studies, into a reliable assessment system that is sensitive to individual differences, and similarly, to draw together findings on the development of play into a single reliable and sensitive assessment technique. Then, it will be possible to compare the two strands of development.

ASSESSING PRAGMATIC DEVELOPMENT

Pragmatic development has been studied by means of the analysis of spontaneous speech (Dore, 1974; Halliday, 1975; Greenfield and Smith, 1976), as well as by means of structured elicitation tasks (Snyder, 1976) designed to elicit declarative and imperative functions.

Several classifications have been proposed for the analysis of spontaneous speech. Halliday (1975) provides a set of categories that cover a broad developmental range: instrumental/regulatory/interactional/personal/heuristic/imaginative/informative. Dore's (1975) system is an elaboration of the earlier phases: labeling/repeating/answering/requesting action/requesting answer/calling/greeting/protesting/practicing. In contrast to these relatively elaborate schemes, Bates, Camaioni, and Volterra (1975) restrict their attention to just two pragmatic functions: the imperative and the declarative.

All of the classification systems proposed to date are based on the examination of utterances from a small number of children. A prime motivation for introducing pragmatic analyses has been the claim that pragmatic function is not perfectly correlated with linguistic form; thus, formal devices cannot be used as the only basis for classification (deVilliers and deVilliers, 1978). Sometimes intonation is a helpful basis (Dore, 1975; Halliday, 1975), but not always (Bloom, 1973). Thus, researchers have a great deal—perhaps too much—freedom in devising a system of categories, and a paucity of means for evaluating the system.

There is not yet a solution to this problem. The criterion of simultaneous emergence, applied in the domain of syntax by Braine (1976) and in the domain of pragmatics by Halliday (1975) may be useful in devising a classification system. However, this criterion alone is unlikely to be adequate because genuinely distinct functions may appear at the same time, or conversely, differences in emergence may reflect a sampling error. The system used in this study is based on the authors' estimate of the consensus among researchers. Most classification systems include a division between declarative and imperative, between affirmation and negation (and usually a subdivision among negations along the lines of Bloom, 1970), between requests for objects and events versus requests for information, and between reference to immediately perceivable objects or events and reference to absent objects or events. Some of these distinctions may ultimately be assigned to semantics, rather than pragmatics. DeVilliers and deVilliers (1978) discussed the possible dividing lines between these two domains.

To a certain extent, sampling problems can be reduced by means of standardized elicitation tasks. These are most easily constructed for declarative and imperative functions. Snyder (1978) distinguished two aspects of declaratives. Greenfield and Smith (1976) noted that children at the one-word state most often encode that aspect of the situation that is novel or that has most recently changed. They argued that this tendency to encode the novel element is the precursor of the process of presupposition, which is ultimately reflected in the division of meaning within sentences into two parts: that which is presupposed, and that which is asserted. This distinction is approximately the same as that between given and new information (Clark and Clark, 1977). Snyder (1978) engaged children in a repetitive task, such as dropping balls in a bucket, and then handed the child a baby bottle. She scored responses along two dimensions: 1) was there an attempt to communicate this new element? and 2) by what means (gestural, vocal, or verbal) was this communication attempted? Imperative-eliciting tasks were administered by handing the child one part of a desirable toy and showing the child the other part, for example, a xylophone and a mallet. Snyder devised reliable scoring systems with satisfactory scalability for all three dimensions.

In view of the limitations of both the naturalistic and the structured approaches to studying pragmatic development, the authors of this chapter chose to investigate both methods.

ASSESSING PLAY DEVELOPMENT

Symbolic, or pretend, play begins to appear in the second year of life. Central to Piaget's account is the assumption that symbolic play represents a new developmental understanding of the world; like language, symbolic play depends on the ability to represent mentally objects and events. Piaget (1945, 1962) observed three levels of symbolic play after a pre-symbolic period:

1. Pre-symbolic play: Child pretends at own routines, e.g., pretending to eat.
2. Stage I symbolic play: Child pretends at adult's routines, e.g., driving a car.
3. Stage II symbolic play: Child substitutes one item for another, e.g., child uses a block as a toy car.
4. Stage III symbolic play: Planned combinations, e.g., play consisting of sequences of actions resembling real scenes.

Lowe (1975) presented a series of toys to children, ages 12 to 36 months; after a brief period, each set was removed and another set was introduced. The play of the 12-month-old children was primarily classifiable as pre-symbolic; the most common activities were feeding themselves or brushing their own hair. By 18 months, one-third of the children exhibited Stage I play by feeding the doll, and by 30 months all of the children exhibited such play. Lowe's materials were not conducive to symbolic substitution or to planned combinations and she does not report figures on such play, but she does describe examples of both kinds of play from children 30 months old. Lowe did not scale the four types of play.

Nicolich (n.d.) argued that spontaneous, unconstrained play reflects children's developmental level better than does play in a relatively structured situation. She observed five female infants ages 14–19 months for 1 year. The children were given a standard, but large, set of toys and they were observed for 40 minutes at each visit. Nicolich observed a level of relational play prior to pre-symbolic play. She also added two levels of play between Piaget's Stage I and Stage II, for a total of seven categories:

1.	Relational:	Child puts cup on saucer.
2.	Symbolic schema:	(Piaget's pre-symbolic) Child pretends at own routines.
3.	Single symbolic games:	(Piaget's Stage I) Child pretends at adult routines.
4.	Single schema combinations:	Child plays at only one action, but extends it to many objects, e.g., pretends to drink, then has doll drink.
5.	Multi-schema combinations:	Child plays at many actions with many objects, but without realistic sequencing, e.g., pretends to eat, then to drink, then to stir.
6.	Planned single schema game:	(some similarity to Piaget's Stage II) Involves some sort of search behavior, but only one action.
7.	Planned multi-schema game:	(Piaget's Stage III) Tends toward realistic scene, some overall plan, search involved.

Nicholich's data do not provide support for this entire ordering. Levels 6 and 7, for example, emerge at the same time in three of the children, and level 7 appears before level 6 in the other two. Similarly, levels 2 and 3 are not distinguishable from her observations, and levels 4 and 5 are only weakly distinguishable. In sum, only four levels of play can be distinguished: relational/single symbolic/sequential symbolic (no apparent planning or search)/planned symbolic sequences.

Fenson, Kagan, Kearsley, and Zelazo (1976) investigated play development through a somewhat earlier age range, 7 to 20 months. They presented children with a standard set of toys for 20 minutes. Because much of the play they observed was pre-symbolic, they introduced a number of new distinctions. Although no scaling is reported, age trends suggested the following sequence:

1.	Pre-relational:	Play with one toy at a time.
2.	Nonappropriate relational:	Child puts spoon to bottle.
3.	Appropriate relational:	Child puts cup on saucer.
4.	Sequential relational:	Child puts cup on saucer, then spoon in cup.
5.	Symbolic acts:	(Piaget's pre-symbolic plus Stage I) Child pretends to drink or makes the doll drink.
6.	Sequential symbolic acts:	Child pretends to stir, then to drink.

METHOD

Subjects

Twenty white children were tested—two boys and two girls, ages 12 months, 15 months, 18 months, 21 months, and 24 months. They were drawn from a subject pool based on Seattle-area birth announcements.

Procedure

Each child was seen twice within a 2-week period. The first visit comprised a spontaneous play session and a set of structured pragmatics tasks. The second visit comprised a spontaneous language sample. All testing was done in a large homelike room, which was carpeted and had a colorful couch and a window.

Play Sampling   A standard set of toys (Table 1, group 1) was on the floor when the child and parent entered. The parent was asked to be responsive, but to refrain from initiating or suggesting novel play activities. The experimenter remained in the room for about 3 minutes talking with the child and the parent and demonstrating the requested style of interaction. Then, the experimenter explained that children frequently play differently in the presence of a stranger; therefore, the experimenter would leave and return later to give the child a new set of toys. After 10 minutes, the experimenter returned and exchanged the group 1 toys for the group 2 toys (Table 1), which were selected to "pull for" substitution play. Again the experimenter remained in the room for 3 minutes; then he left for the remainder of this second 10-minute observation. All sessions were videotaped with three cameras that together covered nearly all of the room space. During the spontaneous play session, an observer behind a one-way mirror took notes on the play of the child. This record was later supplemented by the videotape for purposes of coding.

Structured Pragmatics Testing   Next, all toys were put away and the experimenter donned a "toy apron," its pockets filled with the toys used in the structured pragmatics tasks. These tasks were administered in a constant order: first the declaratives, then the imperatives. The experimenter began the declarative tasks, patterned directly after those of Snyder, by putting a brightly colored plastic block in the child's pail. Then he took it out and gave it to the child, and gestured or helped the child put it in the pail. Then, another block was presented. If the child would not spontaneously place the block in the pail, the experimenter assisted and then presented a third block. When the child had spontaneously placed three blocks in the pail, a doll was presented. A similar format was followed for all declarative tasks. The imperative tasks were modified somewhat from those of Snyder. (The authors were unable to use her

Table 1. Toys used in play session

Group 1: Imitative symbolic play	Group 2: Symbolic substitution
teapot	large empty container
teapot lid	oversized round block
2 cups	2 hexagonal nesting toys
2 saucers	2 small round blocks
2 plates	2 large round blocks
2 spoons	2 sticks
male doll	male doll (same)
female doll	female doll (same)
baby doll	baby doll (same)
baby bottle	short stick with one rounded end
big doll bed	flat rectangular block
small doll bed	small flat rectangular block
doll blanket	sheet of paper
toy car	thick rectangular block

"two parts of a toy" format because the subjects were not immobilized by a feeding table as were hers.) The experimenter presented the child with an attractive toy packaged so that the child required assistance, for example, a clear plastic purse with plastic keys inside (a complete list of items is given in Dale, 1980). The experimenter and an observer recorded all responses. In cases of disagreement, the final coding was made from the videotape.

Spontaneous Language Sampling For the second session, the parent and child returned to the homelike room that now was furnished with a couch, chairs, slide, and variety of toys, including a playhouse, dolls and stuffed animals, cars and trucks, and a play sink and dishes. In contrast to the restraint suggested for the play session, the child's parent was requested to play with the child as she would normally do. After about 8–10 minutes of play, the experimenter brought out a snack of juice and a cookie. The experimenter left the room for about 15 minutes, returned to put away the toys with the child's help, and said good-bye to the child. A total of 30 minutes was video-recorded for transcription and analysis. The videotape record also was available to provide contextual information.

Coding Procedures

Spontaneous Language Coding Table 2 displays the coding system. Verbalizations, identified as such in borderline cases on the basis of information from the parent and plausibility of the phonetic substitutions required, were coded on two dimensions: dialogue status and pragmatic function. The set of pragmatic function categories represents a conflation

Table 2.   Pragmatic function coding system

Dialogue status
SP—spontaneous utterance. (19[a])
RLA—relevant response or answer to a question. (16)
EIM—elicited imitation of another's speech, including responses to questions such as, *can you say 'doggie'?* (3)
SPIM—spontaneous imitation of another's immediately preceding utterance. (16)
SR—self-repetition of a child's immediately preceding utterance, with no intervening adult utterances. (16)
UNC—unclassifiable. (4)

Pragmatic functions
NAME—verbal naming. Descriptive labels, which are common nouns for the child's environment. (19)
ATTRIB—verbal attributes. Descriptive labels for the child's environment that are perceivable attributes of objects or events, color, shape, location, movement, action. (13)
COMNT—verbal comment. This requires going beyond immediately perceivable information to link with stored knowledge. Included are utterances that are words associated with a given object, event, or attribute of interest, posessives, or customary locations, as opposed to present locations. (13)
TENSE—verbalizations marking tense. Comments on future or past actions. (5)
RQPRES—verbal requests pertaining to present environment. Requests for present objects, for actions, other than giving an object, or for permission or approval. (12)
RQABST—verbal request for an absent object. (5)
RQINFO—verbal request for information. (5)
NONEX—nonexistence verbalization. Negative expressing the absence or disappearance of an object, e.g., *all gone.* (4)
REJECT—verbal rejection. Negative expressing the rejection of an object or action. (4)
DENIAL—verbal denial. Negatives expressing the denial of a proposition, e.g., *Is Daddy at work? No.* (7)
AFFIRM—verbal affirmation. Response expressing affirmation or confirmation of a proposition, e.g., *yeah, okay.* (11)
ATTN—attention-seeking verbalization. (13)
GREET—greetings and other ritualized forms, e.g., *bye-bye, night-night.* (18)
UNIN—unintelligible, but apparently verbal and/or uninterpretable. (17)

[a]number of children (of 20) displaying response in this category.

of categories proposed by Dore, Bates, and others, including some additions that seem relevant for relating language to cognition, for example, separating requests for present objects from requests for absent objects (RQPRES versus RQABST), and separating attributes that are directly perceivable, such as color and shape, from comments that require going beyond immediately perceivable information, such as customary location, possessive, or object associated with given object (ATTRIB versus COMNT). Mean length of utterance (MLU) and rate of spontaneous imitation measures were also computed, for all samples of verbalizations, as marker variables to facilitate comparison with the results of other studies.

Structured Pragmatics Coding   Responses on the structured pragmatics tasks were coded with a system only slightly modified from that
used by Snyder (1978); details on the system are available in Dale (1980).
Responses to the declarative tasks were coded in two ways. The presupposition measure (1-4) reflects whether there was a response to the new
object; if there was, the declarative measure (1-5) reflects how it was communicated to the object. For imperative items, a single coding was made
(1-7). The declarative and imperative measures developed by Snyder are
based on research by Bates et al. (1975) and Sugarman (1976) on the development of naturally occurring communicative acts during the preverbal
and early linguistic periods. The scales reflect two major developmental
trends: first, the growing tendency to attend (by looking, reaching, etc.)
to both the adult and the object in the situation; and second, the increasing use of the vocal channel, first with vocalization and later with verbalization.

Play Coding   A codable play act began when a child picked up an
object and continued until the object was either put down or a different
codable play act was observed, for example, picking up a doll, examining
it, and putting it down (pre-relational); taking the lid off the teapot, holding it, and putting it back on the teapot (functional relational); and, picking up a spoon, putting it in the cup and stirring, then removing it and putting it down (symbolic-known routine). Each play act was coded for the
highest level of play displayed according to the 23-level system summarized in Table 3. (Full details are available from the authors). To be
credited with a given level of play, a child had to exhibit at least two different play acts at that level.

RESULTS

Reliability of Measures

Spontaneous Language Measures   Eight language samples (20% of
the total, unsystematically chosen, comprising 400 utterances) were coded
independently by two observers. The second coder was provided the
orthographic transcription used by the first coder. The following percentages of agreement were obtained for the various levels of coding:

Pragmatic function	88%	(77-100%)
Dialogue status	94%	(84-100%)

Structured Pragmatics Measures   All pragmatic tasks for the first
six children were independently coded by two observers. All disagreements were resolved by viewing the videotape together and arriving at a
consensus. The responses of the next six children were independently
coded by at least two observers, one coding from the videotape alone.

Table 3.   Coding systems for play behaviors

Initial coding level	Revised coding level[a]
I. Pre-relational Play	
1. One object at a time	Pre-relational
2. Banging	
II. Relational Play	
1. Giving object to mother	
2. Nonfunctional relational	
3. Functional relational	Single relational
4. Grouping	
5. Approximation to pretend play	
6. Repeated relational actions	
7. Sequential relational actions	Sequential relational
III. Symbolic Play	
1. Known routines	
a. involving inanimate objects only	
b. self-directed	
c. directed to mother	Single symbolic
d. directed to doll	
2. Repeated symbolic actions	
3. Sequential symbolic actions	Sequential symbolic
4. Planned symbolic actions	Planned symbolic
IV. Symbolic Substitution	
1. Known routines with some symbolic substitution	
a. involving inanimate objects only	
b. self-directed	Single symbolic substitution
c. directed to mother	
d. directed to doll	
2. Repeated actions involving symbolic substitutions	
3. Sequential actions involving symbolic substitutions	Sequential symbolic substitution
4. Planned actions involving symbolic substitutions	Planned symbolic substitution

[a]See Results section, page 162.

Inter-rater reliability for both declarative measures was 100%, for the imperative measure, 91%.

Play Measures   Play coding was done from videotapes by a coder who had usually observed the session live as well. A second coder, working only from the videotape, coded 20% of the play sessions (actually, eight randomly chosen half-sessions). Two types of disagreement were possible: first, a behavior could be recorded and coded by one of the coders and not the other; and, second, two coders would have classified the same behavior in different categories. If the first type of disagreement is included, the percentage of agreement is 77% (67–88%). When reliability is calculated only for behaviors that are coded by both observers, the percentage of agreement is 93% (89–100%).

Spontaneous Language Measures

Figure 1 displays the mean number of pragmatic language categories (functions) produced, which was highly correlated with age ($r = 0.89$, $p < 0.001$). Although the pragmatic categories did not attain scalability (coefficient of reproducibility $= 0.82$, coefficient of scalability $= 0.37$), the apparent order of difficulty is reasonably consistent with that of previous work:

Naming
Greetings and ritualized forms
Attributes, comments, attention-seeking
Requests for present objects, actions, or permission
Affirmation
Denial
Reference to past or future; requests for absent objects; requests for information
Nonexistence, rejection of object or action

Contrary to hypothesis, comments were no less common than attributes. Nonexistence negations were surprisingly rare, probably because the unfamiliar setting made it more difficult for the child to think of absent objects that might be available.

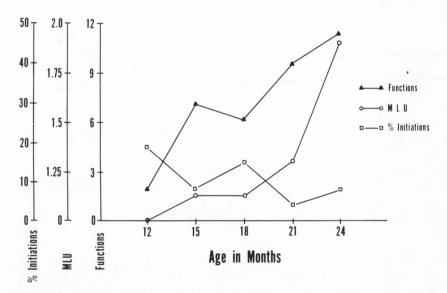

Figure 1.   Number of pragmatic functions manifested, mean length of utterance, and rate of spontaneous imitation.

Figure 1 also includes mean MLU and rate (proportion) of spontaneous imitations for each age group. MLU and age were also highly correlated ($r = 0.70$ $p < 0.01$) although rate of imitation and age were not ($r = 0.36$, n.s.). The boys and the girls did not differ significantly in MLU, but the girls produced significantly more categories than the boys ($p < 0.02$, Mann-Whitney).

Structured Pragmatics Measures

The results of the imperative and declarative tasks were analyzed to determine a productive level of communicative performance for the child. For this analysis, the highest score out of seven imperative categories and five declarative categories was determined for each child. If only one example of a highest category was demonstrated, then the "highest score" was reduced to the next highest demonstrated category. The means of the "highest" imperative and declarative categories for the five age levels are shown in Table 4. The means for the imperative tasks varied from 3.75 for 12-month-olds to 7.0 for 24-month-olds. The imperative tasks were apparently a fruitful attempt to evoke communicative behaviors to assess the development of pragmatic notions. However, the declarative tasks did not show a consistent age trend. In fact, the mean scores for declarative varied only between 2.5 and 3.75. In contrast to the imperative results, there was not a spread of scores across age groups nor a ceiling effect for the older children. Table 4 also reveals some tendency for new information to be communicated verbally to a larger degree with increasing age, but these data do not differentiate the age groups clearly.

Performance on the imperative task was considerably more correlated with age ($r = 0.76$, $p < 0.01$) than was performance on either aspect of the declarative task ($r = 0.16$ for Declarative, n.s.; $r = 0.27$ for Infor., n.s.).

Play

Play acts were initially coded into 23 categories. However, this set of categories is too narrow for useful analysis given only 20 minutes of spon-

Table 4.   Results of structured pragmatics tasks

Age in months	Verbal presupposition responses	Mean "highest" response to declarative tasks	Mean "highest" response to imperative tasks
12	0.04	2.50	3.75
15	0.36	2.50	5.25
18	0.08	3.25	6.00
21	0.29	2.50	6.25
24	0.29	3.75	7.00

taneous play. Two broader systems were evaluated: a four-stage sequence suggested by Piaget's account of play, and a nine-stage sequence suggested by the findings of Nicolich.

The first system is displayed in the left-hand column of Table 3: pre-relational, relational, symbolic, and symbolic substitution play. This sequence is honored by every child in the sample; the coefficient of scalability for these four stages is 1.0. The play of all the children consisted primarily of pre-relational and relational play. There were no general developmental trends in the proportion of each level of play, which is consistent with the lack of correlation between age and mean stage of play.

Table 5 presents the number of children, by sex, at each of the four stages of play. Although there are more girls than boys at the higher levels, the difference in the total mean level of play as a function of sex is not significant. Furthermore, the mean level of play is not significantly correlated with age.

Table 6 presents the performance of each child in the sample according to the nine-stage sequence described in the right-hand column of Table 3. Satisfactory scalability is achieved by these data; the coefficient of reproducibility is 0.95 and the coefficient of scalability is 0.75. Single play acts in higher stages appear before sequential play acts in lower stages. It appears that, as important as the development from relational to symbolic to symbolic substitution is, a more difficult development is from isolated play acts to sequences to planned episodes. For example, a child was more likely to feed the doll with a stick than to pretend to pour into a cup, stir with a spoon, and then pretend to drink. The data do not distinguish between pre-relational and single relational play, because all children demonstrated both types of play. Furthermore, the data do not specify the development order of sequential symbolic substitution and planned sequential play, because very few children exhibited either level of play, and the developmental trend was not consistent.

There are significantly more girls than boys at the higher levels (Mann-Whitney, $p < 0.05$). Figure 2 presents the mean level of play by age and sex. While the mean level of play for girls generally increases with age, it remains nearly constant for boys.

Table 5. Number of children, by sex, producing each category of play

Level	Total	Males	Females
Pre-relational	20	10	10
Relational	20	10	10
Symbolic	17	8	9
Symbolic substitution	8	3	5

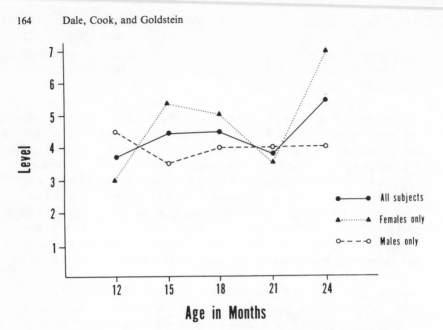

Figure 2.   Mean level of play (nine-level system) at five ages for males and females.

Relationships Among Measures

Following Bates et al. (1977), hypotheses about the relationship between language and thought were distinguished into those that are essentially sequential and those that are essentially correlational. If object permanence is hypothesized to be a prerequisite for noun-use, successful performance on an object permanence task should reliably precede noun use. In this case, a sequential analysis is appropriate; the correlation between the two may be low because of a variable delay between the two. In contrast, object concept and noun-use might both be hypothesized to be separate behavioral manifestations of a single underlying cognitive development. Thus, they should emerge at approximately the same time, although either may appear first. In this case, a correlational analysis is appropriate. Hypotheses of this second type rest on an assumption that there is no direct window on cognitive development and that all tasks, social or nonsocial, language or nonlanguage, reflect cognitive development indirectly in a necessarily multi-factorial way. An analysis of each type is reported below.

For the correlational analysis, there are four play measures: number of categories manifested on the four and on the nine level systems, proportion of symbolic play, and proportion of symbolic substitution play (4Play, 9Play, Symbolp, Substp). There are three spontaneous language

Table 6. Categories of play produced by children (nine-level system)

Age in months	Subject No.	Pre-relational	Single relational	Sequential relational	Single symbolic	Single symbolic substitution	Sequential symbolic	Sequential symbolic substitution	Planned symbol	Planned symbolic substitution
12	1	1	1	1	1	1	0	0	0	0
	2	1	1	0	0	0	0	0	0	0
	3	1	1	1	1	0	0	0	0	0
	4	1	1	1	1	0	0	0	0	0
15	5	1	1	1	1	1	1	1	0	0
	6	1	1	1	1	1	0	0	0	0
	7	1	1	0	0	0	0	0	0	0
	8	1	1	1	1	0	0	0	0	0
18	9	1	1	1	1	0	0	0	0	0
	10	1	1	1	1	0	1	0	0	0
	11	1	1	1	1	1	0	0	0	0
	12[a]	1	1	0	1	1	0	0	0	0
21	13[a]	1	1	0	1	0	0	0	0	0
	14	1	1	1	0	0	0	0	0	0
	15	1	1	1	1	1	0	0	0	0
	16	1	1	1	1	0	0	0	0	0
24	17[a]	1	1	0	1	1	1	1	1	0
	18	1	1	1	1	0	0	0	0	0
	19	1	1	1	1	0	0	0	0	0
	20[a]	1	1	1	1	1	1	1	1	1

[a]Exception to regular sequence.

measures of interest: number of pragmatic functions, MLU, and rate of spontaneous imitation (functions, MLU, Imit); and three structured pragmatics measures: Presup, Dec, and Imp. Three measures are derived from the structured pragmatics tasks: proportion of verbal presupposition (encoding the new object), highest declarative type, and highest imperative type (Presup, Dec, Imp). Table 7 presents the intercorrelation matrix of these measures. Generally, the play measures are well correlated, as are the language measures. However, there is little correlation between the language measures and the play measures. Of the 12 possible correlations between spontaneous language measures and play measures, only three are significant. When age is statistically controlled, most of the coefficients drop; in fact, the correlation between functions and MLU vanishes completely. But the general picture is the same.

A second analysis examined possible sequential relationships between specific language and play categories. Each possible pairing of a language category L and a play category P was examined to determine if either category reliably preceded the other. Perfect sequencing was not expected, given the imprecision of the measuring system, so a sign test was used to compare the number of children for whom L preceded (i.e., appeared in the absence of) play category P with the number for whom P appeared without L. The results of these pairwise comparisons are internally consistent; that is, if a language category L precedes a play category P, so do other language categories that appear to be earlier ones; furthermore, L precedes all play categories that follow P. Similarly, for cases in which a play category P precedes a language category L, P and earlier categories all precede L and later categories. Thus, the results of this large number of comparisons can be presented in abbreviated form in Table 8. Language level appears to predict play level better than play level predicts language level, suggesting that if there are common underlying mechanisms for language and play, they may manifest themselves first in language. The only sequential finding of theoretical interest is that single symbolic play reliably precedes denial, which is closely followed by a package of highly symbolic uses of language: requests for information, requests for absent objects, and tense (reference to the past or future).

DISCUSSION

Pragmatic Functions in Spontaneous Language

The results reported above provide substantial support for the view that the range of pragmatic functions expressed grows steadily during the one-word and very early two-word phase. Furthermore, this development can be observed on the basis of a brief (30-minute) sample collected in a some-

Table 7. Intercorrelations of measures

	Functions	MLU	Imitation	Inform.	Declar.	Imper.	4Play	9Play	Symbolp	Substp
Functions	1.00	0.60[a]	-0.24	0.30	0.06	0.69	0.35	-0.06	0.32	0.21
MLU	-0.07[c]	1.00	-0.19	0.31	0.19	0.59[b]	0.51[a]	0.15	0.34	0.37
Imitation	0.00	0.00	1.00	0.35	-0.04	0.01	-0.30	-0.42[a]	-0.27	-0.31
Inform.	0.13	0.18	-0.29	1.00	0.73[b]	0.39[a]	0.18	0.38	0.16	0.39[a]
Declar.	-0.18	0.12	0.01	0.72[b]	1.00	0.38[a]	0.09	0.11	0.00	0.19
Imper.	0.05	0.12	0.31	0.30	0.40[a]	1.00	0.28	-0.10	0.19	0.18
4Play	0.00	0.35	-0.22	0.09	0.03	-0.06	1.00	0.54[b]	0.78[b]	0.56[b]
9Play	-0.12	0.21	-0.44[a]	0.39[a]	0.11	-0.15	0.59[b]	1.00	0.49[a]	0.55[b]
Symbolp	0.39[a]	0.33	-0.24	0.12	-0.02	0.12	0.80[b]	0.49[a]	1.00	0.60[b]
Substp	0.13	0.35	-0.28	0.36	0.17	0.08	0.55[b]	0.55[b]	0.59[b]	1.00
Age	0.89[b]	0.70[b]	-0.27	0.27	0.16	0.76[b]	0.40[a]	0.00	0.05	0.17

[a] $p < 0.05$.
[b] $p < 0.01$.
[c] Lower half-matrix contains partial correlations with age controlled.

Table 8.   Sequencing of specific language and play categories[a]

Play categories that precede language categories

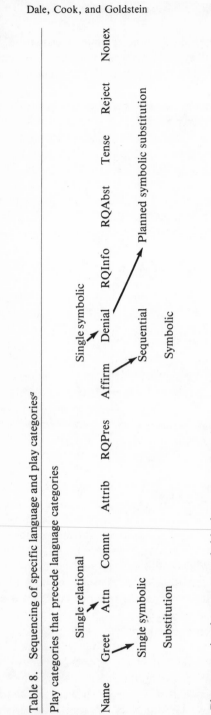

Play categories that are preceded by language categories

[a]Arrows represent a significant (0.05, two-tailed) tendency for one category to precede another.

what unfamiliar setting. However, the attempt of some investigators, for example, Ingram (1974), and Halliday (1975), to posit universal sequences of emergence of these functions is not supported by the cross-sectional data presented here.

Although MLU and the number of pragmatic functions expressed are highly correlated (0.60), this correlation is nonexistent (-0.07) when age is partialed out, reflecting the fact that both measures are highly correlated with age. Number of pragmatic functions expressed is probably a valid measure during the one-word period (at least for the range of functions assessed here), less so because of a ceiling effect when MLU rises substantially above 1.0. The conclusion is that the range of pragmatic functions in the second year of life is measurable and contributes information about language development not tapped by a measure of syntactic development such as MLU.

Structured Pragmatic Tasks

In general, the data from the imperative tasks resemble those of Snyder (1978) more than do the data from the declarative tasks, both in terms of correlation with age and with other language measures. Snyder interviewed children in their own homes, which may account for some of the difference. Also, she administered 10 tasks of each type, whereas only six tasks of each type were administered in this study. Both of those differences were necessary to produce a tool with potential clinical usefulness. It should be noted that all results were in the predicted direction, both with respect to the sign of the correlation coefficients, and the overall tendency to encode the new aspect of the situation.

Development of Play

A regular order of emergence of categories of play was observed, both with respect to a four level Piaget-derived system and a nine level Nicolich-derived system. The similarity of these results to those of Nicolich are even more striking in view of the fact that Nicolich observed children at home, whereas the data in this study were collected in a laboratory setting. Thus, the somewhat distinct dimensions of relational/symbolic/substitution play and of single/sequential/planned episodes appear to be well supported, although there is much individual variation within any one level as to the content of play.

The absence of correlation between level of play and age is surprising in view of the strong scalability of these cross-sectional data. It may simply reflect the small sample size at each age ($N=4$), or it may mean that individual differences in rate of play development are greater than developmental differences in this restricted age range. Another explanation may lie in the role of sex differences. Somewhat unexpectedly, girls appear to be more advanced in their play than do boys. Furthermore, level of play is correlated with age for girls, although not for boys. Fein (1975) suggested that play may be stimulus specific. In this study, each child was observed playing with two sets of toys. While both sets of toys included dolls, one set also included toy dishes, beds, and a car, while the other included blocks and sticks. It is possible that an interaction between sex, age, and type of toy is responsible for some aspects of our results, although the limited sample in this study makes this hypothesis impossible to test.

In summary, a brief (20-minute) sample of play can be reliably coded and evaluated with respect to regular sequence of development across an important, but generally difficult to assess, age span, 12 to 24 months. Mean level of play increases for girls with age, although it does not for boys.

Pragmatics and Symbolic Play

The correlations shown in Table 7 are not consistent with a close relationship between early language development and symbolic play. It is concluded that early language development is not closely tied to symbolic play.

An alternative interpretation of these essentially negative findings is that either the play assessment or the language assessment did not accurately estimate each child's level. The play measures failed to reflect overall developmental differences. However, the findings, with respect to sequence of development, are entirely consistent with other research in the field, as discussed above. The pragmatic function measure, although not scalable, was reasonably consistent with other work, and it reflected developmental differences.

There are at least two plausible interpretations of these findings. The first is that level of symbolic play is not closely tied to other aspects of cognitive development, despite Piaget's claim. Certainly a great deal of recent work on infant development has shown that various dimensions of infant cognition are not highly correlated, especially when age is partialed out (Lewis, 1976; Uzgiris and Hunt, 1975). If this interpretation is correct, it can only be concluded that early language development is not closely tied to symbolic play, and that it may or may not be related to other aspects of cognitive development. Bates (1976) and Snyder (1978), for example, argued for the importance of means-end relationships.

A second interpretation, however, is that early language and cognitive development are indeed relatively independent. The rough correspondence between them probably results from the importance of physiological development and general experience for both. The area of early language-cognition relationships has been the subject of many theories, but much more data are necessary before conclusions can be drawn.

The analysis of specific language and play categories reported in Table 8 does not substantially alter these conclusions. There is no overall trend for play categories to emerge before language categories. There is just one sequential finding of theoretical interest: single symbolic play reliably precedes denial and a group of highly symbolic uses of language.

A single cross-sectional study cannot be viewed as definitive evidence on these questions. Replications, both cross-sectional and longitudinal, are needed. Two additional methods might be used to extend these findings. The first is the investigation of pragmatics and play in other populations. Young hearing-impaired and Down's syndrome children are now being tested. To the extent that language development is a multi-determined process, there is no reason to expect the results from the three populations to be identical. Moore et al. (1977), for example, observed a high correlation between MLU and object permanence for a group of Down's syndrome children, even though similar work with normal children has not found such a correlation. A second method, of both theoretical and clinical significance, would be the use of training studies, for example, an investigation of whether acceleration of symbolic play facilitates language development. The chief problem of such an investigation would be devising a procedure for developing symbolic play that was not itself highly verbal, so that an effect on language development might be direct and not mediated by symbolic play.

ACKNOWLEDGMENTS

We wish to thank Diana Hughes for her help in conducting the experiment and in the design of the coding systems. We are also grateful to Carol Stoel-Gammon for her helpful comments on this paper. Requests for reprints should be sent to the first author, Child Development and Mental Retardation Center, University of Washington WJ-10, Seattle, Washington 98195.

REFERENCES

Austin, J. L. 1962. How To Do Things With Words. Oxford Univ. Press, Inc., New York.

Bates, E. 1976. Pragmatics and sociolinguistics in child language. In: D. Morehead and A. Morehead (eds.), Normal and Deficient Child Language, pp. 411–463. University Park Press, Baltimore.

Bates, E., Camaioni, L., and Volterra, V. 1975. The acquisition of performatives prior to speech. Merrill-Palmer Q. 21:205–226.

Bates, E., Benigni, L., Bretheron, I., Camaioni, L., and Volterra, V. 1977. Cognition and Communication from 9–13 months: A correlational study. Program on Cognitive and Perceptual Factors in Human Development Report No. 12, Institute for the Study of Intellectual Behavior, University of Colorado, April.

Blank, M., Gessner, M., and Esposito, A. 1979. Language without communication. J. Child Lang. 6:329–352.

Bloom, L. 1970. Language Development: Form and Function in Emerging Grammar. M.I.T. Press, Cambridge, Mass.

Bloom, L. 1973. One Word at a Time. Mouton, The Hague.

Bowerman, M. 1978. Words and sentences: Uniformity, individual variation, and shifts over time in patterns of acquisition. In: F. D. Minifie and L. L. Lloyd (eds.), Communicative and Cognitive Abilities—Early Behavioral Assessment, pp. 349–396. University Park Press, Baltimore.

Braine, M. D. S. 1976. Children's first word combinations. Monogr. Soc. Res. Child Dev. 41(1, Serial No. 164).

Brown, R. 1973. A First Language. Harvard University Press, Cambridge, Mass.

Clark, H. H., and Clark, E. V. 1977. Psychology and Language: An Introduction to Psycholinguistics. Harcourt Brace Jovanovich, Inc., New York.

Dale, P. S. 1980. Is early pragmatic development measurable? J. Child Lang. 7: 1–11.

deVilliers, J. G., and deVilliers, P. A. 1978. Semantics and syntax in the first two years: The output of form and function and the form and function of the input. In: F. D. Minifie and L. L. Lloyd (eds.), Communicative and Cognitive Abilities—Early Behavioral Assessment, pp. 309–348. University Park Press, Baltimore.

Dore, J. 1974. A pragmatic description of early language development. J. Psycholinguist. Res. 4:423–430.

Dore, J. 1975. Holophrases, speech acts, and language universals. J. Child Lang. 2:21–40.

Ervin-Tripp, S. 1974. The comprehension and production of requests by children. Papers and Reports on Child Language Development, No. 8, pp. 188–196. Committee on Linguistics, Stanford University.

Ervin-Tripp, S., and Mitchell-Kernan, C. (eds.). 1977. Child Discourse. Academic Press, Inc., New York.

Fein, G. 1975. The development of play: Style, structure, and situation. Paper presented at the biennial meeting of the Society for Research in Child Development, April, Denver.

Fenson, L., Kagan, J., Kearsley, R. B., and Zelazo, P. R. 1976. The developmental progression of manipulative play in the first two years. Child Dev. 47: 232–236.

Greenfield, P., and Smith, P. 1976. The Structure of Communication in Early Language Development. Academic Press, Inc., New York.

Halliday, M. A. K. 1975. Learning How to Mean. Elsevier-North Holland Publishing Company, New York.

Ingram, D. 1974. Stages in the development of one-word utterances. Paper presented to the Stanford Child Language Research Forum, April, Stanford.

Jeffree, D., and McConkey, R. 1974. Extending language through play. Spec. Educ. 1:13–16.

Lewis, M. (ed.). 1976. The Origins of Intelligence. Plenum Publishing Corp., New York.

Lovell, K., Hoyle, W., and Sidall, M. 1968. A study of some aspects of the play and language of young children with delayed speech. J. Child Psychol. Psychiatry 9:41–50.

Lowe, M. 1975. Trends in the development of representative play in infants from one to three years—An observational study. J. Child Psychol. Psychiatry 16: 33–47.

Moore, K., Clark, D., Mael, M., Dawson-Myers, G., Rajotte, P., and Stoel-Gammon, C. 1977. The relationship between language and object permanence development: A study of Down's infants and children. Paper presented at the biennial meeting of the Society for Research in Child Development, March, New Orleans.

Morehead, D. M., and Morehead, A. 1974. From signal to sign: A Piagetian view of thought and language during the first two years. In: R. L. Schiefelbusch and L. L. Lloyd (eds.), Language Perspectives—Acquisition, Retardation, and Intervention, pp. 153–190. University Park Press, Baltimore.

Nicolich, L. McC. Beyond sensori-motor intelligence: Assessment of symbolic maturity through analyses of pretend play. Unpublished paper, Douglass College, Rutgers University.

Piaget, J. 1962. [Play, Dreams and Imitation in Childhood.] (C. Gattegno and F. M. Hodgson, Trans.) W. W. Norton & Co., New York. (Originally published, 1945.)

Snyder, L. S. 1978. Communicative and cognitive abilities and disabilities in the sensorimotor period. Merrill-Palmer Quarterly 24:161–180.

Sugarman, S. 1976. Some organizational aspects of preverbal communication. In: I. Markova (ed.), The Social Context of Language. John Wiley, New York.

Uzgiris, I. C., and Hunt, J. McV. 1975. Assessment in Infancy: Ordinal Scales of Psychological Development. University of Illinois Press, Champaign, Ill.

Weiner, E., and Weiner, B. 1974. Differentiation of retarded and normal children through toy-play analysis. Multivariate Behav. Res. 9:245–252.

The Form and Function of Children's Gestures Accompanying Verbal Directives

Louise Cherry Wilkinson and Karen L. Rembold

It has become increasingly clear that children manifest a high degree of social and communicative competence at an early age. One of the ways that children actively influence their environment is by expressing their wants and needs to others by means of verbal directives. This study examines how children use directives in conjunction with their nonverbal gestures and how this usage changes during the period of rapid language development—the third year.

A directive is a request for action that can either be direct, taking the form of an imperative *(Give me some water),* or indirect, taking the form of a question *(Will you give me some water?)* or a hint *(I sure could use something to drink).* One readily observable aspect of directives is that they are social. One cannot request action from another person without somehow communicating with that other person. For adults, the social nature of a directive is usually communicated by either looking at the person in question while issuing the directive, or by touching them or mentioning their name in connection with the directive (Duncan and Fiske, 1977).

Not all socially directed imperatives, questions, and hints are directives, for example, jokes and insults. To distinguish directives from nondirectives, Labov and Fanshel (1977) formulated the Rule of Requests and the Rule of Indirect Requests. The Rule of Requests states that in

This research was supported by a grant to Louise Cherry Wilkinson by the Graduate School Research Committee and the Wisconsin Alumni Research Foundation.

order to issue a directive, the speaker must furnish the listener with an imperative to perform a specific action at a specific time, and the listener must believe the following:

1. There is a need for the action.
2. There is a need for the request (i.e., the listener would not perform the action without being requested to).
3. The speaker has the authority to tell the listener to perform the action.
4. The listener has the ability to perform the action.
5. The listener has either the willingness or the obligation to perform the action.

If all of these conditions are present, then the speaker will be interpreted as making a valid request for action.

The Rule of Indirect Requests states that in order to make an indirect request, the speaker must address a request for information, or an assertion, to the listener about one of the following:

1. The existential status of an action to be performed by the listener.
2. The consequences of performing such an action.
3. The time at which such an action could be performed.
4. Any of the preconditions for a valid request given in the Rule of Requests.

If all of the other preconditions stated in the Rule of Requests are in effect, the speaker is understood to be making an indirect request for action.

There have been no systematic examinations of how the relationship between verbal directives and the nonverbal behaviors that accompany them change during the preschool years. However, there have been several studies of preschool children's production and comprehension of directives (see Ervin-Tripp, 1977; Garvey, 1975; Read and Cherry, 1978; Shatz, 1975). Taken together, these previous studies have provided information about preschool children's developing communicative ability to communicate their needs and wants to others.

For example, Garvey (1975) examined production of and responsiveness to directives by children ages 3 to 5. She found that the most common form of directive was the direct request, and the majority of directives were acknowledged by child listeners. Her data also show that indirect requests occurred with more frequency and were more often successful in eliciting a response from older listeners than from younger children.

Read and Cherry (1977) found that most of the directives elicited from 4-year-old children were in a verbal form (e.g., *Give me the ham-*

mer), whereas the most common form of directives elicited from 2-year-old children was the gestural form (e.g., pointing to a desired object). Read and Cherry found that 2-year-olds could control their use of gesture in forming directives (e.g., by varying gestures from subtle ones to straightforward ones) although they apparently had less ability to control their speech in forming directives. In addition, they found 2-year-olds using gestures when their verbal directives were not immediately comprehended. These observations led Read and Cherry to conclude that "systematic modification to elicit listener cooperation is achieved first in the gestural modality." This finding is important because it reinforces the importance of nonverbal behavior to the language-learning child, and suggests how the function of gestures in relation to verbal directives may change over time.

The heavy reliance on gestural directives found by Read and Cherry among 2-year-olds, who are novices to the language game, and the relative absence of gestural directives found among 4-year-olds, who are more linguistically skilled, provides support for the viewpoint that language is an emerging socio-cognitive skill in which there is continuity between gestural and verbal means of communication during the course of development.

Other research supports the view that gestural and verbal communication forms are continuous (Bruner, 1975; Dore, 1975; Trevarthen, 1974). Although most of these studies focus on nonverbal behaviors as precursors to linguistic development, and hence imply that nonverbal behavior decreases as verbal behavior increases, there also is research (Jancovic, Devoe, and Wiener, 1975) that suggests that nonverbal behavior increases in amount, and becomes more complex over time, in much the same way that verbal behavior increases in complexity over time.

One reason for this discrepancy in results may be that different aspects of nonverbal behavior have been observed in different studies. For example, it may be that the function of nonverbal behaviors vis-à-vis linguistic behavior may change as the child becomes linguistically skilled; this change in function may, in turn, affect the form of the nonverbal behavior that predominates in the child's repertoire. As the child's language ability increases, for example, nonverbal behavior may supplement and extend the verbal message rather than act as a substitute for the verbal component. As a result, certain nonverbal behaviors, such as pointing, that serve to communicate a message when verbal skills are lacking, may decrease as the child ages, whereas nonverbal behaviors such as expressive hand gestures, which can serve to elaborate a verbal message, may increase in number as well as in complexity as the child ages. This hypothesis is consistent with the Jancovic et al. (1975) data, although Jancovic et al. provide a different interpretation for their results.

FUNCTION OF GESTURES

There has not been a systematic examination of both the form of various gestures used by young children, as well as the function of these gestures in relation to the child's verbal expression, even though some researchers (e.g., Bruner, 1975) have carefully examined the communicative functions of the nonverbal behavior of prelinguistic children. Examination of the types of nonverbal behaviors that seem meaningful for language-learning children, as well as of the functions that these nonverbal behaviors fulfill in relation to the child's verbalizations, is needed. A system of analysis, which was devised for this study, emphasizes the function of nonverbal behaviors vis-à-vis verbal ones, and discriminates the following dimensions of behavioral form: eye contact with a target object, the adult's body, and/or the adult's eyes; solitary gestural activity or gestural movement involving objects and/or the adult; and gestural proximity versus distance.

There are at least three functions that gestures can serve in relation to verbal directives:

1. A gesture can specify a part of speech that is critical for the adult's compliance with a particular directive, which would remain unclear if the verbal message were considered alone.
2. A gesture can essentially replicate the critical directive information, which is already present in the verbal message.
3. A gesture can symbolize a complete idea by adding another layer of meaning to the verbal message.

A gesture can be either indirectly related or entirely unrelated to the verbal message and it is likely that as children's linguistic ability increases, the manner in which their gestures are related to language will change. For example, one might expect that as children grow older, gestures play less of a specifying role and more of a symbolic or redundant role.

FORMS OF GESTURES

Eye Contact

Many researchers have found that eye contact is a very sensitive and common mode of communication for mothers and their young children. Eye contact is also one of the most important nonverbal behaviors of adults (Duncan and Fiske, 1977; Henley, 1977; Weitz, 1979). For example, Stern (1974) has found that the gaze of 3- to 4-month-old infants toward their mothers significantly increases the probability that their mothers will return the gaze. Schaffer, Collis, and Parsons (1977) have found that while interacting with their 1- and 2-year-old children, mothers looked at the children an average of 90% of the time. For mother-child dyads, two meaningful types of gaze behavior are eye-to-eye contact and eye contact with objects. Children as young as age 1 have been observed to gaze into their mothers' eyes during games such as peekaboo, as if to determine whose turn it is, or to see if their mother is ready to play (Argyle and Ingham, 1972; Bruner, 1975). With regard to objects, Scaife and Bruner (1975) have found that, by the age of 9 months, children are frequently inclined to follow the gaze of an adult when the adult's gaze is directed at an object away from the child. A combination of these two types of behaviors, for example, the child's alternating gazes between an object and an adult's eyes, is cited by Golinkoff (in press) as one of the clearest examples of intentional communication among prelinguistic children. Therefore, because of their importance to the child, instances of eye contact with the adult's eyes and with significant objects are included in this study. Eye contact with the adult's body was included because the child frequently uses an adult's body as an object in play.

Gestural Interactions

Gestural (hand and body) manipulation of objects is perhaps the single most common form of behavior in which young children engage. Piaget (1952) suggested that children learn about causality and language through their manipulation of objects. Learning that the capability for action distinguishes animate and inanimate objects is an important aspect of learning about the world and the use of language (Golinkoff, in press). In this study, the child's gestural interactions with the adult are distinguished from gestural interactions with toys.

As in the case of eye contact mentioned above, the combination of these two types of gestures results in a third, more complex, type of interaction—gestural interaction with an object and an adult simultaneously. Sugarman-Bell (1978) notes that this type of interaction is an indication of truly social behavior on the part of the child. Finally, this study also includes analysis of gestural activity that involves neither objects nor adults—that which occurs in isolation.

Gestural Proximity Versus Distance

Studies of nonverbal behavior generally distinguish gestures that operate on objects within reach from those that operate on objects at a distance (Bruner, 1975; Lyons, cited in Bruner; Shatz, in press). This distinction frequently has been made in the instance of touching an object versus pointing to an object. However, it logically extends to the other categories of gestural interaction in the study, with the exception of solitary gestural activity. A child could touch the adult's body (proximal), or could reach for the adult's body (distal). Along similar lines, the child could interact with both an object and an adult within reach, or the child could interact with both an object and an adult at a distance. For more detailed definitions of all of the dimensions of this coding scheme, and for examples of each, see the chapter Appendix.

THE STUDY

The Data

Three native English-speaking, white, middle class, male children were recruited through newspaper birth records in the Madison, Wisconsin area, to serve as the subjects for the study. These children were observed at age 2 and again when they were 2½ years old.

Audio and video recordings were made of the children in free play sessions with each parent, in their homes. The videotapes were transcribed and were examined for instances of verbal directives. (A full description of the methods of data collection is available in Wilkinson and Rembold, in press.) One- and two-word utterances are not uncommon among 2-year-old children, and the meaning of these utterances is often unclear from the verbalization alone. Therefore, both the verbal and nonverbal context often must be considered in judging whether a specific utterance is a directive. Context is routinely considered by sociolinguists (for example, Hymes, 1974) to be crucial in interpreting speech, and the research of Shatz (1975) demonstrates that even very young children depend heavily on context in decoding verbal information.

One important aspect of the context of children's utterances is the verbal and nonverbal responsiveness of others to their speech. This responsiveness is especially important when one considers that directives are one of the means by which children influence their environment. As a result, verbal directives for this study are defined as lexical or nonlexical verbalizations that appear to fulfill the Rules of Direct or the Rules of Indirect Requests (Labov and Fanshel, 1977), *and* that were responded to by the adult as a direct or indirect request for action. In addition, the following requirements for audio and visual clarity were used: 1) the audio recording for the entire directive sequence was required to be undistorted for both parent and child; 2) both participants were required to be "on camera" for the entire directive sequence; and 3) any object mentioned in the directive sequence was required to be "on camera." After all instances of verbal directives were identified from the tapes and transcripts, two steps were taken. The first step was noting whether an agent, action, or object was verbalized for each directive so that a comparison with any nonverbal indications of these categories could be made. The second step was coding the nonverbal behavior accompanying each verbal directive with respect to its form and function as described above. In other words, the nonverbal behavior was observed in order to determine whether: 1) eye contact was made with an object, the adult's body, and/or the adult's eyes; 2) gestural activity involved an object, the adult, both an adult and an object, or whether it was solitary; 3) gestural activity was performed proximally or at a distance; and 4) the function of the gesture was to specify, duplicate, or symbolize information contained in the verbal directive, assuming that the gesture was directly related to the verbal message.

Results

The results of the analyses, summarized in Tables 1 and 2 show a trend in the increased production of verbal directives at 2½ years compared to 2 years (Dan, Kevin), which is consistent with the Read and Cherry (1977) finding that older preschool children produced more directives in a verbal form in comparison with younger preschool children. This finding is not surprising because 2½-year-olds are more linguistically competent than 2-year-old children. However, Read and Cherry's findings might lead one to expect a corresponding decrease in the number of meaningful (that is, specifying, redundant, or symbolic functions) gestures accompanying the verbal directives, yet no such trend was found. Dan had about the same number of meaningful gestures at age 2 and at age 2½; Harry had more at age 2½ than at age 2; and Kevin had more at age 2 than at age 2½.

There was also a trend (Table 1) toward an increased number of verbalized agents, actions, and/or objects in the directives from 2- to 2½ year olds. This trend also is attributable to a comparative increase in linguistic competence in the 2½-year-old child. Read and Cherry's findings also might lead one to expect a corresponding decrease in the number of agents, actions, or objects specified by gesture. However, there is actually a very slight trend toward an increased number of gesturally specified agents, actions, and objects (Dan, Harry).

Table 1.   Number and proportion of verbal directives

| | | | Focus of verbal directive | | |
Child	Age	Number of verbal directives	Agent	Action	Object
Dan	2	8	0.12	0.62	0.25
	2½	20	0.25	0.80	0.60
Harry	2	19	0.05	0.15	0.33
	2½	18	0.11	0.38	0.16
Kevin	2	1	0.00	0.00	0.00
	2½	7	0.28	0.14	0.42

With regard to gestural form, three promising trends (Table 2) were observed. The first was a trend from gestural interactions dealing solely with objects, to interactions involving adults, and/or adults and objects simultaneously (Harry, Kevin). This finding may reflect the child's increasing ability to engage in more complex social interactions (Bruner, 1975; Sugarman-Bell, 1978). The second trend was from primarily proximal (touching) gestures directed toward adults and objects to those that included distal gestures (Dan, Harry). This finding suggests an increasing decontextualization of gesture, similar to the decontextualization that occurs in language (Blank, Rose, and Berlin, 1978). The third trend observed involved a shift from primarily interactive gestures (with objects, or adults, or both) to those that included solitary gestures. This trend could suggest the child's increased desire for independence, or a growing ability to appreciate movement for the sake of movement, i.e., an appreciation of the more abstract nature of gesture. All of the children tended to interact gesturally more with objects than with adults during their directive sequences and this apparent preference for interaction with inanimate objects did not change with age.

Two trends emerged with respect to the eye contact categories. The first was a trend toward eye contact with the adult's body and/or eyes, as opposed to eye contact primarily with objects (Dan, Harry). This trend may indicate the child's increasing ability to engage in more complex social interaction, paralleling the shift, described above, from gestural interactions with objects to gestural interactions with adults. The second trend in eye contact was a slight tendency for the children to engage in more alternate looking at 2½ years than at 2 years, i.e., looking from an object to the adult, and back to the object again.

This category was not part of the coding scheme, and therefore is not represented in Table 2. Alternate looking may reflect the child's growing ability to engage in complex gaze patterns, although it may reflect more sophisticated social and communicative skills as well. For instances,

Table 2.   Proportion of gestures in each behavioral form

Child	Age	Proximity		Interactions			
		Proximal	Distal	Child with object	Child with adult	Child with adult and object	Child alone
Dan	2	0.92	0.08	0.54	0.15	0.23	0.08
	2½	0.58	0.42	0.42	0.16	0.19	0.23
Harry	2	0.75	0.25	0.68	0.09	0.06	0.17
	2½	0.45	0.55	0.44	0	0.36	0.20
Kevin	2	0.50	0.50	1.00	0	0	0
	2½	0.57	0.43	0.28	0.07	0.36	0.28

Table 3. Proportions of gestures in eye contact forms of behavior

Child	Age	Eye contact			Gestural function				
		With object	With adult's body	With adult's eyes	Specifying	Redundant	Symbolic	Unrelated	No movement
Dan	2	0.64	0.18	0.18	0.33	0.33	0.11	0.22	0
	2½	0.37	0.37	0.25	0.36	0.27	0.09	0.27	0
Harry	2	0.84	0.16	0	0.37	0.16	0	0.47	0
	2½	0.69	0.14	0.17	0.89	0	0	0.11	0
Kevin	2	0.50	0	0.50	1.00	0	0	0	0
	2½	0.71	0	0.29	0.33	0	0.11	0.55	0

Golinkoff (in press) considers this gaze pattern to be one of the clearest forms of intentional communicative behavior.

With regard to the gestural functions, no clear trends emerged from the data (Table 3). The children in this study appeared equally likely to use gestures to specify an ambiguous part of the verbal directive at 2½ years as they were at 2 years; and they were just as likely to use gestures to reiterate part of the verbal directive and to use gestures symbolically at 2 years and at 2½ years. In addition, there was no developmental trend with respect to gestures that were related or unrelated to the verbal directive. At both 2 and 2½ years, however, the children were more likely to accompany their directives with gestures that were related to the verbal context, as opposed to gestures that were unrelated.

Conclusion

In summary, the findings from this study demonstrate the importance of gesture to the preschool child at age 2 and at age 2½. The three children produced more gestures related to verbal directive content than gestures unrelated to verbal directive content.

The increased gestural specification of agents, actions, and objects in directives, corresponding to increased verbal specification of agents, actions, and objects, suggests that communication in both modes develops rapidly between the second and third year. As children become more aware of grammar, and more facile in expressing it verbally, they also become more skilled in expressing grammar gesturally. This finding supports Jancovic et al.'s (1975) position that nonverbal communication continues to grow in importance as age increases, and does not merely act as a precursor to linguistic development.

It appears that the general function of gestures for young preschool children is to supplement verbal communication. The data suggest that this does not change dramatically between age 2 and age 2½. Nor is there any clear pattern of change in the functions of specifying parts of speech, of duplicating, and of symbolizing the verbal directive. The function of gesture—to increasingly specify the grammatical categories of agent, action, and object—does change, however. This finding, together with the finding of Read and Cherry (1977) that 2½-year-olds use more gestural directives than 4-year-olds, suggests that over time, the role of gesture with regard to directives may be more complex than expected. While the findings of Read and Cherry (1977) seem to indicate that the role of gestural directives decreases in importance as the child becomes more verbally proficient, this data suggest that the role of gestural directives may merely change with an increase in age. Gestures may not necessarily take the place of verbalization as the child becomes more linguistically competent, as Read and Cherry (1977) conclude, but they may increasingly serve to supplement the verbal message.

This study also provides a record of the increasing ability of 2½-year-old children to engage in complex social interactions, both verbally and gesturally. An increased number of verbal directives were produced by 2½-year-olds thus extending the pattern that Read and Cherry (1977) found among 2½- and 4-year-olds; and more agents, actions, and objects were verbalized in these directives. In addition, children of that age produce more gestures that involve interactions with adults; they engage in more interactions that involve both adults and objects; and they engage in more, and more complex, eye contact with adults.

Research focusing on the gestures that accompany verbal directives of older children, or on gestures that accompany the verbal directives of children to their peers, would greatly contribute to our knowledge of the role of gesture in relation to directives. Finally, considerable information on the function of gestures in general could be obtained by studying gestures in young children that accompany forms other than directives.

ACKNOWLEDGMENT

The authors gratefully acknowledge Philip Dale for his helpful comments on an earlier draft of this paper.

REFERENCES

Argyle, M., and Ingham, R. 1972. Gaze, mutual gaze and proximity. Semiotica 4(1):32–49.

Blank, M., Rose, S., and Berlin, L. 1978. The Language of Learning: The Preschool Years. Grune & Stratton, New York.

Bruner, J. 1975. From communication to language: A psychological perspective. Cognition 3:225–287.

Dore, J. 1975. Holophrases, speech acts and language universals. J. Child Lang. 2(1):21–40.

Duncan, S., Jr., and Fiske, D. 1977. Face to Face Interaction: Research, Methods and Theory. Laurence Erlbaum Associates, Hillsdale, N.J.

Ervin-Tripp, S. 1977. Wait for me, roller skate! In: S. Ervin-Tripp and C. Mitchell-Kernan (eds.), Child Discourse. Academic Press, Inc., New York.

Garvey, C. 1975. Requests and responses in children's speech. J. Child Lang. 2: 41–63.

Golinkoff, R. The influence of Piagetian theory on the study of the development of communication. In: I. Sigel, D. Brodzinski, and R. Golinkoff (eds.), Piagetian Theory and Research: New Directions and Applications. Laurence Erlbaum Associates, Hillsdale, N.J. In press.

Henley, N. 1977. Body Politics: Power, Sex, and Nonverbal Communication. Newbury House Publishers, Rowley, Mass.

Hymes, D. 1974. Foundations in Sociolinguistics. University of Pennsylvania, Philadelphia.

Jancovic, M., Devoe, S., and Wiener, M. 1975. Age-related changes in hand and arm movements as nonverbal communication: Some conceptualizations and an empirical exploration. Child Dev. 46:922–928.

Labov, W., and Fanshel, D. 1977. Therapeutic Discourse: Psychotherapy as Conversation. Academic Press, Inc., New York.

Piaget, J. 1952. The Origins of Intelligence in Children. International Universities Press, Inc., New York.

Read, B., and Cherry, L. 1977. Children's spontaneous use in elicited situations. In: W. Beach, S. Fox, and S. Philosoph (eds.), Papers presented at the 13th Regional Meeting, Chicago Linguistic Society, Chicago.

Read, B., and Cherry, L. 1978. Preschool children's production of directive forms. Discourse Processes 1(3):233–245.

Scaife, M., and Bruner, J. S. 1975. The capacity for joint visual attention in the infant. Nature 253(5489):265–266.

Schaffer, H., Collis, G., and Parsons, G. 1977. Vocal interchange and visual regard in verbal and preverbal children. In: H. R. Schaffer (ed.), Studies in Mother-Infant Interaction. Academic Press, Inc., London.

Shatz, M. 1975. On the development of communicative understandings: An early strategy for interpreting and responding to messages. Unpublished doctoral dissertation, University of Pennsylvania, Philadelphia.

Shatz, M. On mechanisms of language acquisition: Can features of the communicative environment account for development? In: L. Gleitman and E. Wanner (eds.), Language Acquisition: The State of the Art. In press.

Stern, D. 1974. Mother and infant at play: The dyadic interaction involving facial, vocal and gaze behaviors. In: M. Lewis and L. Rosenblum (eds.), The Origins of Behavior, Vol. 1: The Effect of the Infant on its Caregiver. John Wiley & Sons, Inc., New York.

Sugarman-Bell, S. 1978. Some organizational aspects of preverbal communication. In: I. Markova (ed.), The Social Context of Language. John Wiley & Sons, Inc., New York.

Trevarthen, C. 1974. Conversations with a two-month old. New Sci. 62(896): 230–235.

Weitz, S. 1979. Nonverbal Communication. Oxford Univ. Press, Inc., New York.

Wilkinson, L. C., and Rembold, K. 1980. Preschool children's production of gestural directives. Lang. Sci. 2:127–143.

APPENDIX

Proximal (Touching)

$C \times O$ Child interaction with object. A gesture is considered to possess a $C \times O$-proximal form if the child intentionally and actively touches an object, as in holding, grasping, or manipulating. Apparently accidental contact with an object, such as brushing against a toy, or non-active contact, such as resting against a couch, are not included.

$C \times A$ Child interaction with adult. A gesture is considered to possess a $C \times A$-proximal form if the child intentionally touches the adult. Gestures falling into this category include climbing on an adult's body, tapping an adult to gain attention, and grasping any part of the adult's body. Accidental or non-active, ongoing sequences, such as bumping into an adult or sitting in an adult's lap, are not included in this category.

$C \times O \times A$ Child interaction with adult and object simultaneously. A gesture is considered to possess a $C \times O \times A$-proximal form if the child and adult simultaneously and intentionally touch an object. Examples of gestures included in this category are handing an object to an adult, taking an object from an adult, and playing with an object that is being held by an adult. Accidental or non-active sequences, such as a book lying unattended in a child's or in an adult's laps, are not included in this category.

Distal (Not touching)

$C \times O$ Child interaction with object. A gesture is considered to possess a $C \times O$-distal form if the child intentionally interacts with an object at a distance, such as pointing to, nodding toward, or reaching for an object.

$C \times A$ Child interaction with adult. A gesture is considered to possess a $C \times A$-distal form if the child intentionally interacts with the adult from a distance, such as pointing to, nodding toward, or reaching for the adult.

$C \times O \times A$ Child interaction with adult and object simultaneously. A gesture is considered to possess a $C \times O \times A$–distal form if the child intentionally interacts with an object and an adult simultaneously, when both the adult and the object are at a distance. Examples of gestures in this category are the child's throwing an object to the adult (or similarly receiving a thrown object), the child reaching for an object in the adult's hands, and the child's pointing to an object that the adult is already pointing to (or vice versa).

Solitary-C (Child acting alone)

Gestures falling into the C category are those in which the child interacts neither with the adult nor with an object, either proximally or at a distance, but makes isolated body movements that appear to be related to the directive. Examples of gestures in this category would be a child waving his arms up and down agitatedly, opening and closing his hand, or hitting his elbow with his fist.

EYE CONTACT CATEGORIES

Direction of eye contact is determined by the child's eyes when they are clearly in view of the camera, and by head movements when these movements appear to clearly indicate the direction of gaze.

Eye/Object

The child makes eye contact with a significant object, such as one being played with, pointed to, or talked about. Gazing into the distance or at nonsignificant objects (nonsignificant with respect to the directive) is not included in this category.

Eye/Body

The child makes eye contact with any part of the adult's body, except for the adult's eyes.

Eye/Eye

The child makes eye contact with the adult's eyes, whether the adult appears to return the child's gaze or not (although it's a rare circumstance when the adult doesn't return the gaze).

GESTURAL FUNCTION CATEGORIES

Gestures Directly Related to Verbal Directive Content

Specific   A gesture is determined to have a specifying function if it serves to specify a part of speech (e.g., noun, verb, pronoun, adjective) the meaning of which is ambiguous when the verbal message is taken alone, yet is essential information for the adult to have in order to comply with the child's directive.

> Example A   Dan: Uh, Daddy, Daddy, take that.
>   Father: You want me to take this?

Dan is playing with some plastic rings on the floor. He picks up one of them, and with a wide gesture, holds it out to his father saying, "Uh, Daddy, Daddy, take that." By holding out the ring to his father and indicating that his father take it, Dan specifies what he means by the pronoun "that."

Redundant   A gesture is considered redundant if it adds no new information that the adult must have for compliance with the child's directive, but which simply reiterates part or all of the verbal message nonverbally.

> Example B   Dan: A-ah, oh, pway baw (play ball).
>   Father: You're not a very good thrower, though.

Dan and his father have been playing with another toy when Dan directs his father to play ball with him. As he talks, Dan takes the ball, crawls away from his father, and throws the ball to him. The function of this gesture is one of redundance, because the information conveyed by throwing the ball to the father has already been conveyed in the verbal directive.

Symbolic   A gesture is considered to have a symbolic function if it involves acting upon an object that appears to be a substitute for the genuine object of intention, or if an action is abbreviated so that the shortened gesture appears to stand for another, more complete gesture.

> Example C   Dan: Teecoh (tickle).
>   Father: What do you want to do to Daddy?

Dan grabs a pillow from the sofa and pulls it onto his father's lap. Then Dan falls onto the pillow and digs his hand into the pillow as if tickling it, laughing and saying "Teecoh." From his father's comment "What do you want to do to Daddy?" we can see that the father interprets Dan's tickling of the pillow as symbolic, that is, representing a person to be tickled.

Gestures Not Directly Related to Verbal Directive Content

Gestures falling into this category are either totally unrelated to the verbal directive or they are indirectly related, such as ongoing movement that involves the directive's subject matter, or a demonstration of affective states.

> Example D   Dan: Ca cuz, cacuz.
>   Father: Do you need more crackers?
>   Dan: Yes, yes...

While making his request, Dan puts his arms on the sofa, then turns so that the side of his face is on the sofa. Then he makes movements with his feet as if to get onto the sofa, and kicks his feet. These motions appear to be completely unrelated to Dan's directive concerning crackers.

Parental Influences on Language Development

It has been less than 12 years since the investigation of adult speech to young children began. Somewhat misleadingly called "motherese," this topic is now one of the most fruitful areas of research. Snow, in Chapter 12, and Cross, in Chapter 13, discuss why descriptive data were so slow in being collected, and the extent to which the data, once collected, disconfirmed a number of widely held assumptions about the degraded quality of the linguistic data available to children.

Now that it is a well established fact that adult-child language differs in many ways from adult-adult language, research in this area has changed, in Catherine Snow's apt phrase, "from input to interaction." This characterization is appropriate in three senses. First, many of the most important aspects of the special quality of adult-child communication concern the nature of interaction: special devices for attention-getting and attention-holding, patterns of topic-initiation and topic-continuation, and other characteristic ways in which conversation partners respond to each other. Snow's hypothesis concerning the importance of experience with games and routines in providing an opportunity to learn structure through "slot filling" is a generalization and a downward extension of this finding to the prelinguistic and very early linguistic periods.

Second, the process that underlies this communication style is interactional. In effective parent-child communication, meaning is primary. Neither partner is excessively concerned with linguistic form; each partner fits a meaning as best as he or she can to the other's utterance, then responds to that meaning. To the extent that either partner shows a lack of attention, understanding, or interest in that meaning, the other partner is likely to modify his or her utterance. As a result, parents' utterances are made just simple enough for the child.

The third sense, which is based on a slightly different meaning for the word interaction, is tied both to the statistical sense of the word and to the Piagetian sense, as in the phrase "development is the interaction of the organism and the environment." The point here is that linguistic input to the child will have an effect, but only as a function of the child's current level of development. The child learns from phenomena that attract attention and present a challenge because they are at the "growing edge" of his or her ability. Thus, at different points in development, the same experience may have very different effects. Both Nelson's theoretical model in Chapter 14 and Cross' methodological paper are concerned with this point.

For obvious ethical and practical reasons, a direct experimental-manipulative test of the importance of adult-child language cannot be conducted. Therefore, the testing in this section is limited to indirect correlational methods with their inherent ambiguity (is the mother teaching the child, or just responding to the child's language?), and small-scale experiments. Cross points out some conceptual and methodological problems that must be faced in this research. Nelson suggests some innovative methodologies. Cross is dubious about the value of experimental work. As is pointed out in the introduction to Section III, both experimental and correlational methods have limitations, and only by combining them can researchers hope to clarify causal relationships.

The study of speech to exceptional children may also be helpful because with various disabilities, highly correlated aspects of language may be partially disentangled. For example, it is not yet clear whether children's comprehension, or their production level has the greatest influence on parental speech. The two are highly correlated in normal children, but less so in language-impaired populations, therefore, comparisons of adult speech to children with varied patterns of abilities may clarify this issue. The little evidence now available on speech to impaired children is mixed; Cross reports studies that suggest substantial differences in speech to children with various disabilities, whereas other studies find overall similarities in speech to children who are matched on intellectual and/or language level.

Academics interested in children are often asked for advice. Most often they are reluctant to give it because they are intimately aware of the limitations of the understanding of human development. Nevertheless, the evidence now available does suggest an answer to any parent who wishes to know how to facilitate a child's language development, an answer that has been expressed very well by Roger Brown:

> Believe that your child can understand more than he or she can say, and seek, above all, to communicate. To understand and be understood. To keep your minds fixed on the same target... There is no set of rules of how to talk to a child that can even approach what you unconsciously know. If you concentrate on communicating, everything else will follow.[1]

What children need, above all, are parents who believe that it is both possible and valuable to communicate with them.

---

[1]Roger Brown. 1977. Introduction in Catherine A. Snow and Charles Ferguson (eds.), Talking to Children. Cambridge University Press, New York. p. 28.

Social Interaction and Language Acquisition

Catherine E. Snow

The aim of this chapter is to assess the importance of social interaction at three points in the acquisition of language and communication. For each of these points, the available research on the effect that social interaction might have on the child's discovery of the principles of communication and language is discussed. The assumption underlying this approach is that it is useless to discuss or evaluate any general hypothesis about the role of social interaction in language acquisition. What is needed, in order to establish the theoretical implications of research already completed and to guide future research efforts, are predictions of the effects of specific social experiences in the child's life on specific aspects of his communicative and linguistic growth.

Therefore, the weakest of the various hypotheses about the role of social interaction in language acquisition—that there is some positive effect—is not discussed here. It is clear that the child's access to social interaction with warm and caring adults is necessary for normal physical and cognitive development, and that the lack of sufficient access to such interaction will lead to a general developmental deficit. The general hypothesis, then, that access to social interaction is a prerequisite to normal language acquisition, is too weak to generate interesting testable predictions.

Instead, hypotheses that state that specific experiences in the life of the infant or child contribute to or are prerequisites to the acquisition of specific communicative abilities are discussed. The hypotheses presented are specific enough to be evaluated and general enough to have interesting and important theoretical implications. Specific predictions for various points in the child's development are discussed, and language acquisition is treated as a special case of the acquisition of communicative ability. It is assumed that the same principles relevant to the acquisition of a first language are relevant to the acquisition of a second language, at least in childhood, and that second language acquisition data can, therefore, be used to test hypotheses about the relevance of certain social experiences.

The role of social interaction in language acquisition during the early stages of language acquisition is not discussed. This omission may seem paradoxical because it is for precisely that age period, 18–36 months, that most researchers try to link aspects of the social environment to advances in linguistic development. (See, for example, Cazden, 1965; Cross, 1977, 1978; Nelson, Carskaddon, and Bonvillian, 1973; Newport, Gleitman, and Gleitman, 1977.) Nonetheless, the period of early language acquisition may give the least basis for making a case that social interaction contributes to the development of communication and language. The difficulty of finding any effect of social interaction during the third and fourth years of life on communicative development probably results not from the absence of any effect, but from the fact that almost all children are in a nearly optimal situation for language acquisition during this age.

After children start to talk, the variation between children in the availability of appropriate social experience decreases. This restricted variation may well result from the nature of conversation and conversational rules. The basic principle of conversation is the organization of a series of utterances by two or more speakers around a single topic. This principle dictates that a large percentage of the utterances addressed to children will be semantically and syntactically simple because they will be related to the child's own remarks, and to the conversational topics introduced by the child. Another principle of conversation is that speakers should be responsive to one another; that is, questions should be answered, comments should be acknowledged, and directions should be followed. This principle ensures that the speech addressed to children will be quite redundant because the child's failure to respond occasions a conversational breakdown, which leads to repetition (Bohannon and Marquis, 1977). Furthermore, the principle of responsiveness implies that incomprehensible utterances must be clarified. The adult's need to clarify the meaning of a child's utterances leads to the use of explanations and clarification questions, and the potential of that practice for providing information about the structure of language has been widely discussed (Cherry and Lewis, 1976; Nelson, Carskaddon, and Bonvillian, 1973). Any interlocutor who knows the basic principles of carrying on a conversation will provide the child with highly usable information about the nature of language, as long as the child's own competence in the language is sufficient to elicit application of the conversational rules. In the case of the prelinguistic child, however, or of the child in the first stages of second language learning, the conversational principles apply less stringently because the prelanguage learner need not be treated as a potential conversational partner. In this chapter, hypotheses about the role of social inter-action in furthering the child's discovery of the principles of communica-tion during the prelinguistic period and during the first stages of second language acquisition are discussed because, in these situations, the natu-rally occurring variation is large enough to have an observable effect.

Even for those periods of development that are associated with a fairly large variance in the quality of the social experience available to the child, it is not always easy to demonstrate that the hypothesized effect has occurred. The positive effect of some bit of social experience or linguistic input is very likely, for example, to be stage-related. Expanding children's utterances, or modelling some particular sentence type, may have a very dramatic positive effect on the linguistic progress of children who are at precisely the right point of language development to benefit, but this ef-fect may not be visible in a large group of children in which many are not at the sensitive stage (Cross, this volume). Furthermore, some social expe-riences may have threshold rather than incremental effects on communi-cative development. In this case, the occurrence of a relatively rare event at the crucial moment could have enormous impact which is, however, relatively hard to identify (Nelson, this volume; Snow, 1977).

CONTINGENT RESPONDING

The first hypothesis discussed is that the development of communicative ability during infancy depends crucially on experiences of contingent re-sponding. Only by noticing that his own behaviors have a predictable ef-fect on the world can the infant develop the notion of signal, which is the first stage in developing the ability to communicate. Because of their physical helplessness, newborns have, at least in the absence of the extra-ordinary apparatus designed by experimental psychologists, very little op-portunity to affect the objects or events in the world directly. A 1-year-old can build a tower, knock over a glass, kick a ball, make pencil marks on paper, rip pages out of books, and in countless other ways, can observe the contingencies between his own behaviors and changes in the world. A newborn, who is unable to grasp, to locomote, or to maintain an unsup-ported head or torso position, must rely on his caregivers to mimic cause and effect relationships for him. Only in interaction with caregivers does the young infant have experiences of effectiveness. For example, the in-fant moves his gaze to the adult's eyes, and the adult smiles and says "Hello"; the infant vocalizes "goo" and the adult vocalizes "goo." Ex-perience with such contingent responding may be the source of the infant's knowledge regarding signals. It has been widely suggested that in-fants' experiences with contingent responses contribute to their social and cognitive development (Ainsworth and Bell, 1974; Lewis and Goldberg, 1969). The hypothesis presented here is much more specific: learning to signal depends on having experienced contingent responses.

The ability to signal can be seen as one of the first steps in the development of the ability to communicate (Snow, 1979). A signal is defined as a behavior of a more or less constant form produced with the expectation that it will have some predictable effect in a certain class of receivers. A signal is, therefore, more sophisticated than a simple expectation of effect, in that it does involve interpersonal contact. It does not, however, require arbitrary, conventionalized, or mutually agreed upon behaviors, as does the later use of words.

Learning to signal involves learning that certain behaviors are responded to predictably by certain people, and intentionally applying that knowledge.

The hypothesis that experience with contingent responses is the source of the infant's knowledge about signals has the following testable implications: 1) infants who have never experienced contingent responses will not learn to signal, 2) up to a certain point at least, greater frequency of experience with contingent responses will decrease the age at which infants learn to signal, 3) greater frequency of experience with contingent responses will decrease the age at which infants learn new signals, and 4) greater frequency of experience with contingent responses increases the ease with which more complex contingencies can be learned.

All infants who develop normally have access to significant amounts of contingent responding. Studies of mother-infant interaction typically report that the most frequent maternal behaviors to infants are vocalizing, smiling, and touching (Lewis and Ban, 1977). These behaviors are often (although not always) produced in response to infant behaviors (Snow, deBlauw, and van Roosmalen, 1979) and thus provide experience with contingent responding. Such contingent experiences occur, in fact, with considerable frequency in infants' lives. In one study of mother's interactions with infants between the ages of 3 and 6 months, stereotyped responses to specific behaviors (for example, saying "Pardon you" after the infant burped or "Oh, dear" after he coughed, imitating infant vocalizations) occurred an average of 8.4 times an hour at 3 months of age, and 13.3 times an hour at six months of age (Snow, deBlauw, and van Roosmalen, 1979). These observations were made during periods of potential social interaction, for example, times when the baby was awake but was not being breast or bottle fed, and when the mother was in the same room. Obviously, the infant does not have constant exposure to this frequency of contingent responding. The relevant data for assessing the infant's potential for learning on the basis of contingent responses are not the density of such responses during observation sessions, but their total frequency over the course of a day or a week. It seems likely that an infant has access to potential social interaction 3–4 hours a day throughout his first 6 months. The observed frequencies, then, of 8.4 and 13.3 contingent responses per hour of potential social interaction, could be extrapolated to an estimate of approximately 25 and 40 contingent responses per day at 3 and at 6 months, respectively. This represents a sufficient amount of exposure to suggest that the experience of contingent responding may play a crucial role in the discovery of signals.

A wider review of the literature on mother-infant interaction, however, suggests that access to contingent responding might be limited to infants brought up in middle class homes in North America or Britain. Studies of mother-infant interaction in other cultures report that talking to babies, smiling at them, tickling them, imitating them, and showing other forms of social, contingent behavior to them is a relatively infrequent experience for many of the babies in the world. For example, it has been reported that the following groups of mothers talk to and play with their babies much less than is generally observed among middle class North Americans: Zambians (Goldberg, 1972), the Kikuyu (Liederman and Liederman, 1977), the Zincanteco (Brazelton, 1972), Guatemalan Indians and mestizos (Kagan and Klein, 1973), Japanese (Caudill and Weinstein, 1969), and lower class Americans (Tulkin and Kagan, 1972).

The relative unavailability of contingent smiling and vocalizing to infants in Mexico, Zambia, Japan, Guatemala, and Kenya seems to suggest that experience with such contingent responses cannot be a prerequisite to normal communicative development. It is striking, however, that in precisely those cultures that seem to provide little response to infant behaviors like smiling, laughing, and vocalizing, infant distress behaviors such as fussing and crying are responded to much more promptly and reliably than is typically the case in North America or Western Europe. Especially in cultures where babies are carried in a sling on the mother's hip or back for much of the time during the first 6–12 months, response to distress signals can be extremely prompt. The most frequent response to an infant's distress signal is feeding. It has been reported that Zincanteco infants in the Mexican highlands feed between one and two times an hour during their first 4 months (Brazelton, 1977). The contrast between this frequency and the minimum 2½-hour interfeed interval recommended for "demand fed" American babies, or the 4-hour interval enforced for "schedule fed" babies, suggests that babies who are carried and are fed promptly in response to minor distress signals may have a great deal of experience with contingent responding despite the infrequency of playful and purely social response. They may, in fact, experience more contingent responding than the North American and Western European babies who experience a few long play sessions each day but whose distress behaviors may not be responded to for several minutes. On second analysis, then, the cross-cultural literature on mother-infant interaction supports the notion that all babies growing up in normal circumstances have access to significant amounts of contingent responding to their own behaviors. Cultural differences may affect the type of infant behaviors that elicit the contingent responding, but some sort of contingent responding seems to be universally available.

Whether there is any evidence concerning the efficacy of contingent responding in contributing to the development of communication, aside from the very weak argument that contingent responding is universally available and, therefore, could have the hypothesized effect is not known. The only adequate way to test the hypotheses presented above is to compare two groups of infants who had had different amounts of access to contingent responding on their development of the ability to signal and to learn complex contingent relationships. The effect of contingent responding during the first few months on the development of communicative behavior has not been tested, although positive effects of experience with contingent responding on the ability to learn an operant response have been found for 4- to 6-month-olds (Finkelstein and Ramey, 1977) and for 8- to 10-month-olds (Riksen-Walraven, 1977). Furthermore, positive effects of frequent contingent responses to fussing and smiling during the first 3 months and on developmental assessments at nine months have been reported (Beckwith et al., 1976).

Indirect support for the notion that contingent responding contributes to the development of communicative facility comes from several studies of the effects of early intervention and maternal training carried out with various groups of normal and high risk infants. For example, one of the primary effects of the early intervention program designed by Meltzl (1978) is to increase the likelihood that infants will receive contingent responses. Similarly, the positive effects on language acquisition of extensive physical contact between mother and infant during the period immediately after birth (Ringler, 1980; Whiten, 1977) may be mediated by the mother's resultant greater sensitivity to the infant's signals and her improved ability to respond appropriately to those signals. The most long-lasting effects on children's cognitive and linguistic development have been obtained as a result of home intervention programs that attempted to modify the mother-child interaction (Bee et al., 1969; Madden, Levenstein, and Levenstein, 1976). Maternal behavioral variables that seem to reflect the tendency to provide contingent responses correlate significantly with the child's language achievements at age 3 (Elardo, Bradley, and Caldwell, 1977) and with IQ at age 4 (Bradley and Caldwell, 1976). The amount of social interaction available to the child before 3 months has been shown to be directly relevant to developmental quotients in the second half of the first year (Cohen and Beckwith, 1977).

Additional indirect support for the hypothesis that contingent responding contributes to the development of signaling ability—and, therefore, of language—comes from: 1) studies of disturbed interaction between mothers and high risk infants such as prematures, small for dates, and those who have suffered respiratory distress syndrome (Field, 1977; Field et al., 1978; Osofsky, 1976), and 2) reports that these groups of infants are excessively represented among the population of language- and learning-disabled (Field et al., in press; Goldstein, Caputo, and Taub, 1976; Gottfried, 1973; Pasamanick, Constantinou, and Lillienfeld, 1956; Smith et al., 1972). Although the alternate hypothesis of a direct link between perinatal stress and developmental lag or deviancy cannot now be excluded, the degree of heterogeneity in the ultimate achievements of perinatally stressed infants suggests that morbidity or prematurity may have deleterious effects on development only if it results in a disturbed pattern of mother-infant interaction during the several months after birth. If the adult caregiver can, despite the inherent difficulty of caring for the physiologically suboptimal infant, learn to understand the significance of the infant's behaviors and to respond predictably and contingently, subsequent language disabilities may be avoided.

In summary, there is no direct evidence linking experience with contingent responding to the development of any specific communicative ability. There is, however, a general recognition of the importance of experience with contingent responding for normal cognitive development, and there are three sources of indirect evidence supporting the more specific hypothesis: 1) all normally developing babies in all cultures do have access to significant amounts of contingent responding, 2) early manipulations of the mother-infant interaction, which have been shown to contribute to communicative development, increase the likelihood of contingent responding to infant behaviors, and 3) groups of infants who are at risk for impaired communicative development show behaviors during infancy that make it very hard for caregivers to provide contingent response.

PLAYING GAMES

The second social experience that may contribute in a crucial and specific way to the development of communicative abilities—especially during the second half of the first year—is games and playful routines. Many possible effects of games have been hypothesized. (See, for example, Bruner, 1975a, 1975b, 1977; Snow et al., in preparation.) These hypotheses include the following:

1. Experience with games during which the caregiver has finely adjusted the temporal aspects of his or her behavior so that the infant has an optimal opportunity to participate contributes to the child's knowl-

edge of conversational rules and development of conversational skill. Very subtle fine tuning by mothers to their infants' behavior has been described by Trevarthen (1977), and some variability in the ability to do this by Brazelton, Koslowski, and Main (1974).

2. Engaging frequently in game playing and in well-practiced routines contributes to the child's ability to use language with a social function, as reflected in his learning expressions such as *hi, bye-bye, thank you,* and proper nouns, and in his use of vocalizations and words to demand objects and attention from adults (Nelson, 1973).

3. Infants learn about the potential for combining words with actions and with other words in presyntactic sequences from experience with games and routines in which words or actions fill predictable slots (for example, the word peekaboo fills the slot after reappearance in the game, *peekaboo;* and the actions of patting, rolling, throwing, fill slots in the word and action game, patty-cake.

The third hypothesis, that experience with games and routines develops the child's skill in slot filling, is the basis of the present section. There are two separate arguments that must be made: 1) game playing contributes to skill in slot filling, and 2) skill in slot filling has some relevance to language ability. The argument that language is acquired as a set of rules for filling up slots in the interaction can be made most strongly for the earliest stages of language acquisition, when single word utterances clearly are slotted into familiar environmental or discourse contexts. It is not just social routine words such as *hello, good-bye,* and *thank you* that are used at points in the interaction, which are defined by what has come before, but common nouns and verbs used referentially also are learned by being produced at certain points in practiced social routines. For example, routines like "Where's your nose? Where are your eyes? Where are your ears?" are frequently heard expressions that have a game-like structure. Early word combinations do not result from rules allowing a maximally productive combination of words from different classes. Rather, the early word combinations reveal that few words are fully analyzed as separate units, and others are used only in certain combinations or slots (Ingram, 1978). Obviously, with the introduction of multilevel syntactic analysis and true syntactic rules, the child's serial constructions must be analyzed and the syntactic relations among the parts defined. However, there is no evidence that this occurs during the early stages of sentence production, when the child is limited to utterances of a few words. In fact, analyses of the seemingly long and complex utterances of children as old as 4 or 5 years reveal that many of these utterances can be explained as concatenations of memorized chunks (Clark, 1974, 1977) and imitations of adult utterances (Van der Geest, 1977), not as the product of transformational rules for combining underlying sentences (Ingram, 1975). The position that the syntactic knowledge of 4- to 5-year-olds is much more limited than has traditionally been assumed receives additional support from the discovery of children's inability to differentiate between grammatical and ungrammatical utterances in imitation or comprehension tasks at this age (Bohannon, 1976).

The essence of learning the rules of a game consists of learning at which point to make which response. Babies begin to receive practice in simple games when they are a few months old, at which time their caregivers start introducing tickling games such as This Little Pig Went to Market and Round and Round the Garden. The infant's role in these games involves only: a) attending during the first phase, and b) laughter at the end of the game. As the game structure develops, the occurrence of subsequent turns comes to depend on the infant's having taken his turn. For example, in patty-cake, patty-cake, successful play depends on the infant's having made the appropriate clapping, rolling, and throwing motions, and in give-and-take routines, the infant must accept and give items for the game to be continued. The infant's task of acquiring skill for these games requires: 1) learning what actions must be performed, and 2) learning at what point in the routine those actions must be inserted. The second skill often poses more of a problem than the first. One 28-month-old boy, for example, responded to having any toe touched by laughing and saying "Wee wee wee home," a clear example of knowing one of the turns in the game This Little Pig but not knowing in what slot it comes.

The infants' turns in early games and routines most often consist of gestures rather than vocalizations, and early words are often introduced as accompaniments to those gestures before they replace the gestures entirely. The greater availability of gestural signals than vocal communication signals to the child age 6–18 months is revealed not only by the ontogeny of turns in games, but from several other sources as well, for example:

1. The precocity of first language signers as compared to first language speakers. Many reports of deaf children learning sign language as a first language from their deaf parents suggest that all the major milestones of communicative development (use of first sign, size of vocabulary at 12 months, use of first two- and three-sign combinations) are several months advanced for first language signers over first language speakers (Moores, 1974; Schlesinger and Meadow, 1972).

2. The widespread and sophisticated use of gesture by hearing children at an age when their vocal development is still limited. For example, Nathaniel, at age 20 months, used the 12 gestures listed in Table 1 when his spoken vocabulary consisted of five words and he used ges-

tures to differentiate between homophonous productions of different words. He used *tata* to mean 'all gone,' in situations where he had finished eating or drinking something, or when something disappeared, and to mean 'all done,' when indicating completion of some action such as placing a block on a tower, putting some article of clothing on, and finishing a book. The vocalization, which was identical in both cases, was accompanied by a gesture of holding his hands open, palms facing up and forward, for 'all gone,' and the gesture of extending his arms fully for 'all done.'

3. The ubiquitous use of gesture to support verbal communication by children in the later stages of language acquisition. Wilkinson and Rembold (this volume) reported, for example, that gesture is widely used by 2-year-olds in supplementing or in substituting for verbal communication.

4. The widespread use of gestural communication by mothers to infants in the prelinguistic stage (Reilly, Zukow, and Greenfield, 1980) and to older children (Garnica, 1978; Stella Prorok, 1978).

5. The effectiveness of sign in language training, not only for deaf and hard of hearing children who have limited access to auditory input (Sørenson and Hansen, 1980) but also for autistic children (Bonvil-

Table 1.   Gestures used by Nathaniel at 20 months of age

Gesture	Gloss	Accompanying vocalization
Both arms extended forward, hands open	Give me X	Variable
One arm extended upward, hand open	Open the door	Variable
One arm and index finger extended	Look at X	None
Head aversion	Don't	Variable
One arm extended backward, hand open	Help me	Variable
Taking adult's hand	Fix X/open X	None
Waving	Let's go	Variable
Sitting on heels	Carry me	None
Both arms extended above head	Help me into highchair	None
Sticking out tongue	Let's play a game naming body parts	None
Pushing against wall with one hand	Get up	None
Both hands opened in front of shoulders	All gone	Tata
Both arms extended sideways	All done	Tata

lian and Nelson, 1976; Bricker, 1972; Miller and Miller, 1973) and children who show a specific language deficit (Yamada, Kriendler, and Haimsohn, 1978). In fact, sign language has been used successfully with multiply-handicapped children who show motor deficits as well as hearing loss and mental retardation and a resultant severe delay in the acquisition of spoken language (Fenn, 1974).

It is not clear why gestural communicative systems are so ubiquitous, so precocious, and so much easier to learn than spoken language. Some of the features of gestural communication that might make it easier to understand and to use than spoken language are its iconicity (Brown, 1977), the possibility of slowing down its presentation without distorting the signal (Yamada et al., 1978), the fact that its production can be facilitated by molding the young signer's hands into the appropriate shape in a way that has no parallel for spoken language, and the fact that grosser motor responses are used in signing than in speaking. Perhaps the most important reason is the fact that signed communication is carried out using the same sorts of motor behaviors that produce effects in the physical world. It is not surprising that a child who is actively involved in learning about how his own actions produce effects in the world—which is essentially what he spends his time doing during the sensorimotor period—should expect that the same sorts of motor behaviors that operate directly on the world will operate on people as well. The robustness of the tendency to use gestural communication is demonstrated by the findings that deaf children deprived of any gestural input by the oral convictions of their parents and teachers nonetheless generate a sign language spontaneously (Feldman, Goldin-Meadow, and Gleitman, 1977). Unfortunately, a study of deaf children who were raised in an oral context in Holland, which was carried out at the Institute for General Linguistics, University of Amsterdam, under the direction of B. Tervoort, found no similarly rich use of gestural communication by the children. In fact, the most striking aspect of the children's behavior in the Dutch study was that they used less gesture than children with normal hearing (LeGrand, 1978). Thus, in addition to being deprived of oral input and the chance to learn spoken language by their deafness, the Dutch children were being cut off from normal use of gestural communication by their parents' extreme unwillingness to use or to respond to gesture.

Given the naturalness of action and gesture as means of communication for the young child, it becomes clearer how extensive experience with game playing could contribute to communicative development. Games and other social routines involve practicing precisely those skills that enable the child to communicate: 1) taking his turn in a social interaction, 2) following the rules for how his turn should be filled in, and 3) within the limits prescribed by the rules of the game, varying the exact content of the turn. One would expect, then, that extensive early experience with games and other social routines would contribute to the early communicative use of gestures, and subsequently, perhaps to the early use of words.

Once again, as for the hypothesis regarding the effects of experience with contingent reinforcement, the only supporting evidence takes the form of a demonstration that game playing occurs with sufficient frequency and repetitiveness that it could indeed contribute to language acquisition as hypothesized. Furthermore, most cultures seem to have many games and verses that are typically used with young children, and that require some participation by the child.

In a study of game playing at ages 3 to 6 months between mother-infant pairs in England and in Holland, it was found that games were played with a mean frequency of 2.0 times per hour of potential social interaction at 3 months, and 4.3 times per hour at 6 months (Snow et al., in preparation). Applying the same sort of extrapolation from observed frequency used above for contingent responses, it can be estimated that the average baby experiences about six games a day at 3 months and 13 games a day at 6 months. If it is assumed that the average daily frequency throughout the first 6 months is six (assuming a more or less linear increase from 0 at birth to 13 at 6 months), then the average baby has experienced more than 1,000 episodes of game playing during this first half year.

The potential effectiveness of these 1,000 game playing episodes in teaching the infant something about communication is greatly increased by the fact that in the average family, only about five different games are played frequently. In fact, the structural similarity of the games played in the Dutch and in the English groups studied was striking, despite the use of different rhymes and verses by the two language groups. Infants have, then, a great deal of experience in playing a small number of games, and the games played in different cultures and different language groups are similar enough in structure that they all teach the same lessons about the nature of language and communication.

The development of the game structure between 3 and 6 months suggests more specifically how playing games teaches children to communicate. At 3 months, the typical game consists of two turns: the mother recites some verse that provides an opportunity to tickle the infant at the end, and the infant laughs. After playing many tickling games, the infant is able to recognize the first line of the verse as a sign that he will be tickled. At this point, mothers often start to segment their turn, pausing after the beginning of the verse to allow the infant a chance for an anticipatory response. At this point, the game has the following structure: the mother "warns" that she is going to tickle the infant by reciting the first line of the verse; the infant responds anticipatorily; the mother tickles; and the infant laughs. In subsequent developments (after 6 months), the infant recognizes that he can initiate the game by, for example, lying down in the tickling position, or by making tickling motions on his own or his mother's body. By virtue of their being embedded in a familiar and often practiced game structure, the infant's behaviors thus are interpreted as attempts at true communication. The infant is enabled to achieve communication with the simple repertoire of behaviors within his competence. Bruner (1977) demonstrated, for example, how behavior that occurs in the course of give-and-take games with older infants is made meaningful by the structure of the game.

There is no experimental evidence that experience with game playing contributes to the acquisition of skill in turn-taking, slot filling, or the use of social words and expressions. The same sorts of indirect evidence as were offered in support of the hypotheses about contingent responding can be presented for the role of game playing in communicative development: 1) game playing is universal, frequent, and repetitive, and thus, could have the hypothesized effects, 2) intervention programs that have been shown to increase children's scores on tests of linguistic and cognitive ability explicitly incorporate games or greatly increase the likelihood that caregivers will initiate games with their infants (Madden et al., 1976; Riksen-Walraven, 1977), and 3) the perinatal factors associated with increased risk of later language disability produce jumpy, easily overexcited, socially nonresponsive infants, with whom it is very hard to engage in the behaviors that lead up to game playing in early infancy (Field et al., 1978).

Somewhat more direct evidence of the efficacy of game playing in teaching communication comes from the scattered reports of infants who have learned specific communicative behaviors in the context of games, for example, signals to the mother to continue with the action in bouncing games (Bruner, 1975b), *please* and *thank you* in give-and-take games (Bruner, 1977), hiding one's face as a request to initiate peekaboo (Bruner and Sherwood, 1976; and Ratner and Bruner, 1978), or hand-clapping as a request to initiate patty-cake (Snow, 1979). Clearly, in these individual cases, experience with specific games and routines led to specific learning, and created a situation in which the child was engaging in more complex or more precocious communication than he would have been capable of without the game playing experience. What has not been demonstrated is that a great deal of experience with games facilitates learning and generalizing the principles of social communication such as turn-taking, use of arbitrary, conventionalized behaviors to communicate, and filling in slots in discourse or within utterances in appropriate ways.

SECOND LANGUAGE ACQUISITION

Childhood second language acquisition may offer the clearest test case for the importance of social interaction in language acquisition. Unlike first language learners, second language learners differ considerably from one another in the availability of interaction with native speakers. These individual differences are derived from the social situations in which different second language learners find themselves, and from their skill in establishing social interactions with native speakers. Furthermore, many of the hypothesized processes of first language acquisition such as imitation of adult utterances, and memorization of large linguistic chunks, are much more evident in second language acquisition because older second language learners have better memories. The subject Joe, studied by Huang and Hatch (1978), for example, could use imitated sentences like *Get out of here* and *It's time to eat and drink* during the time when his productive capacity in English was limited to one-word utterances.

Studies of the verbal environment of second language learners have been primarily motivated by sociolinguistic questions about the nature of "foreigner talk." The studies of foreigner talk (see, for example, Ferguson, 1975; Meisel, 1975; and Workgroup on Foreign Workers' Language, 1978) have generally suggested that input to second language learners does not show the characteristics of simplicity and clarity typical of speech to young first language learners. Especially striking is the use of grammatically incorrect utterances in foreigner talk, unlike speech to children, which is characterized by an extremely low frequency of mistakes, false starts, and syntactic confusions. It seems very likely that the differences between foreigner talk and speech to young first language learners concern the difference in the topics being discussed. Because the topics discussed with young children are relatively simple and concrete, syntactically simple utterances can adequately encode the propositions the adult speakers wish to express. Speech to older language learners, however, is not generally limited to discussion of labels, locations, actions, agents, attributes, and possession. Because much more complex topics are being discussed, limitation to the extremely simple set of syntactic structures and vocabulary familiar to the beginning second language speakers causes distortions, incorrect deletions, and ungrammatical simplifications typical of foreigner talk (Snow and Hoefnagel-Höhle, 1978b).

If it is the semantic complexity of the speech addressed to foreigners that accounts for the specific foreigner talk characteristics, then speech to young second language learners might be expected to be more like speech to first language learners, thus providing a good basis for distilling the structure of the adult language. In a study of the linguistic environment of 13 English speakers in Dutch kindergarten, primary, and secondary school classrooms, it was found that speech to the English-speaking children was simpler than speech to their native Dutch-speaking classmates, but that the incidence of incorrect language models was almost zero (Snow and Hoefnagel-Höhle, 1978b). Evidently, the concreteness and inherent simplicity of the topics being discussed with the schoolchildren enabled their interlocutors to avoid classic foreigner talk characteristics.

The hypothesis about the importance of social interaction in language acquisition that can be most effectively tested using the second language learning situation concerns the quantity of speech heard. The English-speaking children studied were exposed to Dutch almost exclusively in the course of the school day because their families continued to use English at home. They heard utterances addressed by their teachers and classmates to the entire classroom, as well as some utterances addressed specifically to them. These specifically addressed utterances were relatively simple, but the speech addressed to the class as a whole was also syntactically quite simple, was related to ongoing events or visual displays available in books or in the classroom itself, and frequently was interpretable on the basis of the responses to it by the other children. The children studied differed greatly in the amount of Dutch heard, and in the amount directed specifically to them, as well as in their speed in acquiring Dutch. The variation in the total amount of Dutch heard enables one to test hypotheses about the amount of exposure to a language required in order to learn that language. It was found, in fact, that the best predictor of the subjects' subsequent achievements in Dutch was the total amount of comprehensible speech they heard. The number of utterances heard correlated highly with the subjects' performance on comprehension, repetition, translations, and morphology tests administered 4–5 months later. The percentage of the utterances heard that was addressed specifically to the English speakers did not correlate significantly with their subsequent achievement in Dutch, possibly because those classrooms that provided the greatest opportunity for individual conversations were also the noisiest classrooms, those in which the total amount of comprehensible speech heard was quite small (Snow and Hoefnagel-Höhle, 1978b).

It is, of course, not surprising that the amount of speech heard correlated with speed of acquisition. The children participating in this study were receiving no formal instruction in Dutch, so the speech they heard was their only source of information about the Dutch language. What is surprising is the amount of speech the learners had to hear in order to learn Dutch at all. The fastest second language learners were the teenagers (Snow and Hoefnagel-Höhle, 1978a), who were hearing more than 2,000 Dutch utterances a day. Children who heard fewer than 400 Dutch utterances a day did not acquire any Dutch at all in the course of several months' attendance at Dutch schools. Of course, even 2,000 utterances a day is a considerably lower rate than is heard by 1- to 2-year-old first language learners from their caregivers, and the fact that the teenagers could speak a fair amount of Dutch after only 4–5 weeks exposure to about 2,000 utterances a day suggests that they are very efficient second language learners. (See Snow and Hoefnagel-Höhle, 1978a for further evidence on age differences in second language learning ability.) It seems that older children are able to acquire a second language after much less exposure to it than young first language learners require.

CONCLUSION

This chapter presents three specific hypotheses about the role of social interaction in contributing to the development of communicative and linguistic ability in the hope of freeing investigation into the importance of social interaction from nonspecific theorizing about the nature-nurture controversy. Assessing hypotheses about the contributions of specific social experiences to the learning of specific communicative or linguistic skills should provide a greater understanding of the process of language acquisition, an understanding that is not promoted by general statements about the relative importance of innate and environmental factors.

ACKNOWLEDGMENTS

I would like to express my appreciation to Akke de Blauw, Clara Dubber, Marian Hoefnagel-Höhle, and my other colleagues at the Institute for General Linguistics, University of Amsterdam, where the research and the ideas discussed in this chapter developed.

REFERENCES

Ainsworth, M., and Bell, S. 1974. Mother-infant interaction and the development of competence. In: K. Connolly and J. Bruner (eds.), The Growth of Competence, pp. 97–118. Academic Press, Inc., New York.
Beckwith, L., Cohen, S., Kopp, C., Parmelee, A., and Marcy, T. 1976. Caregiver-infant interaction and early cognitive development in preterm infants. Child Dev. 47: 579–587.
Bee, H., Van Egeren, L., Streissguth, A., Nyman, B., and Leckie, M. 1969. Social class differences in maternal teaching styles and speech patterns. Dev. Psychol. 1:726–734.
Bohannon, J. 1976. Normal and scrambled grammar in discrimination. Child Dev. 47:669–681.
Bohannon, J., and Marquis, A. 1977. Children's control of adult speech. Child Dev. 48:1002–1008.
Bonvillian, J., and Nelson, I. 1976. Sign language acquisition in a mute autistic boy. J. Speech Hear. Disord. 41:339–347.

Bradley, R., and Caldwell, B. 1976. The relation of infants' HOME environments to mental tests performance at 54 months: A follow-up study. Child Dev. 47: 1172–1174.

Brazelton, T. 1972. Implications of human development among the Mayan Indians of Mexico. Human Dev. 15:90–111.

Brazelton, T. 1977. Implications of infant development among the Mayan Indians of Mexico. In: P. Liederman, S. Tulkin, and A. Rosenfeld (eds.), Culture and Infancy, pp. 151–187. Academic Press, Inc., New York.

Brazelton, T., Koslowski, B., and Main, M. 1974. The origins of reciprocity: The early mother-infant interaction. In: M. Lewis and L. Rosenblum (eds.), The Origins of Behavior, Vol. 1: The Effect of the Infant on Its Caregiver, pp. 49–76. John Wiley & Sons, Inc., New York.

Bricker, D. 1972. Imitative sign training as a facilitator of word object association with low-functioning children. J. Ment. Defic. 76:509–516.

Brown, R. 1977. Why are signed languages easier to learn than spoken languages? Keynote address, National Association for the Deaf.

Bruner, J. 1975a. From communication to language: A psychological perspective. Cognition 3:255–285.

Bruner, J. 1975b. The ontogenesis of speech acts. J. Child Lang. 2:1–20.

Bruner, J. 1977. Early social interaction and language acquisition. In: H. R. Schaffer (ed.), Studies in Mother-infant Interaction. Academic Press, Inc., New York.

Bruner, J., and Sherwood, V. 1976. Early rule structure: The case of peekaboo. In: J. Bruner, A. Jolly, and K. Sylva (eds.), Play: Its Role in Developmental Evolution, pp. 277–285. Penguin, Harmondsworth, England.

Caudill, W., and Weinstein, H. 1969. Maternal and infant care in Japan and America. Psychiatry 32:12–43.

Cazden, C. 1965. Environmental assistance to the child's acquisition of grammar. Unpublished doctoral dissertation, Harvard University, New Haven, Conn.

Cherry, L., and Lewis, M. 1976. Mothers and two-year-olds. In: N. Waterson and C. Snow (eds.), The Development of Communication, pp. 189–197. John Wiley & Sons, Inc., London.

Clark, R. 1974. Performing without competence. J. Child Lang. 1:1–10.

Clark, R. 1977. What is the use of imitation? J. Child Lang. 3:341–358.

Cohen, S., and Beckwith, L. 1977. Caregiving behaviors and early cognitive development as related to ordinal position in preterm infants. Child Dev. 48:152–157.

Cross, T. 1977. Mothers' speech adjustments: The contribution of selected child listener variables. In: C. Snow and C. Ferguson (eds.), Talking to Children, pp. 151–188. Cambridge University Press, New York.

Cross, T. 1978. Motherese: Its association with the rate of syntactic acquisition in young children. In: N. Waterson and C. Snow (eds.), The Development of Communication, pp. 199–216. John Wiley & Sons, Inc., London.

Elardo, R., Bradley, R., and Caldwell, B. 1977. A longitudinal study of the relation of infants' home environment to language development at age three. Child Dev. 48:595–603.

Feldman, H., Goldin-Meadow, S., and Gleitman, L. 1977. Beyond Herodotus: The creation of language by linguistically deprived deaf children. In: A. Lock (ed.), Action, Gesture and Symbol, pp. 351–414. Academic Press, Inc., New York.

Fenn, G. 1974. Language without Speech. British Association for Applied Linguistics, Edinburgh.

Ferguson, C. 1975. Towards a characterization of English foreigner talk. Anthropol. Linguist. 17:1–14.

Field, T. 1977. Effects of early separation, interactive deficits, and experimental manipulations on infant mother face-to-face interaction. Child Dev. 48: 763–771.

Field, T., Goldberg, S., Dempsey, J., and Shuman, H. Speech disturbance and minimal brain dysfunction: A five-year follow-up of RDS. In: T. Field, A. Sostek, S. Goldberg, and H. Shuman (eds.), Infants Born at Risk. Spectrum Pubs., Inc., New York. In press.

Field, T., Hallock, N., Ting, G., Dempsey, J., Dabiri, C., and Shuman, H. 1978. A first-year follow-up of high-risk infants: Formulating a cumulative high-risk index. Child. Dev. 49:113–131.

Finkelstein, N., and Ramey, C. 1977. Learning to control the environment in infancy. Child Dev. 48:806–819.

Garnica, O. 1978. Nonverbal concomitants of language input to children. In: N. Waterson and C. Snow (eds.), The Development of Communication, pp. 139–147. John Wiley & Sons, Inc., London.

Goldberg, S. 1972. Infant care and growth in urban Zambia. Hum. Dev. 15:77–89.

Goldstein, K., Caputo, D., and Taub, H. 1976. The effects of prenatal and perinatal complications on development at one year of age. Child Dev. 47:613–621.

Gottfried, A. 1973. Intellectual consequences of perinatal anoxia. Psychol. Bull. 80:231–242.

Huang, J., and Hatch, E. 1978. A Chinese child's acquisition of English. In: E. Hatch (ed.), Second Language Acquisition. Newbury House Pubs., Rowley, Mass.

Ingram, D. 1975. If and when transformations are acquired by children. In: D. Dato (ed.), Georgetown University Roundtable on Languages and Linguistics 1975, pp. 99–127. Georgetown University Press, Washington, D.C.

Ingram, D. 1978. On the productive and analytic nature of grammatical rules in the language of children with syntactic delay. Paper presented at the First International Congress for the Study of Child Language, April 7–12, Tokyo, Japan.

Kagan, J., and Klein, P. 1973. Cross-cultural perspectives on early development. Am. Psychol. 28:947–961.

LeGrand, M. 1978. Koen, Annette en Els: De interactie tussen een moeder en haar dovevkind (Koen, Annette and Els: The interaction between a mother and her deaf child.) Unpublished master's thesis, University of Amsterdam.

Levenstein, P. 1976. Cognitive development through verbalized play: The mother-child home programme. In: J. Bruner, A. Jolly, and K. Sylva (eds.), Play: Its Role in Development and Evolution, pp. 286–297. Penguin, Hammondsworth.

Lewis, M., and Ban, P. 1977. Variance and invariance in the mother-infant interaction: A cross-cultural study. In: P. Liederman, S. Tulkin, and A. Rosenfeld (eds.), Culture and Infancy, pp. 329–355. Academic Press, Inc., New York.

Lewis, M., and Goldberg, S. 1969. Perceptual-cognitive development in infancy: A generalized expectancy model as function of the mother-infant relationship. Merrill Palmer Quarterly 15:81–100.

Liederman, P., and Liederman, G. 1977. Economic change and infant care in an East African agricultural community. In: P. Liederman, S. Tulkin, and A. Rosenfeld (eds.), Culture and Infancy, pp. 405–438. Academic Press, Inc., New York.

Madden, J., Levenstein, P., and Levenstein, S. 1976. Longitudinal IQ outcomes of the mother-child home program. Child Dev. 47:1015–1025.

Meisel, J. 1975. Auslanderdeutsch und Deutsch ausländischer Arbeiter. [Foreigner—German and the German of foreign workers.] Zeitschrift für Linguistik und Literaturwissen schaft. [J. Linguistics and Literature.] 5:18.

Metzl, M. 1978. Teaching parents to stimulate their infants as a strategy for enhancing infant development. Paper presented at the First International Congress for the Study of Child Language, April 7–12, Tokyo, Japan.

Miller, A., and Miller, E. 1973. Cognitive developmental training with elevated boards of sign language. J. Autism Child. Schizo. 3:65–85.

Moores, D. 1974. Nonvocal systems of verbal behavior. In: R. L. Schiefelbusch and L. L. Lloyd (eds.), Language Perspectives—Acquisition, Retardation and Intervention, pp. 377–417. University Park Press, Baltimore.

Nelson, K. 1973. Structure and strategy in learning to talk. Monographs of the Society for Research in Child Development, No. 149, 38, Nos. 1 and 2.

Nelson, K. E., Carskaddon, G., and Bonvillian, J. 1973. Syntax acquisition: Impact of experimental variation in adult verbal interaction with the child. Child Dev. 44:497–504.

Newport, E., Gleitman, H., and Gleitman, L. 1977. Mother, I'd rather do it myself: Some effects and noneffects of maternal speech style. In: C. Snow and C. Ferguson (eds.), Talking to Children, pp. 109–149. Cambridge University Press, London.

Pasamanick, B., Constantinou, F., and Lillienfeld, A. 1956. Pregnancy experience and the development of childhood speech disorders: An epidemiologic study of the association with maternal and fetal factors. Am. J. Dis. Child 91: 113–118.

Osofsky, J. 1976. Neonatal characteristics and mother-infant interaction in two observational situations. Child Dev. 47:1138–1147.

Ratner, N., and Bruner, J. 1978. Games, social exchange and the acquisition of language. J. Child Lang. 5:391–402.

Reilly, J. S., Zukow, P. G., and Greenfield, P. M. 1980. Facilitating the transition from sensorimotor to linguistic communication during the one-word period. In: D. Ingram, F. C. C. Peng, and P. Dale (eds.), Proceedings of the First International Congress for the Study of Child Language, pp. 198–225. University Press of America, Lanham, Md.

Riksen-Walraven, M. 1977. Stimulering van de vroeg-kinderlyke ontwikkelung. (Stimulation of early childhood development). Unpublished doctoral thesis, University of Nijmegen.

Ringler, N. 1980. The effects of postpartum mother-infant reciprocal transactions on the development of meaning and language. In: D. Ingram, F. C. C. Peng, and P. Dale (eds.), Proceedings of the First International Congress for the Study of Child Language, pp. 226–245, University Press of America, Lanham, Md.

Schlesinger, H., and Meadow, K. 1972. Sound and Sign. University of California Press, Berkeley.

Smith, A., Flick, G., Ferriss, G., and Sellman, A. 1972. Prediction of developmental outcome at seven years from prenatal, postnatal, and perinatal events. Child Dev. 43:495–507.

Snow, C. 1977. Mothers' speech research: From input to interaction. In: C. Snow and C. Ferguson (eds.), Talking to Children. Cambridge University Press, London.

Snow, C. 1979. The role of social interaction in language acquisition. In: A. Collins (ed.), Children's Language and Communication. Lawrence Erlbaum Associates, Hillsdale, N.J.

Snow, C., de Blauw, A., Dubber, C., and van Roosmalen, G. Playing Games with Babies. In preparation.

Snow, C., de Blauw, A., and van Roosmalen, G. 1979. Talking and playing with babies. In: M. Bullowa (ed.), Before Speech, pp. 269–288. Cambridge University Press, London.

Snow, C., and Hoefnagel-Höhle, M. 1978a. The critical period for language acquisition: Evidence from second language learning. Child Dev. 49:1263–1279.

Snow, C., and Hoefnagel-Höhle, M. 1978b. The linguistic environment of school-age second language learners. Unpublished.

Sorenson, R. K., and Hansen, B. 1980. The sign language of deaf children in Denmark. In: D. Ingram, F. C. C. Peng, and P. Dale (eds.), Proceedings of the First International Congress for the Study of Child Language, pp. 400–438. University Press of America, Lanham, Md.

Stella Prorok, E. 1978. Mother-child verbal interchanges: A field descriptive study with Brazilian children aged one to three. Paper presented at the First International Congress for the Study of Child Language, April 7–12, Tokyo, Japan.

Trevarthen, C. 1977. Descriptive analyses of mother-infant communicative behavior. In: H. R. Schaffer (ed.), Studies in Mother-Infant Interaction, pp. 227–270. Academic Press, Inc., New York.

Tulkin, S., and Kagan, J. 1972. Mother-child interaction in the first year of life. Child Dev. 43:31–41.

Van der Geest, T. 1977. Some interactional aspects of language acquisition. In: C. Snow and C. Ferguson (eds.), Talking to Children, pp. 89–108. Cambridge University Press, London.

Whiten, A. 1977. Assessing the effects of perinatal events on the success of the mother-infant relationship. In: H. R. Schaffer (ed.), Studies in Mother-Infant Interaction, pp. 403–426. Academic Press, Inc., New York.

Workgroup on Foreign Workers' Language. 1978. Nederlands tegen buitenlanders (Dutch addressed to foreigners). Publication No. 18, Institute for General Linguistics. University of Amsterdam.

Yamada, J., Kriendler, J., and Haimsohn, M. 1978. Simultaneous communication triggers language acquisition. Paper presented at the First International Congress for the Study of Child Language, April 7–12, Tokyo, Japan.

Parental Speech as Primary Linguistic Data
Some Complexities in the Study of the Effect of the Input in Language Acquisition

Toni G. Cross

A considerable amount of research has addressed the question of whether parental speech—the speech children are presumed to use as primary linguistic input—is substantially different from the casual speech of adults. As Snow (1977a) noted, this type of research often was undertaken to refute a major premise of the nativistic account of language acquisition prevailing during the 1960s—that children acquiring the structural complexities of their local language did so on the basis of misleading and confusing evidence. Two assumptions, first, that the child's linguistic environment was the same as adult conversational speech, and second, that much of this speech consisted of "false starts, disconnected phrases, and other deviations from idealized competence" (Chomsky, 1972), allowed nativists at that time to conclude that linguistic experience was largely irrelevant in the acquisition process, serving merely to trigger an innate and specialized language-learning program into operation.

Underlying this argument was a very simple approach to the question of how the child acquires language. In general terms, the problem of explaining language-acquisition was believed to be analogous, conceptually, to the process of discovering the contents of a sealed, opaque box. That is, in order to determine its internal structure and manner of

Part of the research discussed in this chapter was supported by grants from the Australian Research Grants Committee.

operation, it was simply necessary to compare the structure of the input (parental speech) with the structure of the output. This simple "black-box" methodology was recommended explicitly by Chomsky (1965, 1972) and by McNeill (1966) among others, and was spelled out clearly by Fodor (1966):

> If the linguistic information in the child's data closely approximates the lin-guistic information he must master, we may assume that the role of intrinsic structure is relatively insignificant. Conversely, if the linguistic information at which the child arrives is only indirectly and abstractly related to the data pro-vided by the child's exposure to adult speech, we shall have to suppose that the child's intrinsic structure is correspondingly complex (p. 107).

This chapter suggests that acceptance of this simple conceptualiza-tion of the problem has impeded the development of firm statements about the role of parental speech in child language-learning, and is con-tinuing to do so. For instance, in her introduction to a detailed and careful analysis of the correlation between maternal and child speech, Newport (1976) refers to Fodor's methodological argument and, in drawing con-clusions from her results, she appeals to it quite explicitly. It is argued here that this characterization of the problem has allowed researchers to overlook much of the complexity in the relationship between the child's mind and the operation of external factors, and that this, in turn, has led to the tendency to draw simplistic, and therefore probably erroneous, conclusions about the limited role of variation in parental speech in the acquisition process. Furthermore, it can be argued that experimental designs based on this conception have contributed to the ambiguity and inconclusiveness of investigations of the effects on children's progress of manipulating various aspects of the input.

What follows is a discussion of some complex issues in the study of the relationship between the input and the output—the complexity of which is usually overlooked in the design and interpretation of such studies—and some suggestions for solving these problems.

MOTHERS' SPEECH RESEARCH

It is now clear that the speech styles used by adults in addressing young children differ markedly from the styles they use in adult conversations. Several comparison studies (for example, Broen, 1972; Snow, 1972; Phillips, 1973; Remick, 1976; Newport, 1976) demonstrate, on many pa-rameters, that the speech addressed to young children barely overlaps with speech addressed to older children or adults. Thus, the assumption that children learn from an input that predominantly resembles normal adult speech is now clearly untenable. For example, it has been shown that parental speech is syntactically simpler and more regular than adult speech; it is spoken more fluently and less rapidly; and it contains far fewer errors or distortions of surface structure or canonical form. Consistent results like these cast considerable doubt on the assertion that the child's input is largely ill-formed and garbled. Furthermore, replicated descriptive work has generally shown that there is only very slight irregularity, error, or disfluency in parental speech—a finding that is inconsistent with the conclusion that the input is unfavorable or misleading for the child. In fact, in keeping with the black-box argument, a number of researchers and reviewers have drawn the conclusion that because the child's task can thus be considered much simpler than most nativists had supposed, it is justifiable to credit the child with much less specificity and detail in intrinsic structure.

The notion that the black-box analogy is appropriate to encapsulate the child's role in the acquisition process (whether used to support nativist or more interactionist positions) is seriously misleading. (See Cross, 1979, for a more detailed discussion of this argument.) It has led to a vast oversimplification of the issue and hence to inadequate research designs and misinterpretation of results. Although Chomsky uses the analogy himself, he reminds readers that it involves the simplifying assumption that the acquisition process is somehow instantaneous (Chomsky, 1976). Such an assumption is acceptable, he argues, only when one accepts the further assumption that children acquire most important aspects of language extremely quickly. Moreover, once it is admitted that, in reality, the process is a continuous acquisition of changing structural knowledge which, albeit rapid, probably extends over several years of early childhood, then several issues emerge to complicate the model. It seems obvious that the child's learning capacities will be different at different stages of development, and that children will process the input differently at various stages, both in terms of what they already understand about the structure and functions of language, as well as in terms of developments in the sophistication of their learning strategies.

Moreover, research has suggested that the notion of developmental complications also should be incorporated into the input side of the equation. Recent studies investigating the determinants of maternal speech adjustments, despite minor differences in interpretation, have shown clear developmental trends in many features of this speech style (for example, Moerk, 1972, 1974; Cross, 1975, 1977a, 1979; Newport, 1976; Snow, 1977b; Morris, 1979; Wells, 1979). In general, these changes indicate that as children mature, parental speech increasingly resembles adult conversational speech. Early studies (Broen, 1972; Snow, 1972; Phillips, 1973; Moerk, 1974) showed significant changes in complexity, fluency, redundancy, etc., with mothers speaking to children of different ages. More recent, detailed analyses (for example, Cross, 1975, 1977a; Newport, 1976;

Morris, 1979) demonstrate that such changes are related to the changes that are taking place in the child's comprehension and production of speech, that is, in the output side of the black-box relationship.

Several lines of research support this conclusion. First, there are replicated results which, to varying extents, show considerable correlation between measures of children's language and their mothers' speech adjustments. This correlation strongly suggests that maternal speech adjustments are made in response to feedback from the child's communicative competence in conversational interaction.

Even clearer evidence of this feedback account comes from a recent comparison of seven mothers speaking to their infants before the infants could comprehend or produce speech (between the ages of 3 and 7 months) with the same mothers addressing their older toddlers (16 to 25 months) who were just beginning to produce recognizable words and phrases (Cross 1978b). In that study, 62 features of maternal speech (including syntactic, semantic, speech style, and discourse adjustments) were compared, and 46 were found to differentiate significantly the speech styles.

In addition, despite the fact that a large proportion of the variance in parental speech features can be attributed to variation in their children's linguistic abilities, the evidence also suggests that once children are equated for linguistic maturity, differences in their individual behavioral and interaction styles in conversational situations can also influence their mothers' speech features.

Cross, Morris, and Nienhuys (in press) compared maternal speech to prelinguistic hearing children at 6 and 12 months with maternal speech to hearing 2-year-olds, and to prelinguistic hearing-impaired 2- and 5-year-olds. They found considerable differences among the groups in syntactic and referential features. A similar result was obtained by Cross (1977b), who found differences in maternal speech to linguistically-matched aphasic 4-year-olds and normal 2-year-olds. However, many of these differences disappeared when the aphasic children's mothers were recorded addressing their normal 2-year-old children. Supportive results were obtained in a recent study that found considerable differences in maternal speech to linguistically-and intellectually-matched normal and Down's syndrome children (O'Kelly-Collard, 1978). All these results strongly suggest that the child's actual behavior (verbal and nonverbal) in the conversation situation is also a major determinant of maternal speech adjustments.

More direct support for the child's role in influencing the quality of his or her own linguistic experiences is provided by two studies that examined more specific aspects of mother-child interaction. Lieven (1978) was able to show that two children at similar stages of development elicited different proportions of expansions and self-repetitions in the speech of both the observer and their mothers. This is consistent with earlier work (Cross, 1973, 1975) that showed that several aspects of maternal speech are sensitive to the child's responsiveness in the conversation. Expansions and semantic extensions were elicited by the maturity of the child's previous contribution to the conversation, and most forms of self-repetition were contingent on the child's lack of response or on the inappropriateness of the response. Additional evidence of the child's role is also suggested by a much earlier but highly relevant finding by Snow (1972). In a study that compared mothers instructing their children in a face-to-face situation with mothers providing similar instructions in their children's absence (leaving tape recordings of their instructions), Snow found differences in the quantity, complexity, and redundancy of their speech.

These results are interesting because they consistently indicate that differences in children's communicative abilities and, consequently, in their conversational behaviors, are responsible for much of the variation that occurs naturally in parental speech adjustments.

METHODOLOGICAL IMPLICATIONS

Design Decisions

As discussed in Cross (1979), the existence of moderate-to-strong developmental trends in most aspects of parental speech holds at least three major implications for the design of investigations into the effect of variation in the input.

First, because much of the naturally-occurring variation seems to be the result of maternal speech adjustments to the children's levels of communicative ability, such studies will require careful controls for children's ability. If researchers wish to draw conclusions from correlations between maternal speech features and subsequent language development, such controls are necessary to ensure separation of the effects of the children's abilities on their mothers' adjustments from the effects of the latter on the child's development. Without this step, it will be impossible to conclude that the direction of cause and effect is from mothers' speech to child language ability rather than from child ability to maternal speech. Thus, it seems important to restrict variation in child ability as much as possible whenever the effect of variation in the input is under investigation.

Second, it is important to be aware of the strong likelihood that both the degree and direction of correlation between aspects of parental speech and child ability may alter from stage to stage throughout development. The quite strong correlations between input and output features that have been demonstrated during the period when children first produce patterned speech (for example, by Cross, 1977a, 1979; Newport, 1976) do not seem to be present either in the prelinguistic period (Phillips, 1973; Snow, 1977b; Morris, 1979) nor much after age 4 (Fraser and Roberts, 1975). Moreover, Moerk (1974, 1977) and Cross (1979) found evidence for non-linear relationships between child maturity and some features of maternal speech, specifically for expansions, semantic extensions, and some question forms.

Such fluctuations in developmental trends indicate the need for designs that investigate the effect of input variation stage by stage. Naturalistic research based on wide variation in child samples (for example, Newport, Gleitman and Gleitman, 1977) may fail to produce positive results simply because effects on children at one particular stage of development are cancelled out by non-effects (or even negative effects) of the same features at other stages. Furthermore, the possibility discussed by several authors (for example, Brown, 1973; Cazden, and Brown, 1975; Nelson, this volume) that at certain points in development children may be more or less ready, or primed, for specific linguistic acquisitions, or that aspects of the language they are acquiring may be more or less sensitive to variation in specific parental features, also highlights the possibility that the effects of the input may be stage-dependent.

A less obvious consequence of correlation between aspects of parental speech and child ability is attributable to the fact that strong linear correlations with child maturity mean that such features are present in maternal speech in their highest or lowest concentrations when children are least mature (Cross, 1979). As generally occurs in development, it is highly probable that children exhibit their most rapid rates of development at these early stages. Thus, naturalistic follow-up studies (of which there have been a number in recent years) run the considerable risk of confounding the relatively rapid developmental rates of immature children with the effects of extreme concentrations of various features in their inputs.

The observation that variation in parental speech is influenced by variation in children's spontaneous communicative behavior in conversational situations, as well as by developmental level, provides an added dimension of complexity to the methodology of researching cause and effect in this area. It seems that, by virtue of their individual styles of interaction with their parents, children can exercise a direct influence over the amount and quality of the linguistic input their parents produce in conversation with them. For this reason, it may still be premature to transport such aspects of the interaction situation into the laboratory. Rigid experimental procedures, which do not permit children to spontaneously influence the adult's conversational style (for example, those which, by design, neutralize the child's contribution to the input and thus his or her role in the acquisition process), can tell us only what can or cannot affect child learning; they will not tell us what factors do in fact influence development in natural circumstances. Failure to design studies that take account of the child's role may be a major cause of the conflict in results with experimental manipulation of variation in features like expansions or semantic extensions in the input (for example, Cazden, 1965; Feldman, 1971; Cross, 1973; Nelson, Carskaddon, and Bonvillian, 1975; Nelson, 1978).

As Wells (1980) pointed out, one of the major problems in studying the role of external factors in language acquisition is that the area lacks a coherent theoretical framework, and thus, an appropriate methodology for handling dyadic interaction. This makes it difficult to encompass the inherent complexity of the two-way cause and effect relationships that apply between child and parent in development. Until an adequate perspective is achieved, it is not particularly surprising that researchers produce different results (and different interpretations of results) depending on their methodological choices, that is, the stage of development they choose, the variation in the child samples they select, and the choice of experimental or observational methods of investigation.

Operational Definitions

If one does adopt an interactional perspective in the study of the input, one is also confronted with problems of operational definition and of data analysis. Indeed, it is very likely that complex interactions may occur at many levels of analysis in natural situations. The possibility of such specific interactions has not generally been appreciated in previous research and, at present, cannot be readily duplicated in experimental procedures. The foregoing discussion suggests that most attempts to demonstrate that variation in features of the input causes variation in developmental progress have suffered from simplistic conceptions of the relationships that may exist between the dependent and independent variables. However, the ambiguity in previous findings also may have been produced by failure to allow for more subtle interactions between variables and for the possibility that different input variables may have differential impacts on, or relationships to, language development.

First, as Cazden (1972) pointed out, insufficient consideration has been given to a basic assumption of the empirical method:

> The actual X (variable) in any experiment is a complex package of what will eventually be conceptualized as several variables. Once a strong and clear-cut effect has been noted, the course of science consists of further experiments which refine X, teasing out those aspects that are most essential to the effect (Campbell and Stanley, 1963, p. 203, cited in Cazden 1972).

Of course, this also will be true of the natural experimental methodology that has become a basic tool in child language studies. Any single variable isolated from the data of natural parent–child conversations is only a theoretical construct, the researcher's categorical imposition on the data. It is therefore probable that many parental variables may, in nature, turn out to be comprised of a collection of independently-acting causal features that will eventually be isolated and redefined. There is also the possibility that such "packages" may contain confounding sub-variables that may either inhibit or enhance the observation of the effects of other sub-variables. For instance, a series of analyses by Cross (1978b) suggest that within the broad category of maternal repetitions, partial repetitions and exact repetitions have contradictory effects on development in the early stages. Similarly, it seems plausible to explain the conflicting outcomes of experimental manipulations of expansions by Cazden (1965), Feldman (1971), and Nelson et al. (1975) in terms of small, but telling, differences in their operational definitions of the expansion treatments.

Two possibilities, then, should be guarded against in observing or manipulating input variables which, as Cazden has argued, may interact in natural situations to produce effects on language development. One is the danger of lumping together, in a single working definition, classes or sub-classes of variables that do not behave compatibly in natural conditions; the other is the complementary danger of pulling apart sub-categories of variables that may act in concert, or may interact in subtler, but as yet, unknown ways.

At least two steps can be taken to guard against the drawing of either too fine or too broad a distinction between the features to be manipulated. The first is returning to naturalistic investigations of spontaneous parent–child conversations to permit conclusions to be drawn about the natural interactions between and within categories of features before isolating variables in experimental manipulations. The other is to define classes of features as finely as possible, and to analyze the data at several categorical levels simultaneously, that is, to investigate separately the effects on child linguistic growth of the overall categories, and as many subcategories of input features as possible. The adoption of such procedures should help to clarify at least some of the complexity that an interactionist approach seems to entail.

If it is still premature to take the investigation of the input-output relationships into the laboratory, it is certainly not too early to take some manipulative techniques into the exploration of natural data. Several of the comparative studies mentioned in this chapter (for example, Cross 1977b, 1978a, 1978b; O'Kelly-Collard, 1978; Morris, 1979) used methods of manipulating either the dependent or the independent variables by selecting contrasting groups of parents and children. In those studies, two or more groups of dyads, which were equated for child language ability, were selected on the basis that the variable of interest differentiated them. For instance, in Morris's comparison, the presence or absence of feedback from the child was manipulated by comparing mothers addressing both hearing and hearing-impaired children. In Cross's study of factors associated with rate of development, groups of children who had different rates of development were compared. While research on such questions remains in the exploratory phase, the use of such contrast groups may be a useful method of producing specific hypotheses for more rigorous experimental research in later phases.

Unfortunately, there also are limitations that hamper this type of design, as can be seen in the above studies. One major difficulty lies in the selection of contrast groups on the basis of a single differentiating variable. This type of design requires that very precise matching procedures be used in order to eliminate the contribution of extraneous factors that may be correlated with the focal variable. This is a demanding enterprise at any time but, because of the ignorance of the interaction between variables in natural settings, it becomes extremely risky at the early stages of research. Nevertheless, as long as the temptation to draw definitive conclusions from such contrasts is avoided, and the design is used only as an interim heuristic for the generation of specific hypotheses, the procedure may have considerable value.

Differential Influences in the Input

The designs of many studies of the role of parental speech features are based on the assumption that effects, if they occur, will be evident in promoting the developmental process as a whole. This assumption may be unwarranted. As early as 1972, Cazden drew attention to a distinction in the ways aspects of the input may vary in their effects on development—a distinction that has not since been implemented in research. Cazden argued that there may be features that have "pervasive" influences on development (for example, the opportunity for engaging in conversation or the total amount of speech heard) and features that may have "differential" or specific influences. Furthermore, the possibility of differentiating features in terms of positive effects, non-effects, or even negative effects has been neglected, in all but one study. Newport et al. (1977), although using a correlational follow-up design that did not entirely overcome the problems raised in this chapter, produced results which, they argued, supported the hypothesis that the syntactic simplifications in parental speech may have merely threshold effects in aiding language development. Newport (1976) also argued that specific aspects of parental syntax, for example, the deletion of preverbal material in yes/no questions, the frequent use of imperatives, and the complexity of Wh-questions may have negative effects on language development. On the other hand, Cross (1978a), while providing consistent results for most syntactic features, also found evidence to suggest that several discourse adjustments may incrementally produce positive or facilitative effects on development (see also Ellis and Wells, 1980). A conclusion that may be drawn from such results is that different aspects of the input may be involved in the learning process in different ways and in different degrees. The results suggest that variation in syntactic simplification may have little impact on development, but variation in expansions, repetitions, or in the use of specific syntactic constructions and speech functions may have direct consequences on both course and rate of development.

By considering the process itself, the notion of differential influences perhaps becomes a little clearer. Cazden suggested that different aspects of language development should be conceptualized as lying on a continuum that ranges from aspects that are relatively impervious to environmental variation (in her terms, language universals) to those that are environment-sensitive, which she considered to be more language-specific features. She provided some examples:

> On one level of discussion, grammatical structure as a whole can be considered more universal than vocabulary, which is more language specific; on another level, within grammatical structure, aspects of word order, such as subject-verb-object, may be more universal than details of noun and verb morphology, which are more language specific (Cazden, 1972, p. 103).

Newport et al., in examining partial correlations (controlling for linguistic ability) between some specific details of maternal speech and several aspects of the child's subsequent growth in spontaneous speech, argued that their data required just such a distinction. More general aspects of the child's grammar, such as basic structure, seemed to be relatively insensitive to variation in maternal syntax, whereas several specific structural acquisitions, such as aspects of the English auxiliary system, were significantly associated with specific constructions in the mother's speech.

Because it is possible that specific features of the input may differentially influence aspects of language development (and may interact with each other in various ways in doing so) and because the developmental process may respond differentially and selectively to such influences, the possibility for complexity is almost unlimited. For these reasons one could predict, with some confidence, that simple experimental-style manipulations of features in the input will have ambiguous or conflicting outcomes.

Stage-Dependent Effects

Obviously the picture is complicated even further by the strong indications in the literature that some features will have stage-related effects on development while others may have continuous or consistent effects throughout development. The observation that there are categories of parental speech features that wax and wane in incidence throughout development, irrespective of their effects, while others simply increase, decrease, or remain stable (Moerk, 1977; Cross, 1977a, 1978b) further complicates the problems confronted by the researcher. Such considerations not only pose large problems for the timing of investigations, but also for the interpretation of their results. It is becoming increasingly clear that relationships found between the input and the output at specific stages (including both effects of the child on the parent, and of the parent on child) may not apply at other stages of development.

Problems of Timing

It also seems likely that the study of the effects of maternal speech may pose timing problems of a different kind. Both Cazden (1965) and Nelson et al. (1975), in their experiments on the effects of expansions and semantic extensions, came to similar decisions about the frequency and duration of the experimental treatments that would be required for effects to become measurable. However, the latter investigation, because of a vacation period, was actually spread over a longer time period. It may have been that this additional time (although there was actually slightly less exposure overall in the latter study) was sufficient to allow the effects of the expansion treatment to reach levels of significance that were not apparent in Cazden's experiment.

Moreover, the time element may interact with the specific effects of maternal speech features in several ways, confounding the results of both naturalistic and experimental studies. Different maternal features, as well as different aspects of language development, may require differing amounts of exposure for effects to become apparent. Thus, Cazden's notion of a continuum of sensitivity to environmental influences could include specific variables like the duration, frequency, and intensity of exposure that are necessary to bring about a change in different aspects of the dependent variable. It could be argued that aspects falling on the universal side of Cazden's continuum may require much wider variations in these parameters to bring about significant variation in the dependent variable; and conversely, that the more language-specific aspects may be responsive to smaller variations in the input. It would then become an empirical matter to establish the degree of exposure necessary in the case of each feature and each aspect of development, not a matter for arbitrary decision, as it is now.

Under the heading of timing, the possibility of delayed effects in the interaction between features of input and aspects of child learning can also be included. For instance, several discussions of the role of imitation in child language-learning suggest that the effects may remain hidden over the short term, appearing only at much later stages of development

(Bloom, Hood, and Lightbrown, 1974; Bloom, 1976; Ferrier, 1978). This may also be the case for various features of the input and, once again, there is the possibility that features may differ in this respect.

Conversely, it is possible that some interactions may have only short term effects on the developmental process—effects that disappear at later stages of development. In a study of twins, one of whom had received formal language training prior to preschool experiences, Luria and Yudovich (1971) found that the effects of training were later obliterated as the untrained twin at kindergarten rapidly achieved his brother's level of ability. Moreover, the possibility that specific interactions between maternal speech features and aspects of development may vary with respect to durability of effects can also be conceived of as interacting with other aspects of timing (for example, with stage of development or exposure), which further complicates the methodological picture.

CONCLUSION

Few of these issues have been given serious consideration in recent discussions on the role of parent speech. And, no study that takes into account all of the sources of complexity discussed here has yet been reported. In fact, it will probably be impossible to conduct such a study because of time, personnel, and budget limitations faced by most researchers. Nevertheless, the discussion of the problems in itself should prove useful, if only to ensure that the complexity of the issue is not underestimated, and to encourage researchers to proceed in smaller steps in their attempts to solve these problems. The surest route to obtaining clear answers is first, to survey the hazards along the way and then, plan a course to avoid or overcome them.

REFERENCES

Bloom, L., Hood, L., and Lightbrown, P. 1974. Imitation in language development: If, when and why. Cogn. Psychol. 6:380–420.
Bloom, L. 1976. An integrative perspective on language development. Papers and Reports on Child Language Development. Stanford University, Stanford, Cal.
Broen, P. A. 1972. The Verbal Environment of the Language-Learning Child. ASHA Monograph. No. 17.
Brown, R. 1973. A First Language: The Early Stages. Harvard University Press, Cambridge, Mass.
Brown, R. 1977. Introduction. In: C. E. Snow and C. A. Ferguson (eds.), Talking to Children: Language Input and Acquisition, pp. 1–27. Cambridge University Press, Cambridge.
Campbell, D. T., and Stanley, J. C. 1963. Experimental and quasi-experimental designs for research on teaching. In: N. L. Gage (ed.), Handbook of Research on Teaching. Rand McNally, Chicago.
Cazden, C. B. 1965. Environmental assistance to the child's acquisition of gram-

mar. Unpublished doctoral dissertation, Harvard University, Boston.

Cazden, C. B. 1972. Child Language and Education. Holt, Rinehart & Winston, Inc., New York.

Cazden, C. B., and Brown, R. 1975. The early development of the mother-tongue. In: E. H. Lenneberg and E. Lenneberg (eds.), Foundations of Language Development, Vol. 1. Academic Press, Inc., New York.

Chomsky, N. 1965. Aspects of the Theory of Syntax. M.I.T. Press, Cambridge, Mass.

Chomsky, N. 1972. Language and Mind. 2nd Ed. Harcourt Brace Jovanovich, Inc., New York.

Chomsky, N. 1976. Reflections on Language. Pantheon Books, New York.

Clark, R. 1977. What's the use of imitation. J. Child Lang. 4:341–358.

Cross, T. G. 1973. The role of parent-child discourse patterns in the young child's acquisition of language. In: D. Riegel (ed.), Language Development and Disorders. Wilke & Co., Melbourne.

Cross, T. G. 1975. Some relationships between motherese and linguistic level in accelerated children. Papers and Reports on Child Language Development. Stanford University, Stanford, Cal.

Cross, T. G. 1977a. Mothers' speech adjustments: the contribution of selected child listener variables. In: C. E. Snow and C. A. Ferguson (eds.), Talking to Children: Language Input and Acquisition, pp. 151–188. Cambridge University Press, Cambridge.

Cross, T. G. 1977b. Developmental aphasia, language delay, conversational deprivation. In: G. V. Stanley and K. W. Walsh (eds.), Brain Impairment: Proceedings of the 1976 Brain Impairment Workshop. Melbourne University Press, Melbourne.

Cross, T. G. 1978a. Motherese: Its association with rate of syntactic acquisition in young children. In: N. Waterson and C. E. Snow (eds.), The Development of Communication. John Wiley & Sons, Inc., London.

Cross, T. G. 1978b. Mother-child interaction in the study of child language development. Unpublished doctoral thesis, University of Melbourne, Melbourne.

Cross, T. G. 1979. Mothers' speech adjustments and child language learning: Some methodological considerations. Lang. Sciences 1:3–27.

Cross, T. G., Morris, J. E., and Nienhuys, T. G. Linguistic feedback and maternal speech: Comparisons of mothers addressing hearing and hearing-impaired children. First Language. In press.

Ellis, R., and Wells, G. 1980. Enabling factors in adult-child discourse. First Language. 1:1–16.

Feldman, C. 1971. The effects of various types of adult responses in the syntactic acquisition of two- to three-year-olds. Unpublished manuscript, University of Chicago, Chicago.

Ferrier, L. 1978. Some observations of error in context. In: N. Waterson and C. Snow (eds.), The Development of Communication. John Wiley & Sons, Inc., London.

Fodor, J. A. 1966. How to learn to talk: Some simple ways. In: F. Smith and G. Miller (eds.), The Genesis of Language: A Psycholinguistic Approach, pp. 105–122. M.I.T. Press, Cambridge, Mass.

Fraser, C., and Roberts, A. 1975. Mothers' speech to children of different ages. J. Psycholinguis. Res. 4:9–16.

Lieven, E. V. M. 1978. Conversations between mother and young children: Individual differences and their possible implications for the study of language learning. In: N. Waterson and C. Snow (eds.), The Development of Communication. John Wiley & Sons, Inc., London.

Luria, A. R., and Yudovich, F. 1971. Speech and Development of Mental Processes in the Child. Penguin Books, Harmondsworth, Middlesex.

McNeill, D. 1966. The creation of language by children. In: J. Lyons and R. Wales (eds.), Psycholinguistic Papers, pp. 99–115. Edinburgh University Press, Edinburgh.

Moerk, E. L. 1972. Principles of dyadic interaction in language learning. Merrill Palmer Quart. 18:229–257.

Moerk, E. L. 1974. Changes in verbal child-mother interactions with increasing language skills of the child. J. Psycholinguis. Res. 3:101–116.

Moerk, E. L. 1977. Pragmatic and Semantic Aspects of Early Language Development. University Park Press, Baltimore.

Morris, J. 1978. The nature and determinants of mothers' speech adjustments. Unpublished honors thesis, University of Melbourne.

Morris, J. E. 1979. Propositional content of maternal speech. Paper presented at the Second National Language and Speech Conference, November 1979, Melbourne.

Nelson, K. E., Carskaddon, G., and Bonvillian, J. 1975. Syntax acquisition: Impact of experimental variation in adult verbal interaction with children. Child Dev. 44:497–504.

Newport, E. L. 1976. Motherese: The speech of mothers to young children. In: N. Castellan, D. Pisoni, and G. Potts (eds.), Cognitive Theory, Vol. 2. Lawrence Erlbaum Associates, Hillsdale, N. J.

Newport, E. L., Gleitman, L., and Gleitman, H. 1977. Mother, I'd rather do it myself: Some effects and non-effects of maternal speech style. In: C. E. Snow and C. A. Ferguson (eds.), Talking to Children: Language Input and Acquisition, pp. 109–149. Cambridge University Press, Cambridge.

O'Kelley-Collard, M. 1978. Mothers' speech to Down's Syndrome children. Unpublished masters thesis, La Trobe University, Melbourne.

Phillips, J. 1973. Syntax and vocabulary of mothers' speech to young children: Age and sex comparisons. Child Dev. 44:182–185.

Remick, H. 1976. Maternal speech to children during language acquisition. In: W. von Raffler-Engle and Y. Lebrun (eds.), Baby Talk and Infant Speech. Swets & Zeitlinger, Lisse, Netherlands.

Snow, C. E. 1972. Mothers' speech to children learning language. Child Dev. 43: 549–565.

Snow, C. E. 1977a. Mothers' speech research: From input to interaction. In: C. E. Snow and C. A. Ferguson (eds.), Talking to Children: Language Input and Acquisition, pp. 31–49. Cambridge University Press, Cambridge.

Snow, C. E. 1977b. The development of conversations between mothers and babies. J. Child Lang. 4:1–22.

Wells, G. 1980. Apprenticeship in meaning. In: K. E. Nelson (ed.), Children's Language, Vol. 2, pp. 45–126. Gardner Press, Inc., New York.

Toward a Rare-Event Cognitive Comparison Theory of Syntax Acquisition

Keith E. Nelson

The topic of this chapter is how new syntactic constructions are introduced into the young child's first language. It concerns how children can be aided or hindered by the input they encounter, and it is about ways to study that question. Theoretical notions about syntactic development and the role of rare events are developed, in this chapter, in more detail than appears in previous works (for example, Nelson, 1977a, 1977b; Nelson, Carskaddon, and Bonvillian, 1973; Nelson et al., 1979a, 1979b). This chapter also examines the extant data bearing on the theory, and discusses means of supplementing such data.

CENTRAL ASSUMPTIONS OF
A RARE-EVENT COGNITIVE COMPARISON THEORY

Assumption 1 To fully master syntactically governed language, the child must engage in active communication in appropriate contexts with partners who are fluent in the language and who display (separately or in combination) a full range of grammatical structures. This assumption, as well as the remaining assumptions apply to sign language, speech, or any other language mode that constitutes the child's first language. Tentatively, it is further proposed that many aspects of second-language acquisition fit this rare-event model (Nelson, 1977b).

Assumption 2 Adults and older children do not directly teach young children to use syntactically well-constructed sentences; they do not know how to do such teaching, and they produce sentences that for the most part, play no essential role in the child's learning of syntax, although the sentences may be vital to acquisition of discourse and other skills (Shatz, in press). Nevertheless, at certain points in development, particular kinds of adult replies to the child are crucial for the child's syntactic progress.

Assumption 3   At any point in syntax development, the child must find relevant examples within an input set of sentences that are predominantly irrelevant. The child must derive information about syntactic structures from a process of cognitive comparison between structures already present in the child's system and certain partially contrasting structures used by others.

Assumption 4   When a cognitive comparison occurs between a new sentence structure, for example, *the boy will run* and a current sentence structure, for example, *the boy ran*, three outcomes are possible: 1) there is no discrepancy between the structures, and the child codes this as confirmation of the usefulness of the current structure, 2) a discrepancy exists, but the child cannot code the nature of the discrepancy, or 3) a codable discrepancy is noted. Only in the third case does the child's language system gain information from explicit differences between current structures and sentence structures in the input set.

Assumption 5   Codable discrepancies are rarely noted by the child. This is because there are limitations of memory, attention, and motivation, and because most of the highly specific kinds of new sentences children require for comparison at each stage do not occur very frequently in input. A complete absence of such required forms for a period will lead to a plateau in syntax acquisition; conversely, a relatively high incidence of such forms will tend to accelerate the child's progress (an assumption directly tested in several of the studies presented below).

Assumption 6   The particular new sentence examples or replies required for syntactic advances in the child's system shift as one moves from one area of syntax to another, or from one stage to the next.

Assumption 7   The number of codable discrepancy comparisons that are required before a child revises his or her system to incorporate the new form may vary from child to child and from form to form, but research to date suggests that this number can be surprisingly low and may decline as development proceeds. Of course, some advances in language may be gradually realized after the child considers thousands of examples. However, the child more often makes a specific change in syntax after considering and coding only a small number (speculatively, 1 to 60) of discrepancies between his or her own sentence structure and that of adults. Again, only those rare discrepancies that are actually noticed and coded could be useful to the child (see also, Nelson, in press).

The above assumptions explain why the theory is termed a *rare-event cognitive comparison theory*. The (typically) rare events absolutely necessary to the child's advances in syntax are the successful comparisons between input constructions and closely related constructions already in the child's syntactic system. A few infrequent events in the midst of a vast amount of language interchange, and a small amount of the right kind of input information that the child closely attends to and analyzes comprise the core of developmental change in syntax, according to the theory. Thus, the nature of syntactic development reflects the nature of cognitive development generally. Research on phonological development, semantic development, and sensorimotor development also demonstrates that the child will ignore extensive input yet will show rapid learning when appropriate rare events are noticed and coded (Nelson, 1977a, 1978, in press).

Assumption 8   The probability that the child will actually code potentially useful input exemplars will vary with the broader temporal and conversational patterns in which exemplars—and exemplar-displaying devices such as recasts—are embedded. This assumption carries many corollaries, two of which deserve note. One is that different rules of syntax may require (or "prefer") different complex patterns for ready processing and acquisition by the child. For example, the conversational patterns that may best display informative questions to the child could prove to be very unlike patterns that best display sentences with essential subject-verb agreement data. A second corollary is that although the child's speed in acquiring a rule is likely to be correlated roughly with the frequency of relevant and timely rule exemplars in input, this correlation should break down for certain forms to the extent that mothers (and other input sources) tend to use these forms with declining conversational appropriateness as their frequencies of using the forms increase.

Assumption 9   To understand how the child moves from no mastery of a form to complete mastery, it is necessary to consider four partially overlapping phases: 1) preparation, in which encounters with the form and related forms do not lead to analysis but do lead to a readiness for the attention and analysis deployed in the next phase; 2) analysis, in which the child attends to and tries to code the input forms in relation to the system that has been established to that point; 3) assessment of new form analyses, involving attempts to use newly analyzed forms in production and comprehension, a phase that clearly may lead back to further analyses until some analysis of the form proves adequate; and 4) consolidation of the new acquisition in the system, ensuring that it will not become unstable or be forgotten. A complete account of a form's acquisition would specify for each of these stages the required input and the way in which the child processes and retains elements of the input. If the child draws upon memory of prior examples and prior attempts at analysis when a new attempt at analysis occurs, then both long-term and short-term memory processes need to be described. In one study described below, a beginning in this direction is provided.

Assumption 10   Many kinds of discourse sequences are useful in displaying the syntactic information the child must analyze in order to acquire a new form. (Elaboration on this topic is provided by Nelson, 1978, in press.) Some of these may involve discourse sequences in which the child is merely an adjunct to, rather than a direct participant, in the conversation. However, among the most useful discourse exchanges are "recast comparisons" in which the following sequence occurs: the child produces a sentence, for example, *The unicorn yawned,* that is immediately given a reply such as *The unicorn stretched and yawned, didn't he?* that retains the basic meaning of the child's sentence but displays it in a new sentence structure, thereby allowing a short-term comparison with the child's own, related sentence. (For additional discussions of discourse sequences potentially useful to the child, see Brown, 1968, Moerk, 1972, and Snow and Ferguson, 1977.)

THE SHADOW INVESTIGATION

Ideally, descriptions of a child's acquisition of a new form should specify exhaustively the most relevant input the child has encountered and should detail precisely when the child first used the new form. The first study presented in this chapter aims toward this ideal more so than prior studies have, by "shadowing" two children fairly intensively over a period of about one month. Despite initial trepidation in choosing this direction, it was found that such shadowing could make sense to mothers and that it could be done without much intrusion into these two children's established patterns of activities. For both children, the shadowing usually was done only on weekdays, with morning, afternoon, and late afternoon periods included. The total time spent directly in interacting with each child or within earshot of each child—so that written records could be made of target and control utterances—was over 44 hours across 36-37 days (including unsampled weekends).

In this shadow investigation (Nelson and Denninger, 1977), the child's productions were extensively sampled but were chosen selectively both with respect to the targets for possible acquisition and to the input manipulations designed to encourage acquisitions. From pre-study sampling, it was known that these two 3-year-olds had not yet acquired tag questions or passive constructions. During the study, the children's use of both kinds of forms were watched for but only the tag questions were included in input manipulations that were expected, on the basis of the above theories, to speed acquisition, while the passives served as a control.

Both children began to use tag question forms, but not the passive constructions. Because the input manipulations consisted of child-experimenter conversations, in which the experimenter provided recast replies that included the targeted-for acquisition tag questions and did not include passives, it was inferred that the recast constructions were helpful in the children's acquisition of the tag question forms. This point is supported by additional evidence, presented below, from other experiments.

The unique insight that the shadow experiment data offer concerns temporal processes involved in acquiring a new syntactic construction. The recasting by experimenters was done in 10–20 minute intervention (with observation, also) periods interspersed with longer observation-only sessions, in which no recastings and no tag questions were provided. Overall, there was much more observation time than intervention time—for Child A the respective times were 47.5 and 20.0 hours, for Child B they were 34.5 and 9.5 hours—therefore, the child's first use of a tag question could occur either very close to an input example or removed in time by hours or days. (Tags by these children's parents, as is true for most parents, were extremely rare in speech directed to the children.) For Child A, her first apparent use of a tag question occurred minutes after an experimenter had last used a tag question. In this instance, then, the initial appearance of the form in the child's language could have been based on a fairly short-term memory of a recent example that may have been different in detail, but of the same form in input. In the case of Child B, however, it seemed that longer-term storage of input must have been involved because the first instance of tag question production was noted one morning at 9:47—before any experimenter tags had been used, and 20 hours and 37 minutes (overnight) after the last tag question had been produced by the experimenter. If only the most recent input was involved in the kind of comparisons between input and the child's own syntactic system that are described in the above theory, then the results for Child B point toward storage, an input exemplar—or the comparison based upon it— and retrieval nearly a day later of such information to guide production. Of course, if information based upon many input exemplars of tag questions are stored and retrieved, then even longer-term retrieval processes are suggested by these findings. Beyond this initial investigation of the temporal relation between input and acquisition, what remains to be specified are the details of information storage and retrieval across minutes, hours, days, and perhaps weeks or months, which allow the child to make the necessary comparisons cognitively for constructing a new syntactic rule.

FURTHER EVIDENCE FOR THE EFFECT OF
INPUT VARIATIONS ON SYNTACTIC PROGRESS

Two further experiments share with the shadow study the goal of relating experimentally determined input variations to children's progress in syntax. The first experiment (Nelson et al., 1973) was conducted at a time (1971) when positive evidence for such relations was lacking. The existing data had been interpreted as showing that adults' replies, including subsets of what in this paper is termed recasts, have little or no effect on syntactic development. This investigation, in contrast, demonstrated that children who experienced an increased use of recast replies by adult experimenters were children who progressed in syntax more rapidly than children in groups in which no adult intervention replies in recast form were furnished.

This result, although a positive one, left open the details of the interchange process because both the intervention and the outcome were based upon fairly broad procedures in that experimenters used any contextually appropriate recasts they could invent and in that the several measures of syntactic advance were also on the general side (for example, mean length of utterance in words (MLU), and verb phrase index).

The final experimental study (Nelson, 1977a) was, in several respects, more sharply focused. The recasts used were quite specific; they were adult replies directed at particular question forms (for example, tag questions) or verb forms (for example, future tense verbs) which, as baseline measures revealed, were lacking in the child's system. In addition, the outcome measures were also interlocked with the specifics of the baseline and intervention forms; that is, the study asked whether children who received particular kinds of recasts, for example those incorporating contextually-appropriate tag questions, were able to begin using the targeted form for the first time during the intervention period. The answer was clear. Children did acquire use of the specific verb and question forms, apparently as a result of the experimentally provided recasts. The children's uses of the new forms (as was true also in the shadow study) occurred in spontaneous sentences rather than in imitative utterances (Nelson, 1977a).

In each of the studies mentioned above, it is important to recognize that the experimenters were not the only sources of the recast replies that proved helpful to the children's progress in syntax. Rather, in congruence with the theoretical propositions of a rare-event cognitive comparison theory, it is likely that the children were already hearing a few recasts

from parents and that the outcomes rested on an increased availability of
the recast replies central to the child's cognitive comparisons of input
forms with present-system forms. If this is so, then in observational
studies, mothers who use relatively many recasts should make available
more of the exchange information a child requires. Consequently, such
mothers should have children who (at least during certain phases of syntactic growth) progress more rapidly in syntax than do children whose
mothers use recasts relatively infrequently. This idea is assessed empirically in the next section of this chapter. The construction of an adequate
theory of language acquisition will require more work of this nature, that
is, detailed analyses of possibly convergent data from a variety of experimental and observational paradigms (Furrow, Nelson, and Benedict,
1979; Nelson, 1977b; Nelson et al., 1979a; Shatz, in press).

OBSERVATIONAL DATA

The results reported here come from a sample of 19 children and their
mothers. Both were observed when the children were 22 months old and
then when they were 27 months old. This project, the Fiffin Project, is
described in more detail in previous reports (Nelson, 1978; Nelson and
Bonvillian, 1978; Nelson, Bonvillian, and Kaplan, 1977). The central
measures of language use are the children's advances in language between
22 and 27 months, as correlated with the 22-month data on mother's language use with the children. In short, the analyses center on whether individual differences between mothers, in their use of recasts and other
constructions at an initial point in time, are predictive of children's differential rates of subsequent syntactic progress.

Two forms of recasts were distinguished. Simple recasts were
mothers' replies that maintained reference to the same basic meaning in
the child's preceding utterance with structural changes that were confined
to just one of three major sentence components—subject, verb, or object.
(These simple recasts included one subcategory, expansion, a reply that
formed a grammatically complete sentence while utilizing all the words, in
their original order, from the child's incomplete utterance (compare, for
example, Brown and Bellugi, 1964; Nelson, 1977a; Nelson et al., 1973).)
Complex recasts involved structural changes in two or three of these components. It was assumed that the 22-month-old's ability to analyze and
make use of the structurally new information in recasts would have
definite limits, and therefore that the children would make better use of
simple recasts.

As it turned out, this simple-versus-complex distinction was valuable
in understanding the possible roles of maternal input. A high proportion
of simple recasts in mothers' replies was correlated $+0.47$ ($p < 0.05$) with

the children's rapid growth in MLU. Similarly, the same measure for the mothers was positively associated with auxilary verb growth in the children's language ($r = +0.47$, $p < 0.05$). In contrast, the mothers' use of high proportions of complex recasts were negatively related to both measures of language growth; for auxiliary verbs $r = -0.61$, for MLU $r = -0.29$ (Pearson r's in each case).

Thus, it seems that recasts that display relatively simple structural changes—changes in comparison with the children's utterances that preceded the recasts—are useful to the child at around age 2. Other replies to the children are less valuable for the children's linguistic growth, as Table 1 shows. For example, mothers' replies that are imitations of the children's preceding utterances or that (unlike recasts) substantially change the topic (compare, for example, Cross, 1977) are not significantly associated with growth in MLU verbs, or noun phrases. Of course, as the theory outlined above suggests, different types of recasts and other replies may well play different roles as the child's language levels shift between ages 1 and 6. From this Fiffin Project data and from other recent reports (Newport, 1977; Wells, 1980), it also is clear that fairly differentiated analyses of mothers' speech are necessary because general measures like mothers' MLU or discrepancy in MLU between mother and child are correlated only at low positive or negative levels with measures of children's linguistic advances.

CONCLUSION: RECASTS AND BEYOND

Mothers vary in the proportion of simple recasts mixed in their conversational replies to children. Furthermore, in congruence with the theory stated at the beginning of this chapter, frequent recast use seems to promote linguistic growth. This interpretation is supported by considerable complementary evidence from a series of experimental studies. In these

Table 1.   Correlations between maternal speech and children's syntactic growth

Increased syntactic complexity by child between 22 and 27 months	Mutually exclusive categories of reply by mother to 22-month-old			
	Simple[a] recasts	Complex recasts	Imitations	Topic changes
MLU	+0.47*	−0.29	+0.00	−0.43
Auxiliaries	+0.47*	−0.61**	+0.02	−0.35
Verbs overall	+0.37	−0.58**	−0.25	−0.01

*$p < 0.05$.
**$p < 0.01$.
[a]This category includes "expansions," replies that keep the elements and order of elements of the child's incomplete sentence but add new elements to form a grammatically complete sentence (compare, for example, Brown and Bellugi, 1964).

studies, the experimenters were, in effect, mimicking what some mothers seem to do actually and without instruction—using recasts often but with contextual appropriateness. It seems reasonable to conclude that the recasts may have facilitated the children's language growth by providing structural information in a way that the children would notice and analyze.

The strong pattern of complementary evidence implicating recasts as one powerful element in syntactic development needs to be extended in future work to encompass additional forms, additional developmental phases, and languages other than English. Beyond that, it should be noted that in the rare-event cognitive comparison theory, recasts are just one example of the kind of input reply or element that could facilitate the child's completion of the cognitive analyses necessary for introducing new forms into his or her language system. One direction for future work is to differentiate further, types of recasts and to specify the whole range of input variations that influence the child's acquisition of new syntactic forms. One additional illustration of how input is related to syntactic progress follows. For the 19 children in the Fiffin Project, the rate of auxiliary verb growth (22–27 months) was strongly and positively associated ($r = +0.84$ $p < 0.001$) with the discrepancy between mother and child in complexity of auxiliary verbs at the beginning of the growth period. Far from suggesting, as some writers have, that mothers should always be fine-tuned in their complexity and should use language that is only slightly more complex than the child's language, this outcome indicates that for some forms and some developmental periods, a considerable discrepancy in complexity provides the child information that aids acquisition of new syntactic forms.

Another major direction for future work is the idea that for different language skills and for different developmental periods, different input or conversational variations may be crucial. In addition to further work concerning acquisition of new syntactic forms as related to recasts and other possible replies, the area of discourse structure within and across developmental periods is an ideal topic for research. How the child's various skills in discourse at ages 3, 4, 5 or later are related both to current conversational input and to the structure of conversational changes earlier in development is a question that needs to be extensively researched. The research could build on some of the excellent groundwork of discourse analysis of the last five years (for example, Bates, 1976; Dore, 1978; Ervin-Tripp and Mitchell-Kernan, 1977; Garvey, 1975; Hall and Cole, 1978). The measure of discourse structure employed in the Fiffin Project was a turn-taking measure, the average number of speaker turns (C-M-C-M-C = 5 turns) pertaining to the same topic. This measure showed highly contrasting relations to language skill for different developmental periods. For the 22–27 month period, turns in mother-child discourse were not associated strongly with any measure of progress for the children. However, long chains of turns on the same topic by mother-and-22-month-old dyads were highly correlated with the children's skill as 4½ year-olds in communication, in generating highly communicable, precise linguistic descriptions (compare, for example, Glucksberg and Krauss, 1967, for a similar measure).

Because early studies of child language and adult input language were usually based on very few subjects, the degree of similarity between different input sources and between different children was often overestimated. In fact, the degree of individual variation in children's language growth and in the conversations they encounter is surprisingly high (compare, for example, Nelson, 1979 and Nelson et al., 1979b). The clear implication is that when different children look for rarely-occurring but essential language events, they may end up looking at very different patterns of input. What one child finds entirely in her mother's input and on a rapid and smooth developmental schedule, another child may find on a more erratic schedule and scattered through the input of brother, cousin, grandmother, mother, father, and babysitter. To incorporate these variations, the theories must allow for alternative ways in which a child will progress toward an eventual congruence between his syntactic and conversational rules and those of fluent adults. In this regard, it is well to remember the rare-event proposition that most children can succeed in completing the necessary analyses by coding a small amount of the right kind of evidence. This is well-illustrated by instances of bilingual acquisition, in which the child receives all the input in one language from someone who is neither the primary linguistic source nor the primary caregiver for the child (Doyle, 1976; Friedlander et al., 1972).

REFERENCES

Bates, E. 1976. Language and Context: The Acquisition of Pragmatics. Academic Press, Inc., New York.

Brown, R. 1968. The development of Wh questions in child speech. J. Verb. Learn. Verb. Behav. 7:279–290.

Brown, R., and Bellugi, U. 1964. Three processes in the child's acquisition of syntax. Harvard Educ. Rev. 34:133–151.

Cross, T. 1977. Mother's speech adjustments: The contribution of selected child listener variables. In: C. Snow and C. Ferguson (eds.), Talking to Children, pp. 151–188. Cambridge University Press, London.

Dore, J. 1978. Variation in preschool children's conversational performances. In: K. E. Nelson (ed.), Children's Language, Vol. 1, pp. 397–444. Gardner Press (Halsted), New York.

Doyle, A. 1976. Some linguistic and cognitive consequences of early bilingualism. Paper presented to the Canadian Psychological Association, June, Toronto.

Ervin-Tripp, S., and Mitchell-Kernan, C. (eds.). 1977. Child Discourse. Academic Press, Inc., New York.

Friedlander, B. Z., Jacobs, A. C., David, B. B., and Wetstone, H. S. 1972. Time-sampling analysis of infants' natural language environments in the home. Child Dev. 43:730–740.

Furrow, D., Nelson, K., and Benedict, H. 1979. Mothers' speech to children and syntactic development: Some simple relationships. J. Child Lang. 6:423–442.

Garvey, C. 1975. Requests and responses in children's speech. J. Child Lang. 2: 41–64.

Glucksberg, S., and Krauss, R. M. 1967. What do people say after they have learned to talk? Studies of the development of referential communication. Merrill Palmer Quart. 13:309–316.

Hall, W. S., and Cole, M. 1978. On participants' shaping of discourse through their understanding of the task. In: K. E. Nelson (ed.), Children's Language, Vol. 1, pp. 445–466. Gardner Press (Halsted), New York.

Moerk, E. 1972. Principles of interaction in language learning. Merrill Palmer Quart. 18:229–258.

Nelson, K. E. 1977a. Facilitating children's syntax acquisition. Dev. Psychol. 13: 101–197.

Nelson, K. E. 1977b. Aspects of language acquisition and use from age two to age twenty. J. Am. Acad. Child Psychiatry. 16:584–607. Also appears in S. Chess and A. Thomas (eds.), Annual Progress in Child Psychiatry and Child Development, Vol. 11. Bruner/Mazel, New York.

Nelson, K. E. 1978. Theories of language acquisition. Paper presented to The New York Academy of Sciences, March, New York.

Nelson, K. E. (a) Theories of the child's acquisition of syntax: A look at necessary, catalytic, and irrelevant components of mother-child conversation. Annals of the New York Academy of Sciences. In press.

Nelson, K. E. (b) Experimental gambits in the service of language acquisition theory: From the Fiffin Project to operation input swap. In: S. A. Kuczaj (ed.), Language Development: Syntax and Semantics. Lawrence Erlbaum Associates, Hillsdale, N.J. In press.

Nelson, K. E., and Bonvillian, J. D. 1978. Early language development: Conceptual growth and related processes between 2 and 4½ years of age. In: K. E. Nelson (ed.), Children's Language, Vol. 1, pp. 467–556. Gardner Press (Halsted), New York.

Nelson, K. E., and Denninger, M. 1977. The shadow technique in the investigation of children's acquisition of new syntactic forms. Manuscript, New School for Social Research, New York.

Nelson, K. E., Bonvillian, J. D., and Kaplan, B. J. 1977. Early conceptual growth and its relation to later conceptual growth and syntactic skill. Paper presented to the Society for Research in Child Development, March, New Orleans.

Nelson, K. E., Carskaddon, G., and Bonvillian, J. D. 1973. Syntax acquisition: Impact of experimental variation in adult verbal interaction with the child. Child Dev. 44:497–504.

Nelson, K. E., Denninger, M., Kaplan, B. J., and Bonvillian, J. D. 1979a. Varied angles on how children progress in syntax. Paper presented to the Society for Research in Child Development, March, San Francisco.

Nelson, K. E., Denninger, M., Bonvillian, J. D., and Kaplan, B. J. Maternal input adjustments and non-adjustments as related to children's linguistic advances and to language acquisition theories. Penn. State Univ. In preparation.

Newport, E. 1977. Motherese. In: N. J. Castellan, D. B. Pisoni, and G. R. Potts (eds.), Cognitive Theory, pp. 177–217. Lawrence Erlbaum Associates, Hillsdale, N. J.

Shatz, M. On mechanisms of language acquisition: Can features of the communicative environment account for development? In: L. Gleitman and E. Wanner (eds.), Language Acquisition: The State of the Art. Lawrence Erlbaum Associates, Hillsdale, N. J. In press.

Snow, C., and Ferguson, C. (eds.). 1977. Talking to Children. Cambridge University Press, London.

Wells, G. 1980. Apprenticeship in meaning. In: K. E. Nelson (ed.), Children's Language, Vol. 2, pp. 85–193. Gardner Press (Halsted), New York.

Elicitation Strategies in Parental Speech Acts

Ben G. Blount

This chapter addresses the question of how parents create interactional contexts for children by attracting their attention with special features of speech. A brief review of the literature on the speech register that is commonly called baby talk is presented, and the argument that a more broadly defined speech register, parental speech, is useful for assessing the role of speech input in child language acquisition is discussed. The functions of parental speech in establishing joint parent–child action is discussed, and special attention is given to prosodic and paralinguistic features that attract a child's attention. A grammar for the use of those features by English-speaking parents is given, and differences between mother speech and father speech are noted.

In 1964, Charles Ferguson published a paper in a special issue of *American Anthropologist* that seemed, at first, to be of only slight anthropological interest. Indeed, the topic was, as Ferguson (1964) himself noted, only marginally related to linguistics. The paper, "Baby Talk in Six Languages," however, is now well-known in several academic disciplines.

Ferguson's paper is often cited to illustrate the social genesis of constraints on language usage. When adults speak to young children who have only rudimentary knowledge of language, the social interaction has an unusual quality. One member of the interactive dyad can only participate in a limited fashion, using little or no speech, and following essentially none of the established conventions for meaningful social interaction. The other member of the dyad must contribute substantially if the interaction is to be established and maintained. The one-sided nature of the interaction leads adults to utilize special constraints in their speech.

241

The social circumstances determine the speakers' choices of phonological, lexical, and grammatical features of speech. In effect, the social definition of the interactors motivates the use of the appropriate speech register, namely, baby talk.

Although the study of baby talk speech registers made important contributions in the general field of sociolinguistics, its impact on research in child language acquisition was less immediate for several reasons. An early goal of baby talk research was to characterize the regular ways in which the register deviated from standard, or ideal, adult language forms. A comparison of baby talk forms and adult forms offered a basis for rule identification. Consonant cluster reduction, for example, occurs only for certain clusters, and in those cases, only specific forms of reduction occur. In English, for example, *stomach* is reduced to *tummy*, but not to *summy*. Initial [st] → [t], not to [s]. Derivational rules can be written for consonant cluster reductions, and establishing a set of such rules is a goal of linguistic research on baby talk forms.

The interest in derivational and formal analysis has led researchers to produce descriptions of baby talk speech register for several languages (see Ferguson, 1977). Descriptions are available for languages as diverse as English, Marathi, Latvian, Berber, and others. As more descriptions of baby talk register become available, our knowledge of the types of derivational processes expands, and the possibility of discovering universals increases.

Advances in the study of baby talk speech registers do not necessarily mean that an understanding of the relationship between baby talk and language acquisition is broadened. On the contrary, it is possible that on a short-term basis, the interest in language-specific forms has had a limiting effect on the development of a functional perspective of baby talk registers. Baby talk forms were defined as appropriate to a register by convention. In other words, forms by definition had to be widespread, commonplace, and stable. Ad hoc vocalizations and imitations by parents were excluded from baby talk registers because they failed to meet those requirements. As a practical consequence, baby talk was considered to be a register addressed to children who had already acquired some language competence. The role of the register in early acquisition was thereby minimized.

The age-constrained view of baby talk was consistent with and indirectly supportive of the innatist viewpoint on child language acquisition that was predominant in the 1960s. The innatist view attributed only a minor role, if any, to parental speech as a determinant factor in children's acquisition of language. As is well known, the innatist position was that children need only a model language against which they could check their intuitions about language. Baby talk register could serve as a part of the model, but its functional role was believed to be minor.

When an interactional perspective began to be adapted for language acquisition studies in the 1970s, the limitations of an age-constrained view of baby talk speech registers became more apparent. Emphasis shifted from form to function, and the speech of parents to their young children was of interest because of the effects it had on the stimulation and initiation of social interaction between parent and child. The concern with function has led to an interest in parental speech in a broader sense than baby talk speech registers. Age constraints have been reduced, and the socialization roles of speech to children have expanded. The effects of parental speech on children's behavior has become a major focus, enabling researchers to establish a behavioral base against which language acquisition can be assessed.

Recent studies, for example, have shown that parental speech plays a directive role in early interactional development of children, that is, before the onset of true language (Blount, 1972, 1977; Bruner, 1975). Moreover, the emergence of interaction patterns between prelinguistic infants and parents is an important step in the acquisition of communicative skills by infants, skills that lead eventually to acquisition of language.

Context-sensitive patterns of vocal interaction between caregivers and prelinguistic infants have been observed as early as the first few weeks of an infant's life (Lewis and Freedle, 1973). By the time the child is 8 or 9 months old, the frequency and duration of the interaction increases, and infants are more proficient at completing turns and rounds in the interaction cycle. Long sequences of interaction can occur even though an infant's utterances and the parental utterances are devoid of any linguistic meaning. Prelinguistic infants participate in a social interactional system with caregivers, a system that has external boundaries and internal order (Blount, 1972; Bruner, 1975; Freedle and Lewis, 1977; Scollon, 1976).

Several analytical approaches can be used to relate aspects of acquisition to the interactional system. An interactional episode can be analyzed for its event structure to show that caregivers structure events, as in object-exchange games, that they call the attention of infants to the structure, and that they engage them actively in producing the structure (Blount, 1977). Longitudinally, infants learn event structures and participate strategically in them.

A second analytical approach focuses on acts within the event structure. Again, the infant's behavior can be shown to be sensitive to the internal structure of an event. To the extent that an individual act is meaningful, at least part of the meaning is derived from the embedding of the act within the event. For example, children's utterances in the one-word phase of development can have both referential and sentential meaning (Dore, 1975; Greenfield and Smith, 1976). A word can name an entity in a straightforward referential way, as when a child looking at a book points to a picture of a cat and says "kitty." The same utterance can also be part of a larger structural unit, as, for instance, when the word *kitty* is uttered in the context of identifying and naming pictures of animals in a book and is a completion of a parental statement such as *And this is a* _____.

If any given utterance has sentential meaning, then an event-structure perspective is essential for analysis of meaning. Children's one-word sentences seem, as Greenfield and Smith (1976) noted, to be two-person sentences, for which the parent structures the context and the child provides the word. The sentences are strongly embedded in the joint action of the participants in the activity at hand. Moreover, the distinction between referential and sentential meaning is useful in a consideration of children's speech acts. The role of parental support in the acquisition of units larger than words—sentences and speech acts—is highlighted in utterances that have sentential meaning. It is also useful, however to consider parental support in the acquisition of referential meaning.

From the genesis of referentiality, it can be seen that joint parental-infant action is the source of the meaning (Bruner, 1975; Blount and Kempton, 1976). For a child to learn the name of an object, a structured context in the earliest instances of naming behavior is required. Naming can occur because the labeling process is embedded in the structure of the event. Meaning, in each instance, is dependent initially on concerted interaction that is already established as a patterned activity. For instance, a child learns to call a ball *ball* only because of activities with his parents involving a ball. Referential meanings per se appear only later in development, and the same argument applies to sentential meaning. They are derived from event-structured parent-child interaction, because the meaning of an utterance, aside from linguistic meanings, is dependent on the conjoinment of speech and event-structured activity.

For a child to engage in joint action with a parent, considerable interactional support by the parent is obviously necessary, especially in the beginning phases of joint action. Infants must learn to respond to the attention-getting actions of their caregivers. They also must learn to focus their attention on the activity itself at first, and then they must learn that actions are systematic, regular, and later, meaningful. The first of these requirements, attention-getting, is almost solely a parental function. It is also the antecedent for further interaction.

Despite the importance of the directive role of parents in establishing joint action, relatively little is known about what parents do systematically to attract and sustain attention (Blount and Padgug, 1976; and Ninio and Bruner, 1978). This area of parental behavior is not well-documented and is in need of further investigation.

Of special interest are the voicing and prosodic features parents use in their speech and how those are patterned interactionally. In a project directed by the author, 34 prosodic, paralinguistic, and interaction features were identified in the parental speech of English-speaking and Spanish-speaking parents in Austin, Texas. Tape recordings, 20–60 minutes in length, were made of parental speech approximately once a week for 14 weeks. The sample included four English-speaking and four Spanish-speaking families. The age ranges of the children were 9 years–18 years, 2 months (9;0–18;2) for English-speaking children and 8;1–13;1 and 18;1–22;2 for Spanish-speaking children.

Parental utterances during the sessions were coded for each of the speech features. Each feature was scored as present, or absent, for each utterance, which produced a rate measure. To date, several findings have been reported that show that although most parents rely heavily on a few features, primarily, exaggerated intonation, high pitch, and repetition, there are differences in feature usage according to language, sex of speaker, and age of child (Blount and Padgug, 1976, 1977; Blount and Kempton, 1976).

One particularly interesting finding is the distribution of features in the parents' speech according to age differences in the children. Using an entailment analysis, it was shown that co-occurrence restrictions were operating in the parental selection process. Speech features that served primarily to attract attention, those that were used to focus attention, and those that were most closely associated with lexical meaning could occur in the same utterance to children in the lower age range but were restricted to separate utterances in speech to the older children (Blount and Kempton, 1976). This distribution of features may reflect changing parental expectations.

In the early interactions, parents used combinations of features in utterances that did not appear in later interactions. Features in later interaction that served to focus attention were not used in utterances with features that served to attract attention. Parents expected only attentiveness in response to utterances in early interaction, whereas in later interactions, they expected attentiveness and a focus of attention on an activity, each in response to separate utterances.

To investigate the parental interactional usage of the speech features, the following features were employed with the data from the Austin project. Only prosodic and paralinguistic features were included in the analysis because the acoustic properties of parental speech that attract a child's attention was the main concern. Five sessions were selected from the protocols of the three youngest children in the English-speaking sample. All the children were in the transition from the prelinguistic stage to the one-word stage of development. Although some words could be identified in their output, the majority of their utterances were devoid of linguistic meaning. The sessions chosen were ones that matched in age range, within the limitations of the sample size.

In each session, episodes of interaction were identified, and episodes were defined as series of rounds with a focus on a specific topic, set off by periods of verbal inactivity. Episodes were ultimately constrained by a child's attention. Episodes began with a parent attempting to attract a child's attention through speech. If the parent was unsuccessful, then the episode would be very brief, containing usually only a few utterances by the parent, punctuated by silence on the child's part. If, however, the child responded, parents would continue the vocal interactions as long as the child remained attentive and responsive. Once the child turned his attention elsewhere, the episode would end. Parents would then wait several seconds, sometimes minutes, before initiating a new episode.

The initial parental utterance in each episode was analyzed for speech features. The assumptions were that the episode-initial utterance was designed to attract and focus attention, and that features present in the initial utterance would serve as attention-getting devices. Moreover, the distribution of features in the episode-beginning utterances reflected parental strategies in the use of the features to attract the child's attention.

The results of the first part of the analysis are in Table 1. Each category was scored separately for mother and for father speech.

In Table 1, the features are described as parental because native speakers of each language identified them as markers of speech appropriate for addressing children. A given feature might occur also in other forms of speech. From Table 1 it can be seen that almost all of the interactional episodes were initiated by utterances marked with one or more of the selected parental speech features. Only ten utterances of 175 (or 5.7%) lacked these features of parental speech. Of 100 utterances by the mothers, only one utterance did not contain any of the features. The table also shows that the two parents participated approximately to the same degree in each session, except for Miranda's father, whose participation, especially at 13 months, was comparatively slight. Mothers and fathers selected similar features, each showing approximately the same number of different features in their speech. Mothers did, however, tend to use more features per initial utterance than did fathers, although the differences were not great. Finally, no noticeable differences occurred in the usage of features according to the age of the child.

Table 2 provides a list of the prosodic and paralinguistic features and a breakdown by speaker and age of child for the total number of feature occurrences. In this sample, 20 of a possible 34 features occurred in parental speech, but only seven of the features appeared 20 times or more. In order, these are: exaggerated intonation, 106; breathiness, 49; instructional, 37; lengthened vowel, 30; high pitch, 29; falsetto, 28; and low pitch, 20. In addition, no clear-cut developmental or transitional patterns appeared. There are some notable differences between mothers' and

Table 1. Episodes and parental speech features

	Jeanne-Marie		Miranda		Rebecca
	12 mos	13 mos	12 mos	13 mos	14 mos
Number of episodes					
Mother	17	26	21	26	10
Father	26	21	8	9	11
Number of episodes with features in initial utterance					
Mother	16	26	21	26	10
Father	24	18	8	5	11
Total number of features					
Mother	54	57	44	67	33
Father	58	33	17	6	29
Average number of features per utterance					
Mother	3.2	2.2	2.1	2.6	3.3
Father	2.2	1.6	2.1	0.7	2.6
Number of different features					
Mother	14	11	10	14	9
Father	13	11	9	4	9

fathers' speech. Mothers used more falsetto, lengthened vowel, and show a slight tendency to use a creaky voice more often. Fathers used, comparatively, a low pitch more often. Also there are individual preferences in the selection of the features. Miranda's mother relied heavily on the feature instructional (heavy stress and flattened intonation), and Jeanne-Marie's mother and father used more phonetic alteration than did the other parents.

It is also possible from the data in Table 2 to rank-order the number of features for each speaker in each session. These results are in Table 3. The rankings include the most frequently occurring features per speaker. An inspection of Table 3 clearly shows the remarkable similarity across parents. Feature 9, exaggerated intonation, is first in all sessions except one, Miranda's mother, at 12 months. Exaggerated pitch, 7, high pitch, and 8, low pitch, are second-ranked in the protocols of five of the parents and are among the top five features in all but two of the protocols. Again, sex differences appear in the order of the feature ranks. Fathers prefer pitch exaggeration, 7 and 8, whereas mothers rely comparatively more on 6, falsetto, 17, lengthened vowel, and 1, breathiness.

Although composite measures, for example, summations of features across utterances, reveal interesting patterns of parental speech feature

Table 2.   Total number of feature occurrences per speaker[a]

		Jeanne-Marie				Miranda				Rebecca	
		12 mos		13 mos		12 mos		13 mos		14 mos	
		M	F	M	F	M	F	M	F	M	F
1.	breathiness	8	8	13	3	5	1	3	0	4	4
2.	breath held	0	3	0	0	0	0	0	0	0	0
3.	whisper	0	0	0	0	0	1	0	0	2	0
4.	lowered volume	1	0	2	1	2	1	3	0	0	4
5.	raised volume	0	1	0	0	0	0	0	0	0	0
6.	falsetto	6	0	5	1	4	1	6	0	4	1
7.	high pitch	4	1	1	1	2	4	5	1	6	4
8.	low pitch	1	5	1	5	1	0	4	0	0	3
9.	exaggerated intonation	15	17	18	11	10	5	14	3	7	6
10.	singing	0	0	0	0	0	0	0	0	0	0
11.	phonetic alteration	3	5	0	4	0	0	0	0	0	0
12.	creaky voice	4	3	4	1	1	0	3	1	0	0
13.	tenseness	2	2	2	0	0	0	2	0	2	2
14.	nasality	0	0	1	0	0	0	0	0	0	0
15.	rounding	2	1	0	1	0	0	2	0	0	0
16.	phonetic substitution	0	0	0	0	0	0	0	0	0	0
17.	lengthened vowel	1	1	8	1	5	1	9	0	3	1
18.	lengthened consonant	0	0	0	0	0	0	1	0	0	0
19.	shortened vowel	1	0	0	0	0	0	0	0	0	0
20.	shortened consonant	0	0	0	0	0	0	0	0	0	0
21.	slow rate	0	1	0	0	1	0	2	0	2	0
22.	fast rate	2	3	0	0	0	1	1	0	0	2
23.	instructional	0	0	2	4	12	2	11	1	3	2

[a]M means mother and F means father.

usage, it is also instructive to examine individual utterances for patterns and co-occurrence restrictions. A list of the episode-beginning utterances for each speaker was scrutinized for regularities in feature choice. Consistent patterns were observed, and by including only those features that occurred three or more times per speaker per session, it was possible to write formal rules for feature usage for each parent, for each session. These are given in Table 4. For brevity and conciseness of rules only the assigned numbers of the features are used.

The following conventions should be observed in reading the rules. Feature numbers without parentheses and braces are obligatory in occurrence. Feature numbers in parentheses are optional; they may or may not occur, depending on the speaker. Braces indicate that at least one feature

Table 3. Rank order of speech features for each parent[a]

Age in months:	Mothers					Fathers				
	Jeanne-Marie		Miranda		Rebecca	Jeanne-Marie		Miranda		Rebecca
	12	13	12	13	14	12	13	12	13	14
1.	9	9	23	9	9	9	9	9	9	9
2.	1	1	9	23	7	1	8	7	7, 12, 13	1, 4, 7
3.	6	17	1, 17	17	6	8, 11, 23	11, 23	17		
4.	7, 12	6	6	6						
5.		12		7	17, 23					8

[a]Features
  1 Breathiness
  4 Lowered volume
  6 Falsetto
  7 High pitch
  8 Low pitch
  9 Exaggerated intonation
 11 Phonetic alteration
 12 Creaky voice
 17 Lengthened vowel
 23 Instructional

Table 4.   Grammars of parental speech features for each parent per session[a]

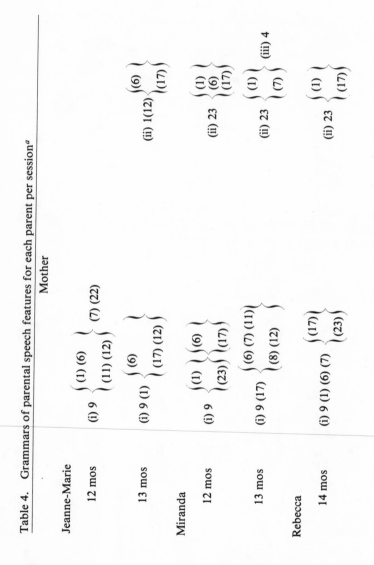

Mother

Jeanne-Marie

12 mos

(i) 9 $\begin{Bmatrix}(1)\ (6)\\(11)\ (12)\end{Bmatrix}$ (7) (22)

(ii) 1(12) $\begin{Bmatrix}(6)\\(17)\end{Bmatrix}$

13 mos

(i) 9 (1) $\begin{Bmatrix}(6)\\(17)\ (12)\end{Bmatrix}$

Miranda

12 mos

(i) 9 $\begin{Bmatrix}(1)\\(23)\end{Bmatrix}\begin{Bmatrix}(6)\\(17)\end{Bmatrix}$

(ii) 23 $\begin{Bmatrix}(1)\\(6)\\(17)\end{Bmatrix}$

13 mos

(i) 9 (17) $\begin{Bmatrix}(6)\ (7)\ (11)\\(8)\ (12)\end{Bmatrix}$

(ii) 23 $\begin{Bmatrix}(1)\\(7)\end{Bmatrix}$ (iii) 4

Rebecca

14 mos

(i) 9 (1) (6) (7) $\begin{Bmatrix}(17)\\(23)\end{Bmatrix}$

(ii) 23 $\begin{Bmatrix}(1)\\(17)\end{Bmatrix}$

Father

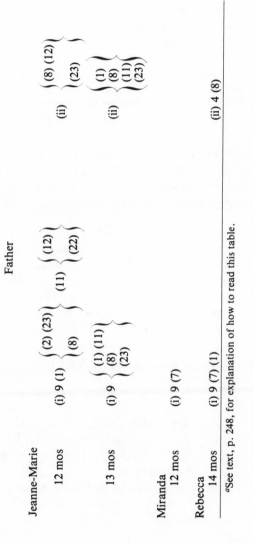

Jeanne-Marie

12 mos   (i) 9 (1) $\left.{(2)\ (23) \atop (8)}\right\}$ (11) $\left.{(12) \atop (22)}\right\}$ (ii) $\left.{(8)\ (12) \atop (23)}\right\}$

13 mos   (i) 9 $\left.{(1)\ (11) \atop {(8) \atop (23)}}\right\}$ (ii) $\left.{(1) \atop {(8) \atop {(11) \atop (23)}}}\right\}$

Miranda

12 mos   (i) 9 (7)

Rebecca

14 mos   (i) 9 (7) (1)   (ii) 4 (8)

aSee text, p. 248, for explanation of how to read this table.

enclosed must be chosen, but numbers in different rows are mutually exclusive. The order of the features on a left-right basis is also important (exclusive of those inside braces). Feature numbers to the left of brackets can occur whether or not any of the features inside the brace occur, but those to the right of the braces can occur only if a feature inside the braces has appeared in the speech. For example, the first rule in Table 4 (Jeanne-Marie's mother; 12 months) reads as follows: use 9, exaggerated intonation; optionally use 1, breathiness, 6, falsetto, 11, phonetic alteration, and 12, creaky voice, with the conditions that at least one of the features must be chosen and that if 1 and/or 6 is chosen, then neither 11 nor 12 can be used, and vice versa; and 7, high pitch and 22, fast rate are optional.

The most complicated rule is for the speech of Jeanne-Marie's father (12 months). The rule is as follows: use 9, exaggerated intonation; 1, breathiness, is optional; 2, breath held, 23, instructional, and 8, low pitch, are all optional, but at least one must appear, and if 2 and/or 23 occur, 8 cannot appear, and vice versa; 11, phonetic alteration, is optional, but it can occur only if 2, 23, or 8 has occurred; and 12, creaky voice, and 22, fast rate, are optional, but one must appear, and if 12 occurs, 22 cannot appear, and vice versa.

Much of the variation and complexity of the feature-usage rules is probably attributable to the small size of the sample. Several patterns, however, stand out and are noteworthy. One is that a natural dichotomy seems to exist between utterances containing exaggerated intonation and those that do not. The latter tend to be marked by 23, instructional, as a non-optional feature by mothers and by 8, low pitch, and 23, instructional as optional features by the fathers. For mothers' utterances containing 9, exaggerated intonation, there is a tendency for 1, breathiness, 6, falsetto, and 7, high pitch, to co-occur and to be mutually exclusive with 12, creaky voice. Rules for fathers in utterances containing 9, exaggerated intonation, appear to be more variable.

Finally, the rules are collapsed across sessions and children, and features that appear in each session are retained, simplified grammars can be written for mothers and fathers collectively. These are shown in Table 5. These grammars reflect, in a core fashion, parental usage for prosodic and paralinguistic speech features in the initial utterances of interactional episodes. They describe the patterns of feature usage in the majority of the utterances that initiate episodes. The high degree of regularity and the high proportion of features that these rules account for allow one to consider them as descriptive grammars. Mothers have two grammatical rules, with two variants of rule (i). The rules read: (i) use 9, exaggerated intonation, and then (a) optionally use 17, lengthened vowel; use 1, breathiness, 6, falsetto, 7, and/or high pitch or 12, creaky voice; or (b) use 9, exag-

Table 5. Composite grammars for mothers and for fathers

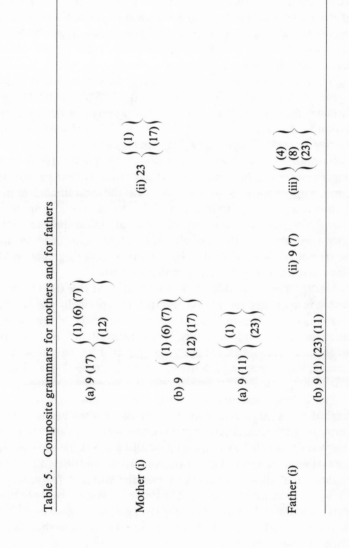

Mother (i)

(a) 9 (17) { (1) (6) (7) / (12) }

(ii) 23 { (1) / (17) }

(b) 9 { (1) (6) (7) / (12) (17) }

Father (i)

(a) 9 (11) { (1) / (23) }

(ii) 9 (7)

(b) 9 (1) (23) (11)

(iii) { (4) / (8) / (23) }

gerated intonation; use 1, breathiness, 6, falsetto, and/or 7, high pitch or use 12, creaky voice, and/or 17, lengthened vowel; and (ii) use 23, instructional, and use 1, breathiness, or 17, lengthened vowel.

An inspection of the grammatical rules for mothers shows a high degree of regularity. There are only minor differences between the two variants of rule one. Feature 17, lengthened vowel, is optional in variant (a) and (b) but it is mutually exclusive with features 1, breathiness, 6, falsetto, and 7, high pitch in variant (b). The variation may be because of small sample size, but it may also reflect individual or possibly dialect differences among speakers.

A second notable aspect of the rules is the segregation of features 9, exaggerated intonation, and 23, instructional. What is interesting about that fact is the separate function those features have in parental speech to children at different ages. As noted above, it was found that parental speech reflects developmentally different parental expectations as to children's responses to the speech (see Blount and Kempton, 1976). Feature 9, exaggerated intonation, was the most important feature in attracting attention, while feature 23, instructional, was the most important in focusing attention. The high frequency of 23 in the mothers' grammar might reflect their effort to focus the children's attention, having already attracted their attention through vision, touch, or some other means. The data are not available to resolve the question, but the segregation of 9 and 23 into two separate rules suggests those efforts.

Fathers have three rules with two variants of rule (i). The rules read (i) use 9, exaggerated intonation and then (a) optionally use 11, phonetic alteration; use 1, breathiness, or 23, instructional; or (b) use 9, exaggerated intonation, optionally use 11, phonetic alteration, 1, breathiness, and/or 23, instructional. (ii) use 9, exaggerated intonation, and optionally use 7, high pitch; and (iii) use 4, lowered volume, 8, low pitch, or 23, instructional.

The grammatical rules for fathers also show high regularity, although there is more variation than for the mothers' rules. Feature 23 contrasts with 1 in variant (a) but co-occurs with 1 in variant (b). Feature 23 also occurs in rule (iii), contrasting with 4 and 8. Rule (iii) contains features that all serve to focus attention, and it may contrast with rules (i) and (ii) along an attention attraction, focus dimension as features 9 and 23 seem to do in mother's speech. The contrast would probably not be as strong, because 23 does occur in rule (i). A greater reliance on 23 is overall characteristic of father speech, and it may be the case that fathers are more concerned than mothers with establishing an immediate focus of attention. Again, the results suggests this explanation.

In summary, English-speaking parents employ numerous prosodic and paralinguistic features in their speech to infants in the transition from prelinguistic to early language phases of development. A core of approximately seven features is used in regular predictable ways in parental utterances that are intended to attract an infant's attention and initiate an interactional episode. Moreover, there are consistent differences between the speech of mothers and of fathers. Mothers tend to use more features per utterance, and their selection of features is less variable. Although mothers and fathers rely more on exaggerated intonation than any other feature, relative emphasis on other features differs. Mothers use comparatively more falsetto, high pitch, and lengthened vowel; fathers use more low pitch, lowered volume, and phonetic alteration.

These usage profiles should be useful for further research in several fundamental ways. A first concern would be to set them in the perspective of broader age range of children. It would be interesting to know if parental speech to children younger than 12 months or older than 14 months would show the same patterning of features or other patterns and features. An expanded age range would provide a basis for assessing the socialization effects of parental speech. A grammar or grammars for parental speech across a broad age range would allow for greater scope in relating the speech to children's acquisition of language. A second productive use would be the experimental measurement, based on the patterns and preferences of speaker usage, of the success of the features in eliciting attention. Measures of the relative efficiency of the features and their patterned usage in attracting infants' attention and sustaining caregiver-infant interaction would raise interesting questions about developmental usage patterns. Patterns of features that are successful interactional devices at one phase of a child's development would not necessarily be functional at other stages, and it would be helpful to know what usage profiles would be early in the prelinguistic phases of development and after the one-word stage was advanced.

A third use of profiles would be a comparison. They could serve as a useful model, for comparative purposes, across languages to identify possible types of parental speech. Differences across languages would be interesting and could be investigated for differential influences on language acquisition. Also, similarities across languages would also be of special interest because they would provide avenues for discovering universals of parental speech. The discovery of a high degree of systematicity in the parental speech samples in English and over a limited age range is an encouraging beginning for that search.

REFERENCES

Blount, B. G. 1972. Aspects of Luo socialization. Lang. in Society 1:236–248.
Blount, B. G. 1977. Parental speech to children: Cultural patterns. In: Saville-Troike, M. (ed.), Linguistics and Anthropology, pp. 117–138. Georgetown Univ. Press, Washington, D. C.

256   Blount

Blount, B. G., and Kempton, W. 1976. Child language socialization: Parental speech and interaction strategies. Sign Lang. Studies 12:251–277.

Blount, B. G., and Padgug, E. 1976. Mother and Father Speech: Distribution of Parental Speech Features in English and Spanish. Papers and Reports on Child Lang. Dev. 12:47–59.

Blount, B. G., and Padgug, E. 1977. Prosodic, paralinguistic, and interactional features of parent-child speech. J. Child Lang. 4:67–86.

Bruner, J. S. 1975. The ontogenesis of speech acts. J. Child Lang. 2:1–19.

Dore, J. 1975. Holophrases, speech acts, and language universals. J. Child Lang. 2:21–40.

Ferguson, C. 1964. Baby talk in six languages. In: J. Gumperz and D. Hymes (eds.), The Ethnography of Communication, pp. 103–114, Special Issue, Am. Anthropol. part 2.

Ferguson, C. 1977. Baby talk as a simplified register. In: C. Snow and C. Ferguson (eds.), Talking to Children: Language Input and Acquisition, pp. 209–235. Cambridge University Press, Cambridge.

Freedle, R., and Lewis, M. 1977. Prelinguistic conversations. In: M. Lewis and L. Rosenblum (eds.), Interaction, Conversation, and the Development of Language, pp. 157–185. John Wiley & Sons, Inc., New York.

Greenfield, P., and Smith, J. 1976. The Structure of Communication in Early Language Development. Academic Press, Inc., New York.

Lewis, M. and Freedle, R. 1973. Mother-infant dyad: The cradle of meaning. In: Pilner, L. Krames, and L. Rosenblum (eds.), Communication and Affect: Language and Thought, pp. 127–155. Academic Press, Inc., New York.

Ninio, A., and Bruner, J. 1978. The achievement and antecedents of labelling. J. Child Lang. 5:1–16.

Scollon, R. 1976. Conversations with a One-Year Old. Univ. of Hawaii Press, Honolulu.

SECTION II

Multilingualism and Reading

The human "faculte de langage" takes on many forms. There are many language abilities that affect each other; some are a function of the psychology of the learner/user, and some are a function of the individual's linguistic environment.

Lee summarizes and reflects on the meaning of a recent and very active line of research on second-language learning in Chapter 16. Current work on second-language learning downplays the role of transfer from first language (the contrastive hypothesis) in favor of a developmental process: the nature of second-language learning is more a function of the second language and general language learning ability, than a function of age or previous language. In many areas, this approach has proven very useful, for example, in making sense of learner errors; but Lee shows that one particularly strong version—the hypothesis that the order of acquisition of grammatical morphemes in English as a second language is invariant across first language experience, and is, in fact, equivalent to the order seen in first-language acquisition of English—is not really tenable on the basis of present evidence.

Oksaar's research, in Chapter 17, is focused on the development of awareness of language in children. In much recent linguistic work, especially that inspired by Chomsky's characterization of linguistic competence, awareness is taken as fundamental. The linguist's basic source of data is appeal to linguistic intuition, that is, conscious judgments by native speakers of the language. However, it is quite clear that language awareness is an ability that must be developed in its own right, and whose parameters of use and development can be studied psychologically. Oksaar's paper addresses the question of the impact of bilingualism on language development, and awareness in particular. The United States is

primarily a monolingual country, and it is seldom realized that the majority of people in the world are bilingual; in fact, the majority of children
around the world receive a substantial portion of their education in a language other than their mother tongue. Thus, researchers in the United
States have only in the past quarter century overcome the old prejudice
(strongly rooted in the late 19th and early 20th century attempt to reduce
immigration and turn up the temperature on the "melting pot") that bilingualism has only harmful consequences for intellectual and social development. It is clear that bilingualism has two important benefits for the
individual: a greater ability to communicate with more people, which pro-
motes social cohesion, and also, a certain liberating effect on aspects of
cognition, including language awareness. One of the most interesting
topics in the study of child development is the relationship among what
might be called primary language development (the ability to speak and
understand oral language), language awareness (metalinguistic ability),
and learning to read. Children begin to develop substantial skill in these
areas when they begin school. Many hypotheses have been advanced concerning the causal relationships among the three; there is undoubtedly a
complex network of effects, and multilingualism is a natural laboratory.

Twentieth century linguistics is characterized by the primacy of oral
language, particularly in American work. Before this time, written language was often taken to be equally important if not more so, for example, classical philology and historical linguistics. The change was, in part,
attributable to the astonishingly varied nature of native American
languages, which neither matched European models nor existed in written
form. However, an unfortunate consequence of this view is that reading
came to be seen as a parasitic process on speech. Reading consisted simply
of translating print to sound—a process which had no direct parallel with
anything in oral language processing—followed by comprehension of
oral language. Recent research demonstrates that reading is a process that
is highly parallel to understanding oral speech; both are essentially hypothesis-testing, prediction processes in which the perceiver constructs a
mental representation on the basis of: a) what is on the page or is present
in the acoustic signal, and b) the reader's knowledge of language and the
world. Reading, like understanding, is a "psycholinguistic guessing
game," in Goodman's felicitous phrase. French, in Chapter 18, assesses
the extent to which reading processes are fully language-independent or
are modified as a function of the particular language being read. The process of interest is indexed by "choice of substantives," which reflects the
fact that it is easier to identify substantives if the reader is using a heavily
semantically-based prediction system. It would be extremely interesting to
set these results in the perspective of results from monolingual Spanish

and monolingual English speaking children to determine whether bilingualism per se has an effect. Given findings such as Oksaar's, this seems quite likely. Comparisons of children who have learned to read by different methods would also be enlightening, because some methods emphasize meaning, whereas others emphasize code-breaking (phonics).

Interpretation of Morpheme Rank Ordering in L₂ Research

Dong Jae Lee

The introduction of cognitive theory into psychology and transformational-generative theory in linguistics prompted researchers in the 1960s to scrutinize more closely the then predominant contrastive analysis hypothesis in second-language learning theory.

Such scrutiny resulted in two new versions of a second-language learning theory, a strong version and a weak version. The strong version proposes that the transfer from the first language (L_1) to second language (L_2) learning is negligible and that L_2 learners generally use common strategies of learning and employ fundamentally similar means in processing linguistic data regardless of the language background, age, varying types of programs, and even the extent of exposure to or instruction of the target language. The weak version of the theory considers transfer as one of the (major) strategies of L_2 acquisition.

Support for both versions is based on the studies of the acquisition order of certain English grammatical morphemes. Such a study was first conducted by Brown (1973). Longitudinal data were collected in a natural communicative situation from three children learning English as their L_1. Brown found that there was a uniform acquisition sequence for 14 morphemes among those three unacquainted children.

Following Brown's study, deVilliers and deVilliers (1973) conducted a cross-sectional study of the same 14 morphemes with 21 children learning English as their L_1. The data were again collected in a natural situation. They reported a significant correlation between the orderings of their own subjects and those of Brown.

Brown's and deVilliers' research methodology was first adopted in second-language research by Dulay and Burt (1973) to study the acquisi-

This research project was supported by a grant from the Office of Research Administration, Univ. of Hawaii, with support also from the State of Hawaii Department of Education. Travel to the First International Congress for the Study of Child Language, held in Tokyo, was made possible by a grant from the Center for Korean Studies, University of Hawaii.

tion order of a subset of the 14 morphemes by children learning English as an L_2. Dulay and Burt's study was cross-sectional, and data were collected with the Bilingual Syntax Measure (BSM), which they had devised with Hernández Chávez to elicit natural speech data. Their subjects were 151 Spanish-speaking children learning English as an L_2 at three geographically different areas. Dulay and Burt found that the children learning English as an L_2 in different areas showed "a common order of acquisition." They also found that, although morpheme acquisition order by L_2 learners closely approximated that of L_1 learners, it was not the same.

Dulay and Burt (1974) then administered the BSM to Chinese-and Spanish-speaking children learning English as an L_2 and found that "the sequences of acquisition of 11 functors obtained from Spanish and Chinese children are virtually the same." Based on this finding, they claimed that "universal cognitive mechanisms are the basis for the child's organization of a target language, and that it is the L_2 system, rather than the L_1 system that guides the acquisition process."

The same research method was adopted by Bailey, Madden, and Krashen (1974) in their study of the morpheme acquisition sequence by adults learning English as an L_2. They claimed in the study that ". . . despite the differences in adult learners in amount of instruction and exposure to English . . . there is a high degree of agreement as to the relative difficulty of the set of grammatical morphemes examined."

Lee (1978) also reported some of the results of research conducted with 30 Korean children learning English as a second language in Hawaii. One of the questions addressed was whether children with varying degrees of exposure to English have similar orders of accuracy rates with respect to recently-studied grammatical functors.

The subjects of the study were 30 students, ages 6–13, enrolled in grades K–6. These students were divided into three groups: 11 children, who had been in Hawaii for 3–12 months were in Group I, 13 students, who had been there more than 1 year but less than 2 years, were in Group II, and six students, who had been there more than 2 years but less than 3 years, comprised Group III.

Each subject was tested with the BSM individually by two persons: the author and a bilingual teaching aide at the children's school. The instructions for administration of the test in the Manual (English edition) were not closely followed. The BSM was used more loosely in order to elicit as much L_2 data as possible because, if followed literally, the corpus of data would have been too small and it would have been possible for a subject to answer the questions in the BSM without using, for example, auxiliary verbs or possessive markers, which the researchers wanted to study. Another equally important reason for not closely following the instructions was to allow further questioning when a child used a grammatical morpheme correctly at one time and incorrectly another time. In this way, the extent of the subject's acquisition of the item could be determined more precisely.

The accuracy of the use of a morpheme was assessed by tabulating its occurrence in obligatory contexts, according to the current general practice, which is based on the hypothesis that:

> One can set an acquisition criterion not simply in terms of output but in terms of output-where-required. Each obligatory context can be regarded as a kind of test item which the child passes by supplying the required morpheme or fails by supplying none or one that is not correct (Brown, 1973, p. 255).

This tallying system, which considers only the occurrence of a morpheme in obligatory contexts without due attention to the use of the same morpheme in non-obligatory contexts, is unsatisfactory and has to be re-examined. One cannot claim, for example, that a subject has learned the plural -s if the subject constantly uses -s for both the singular and plural although his score for the plural would be 100, according to Brown's obligatory-context-only method.

The scoring system used was the ternary system of Dulay and Burt (1974) rather than the binary system of Brown (1973). Of the three scoring methods that Dulay and Burt used, only the Group Means Method was adopted. The results are presented in Figure 1.

The correlations of the performances of the subjects in this study may be computed by Spearman's Rank Order Coefficient, by Kendall's Concordance Coefficient, or by the Pearson Product-Moment Coefficient. All three have been used in previous L_2 research. However, the results shown in Table 1 show that none of the statistics reveal a high level of stability of ordering.

Table 1 shows that, whichever statistical method may be used, the correlations among Groups I, II, and III are non-significant, except that the Spearman's Rank Order Coefficients and the Kendall's Concordance Coefficients suggests only a meager correlation between Groups I and II. In contrast, the Pearson Product-Moment Coefficients show no correlation between Groups I and II. The Pearson Product-Moment Coefficient is computed with the actual percentage of each item as the input, whereas the Spearman's Rank Order Coefficient and Kendall's Concordance Coefficient uses the rank order of the percentage of the items as input in the computation. The accuracy of the latter two is reduced in the process of translating percentages into a rank order. Such a loss is considerable when the number of test items is small, as is true in most L_2 acquisition studies. Usually the number of test items is about ten. For this reason, the Pearson Product-Moment Coefficient was chosen.

Group Means

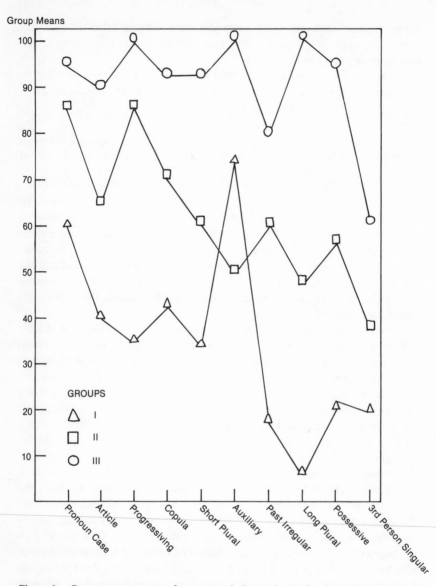

Figure 1.   Group mean accuracy for grammatical morphemes for three Korean groups. (Only limited aspects of these grammatical morphemes were investigated. For details, see Lee, 1978.)

Based on the Pearson Product-Moment Coefficients, Lee (1978) reported that the Korean data did not concur with the claim of Bailey et al. (1974) that "despite the differences in adult learners in amount of instruction [and] exposure to English ... there is a high degree of agreement as to the relative difficulty of the set of grammatical morphemes examined

Table 1. Correlation coefficients between Korean groups I, II, and III[a]

	I/II	I/III	II/III
Pearson Product-Moment	0.3810	0.3576	0.4566
	n.s.	n.s.	n.s.
Spearman's Rank Order	0.5515	0.2270	0.0245
	$p<0.05$	n.s.	n.s.
Kendall's Concordance	0.4667	0.2095	0.0233
	$p<0.05$	n.s.	n.s.

[a]$N=10$ in each group.

here ...." Some might argue here that the results of this study are not comparable with those of Bailey et al. because the subjects of this study were children and Bailey et al. studied adults. Such an age difference, however, should not be a variable according to Bailey et al., who argue that "relative accuracy in adults is quite similar to the relative accuracies shown by children learning English as a second language for the same functors."

In this chapter, the problem of interpreting the rank orders found by recent L_2 researchers is discussed.

Dulay and Burt (1973) claimed that the rank ordering of the grammatical morphemes that they found in their 1973 study was "an order of acquisition." They also claimed that such a rank order is universal after they found that there exists "a high correlation between the rank orders of the morpheme scores of Chinese-speaking subjects and Spanish-speaking subjects" (1974). Bailey et al. called this sequence a "difficulty order," and Larsen-Freeman proposed the term "accuracy order" (1975a).

One of the assumptions for Dulay and Burt's identification of the rank ordering as an order of acquisition seems to be that "... the slice one takes in the continuum will be a microcosm of the developmental process" (Rosansky, 1976). Rosansky found evidence disconfirming such an hypothesis by studying "whether the cross-sectional and longitudinal research findings in second language acquisition research are comparable." She compared cross-sectional rank orders of morpheme accuracy of a Spanish-speaking adolescent with the same subject's longitudinally-derived orders of acquisition over 10 months and found that "... no cross-sectional point appears to resemble the longitudinal developmental order."[1]

Using the results of Lee (1978), the rationale for inferring an order of acquisition, which is a developmental process, can be re-examined from

---

[1]The author of this chapter is conducting a similar research project, which began in April, 1978, with two Korean children to see whether Rosansky's findings will be replicated with Korean-speaking children.

the static data of cross-sectional studies. If Dulay and Burt's claim that the rank ordering of grammatical morphemes is the order of acquisition, then the rank orders of Korean Groups I, II, and III should correlate with each other. Their orders can be seen in Figure 2.

In Figure 2, the rank order of Group II was taken as the base line of comparison because Group II is the median group. As Table 1 shows, the Pearson Product-Moment correlation coefficient of Group I and Group

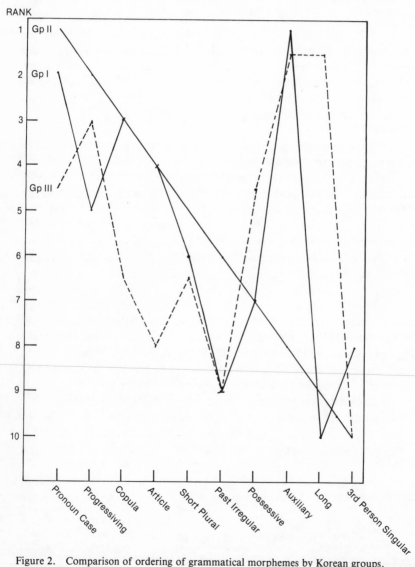

Figure 2.   Comparison of ordering of grammatical morphemes by Korean groups.

II is 0.38, that of Group II and Group III, 0.46, and Group I and Group III, 0.36, all of which are non-significant. Such non-significance is illustrated in Figure 2. This means that the so-called acquisition order of the morphemes in second language acquisition at a particular stage, does not reflect earlier or later stages. The lack of correlation between these three groups also indicates that there ought to be three acquisition orders for Korean children alone. Therefore, the claim that such an order is universal, regardless of the language backgrounds of L_2 learners, is dubious. This is true, even when the rank ordering is interpreted as a difficulty order or an accuracy order, as is discussed below.

The differences in difficulty orders (or acquisition orders, for that matter) of different groups are the result of variant rates of progress (in terms of the rationale of those who claim rank order to be either acquisition order or difficulty order). For example, in this data, Group II children showed an accuracy rate of 64% with the article, whereas Group I children showed only 39%, a difference of 25%. On the other hand, with the progressive –ing, Group II showed an accuracy rate of 85% and Group I, 34%, a difference of 51%. These differences, rather than the absolute performance at a particular stage of L_2 learning, would be a more valuable metric for measurement of difficulty and ease of acquisition. The inference of difficulty order (or acquisition order) becomes even more dubious when one considers that unlearning or regression takes place in the learning process. The case in point is the auxiliary, be. Its accuracy rate in Group I, which was 73%, decreased by 24% to 49% in Group II. From this perspective, it is not certain whether the rank ordering can be interpreted as a difficulty order.

Some researchers have suggested that rank ordering be called an accuracy order.[2] Larsen-Freeman (1975a) stated that the term "may be more precise in describing a measure of the percentage of times a subject *accurately* supplies a morpheme in an obligatory context."[3] She further refined it as an accuracy order for a specific task, the task being speaking, as compared to listening, reading, writing, and imitating (1975b).

However, it would be very difficult to identify the rank order as the accuracy order of speaking, because most of the rank orderings available now are based on data not gathered from natural communicative situations but elicited by instruments such as the BSM or the Second Language Oral Production English Test (SLOPE). The use of these elicitation in-

---

[2]The "accuracy" will vary depending upon which scoring method is used, i.e., Brown's binary or Dulay and Burt's ternary scoring method. It will also make a difference whether only Brown's "output-where-required" or also the "output-where-not-required" are included in the calculation.

[3]In her 1975a study, Larsen-Freeman used four other L_2 acquisition testing instruments along with the BSM, which she used to measure the special task of "speaking," and found that her BSM results correlated with those of Dulay and Burt.

struments as bona fide tools for eliciting L_2 performance data seems to derive a raison d' être from Brown's (1973) statement:

> This performance measure, the percentage of morphemes supplied in obligatory contexts, should not be dependent on the topic of conversation or the *character* of the interaction (p. 255, emphasis added).

However, L_2 performance is quite different from L_1 performance, particularly in the learning stages of children and throughout most adults' lives. The gap between the performance in a natural oral communicative situation and that in a situation other than natural is much greater in L_2 than in L_1, and the earlier the child is in the learning process, the greater the gap. A natural oral communication situation is one that forces a speaker "to use the patterns with appropriate vocabulary items at normal speed for [oral] communication" (Lado, 1964). In particular, the performance gap of the grammatical functors being investigated in these two situations is greatly affected by variables on which "the performance measure, the percentage of morphemes supplied in obligatory contexts, should not be dependent [in L_1 speech]."

Such variables, among others, are the memory span in L_2 (which is shorter than in L_1), the length of the sentences, the mode of discourse—the answer mode versus the creation mode—and, the artificial introduction of grammatical concepts to the subject's consciousness (as in the Slope Test, Krashen and Pon, 1975). Memory span and sentence length, of course, are factors in any L_2 language performance, regardless of the character of interaction. However, the BSM, the most frequently used data-eliciting instrument, possesses problems with the mode of discourse, for example, the answer versus the creation mode.

Dulay and Burt (1974) stated that the "aim of the BSM is to elicit natural speech from children." However, the BSM cannot adequately measure the whole spectrum of natural speech because of its character of interaction. What is required of the student by the BSM is mostly the answer mode of speech. This is only one aspect of the speech spectrum, which includes, among others, the creation modes of question, description, command, and proposal. The answer mode consists mainly of patterning after the grammatical functors used in the questions or using sentence fragments, which are shorter in length, and therefore easier than the comparable full-length sentences.

It is very often observed that L_2 learners in the early stages respond satisfactorily to such questions as *Where is this dog going?* by answering, *The dog is going to the house.* However, when they are told to ask a question to the same effect, they cannot construct the question properly, and produce sentences like, *Where're you going, this dog?*

In order to find out whether the answer mode and creation mode are the same, three 1-hour taped speech protocols for two Korean speakers learning English in Hawaii were examined. Their ages were 6 (subject A) and 9 (subject B). The first protocol was taped after they had been in the U.S. for 6 months, the second, for 6½ months, and the third, for 7 months. Each twice-monthly session was carried out with the two children and a research assistant who is a native speaker of English. The transcripts were scored in Dulay and Burt's ternary system. The same ten grammatical functors used in other research described in this chapter were studied.

The comparison of their performances in the answer and creation modes is shown in Table 2. Deleted from the table are those items that did not occur frequently enough, and for which the possibility of chance was great.

Both subjects showed considerably better performance in the answer mode with respect to all the functors, except for –ing in the case of Subject B. No explanation is given here for this regression in the answer mode. These results demonstrated that the character of interaction on which the "performance measure, the percentage of morphemes supplied in obligatory contexts, should not be dependent [in L_1 speech]" is a variable on which the performance of L_2 learners is indeed dependent.

These results also proved that L_2 eliciting instruments such as the BSM do not measure the whole spectrum of speech, and the result cannot be called the accuracy order of the special task of speaking. The rank order, therefore, must be interpreted as the accuracy order of the grammatical morphemes only in the answer mode of speech at a particular stage of L_2 learning. This restriction of the interpretation of rank order to a particular mode and time of course should be equally valid regardless of whether the rank order is interpreted as acquisition order or difficulty order.

CONCLUSION

The problem of interpreting rank orders of the accurate suppliance of the grammatical morphemes that several L_2 researchers have found is discussed in this chapter. Such an order cannot be equated with the so-called

Table 2.   Accuracy percentages of answer versus creation modes

	Subject A		Subject B	
	Answer	Creation	Answer	Creation
Auxiliary	38	20	50	33
Progressive -ing	33	23	50	75
Pronoun case	89	61	86	77
Article	81	36	50	42
Short plural			78	24

acquisition sequence because the L_2 performance at a particular learning stage does not reflect either earlier or later stages. In addition, rather than one invariant order, there are at least three variant orders of acquisition for Korean children as far as these findings are concerned.

It was suggested that the different rates of progress be taken into account in interpreting such an order as the difficulty order. The question of whether the order can be called an accuracy order of the special task of speaking was raised because: 1) the character of interaction in L_2 does influence the L_2 performance, at least in the learning stages, and 2) the L_2 data-eliciting instrument used possesses a character of interaction such that the whole spectrum of the subjects' natural speech is not elicited. In view of this, it is proposed that the rank orders may more properly be called accuracy orders of the morphemes only in the answer mode of speaking, at a particular stage of learning.

Whatever the interpretation of the rank orders may be, if the purpose is to study the ontogeny of L_2, cross-sectional studies with the data elicited by artificial instruments do not serve the purpose. More longitudinal studies based on data collected in natural communicative situations should be conducted even though such studies are more time consuming and costly.

ACKNOWLEDGMENTS

The author wishes to acknowledge John Haig for his valuable comments, and Elizabeth Lee for the assistance she provided.

REFERENCES

Bailey, N., Madden, C., and Krashen, S. D. 1974. Is there a 'natural sequence' in adult second language learning? Lang. Learning 24:235–243.

Brown, R. 1973. A First Language. Harvard University Press, Cambridge, Mass.

Burt, M. K., Dulay, H. C., and Hernández Chávez, E. 1975. Bilingual Syntax Measure. Harcourt Brace Jovanovich, Inc., New York.

deVilliers, J., and deVilliers, P. 1973. A cross-sectional study of the acquisition of grammatical morphemes in child speech. J. Psycholinguist. Res. 2:267–278.

Dulay, H. C., and Burt, M. K. 1973. Should we teach children syntax? Lang. Learning 23:235–252.

Dulay, H. C., and Burt, M. K. 1974. Natural sequences in child second language acquisition. Lang. Learning 24:37–53.

Fathman, A. K. 1975. Language background, age, and the order of acquisition of English structures. In: M. Burt and H. Dulay (eds.), On TESOL '75: New Directions in Second Language Learning, Teaching, and Bilingual Education, pp. 33–44. TESOL, Washington, D. C.

Krashen, S. D., and Pon, P. 1975. An error analysis of an advanced learner of ESL: The importance of the monitor. Working Papers in Bilingualism 7: 125–129. Ontario Institute for Studies in Education, Ontario.

Krashen, S. D., Sferlazza, V., Feldman, L., and Fathman, A. K. 1975. Adult performance of the SLOPE test—more evidence for a natural sequence in adult second language acquisition. Lang. Learning 26:145-151.

Lado, R. 1964. Language Teaching: A Scientific Approach. McGraw-Hill Book Company, New York.

Larsen-Freeman, D. 1975a. The acquisition of grammatical morphemes by adult ESL students. TESOL Quarterly 9:409-419.

Larsen-Freeman, D. 1975b. The acquisition of grammatical morphemes by adult learners of English as a second language. Unpublished doctoral dissertation, University of Michigan, Ann Arbor.

Lee, D. J. 1978. Learning strategy of English by Korean children in Hawaii. In: J. H. Koo and R. N. St. Clair (eds.), Bilingual Education for Asian-Americans: Problems and Strategies. Bunka Hyoron Publishing Company, Hiroshima, Japan.

Porter, J. H. 1977. A cross-sectional study of morpheme acquisition in first language learning. Lang. Learning 27:47-62.

Rosansky, E. J. 1976. Methods and morphemes in second language-acquisition research. Lang. Learning 26:409-425.

Linguistic and Pragmatic Awareness of Monolingual and Multilingual Children

Els Oksaar

INTEGRATIVE APPROACH

Very little is known about the linguistic and pragmatic awareness that people, especially children, have about language. The question of awareness concerning language and its use has not attracted much attention probably because many linguists assume that people generally do not pay attention to the language they use, and that the processes of language use are automatic.

This assumption, however, is based only on production, and the important perspective of comprehension is overlooked. In order to investigate the developing linguistic and pragmatic awareness of a child—not only for theoretical but also for pedagogical purposes—methodological strategies that take into account both the speaker's and the listener's point of view must be developed.

Research in this field is at a standstill because, as Kramer (1977) stated, "there are so many controversies that as yet it is impossible to find undeniable main lines." One way out of this dilemma is to extend the investigation to multilingual children. Leopold (1949) observed that "bilingualism helps to break down the intimate association between form and content." Oksaar's studies of Swedish-Estonian (1971, 1976, 1977a) and German-Swedish (in preparation) bilingual children and of a Swedish-Estonian-German trilingual child (1977b) support this observation. Her data suggest that multilingual children, more so than monolingual children, are able to break down the screen which language builds between the human being and reality. They are aware of the arbitrariness of words earlier than monolingual children are. Ianco-Worrall's (1972) data from studies of bilingual children support this point. Oksaar (1977a) showed that they are also more aware of situations into which certain communicative acts fit.

The approach to researching the linguistic and pragmatic awareness of monolingual and multilingual children that is suggested in this chapter involves integrating: 1) evidence from observations of children's metalinguistic behavior on all levels of language, including paralinguistic and kinesic elements, and 2) evidence from observations of their pragmatic behavior, that is, their judgment of the use of language according to its appropriateness in particular situations.

The data discussed here are from a longitudinal project on child language acquisition conducted at the Institute of General Linguistics in Hamburg with monolingual, bilingual, and trilingual children. There is a battery of various tests and observational data that build up a comprehensive corpus. Various test data have been analyzed in 10 publications. Discussed in this chapter are some additional data from tests and from two other methodologies from which statements about children's linguistic and pragmatic awareness can be made: 1) directed conversations conducted in connection with the tests; 2) observations of the behavior of children when they are correcting themselves, and when they are correcting or commenting on the speech of others. In these cases, examples were collected from the children's spontaneous conversations with their parents, caregivers or other children.

All data were collected and analyzed according to the principles of an integrative approach (Oksaar 1975, 1977a). An integrative approach is based on the fact that the child must develop a communicative system and must therefore learn rules of action and interaction. The child not only acquires the ability to produce and understand grammatical and acceptable expressions, but learns to judge the situations in which these are appropriate as well.

A model of description must account for paralinguistic and kinesic factors such as intonation and gestures, as well as for verbal units, including situative elements such as partner, subject, etc. The *communicative act* is the point of departure for research of this kind. A communicative act includes the total frame of action in which the activity of speech occurs. The elements of the communicative act are: 1) partner, 2) subject, 3) verbal elements, 4) paralinguistic elements, 5) kinesics, and 6) the total of the affective behavior characteristics.

The examples discussed below are taken from the data from eight Estonian-Swedish bilingual children in Stockholm, ages 2 years, 3 months (2;3)–6 years, 4 months (6;4); six German-Swedish bilingual children in Hamburg, ages 2;1–7;0; a Swedish-German-Estonian trilingual child whose name is Sven; eight monolingual German children ages 3;0–6;7;

and six monolingual Swedish children, ages 3;1–6;5. All of these children are from upper middle class families. (Bilingualism and trilingualism are referred to as multilingualism.)

Directed Conversations in Connection With Tests

In a picture test, the German-Swedish children were asked, in German, to identify all *blumen* 'flowers' that were pink. On the picture there were also pink blossoms. The German language differentiates between *blume* 'flower' and *blüte* 'blossom'; in Swedish, both are covered by the word *blomma*. On the next day, the same question was given in Swedish. Two children, ages 2;1 and 3;0, identified the blossoms also as flowers; all the other children, ages 3;4–7;0 made correct identifications. In the Swedish task, all were identified correctly, that is for *blomma* both flowers and blossoms were pointed out. Discussion with the children showed that even the 3-year-old, although he had not differentiated between flower and blossom, was aware of the difference between German and Swedish. When the blossom was pointed to and he was asked what it is in German, he correctly answered *blüte*, commenting that in Swedish it is *blomma*.

This kind of observation, that is, tests with additional dialogues with children, is methodologically sound because the combination of test and talk gives more evidence of their knowledge than does the test alone.

In a question play with Swedish-Estonian and German-Swedish children, equivalents in each language were requested in a way that would stimulate the children to give additional information. They were shown a Teddy family: mother, father, son, daughter, grandmother, grandfather, aunt, and uncle. Whereas Estonian and German have the same system as English, that is, the words for grandmother and aunt provide no information as to whether these are maternal or paternal relatives, the Swedish language differentiates between relations through mother and father. There are no words for *grandmother* and *grandfather*; instead, Swedish has *mormor* 'mother's mother' and *farmor* 'father's mother,' *morfar* 'mother's father' and *farfar* 'father's father.' There are no words for *aunt* and *uncle* in the system of relatives; instead, there is *moster* 'mother's sister' and *faster* 'father's sister;' *morbror* 'mother's brother' and *farbror* 'father's brother.'

The Teddy family was introduced to the Swedish-Estonian children in Estonian, showing who is grandmother, aunt, etc. Then, the children were asked "If this was a Swedish family, how do we call the Teddies?" Seventy-five percent of the children said *mormor* 'mother's mother' for grandmother and *moster* 'mother's sister,' thus choosing the maternal side of relationship. At this point, a series of questions and answers arose. For example, they were asked "Could you also say *farmor* 'father's mother' and *faster* 'father's sister?'" All gave an affirmative answer. The next question was "Could you say it in this way also in Estonian?" The answers (in German in the test with Swedish-German children) all revealed that the children reflected on the differences; the only exception was a child (2;1,) in the Swedish-German group who answered "I don't know;" however, he was using both languages in this sphere correctly. A typical answer, in German, from the Swedish-German group was "In German I only say *Großmutter*. In Swedish I say *mormor* and *farmor*." Sven (4;3) spontaneously added "Why is it *mir* and *mich* in German and only *mig* in Swedish?" Up to 3;11 a Swedish-Estonian bilingual child, Sven had been in Germany for only 4 months and had acquired a reasonable communicative competence in a short time (compare, for example, Oksaar, 1977b).

Similar answers and questions very clearly showed that the younger children also had a certain awareness of differences between languages, a kind of comparative analytic ability, which monolingual children—for obvious reasons—lack.

In directed dialogues it often is possible to obtain evidence that the children are aware of certain rules of the second language and that they can give answers concerning its use. It must be stressed, however, that when multilingual children are addressed in language 1 and no answer follows, or the answer is in language 2, no conclusions can be drawn concerning his competence in language 1. The possibility that the child just did not want to answer must be taken into account. It is human beings with individual patterns of behavior who produce language. Some other, less direct ways to obtain information are given below.

1. In case of lexical interferences, ask them about the interference:

> Christina (4;9, Swedish-German): Det war en *Überraschung*. (German) 'that was a surprise.'
> Adult: Vad heter det på svenska? 'What is it in Swedish?'
> Christina: *Överraskning* 'surprise.'

The adult did not refer to a certain word, the child's answer clearly showed that she was aware which foreign item she had used. Compare for example the same situation in Estonian:

> Sven (5;9): Liiga *langweilig* (German) hakkab 'it starts to be very tedious'
> Adult: Kuidas see eesti keeles on? 'How is it in Estonian?'
> Sven: Igav 'very tedious'

2. When the child creates loan translations:

> Sven (6;3) in Estonian (pointing at the neighbors driving): Tule vaata, nad teevad *umwegi* hommikul 'come have a look, they go a roundabout way in the morning.'

He uses a morphosemantic transfer of the German *umweg*.

Adult: Mis tähendab *umweg*? 'What does Umweg mean?'
Sven: Ümbertee (literally) 'roundway.'

Here a new Estonian word was created by loan translation, a process that indicates the child's knowledge of segmentation and the awareness of the components of words.

Monolingual children also develop quite early a kind of awareness of language norms. This awareness can be: 1) directed toward the general norms of language use, or 2) directed toward the child's own norms of language use. Some examples taken from the Hamburg corpus follow.
For the first case:

Heinz (4;0, German) was asked: *Kann Dein Schwesterchen schon gehen*? (literally, 'Can your little sister go already?')
Answer: *Sie geht nicht, sie läuft* (literally, 'She does not go, she runs.') (*Laufen* 'run' for *gehen* 'go' is colloquial.)

Compare, for example, a multilingual child:

Sven (3;8) is correcting his mother, who says in Estonian: *ma lähen Londoni* 'I am going to London.'
He says: *Sa ei lähe sa lendad lennukiga* 'you are not going, you are flying with the plane.

Examples for the second category, where the child keeps to her own norms:

Marie (3;2, German) corrects her mother, who says: *Die dritte Station ist Hauptbahnhof* 'The third station is Central Station.'
The girl says: *Nein, nicht die dritte, dreite* 'no, not dritte, dreite.'
Mother: *Nein, dritte* 'no, dritte.'
Girl: *Nein, dreite, dreite, dreite* 'no, dreite, dreite, dreite.'

Here the principle of analogy is working: *zweite, dreite,* this principle influences the first morphological development, which results in forms such as *leste,* English *readed,* or *gekommt,* English *comed.*

Adult asks Martin (3;5, German):   *Wem gehört das da?* (pointing at a toy) 'To whom does it belong?'
Martin: *Mich* 'me.'
Adult: *Mir, es heißt mir, nicht mich* 'To me, it is to me, not me.'
Martin: *Mir..., nein,mich*! 'To me ..., no, me!

Questions and Comments

Why-questions.   87 percent of all why-questions (598 from 688) had the structure of a simple question-sentence of the type in Swedish *varför heter bilen bil*, in German *warum heißt die Katze Katze*, etc. the formula being: why is the name of X *X*?

Thirteen percent of the why-questions had an additional remark of the type: why is the name of X *X* and not *Y*? Seventy-eight percent of these came from multilingual children.

In why-questions, free morphemes are often connected with kinemes, which also can appear as independent elements in the communicative act:

> Sven (7;1) pointing from the shoulders to the fingertips, in Estonian: Miks see siin on saksa keeles *arm* ja *hand*? Ma mõtlesin, et see (pointing once more) on *hand*. 'Why is this here in German *arm* and *hand*? I thought that this (pointing once more) is *hand*.'

It must be emphasized that he has used these two words according to the German lexical rules for more than two years. He has also used the Swedish words *arm* and *hand* according to the system that makes the similar division as German. Estonian, however, has only one category for the whole phenomenon, *käsi,* and does not differentiate between "arm" and "hand." In all probability, Sven had the Estonian system as a base for his considerations. From this type of questions and comments, which in the Hamburg corpus are well documented, and from the fact that children follow the rules without deviations in their speech, one can conclude that the awareness of the child concerning his language(s), his metalinguistic awareness and ability can reveal itself much later than his systematic control of the rules of the language(s).

Questions about Correctness

> Christina (4;6, Swedish-German) to her mother: Varför säger farbror *mor* och inte *mamma*? 'Why does uncle say mother and not mummy?'
> Sven (4;7) to his father in Estonian: Isa, kuidas on õige, vanaema ütles *söö* piim *ära* ... aga kuidas on õige ... (hesitating) nii öelda? (literally 'Father how is it right, grandmother said eat your milk ... but how is it right ... (hesitating) so one cannot say?')

Questions Concerning the World Around Them   Type: *What is the name of this?* These kind of questions show the awareness of a norm that every thing has a name. Multilingual children ask additional questions of a type: *what is x in y?,* e. g., *Was ist 'Urlaub' in Schwedisch?* 'What is 'Holiday' in Swedish?'

> Peter (4;10, Swedish-Estonian) in Swedish to his mother who is reading to him: Vad är "*skyskrapa*" på estniska? 'What is "skyscraper" in Estonian?'

Questions and Comments Showing Awareness of Segmentation

> Adult to Sven (5;9), who wanted to follow her to the hairdresser's, in Estonian: Sul on juuksuri juures ebamugav istuda, literally, 'It is uncomfortable for you to sit at the hairdresser's.'
> Sven: Mis tähendab *ebamugav?* Mis on *mugav* ja *eba?* 'What does *ebamugav* mean? What is *mugav* and *eba?*'
> Adult explains it and gets a new question: 'How is it in Swedish?'

An interesting connection between form and content, written and spoken language reveals itself through the following question:

> Sven (5;5, reading numbers in Estonian): Üks, kaks, kolm ... kakskümmend 'One, two, three ... twenty'
> (20 = literally "two + ten + suffix.")
> Ema, kas null on *kümmend?* 'Mother, is zero *kümmend?'*
> (The sign 0 is identified as *null* 'zero', 2 as *kaks* 'two', and in this context the spoken form *kümmend* needs an identification.)

Questions and Comments Concerning Words   There are numerous questions and comments about the semantic structures of words, also from other languages, according to the principle of Sinngebung. This principle is the basis for the folketymology of adult language; the prerequisite is the ability of segmentation.

> Sven (5;5, in Estonian): Kas Islandil on ainult jää? 'Has Iceland only ice?'
> Adult: Ei 'no.'
> Sven: Miks ta on siis Island? 'Why is it Iceland, then?'

The Swedish word *is* 'ice' was identified in the name *Island* and discussed in Estonian. One month later, talking about countries, where it is cold:

> Sven (5;6): Aga Islandil võib veel külmem olla ... seepärast et ... ta nimi ongi Island ... sääl on jää 'But on Iceland there it may be still colder ... because of ... its name is thus Iceland.'
> Adult: Ma olen siis Mannheimis 'I am in Mannheim then.'
> Sven (5;4): Miks selle nimi on Mannheim? Kas sääl elavad ainult härrad? Peavad ju ainult härrad elama (laughing)! (literally, 'Why is its name Mannheim? Do there only gentlemen live? There must of course only gentlemen live (laughing)!'

The German town name *Mannheim* (*Mann* + *heim* 'man + home') was analyzed by the child, and interestingly he translated German *Mann* as Estonian *härra* 'gentleman,' although he was using Estonian *mees* 'man' frequently. His quick answer to his own question shows that during this process, language "defines experience" (Sapir, 1931) for him. His laughing, however, is ambiguous. It could signal his delight for having found a good answer himself, or it could show that he utters it with a sense of humor.

The awareness of the semantic structure of a word is evident also in the following dialogue, which reveals the associative network of the word. It gives empirical support for Sapir's (1931) theory that language is "a guide of social reality" and it "actually defines experience for us by reason of its formal còmpleteness and because of our unconscious projection of its implicit expectations into the field of experience," at the same time showing that this seems to be still stronger in the case of children.

Sven (6;3) commenting on the name of another German town in Estonian:
See on imelik, et pandi Norderstedt nimeks. 'It is strange that it got the name of Norderstedt.'
Adult: Miks? 'Why'
Sven: Siis peaks sääl ju palju lund olema. 'Then there ought of course to be much snow.'
Adult: Miks lund? 'Why snow?'
Sven: Norden! 'North!' (smiling)

The following communicative acts reveal awareness of lexical and semantical rules:

Sven (5;5, in Estonian):   Jookseme nüüd käest kinni! 'Let us now run hand in hand!'
Mother: Ma ei jõua joosta, ma olen vana. 'I cannot manage to run, I'm old.'
Sven: Ei ole, siis sa ju oled mu vanaema, (literally, 'No you are not, because then you are my oldmother (= grandmother).') Estonian *vanaema* 'grandmother' contains the lexemes *vana* 'old' and *ema* 'mother.'
Two months later, on a similar occasion:
Mother: Mul on *vanad* jalad, ma ei jõua, (literally, 'I have old feet, I cannot manage.')
Sven (5;7):   Ei, siis su nimi oleks peanud (instead of: pidanud) olema *vana*ema! 'No, then your name must have been oldmother!'

The following word creation reflects segmentation and semantic rules as well as the rules of humor:

Adult speaking with Sven in German about skying: Bist Du ein Anfänger? 'Are you a beginner?'
Sven (7;0):   Ich bin ein Mittelfänger (laughing) 'I am a *Mittelfänger* (mittel 'medium') (laughing).'

Comments on Differences Between Speakers and Languages   After 2 months in Germany Sven (4;1) tells his father in Swedish about his observation concerning German pronunciation:

Mamma säger [fá:tɚr], Helmut säger [fá:ta] 'Mother says [fá:tɚr], Helmut (his German playmate) says [fá:ta].'

In the period of 6 months numerous observations of the following kind were stated:

Sven (4;3):   jag säger [ekehárt], han alltid rättar mig [ekehátt] 'I say [ekehárt], he always corrects me [ekehátt].'

Multilingual children also show an early awareness of languages they do not speak:

Peter (3;9, Swedish-Estonian) to his mother in Swedish: [pɚen ɚmɚerikɚn rikonfɚ́:m] det är min engelska 'Pan American reconfirm that is my English.'

Grandmother: Uno momento.
Sven (4;6, in Estonian):   Kuule, ma ei ole ju itaaliane (instead of: itaallane) 'Listen, I certainly am not an Italian.' (Sven had visited Italy.)

Questions Concerning Linguistic and Pragmatic Competence A special type of question or comment (compare the why-questions) concerns linguistic and pragmatic competence. Sven (5;1) hears his mother saying *Gesundheit*, when his friend is sneezing. He asks (in German) *what do you say, when he is coughing?* adding: *in Swedish you say prosit, when you are sneezing.*

What a child knows about the sociocultural and pragmatic rules of language use is, of course, not always easy to decide. When Kirsten (1;9, German) says [fí:dáŋk] 'many thanks' when she is offered a candy, this utterance and behavior alone are not proof that she is aware of this rule of interaction at the dimension of politeness. Some evidence of the awareness of interactional rules can be obtained in situations when children are playing with their toys, using the most common words in greeting rituals, correcting their puppets, asking them to behave in a certain way, etc. When Christina (2;6, Swedish) said to her puppet: *Kom, säg goddag* 'come, say how do you do,' and she was asked why the puppet had to say *goddag*, she answered *Hon är snäll* 'she is a good girl.'

Correcting Themselves

Corrections are apparent when the correct form comes immediately after a short pause: *Mutti hat gelest . . . gelesen* 'Mummy has readed . . . read.' The data show that multilingual children are more aware of their own lexical and grammatical deviations from the rules than of the phonetical ones. However, if they are spontaneously judging the behavior of others, there is no significant difference between these types of correction.

There is evidence of interlingual awareness when children correct their interferences spontaneously, without any reactions from the surroundings.

Anders (3;8, German-Swedish, commenting a picture book in Swedish):   Det här är en *insel* (German) . . . *ö* 'This is an island.'
Sven (3;4, in Estonian):   Mina olen siin *knänade* (Swedish) . . . (short pause) *põlvede* pääl 'I am here on my knees.'
Christina (5;5, Swedish-German):   Jag *stekker* det i munnen . . . *stoppar* 'I put it into the mouth.'

Stekker is a morphosemantic transfer of German *stecken* 'put.'

Correcting Others

Correcting (Younger) Children The most frequent structures were sentences starting with—in all three languages—an equivalent of *don't say X, say Y,* or *it isn't X, its Y,* type examples:

Ingrid (4;1, Swedish) to Tomas (2;6, Swedish): *Säg inte datt, säg katt!*
'Don't say datt, say katt!'
Mathias (4;8, German) to Jens (2;8, German): *Es heißt nicht nach Susanne,
es heißt zu Susanne* 'It isn't *nach* Susanne, it is *zu* Susanne.'

Correcting Adults   The most frequent structure is the negation of
the special word or form, and giving the correct one, from the point of
view of the child.

Adult in Estonian: ... *eilases* lehes ... või üle*eilases* lehes 'in yesterday's
paper or the day before yesterday'
Sven (6;1):   Miks sa ikka *eilases* ütled? *Eilses* on õige. 'Why do you always
say *eilases*? *Eilses* is right.'

Liis (2;9) to her father, who had used the Estonian idiomatic expression for 'how are you?' *Kuidas käsi käib?* literally, 'how does the hand
go?' *Käsi ei käi, jalg käib* 'the hand does not go, the foot goes.' Older
children, from 5;10 upwards, already have an awareness of ambiguity, according to the data in this chapter because, judging from their paralinguistic and kinesic behavior, they are using corrections of this kind for the
sake of humor. Typical examples of awareness of ambiguity and arbitrariness of words are questions like the following from a boy (9;8) in Estonian: 'why do they (German) say *vor rund drei Wochen,* why not
viereckig?' (*Rund* 'round,' *viereckig* 'quadrangular.')

Connection Between Spelling and Pronunciation

Children who learn to read and to write while they are still very young
have also an early awareness for the connection between spelling and pronunciation. A 4;2-year-old Estonian girl refused to write *Tallinn* with two
l's and n's, because, she said: *I say Talin.*

NONVERBAL ACTIONS

Linguistic and pragmatic awareness may be manifested in cases when children take the words literally and act according to them. The philosophical
question of the "power of language upon thought and action," which has
been discussed since the time of Herder, Wilhelm von Humboldt, and in
our times also as the Sapir-Whorf hypothesis, is seldom mentioned in connection with children (Oksaar, 1977a). The examples of communicative
acts above give evidence of the influence of words on interpreting reality.
There may be a kind of linguistic determinism in certain spheres of the lexical level. However, the phenomenon of "power of language upon
action" can also be observed clearly in the preschool period.
    Type examples: Stephanie (4;1, German) puts handkerchiefs, Ger-
man *Taschentücher* (*Tasche* 'pocket'), into pockets of clothes in the

wardrobe. She answers the why-question of her mother with the following statement: *Taschentücher gehören in die Taschen* 'handkerchiefs belong into pockets.'

Martin (4;2, German) claims bread for his supper. His mother's why-question gets the answer: *Es ist doch Abendbrot,* literally, 'bread of the evening.'

Children also reflect later on language and act according to their interpretations. For example, Sven (6;2) prepares a poem for his German class by simply reading it through. After school he tells his mother that the teacher had wanted it by heart. Sven, in Estonian: Aga õpetaja ütles *auswendig* (German)! Kui oleks ilma raamatuta, siis oleks ju *inwendig* olnud "But the teacher said *auswendig*" (German *aus* 'out'). If it would be without the book, it would of course have been *inwendig* ('in the body' *in* 'in'). Here the influence from his other languages is out of the question, because Estonian has a different structure also in this field, and Swedish resembles German: *utantill* (*ut* 'out') 'by heart,' läsa *innantill* i en bok (*in* 'in') 'read out of a book.'

DEVELOPMENT OF AWARENESS

In the above analyses various age groups were not differentiated because of the small number of children in each group. The data from the longitudinal project, however, show that there are certain age-specific tendencies. Children seem, first of all, to be aware of lexicosemantic regularities—at the age of 3–4 they are mostly responding to deviations from the rules of semantic congruency and choice of lexical items. Deviations from syntactical rules, especially word order, were also observed by both monolingual and multilingual children in this age group, but they did not occur as frequently. Phonological analytical abilities also seem to develop around age 3, although there are individual differences. In Oksaar (1977a) developmental aspects of linguistic and pragmatic awareness are also discussed in the light of earlier and current research. Of course, it is too early for general statements—more studies from various languages are needed. However, because there are both Indo-European and non-Indo-European languages in the corpus, the tendencies can be pointed out, thus presenting a broader basis concerning the type of language. Researchers must, however, be aware of methodological difficulties in classifications: what belongs to morphology in one language, may belong to syntax in another (Oksaar 1971).

It is interesting to observe that multilingual children seem to be aware very early of the function of language as a tool in the sense described by Plato as *orgamem*. When Sven (2;4–2;10) asked for something in Estonian and his parents did not react immediately, the theme was repeated in Swedish, with paralinguistic and kinesic support. This kind of functional code-switching was also found among Swedish-German children.

CONCLUSION

This chapter has shown how the linguistic and pragmatic awareness of monolingual and multilingual children manifests itself and that multilingual children develop early a comparative awareness that presupposes analytical abilities. This happens in a period that Piaget (1923) classified as the preoperational stage (2 to 6 or 7 years). According to him, thinking is, at this stage, egocentric, static, and irreversible. The egocentric thinking is apparent in their inability to act according to various roles. (For a critical discussion of Piaget's concepts compare, for example, Oksaar 1977a).

It seems that such a characterization of children between ages 2 and 6 or 7 does not cover what the child really manages in linguistic and pragmatic awareness. The fact that a preschool child is capable of abstract operations when he asks comparative questions concerning elements of the pronominal system in two languages must be taken into account (compare, for example, page 278). Children use language both as a communicative tool, that is, a social tool, and as an intellectual tool. A revision of the Piagetian stages including these components is necessary.

REFERENCES

Janco-Worrall, A. D. 1972. Bilingualism and cognitive development. Child Dev. 43:1390–1400.
Kaper, W. 1977. Paper presented at the Conference on the Child's Conception of Language, May 4–7, Nijmegen.
Leopold, W. 1949. Speech Development of a Bilingual Child. Vol. 4 Northwestern Univ. Press, Evanston, Ill.
Oksaar, E. 1971. Zum Spracherwerb des Kindes in zweisprachiger Umgebung. [The acquisition of language by children in a bilingual setting.] Folia Linguistica IV:330–358.
Oksaar, E. 1975. Spracherwerb und Kindersprache. [Speech acquisition and child language.] Pädolinguistische Perspektiven. Zeitschrift für Pädagogik 21:719–743.
Oksaar, E. 1976. Prinzipielles zur Entwicklung der linguistischen und kommunikativen Kompetenz im Vorschulalter. [Principles of the development of linguistic and communicative competence in preschoolers.] In: G. Drachmann (ed.), Akten des 1. Salzburger Kolloquiums über Kindersprache, pp. 383–391. Narr, Tübingen.
Oksaar, E. 1977a. Spracherwerb im Vorschulalter. Einführung in die Pädolinguistik. [Speech Acquisition in Preschoolers. Introduction to Paedolinguistics.] Kohlhammer, Stuttgart.

Oksaar, E. 1977b. On becoming trilingual: A case study. In: C. Molony, H. Zobl, and W. Stölting (eds.), Deutsch in Kontakt mit anderen Sprachen, pp. 296–306. Scriptor, Kronberg.

Piaget, J. 1923. Le langage et la pensée chez l'enfant. [The Language and Thought of the Child.] Neuchâtel.

Sapir, E. 1931. Conceptual categories in primitive languages. Science 74:578.

Processing Strategies in Language and Reading

Patrice French

Just as psycholinguistic researchers have moved away from word-for-word (behavioristic) models of language, reading researchers have largely abandoned models that deal exclusively on the level of the single word. The most obvious reason for this trend is that the fluent reader is able to recognize and to integrate and understand the words in a segment of text much faster than the total time required simply to recognize the words concerned (Neisser, 1967). Obviously, recognition and integration cannot happen faster than recognition alone. Thus, the question for reading researchers no longer concerns how words are recognized, but rather, How is normal fluency possible?

The focus of research on the acquisition of reading has shifted in a similar direction. The one-word-at-a-time approach was also applied to reading acquisition with some initial success. Such a model is obvious because children are initially taught to read by recognizing words one at a time. And, for adults who read word-by-word at or below phonation rate for their entire lives, the model seems appropriate. However, such speeds are not considered normal or fluent. At about the fourth grade, most children begin reading much faster, effortlessly instead of haltingly. At this point, reading seems to be less like the serial decoding of printed words and more like the understanding of ordinary speech, except that it is visual and faster. At this stage, the child's performance is no more adequately described by the word-by-word model than is the adult's performance. So the question in reading acquisition research also becomes: how is normal fluency possible?

In this pilot study, the Rapid Serial Visual Presentation (RSVP) technique was used to study comprehension strategies of fourth grade readers that may permit such fluency. When words of a sentence are presented successively at tachistoscopic speeds, subjects typically are not able to report the entire sentence, but rather only two or three words. More fluent adult readers report proportionally more subjects, verbs, and objects than functors and modifiers, as compared to their less fluent counterparts, who report a more random sample (French, 1977a, 1977b). Given the higher information load of substantives, the utility of such a selection is obvious. *Cow ate grass* is a meaningful sample of the sentence, *The fat cow ate the green grass*, but *The fat the* is not.

This priority of processing of subjects, verbs, and objects is at least a candidate for a language-independent strategy. Such a priority may be the most cognitively economical way to get the meaning in sentences in general. It is hard to imagine a language in which analogs of *fat green the* are more useful than *cow ate grass*. Furthermore, that children choose similar words in their earlier (telegraphic) sentences, suggests that such a strategy for identifying important words is one of the earliest and most basic language strategies. *Fat green the* is a much less common utterance than *cow ate grass,* for a toddler. Thus, it was expected that the fourth graders who were the most fluent readers would also exhibit this strategy in the RSVP technique.

However, it is not obvious that the priority of substantives will be an equally good description of the selection abilities of good readers in all languages. Parts of speech across languages vary in their information load. Here, Spanish is used for the initial test of universality because of: 1) the similarity of its orthography (another variable that would be a confound); 2) the easy availability of subjects and, therefore, the opportunity for large scale and repeated studies; and 3) the difference in the information load carried by different parts of speech. For example, *the* is semantically nearly empty in English. One could imagine that it is most cognitively economical to attend to it to the same extent as you are attending to the floor this minute. You would notice it only if it were *not* there or if it were suddenly removed. Thus, your attention is available for more informational aspects of the visual field. However, in Spanish, articles are not semantically empty, but rather they carry gender and number information. They are a source of redundancy and therefore potentially useful in decoding. Thus, the priority of substantives may be less pronounced in children reading Spanish than for adults reading English (French, 1977b).

METHOD.

Fourteen Spanish-English bilingual fourth-grade children were tested with the following measures:

1. RSVP (English)—Individual words of seven-word English sentences were successively flashed on a screen at a rate of 14 words per second.

Immediately after the presentation of each sentence, students wrote down all words that they saw. The presentation/write sequence was repeated for all 16 sentences. The first and last words of a sentence were not included in the analysis because of their greater effective durations.

2. RSVP (Spanish)—Sixteen translation-equivalent sentences in Spanish were presented in the same manner that is described above. Although too few words were seen for any student to recognize, the translation-equivalence of materials, and the possible practice effects were controlled by presenting the English sentences before the Spanish for half of the subjects, and in the reverse order for the other half.

3. SOBAR (English reading) (System of Objectives-Based Assessment of Reading)—This 30-item test of English reading measured decoding, comprehension, vocabulary, word structure, and capitalization.

4. SOBAR (Spanish reading)—This 30-item test was created in parallel to SOBAR to measure the same skills in Spanish.

5. Bilingual Syntax Measure (English Oral Language)—This is a test of English language development.

6. Bilingual Syntax Measure (Spanish Oral Language)—This is a parallel test to the English form above.

RESULTS

The pattern of results for children reading English replicated that for adults, reported in French (1977a, 1977b). Reading ability was significantly correlated ($p < 0.01$) with the number of substantives seen but not with the number of functors/modifiers (see Table 1).

In Spanish, the results are not as clear. Reading ability is only somewhat more highly correlated with the numbers of substantives seen (as compared to functors/modifiers) and the correlation is not significant (see Table 2). That this was the result obtained for adults (French 1977b), suggests that this pattern may reflect the greater information load carried by functors/modifiers in Spanish.

Table 1. Correlations of measures (English speakers)

	(1)	(2)	(3)	(4)
1. Reading (SOBAR)	1.00			
2. Oral language (BSM)	0.07	1.00		
3. Substantives (RSVP)	0.68[a]	−0.06	1.00	
4. Functors/Modifiers (RSVP)	0.38	0.11	0.24	1.00

[a] $p < 0.01$

Table 2.   Correlations of measures (Spanish speakers)

		(1)	(2)	(3)	(4)
1.	Reading (SOBAR)	1.00			
2.	Oral Language (BSM)	0.08	1.00		
3.	Substantives (RSVP)	0.23	−0.18	1.00	
4.	Functors/Modifiers (RSVP)	−0.22	0.23	0.14	1.00

all $p > 0.05$

Thus, while the limited data of this pilot study require caution in interpretation, the results do suggest a substantives-first processing strategy, at least in English reading, and the possibility of language-independent reading strategies. After replication of this study with a much larger sample, more microscopic study of such strategies will be possible as part of the author's ongoing eye-movement research with Professors Fender and Briggs at the California Institute of Technology.

DISCUSSION

Moving away from formal models of language, researchers of language processing have looked at the cognitive strategies that the speaker/hearer uses for encoding or decoding. These processes are not the simple word-for-word interpretation of text or speech, but they suggest higher-order strategies for language processing. Such an approach first became common in child language with Bever's (1970) analysis of strategies used by children for deducing subject-object relations in active and passive sentences (see French, 1975, 1976, for reviews). This represents a theoretical change of direction: the child is seen as processing by means of general cognitive abilities rather than through the workings of an innate Language Acquisition Device. Thus, strategies may differ across individuals, across languages, or they may change with age.

In this study, the RSVP, which has been shown to suggest at least some strategies of reading in adult readers, was used (French 1977a, 1977b). The selection of subjects, verbs, and objects at the expense of less important or less meaningful parts of speech is a type of selection strategy that could help to account for the fluency of normal reading. Furthermore, such a semantic strategy is consistent with the present directions in psycholinguistics. As early as 1966, Slobin showed that semantic processing strategies can obviate the need for complete processing of a sentence. Passives took no longer to comprehend than did active sentences, if the semantic relations of subject, verb, and object were unique. Although *Bill was hit by Bob* requires more syntactic processing than *Bob hit Bill* to discriminate the subject and object, a sentence such as *the leaves were raked by the boy* requires no such processing because who does what to whom is obvious from the meaning of the nouns. Furthermore, simple active affirmative sentences are the most common, far outnumbering the reorganized passive (Goldman-Eisler and Cohen, 1970). Thus, given the unequal information load of various words and the preponderance of a subject-verb-object (SVO) order in English, the selection of SVO and semantic instead of syntactic processing would seem to be the obvious and natural strategy in the processing of English. The most exciting possibility of this pilot work is that an obvious strategy for processing English may be related to reading ability, which suggests that processing strategies are common to both speech and reading.

ACKNOWLEDGMENTS

The author wishes to express appreciation to Drs. Cornejo, D. Gonzales, and C. Fisher of the Center for the Study of Evaluation, UCLA, for providing the data for tests 3, 4, 5, and 6.

REFERENCES

Bever, T. G. 1970. The cognitive basis for linguistic structures. In: J. R. Hayes (ed.), Cognition and the Development of Language. John Wiley, & Sons, Inc., New York.

French, P. L. 1975. Perception and early semantic learning. In: W. von Raffler-Engel, (ed.), Child Language Today, pp. 125–238, The International Linguistics Association, New York.

French, P. L. 1976. Disentegrating theoretical distinctions and some future directions in psycholinguistics. In: E. C. Carterette and M. P. Freidman (eds.), Handbook of Perception, Vol. 7, pp. 445–465. Academic Press, Inc., New York.

French, P. L. 1977a. Child Language and Adult Reading: Evidence for Parallels in Progress. Paper presented at the Second ICU Symposium on Pedolinguistics, Tokyo.

French, P. L. 1977b. Cognitive Strategies in Spanish and English Reading. Paper presented at the 1977 meeting of the American Educational Research Association, New York.

Goldman-Eisler, F., and Cohen, M. 1970. Is N, P, and PN difficulty a valid criterion of transformational operations? J. Verb. Learn. Verb. Behav. 9:161–166.

Neisser, U. 1967. Cognitive Psychology. Appleton-Century-Crofts, New York.

Slobin, D. I. 1966. Grammatical transformation and sentence comprehension in childhood and adulthood. J. Verb. Learn. Verb. Behav., 5:219–227.

SECTION III

Exceptional Language Development

Historically, studies of normal and disabled language development have been conducted in separate disciplines, with little communication between those conducting the studies. There have always been a few exceptions, of course, the most remarkable of which is the work of Roman Jakobson (1968) who attempted to integrate child language, linguistic universals and aphasia; but exceptions such as this one have been infrequent. In the past 15 years or so, the gap has been at least partially bridged on a continuing basis although the traffic thus far has been largely one way: ideas emerging from the study of normal language development have been applied to the disabled. Considering the great theoretical significance of disorders for understanding basic processes of development, the time has come for some traffic to move in the other direction.

There are numerous aspects of knowledge about normal development that are potentially applicable to clinical and educational practice. Many researchers, clinicians, and educators have been intrigued by the relatively uniform sequences of development observed in many areas of language development. These sequences provide a fruitful framework for the design of assessment instruments. It has even been argued that they provide the best guide for sequencing the content of instruction. Others have been interested in research on the role of processes such as imitation and expansion, and features of parental speech to children as a guide for the design of remedial environments. Nevertheless, knowledge concerning the relationships among various aspects of language and between language development and environmental factors does not automatically generalize across populations. Unless it is determined that a particular type of language disability is associated with a similar pattern of development, as is observed in normal children, there is no basis for using predictions based on normal development. Similarly, to the extent that language impairments stem, at least in part, from congenital factors, there are no grounds for assuming a priori that environmental factors will have the same effect as they do for normal children; conversely, factors that play a small role in normal development may play a greater role in remediation. Thus, fruitful interaction between studies of normal and disabled language development is more likely to occur at the level of suggested methodologies, assessment instruments, and hypotheses that will need to be independently evaluated for each population.

The question most often asked about language of handicapped children is whether it is simply a delayed version of normal development (a so-called quantitative difference), or whether it follows a qualitatively different path. To expect a single answer to this question is simplistic. The situation varies from child to child; more importantly, the answer may vary from one aspect of language to another. In any case, the dichotomy between delay and difference has probably been exaggerated. Consider the possibility of a child who is mastering one aspect of development (A) in the normal sequence, but is delayed, while another aspect of language (B) is also mastered in the normal sequence, but is more substantially delayed. With respect to each dimension, the delay versus difference question can be answered "delay," but with respect to the whole process, the hypothetical child is not equivalent to a normal child of any age. In other words, delay in varying degrees amounts to difference. Some particularly interesting possibilities for A-B contrast of this type are: vocabulary-syntax, language function-language form, and comprehension-production. The situation is rendered even more difficult by the fact that very little information is available about the range of variability within the normal population in both rate and qualitative nature of these and other dimensions of language development. Obviously, it is impossible to judge whether a particular pattern of development is delayed or deviant without a good estimate of the range of variability among normal children.

The first four chapters in this section are concerned with the most basic question of all: how to characterize specific disorders. All are guided by the belief that underlying the global language deficit are one or more key difficulties. The assumption amounts to seeing language, like other cognitive functions, as the result of a number of interacting processes, and a disturbance in any one of these will have far-reaching consequences. Bartak and Goode, in Chapter 19, emphasize that a deficit in social comprehension is part of the problem for autistic children, rather than a narrowly linguistic handicap. They also argue cogently against another current hypothesis: the problem lies in defective analytic ability. This hypothesis has been supported by evidence that the left hemisphere is specialized for analytic tasks, whereas the right hemisphere is generally known to be better at just those tasks that autistic individuals do relatively well, spatial tasks and vocabulary, in particular. Butler implicates auditory attention processes in Chapter 20, and she focuses on the inability to resist distraction and ignore irrelevant attention by both young normal children and children with learning difficulties. Cromer, in Chapter 21, demonstrates that a major problem for aphasic children that often is construed as a deficit in handling structure, is actually limited to a deficit in processing hierarchical structure.

Research of this type has both practical significance—it suggests key points for intervention—and theoretical significance—it draws on these tragic "experiments of nature" to map the relationships among various processes. It is, however, very difficult to convincingly prove the case for a "key process" explanation. Observations of differences in mean performance between normal and disabled children on any one task constitute relatively weak evidence. If a child is defined as deficient on something as global as language, the child is almost certainly deficient on any specific measure of that skill. The single correlation is almost uninterpretable because any other measure might have yielded the same result. Thus, it is necessary to compare children's performance on a number of similar tasks. For example, Cromer shows that autistic children indeed do poorly on a hierarchical structure processing measure, but this finding is made more significant by the finding that a very similar sequential structure measure does not show this difference. Another technique that can provide stronger evidence is to determine the correlation between the hypothesized key process and the global measure *within* the two populations. If it is believed that a variable can explain the difference between two groups, the variable ought also to explain some of the variance within the groups. Experimental-manipulative studies that attempt to facilitate the process of interest are also valuable, although by themselves, they too, are limited in interpretive strength. The fact that teaching A leads to the development of B shows that A is sufficient for B, but it cannot demonstrate that it is necessary; it can be shown that this is one way children can learn B, but not that it is the only way, or even the most common way. Laboratory effects do not automatically generalize to normal development. The combination of correlational and experimental-manipulative approaches is far more promising than either is alone.

Haber has taken the most empirical approach. Within a tightly specified domain of repetition of syntactically-structured strings, she compared the usefulness of various measures in distinguishing children in various groups. Her research, described in Chapter 22, is explicitly based on the assumption that some children will exhibit qualitative differences, and others will exhibit quantitative ones. Her most important finding is that the classification can be done, and that the various measures agree well with each other. The research provides an excellent example of how a simple classification of responses into correct versus incorrect is of little use, whereas finer classifications of incorrect responses can provide highly valuable information.

Usuda and Koizumi, in Chapter 23, report an investigation of a little-examined population—children who have regressed in language for unknown reasons (that is, not attributable to true traumatic aphasia in childhood). Even though language usually begins redeveloping relatively quickly, the long-term prognosis for these children is not encouraging, perhaps because the disorder is associated with severe prenatal and perinatal difficulties, or perhaps because the loss was either caused by, or was a contributing factor to, an impaired mother-child attachment. One of their major findings is that regression is not limited to children diagnosed as autistic, but it also occurs in some children diagnosed as mentally retarded. A particularly intriguing finding is that in many cases, other abnormal features were noticed before the language regressed; this finding, if replicated, might have great practical significance. Usuda and Koizumi conclude with a speculative model that implicates defective mother-child attachment as a primary cause for language loss. Here again, there is great difficulty in moving from a correlational finding to a causal inference; biological factors may play an important "third variable"role.

Söderbergh provides the only intervention-oriented chapter in this book. Chapter 24 is especially interesting when read together with Oksaar's Chapter 17 on language awareness because both bear on the question of the relationships among oral language development, reading, and language awareness. For young hearing children, print is first mastered as a representation of the language that the child already knows. Only later will the child learn new vocabulary and grammatical structures through print. It is, therefore, a reasonable speculation that an awareness of the primary language is an important part of learning to read. However, for children with less language, for example, deaf children, print may have to be learned as a primary language itself, without the mediation of another language system or of conscious awareness. A consequence of this view is that print must therefore be functional for the child, just as oral language fills a need in the daily life of the hearing child. Söderbergh's paper is a clear and charming account of how this can be done for preschool children. Of particular note is the way in which errors are viewed as potentially developmental, reflecting genuine, although perhaps partial understanding, as they do in oral language development. There is also a notable dual emphasis on signing and print as primary language modes. All too often, designers of programs for the deaf assume that a choice must be made between the two modes. This is not the case in the Swedish program, as Söderbergh explains in her chapter.

REFERENCE

Jakobson, R. 1968. Child Language, Aphasia, and Phonological Universals. Translated by A. Keiler. Mouton, The Hague.

Central Language Disorders and Social Comprehension in Children

Lawrence Bartak and Marged Goode

There is now considerable evidence from clinical and experimental studies that autistic children have a serious cognitive deficit that includes a marked impairment in language functioning (Hermelin and O'Connor, 1970; Rutter, 1974). However, controversy has continued regarding the relationship between the language disorder in autism and the disabilities present in developmental disorders of understanding of speech. In addition, the extent and the nature of the cognitive deficit in the autistic child remain unclear. A number of researchers have discussed the similarities and differences between autistic and developmentally dysphasic children (Churchill, 1972; Cohen, Caparulo, and Shaywitz, 1976; De Hirsch, 1967; Eisenson, 1971; Sahlmann, 1969). In an attempt to resolve some of these issues, a comparative study of autistic and developmentally receptive dysphasic children was conducted. The findings are presented in detail in Bartak, Rutter, and Cox (1975); Cox, Rutter, Newman, and Bartak (1975); Bartak, Rutter, and Cox (1977); and Baker, Cantwell, Rutter, and Bartak (1976), and are summarized before the results of a new investigation are presented.

SUMMARY OF COMPARATIVE STUDY

In the study, a group of autistic children (N = 19) were compared with a group of developmentally receptive dysphasic children (N = 23) (referred to in this chapter as dysphasic) and with five children who had a mixed or atypical disorder. The groups were closely matched for nonverbal intelligence on the Wechsler Intelligence Scale for Children (WISC) (1949), with a mean IQ of 92–93. All three groups showed a severe impairment in the comprehension of spoken language when tested on the Comprehension Scale A of the Reynell Developmental Language Scales (Reynell, 1969). The children were compared on a variety of standarized cognitive tests, both verbal and nonverbal, and on measures of receptive and expressive language, reading and social competence. In addition, parents were interviewed to obtain a detailed history of the child's language and social development and a systematic account of his or her current social behavior.

Clear differences emerged between autistic and dysphasic samples in patterns of scores on cognitive tests. Both groups seemed to have a disordered ability to process verbal information. However, the impairment seemed qualitatively different in the autistic sample. The disability for this group extended beyond purely verbal material and seemed to encompass the processing of *symbolic* material of several kinds. In contrast to the dysphasic group, they showed little capacity for symbolic play. In addition, the autistic group was less able to extract meaning from written material. Children in each group who could read were given the Schonell R1 test of word recognition (Schonell and Schonell, 1960) to assess mechanical reading skill. The autistic children performed at a higher level than those in the other group. However, when these two groups of children were given a test involving silent reading and understanding (Schonell R3), four of the autistic children could understand the task that required them to write answers to questions about the text just read, and these children performed at a lower level than the dysphasic children who completed this task. The latter did so at a level comparable to that of their performance on the test of word recognition.

The autistic children were also less able to comprehend or express information that was expressed gesturally. The task required association of stimuli with mimed actions. For comprehension, a standarized mimed action was presented to the child and he had to indicate the relevant stimulus; for expression, a stimulus was presented and he was asked to mime the appropriate action associated with it.

Such results might merely reflect a more severe verbal impairment in the autistic group. However, the patterns of cognitive test results (described fully in Bartak, Rutter, and Cox, 1975) seem to support the view that autistic children have problems in extracting meaning, irrespective of level of ability. First, there was a marked difference between the groups on WISC Verbal Scale patterns of sub-test scores. The pattern for the autistic group was very similar to that obtained in an earlier study (Lockyer and Rutter, 1970) of autistic children who were more severely mentally retarded than those in this study. In both studies, the autistic group showed greatest impairment on tasks stressing extraction of meaning rather than rote skills.

In contrast, performance of the dysphasic children on the WISC Verbal Scale subtests was even, suggesting a more specifically verbal impairment that affected all verbal tasks equally. Second, there was a difference between the groups in their performance on two nonverbal tests of intelligence one of which required the child to extract meaning from the visual material (Columbia Mental Maturity Scale), the other of which did not (Raven's Colored Progressive Matrices). Although the dysphasic children performed at the same level on both tests, the autistic children performed relatively better on the Raven's tasks, which did not require extraction of meaning.

In the dysphasic group, the impairment seemed to be more specifically verbal and less specifically related to the extraction of meaning from perceived material. In addition, there was substantially greater *social* impairment in the autistic group.

Two further questions arose from these results. First, there was continuing uncertainty about the nature of the cognitive deficit in autism. There seemed to be a profound cognitive disorder underlying the behavioral disturbance. Second, there was the question of whether social factors such as parental personality traits or patterns of social interaction in the families might be more associated with the occurrence of autism than with a simple disorder of receptive language.

Familial Factors

A systematic study of parents in these two groups showed that there were very few differences between the parents, except for a slight but significant bias toward professional and managerial occupational status in the autistic group. Other than this finding, which has been noted in other studies (Cox, Rutter, Newman, and Bartak, 1975), there were no major significant differences. Measures of obssessionality, emotional warmth and demonstrativeness, and neuroticism were similar in both groups and within normal bounds. Patterns of social interaction in families also displayed no differences.

Accordingly, the question of the underlying nature and origin of the cognitive impairment in autism responsible for the behavioral pattern, which is so clearly demarcated (Bartak, Rutter, and Cox, 1977), remained unanswered because it was unlikely that the difference between the groups was dependent upon familial factors. As noted in Baker, Cantwell, Rutter, and Bartak (1976), autism seemed to be characterized by a different pattern of cognitive skills associated with severe language delay, but in which the disability affects a variety of cognitive functions that generally are not impaired in dysphasic children.

SOCIAL IMPAIRMENT

The finding that the autisitic children were considerably more socially impaired than the dysphasic children, both on a standardized test and on assessment of their behavior in naturalistic settings, suggested that the cognitive deficit might extend to the interpersonal area. There might be an additional deficit in the autistic child that impaired his ability to extract information from social settings. The most elementary skill in this area would seem to be the recognition of affect from facial cues. Therefore, an investigation of children's ability to recognize affect from pictures of human faces was conducted. The work is reported in detail in Goode, Bartak, and James (in preparation). Previous work by Ekman and his colleagues (Ekman and Friesen, 1975; Ekman, Friesen, and Ellsworth, 1972) resulted in the production of a standard set of photographs that show a variety of facial expressions. Little work, however, has been done in assessing children's ability to recognize these expressions. In this study, 12 full faces depicting six different affects (happiness, sadness, surprise, anger, fear, and disgust) were selected from Ekman's series. A standardized procedure was adopted in which three pictures were presented and the child was asked to point to the relevant stimulus following a verbal demand, for example, "show me *sad*." Practice items in the same format were used to determine whether the children understood the nature of the task and whether they could at least sometimes perform it sucessfully. Children were also assessed on a task of nonverbal ability (Raven's Colored Progressive Matrices) that required recognition of relationships among abstract visual patterns, and on a measure of vocabulary comprehension (Peabody Picture Vocabulary Test).

Sample

The sample consisted of groups of normal, autistic, deaf, and dysphasic children. Autistic children met the criteria outlined in an earlier study (Bartak, Rutter, and Cox, 1975). Tables 1 and 2 give details of the size of the groups and their performance on the two ability measures. Findings obtained with the Ekman pictures, which are referred to here as the Social Comprehension Test (SCT), on a sample of 71 normal children ages 4-8 showed that performance correlated with age but little improvement occurred above age 6. In the comparison described below, an attempt was made to match groups of children on their level of language comprehension. For this purpose, a sample consisting of the 30 youngest children was selected from the larger group. A sample of the 15 oldest autistic children who could do the SCT task was selected. Fifteen deaf children were included, all of whom had a hearing loss of at least 40 db below standard reference level on their better ear for the best frequency between 250

Table 1. Mean chronological age and age-range of autistic children and control groups, expressed in years and months

Sample	N	Mean	Range
Normal	30	4;3	3;5-4;9
Autistic	15	9;5	6;8-15;7
Deaf	15	6;4	5;8-7;10
Dysphasic	10	7;7	5;0-11;8

hz and 4,000 hz. The mean hearing loss in this sample was 76 db (range 40-95 db). Ten dysphasic children with normal hearing were selected. Children in the autistic group were significantly older than children in normal and deaf groups.

Thus, the normal, autistic, and dysphasic groups were matched on verbal comprehension, whereas the autistic, dysphasic, and deaf groups were matched on the measure of nonverbal ability. Comparative figures are in Table 2.

Results

An examination of relationships between age, SCT score and other test scores from normal children suggested that the autistic and dysphasic children should do better than normal children because they were older and had higher scores on the nonverbal test of ability. However, findings from earlier research (discussed above) dealing with cognitive deficits in autistic children suggested that autistic children might be impaired on the SCT. Those findings are shown in Table 3. Comparison across groups shows that the autistic children clearly performed worse than normal or deaf children on the SCT ($p < 0.001$). The dysphasic children performed slightly worse than normal or deaf children ($p < 0.05$). There was no difference between the performance of normal children and that of deaf children, and the difference between the performance of autistic and dysphasic children failed to reach statistical significance.

DISCUSSION

The results show that the autistic children had significantly lower scores than the normal and deaf children on a task involving recognition of

Table 2. Mean mental age of autistic children and control groups, expressed in years and months

Sample	Verbal	Nonverbal
Normal	4;9	4;11
Autistic	4;4	6;10
Deaf	3;3	8;1
Dysphasic	4;11	7;9

Table 3.   SCT Scores (maximum = 12)

Sample	N	SCT Scores Mean	s.d.
Normal	30	9.0	1.49
Deaf	15	9.8	1.86
Dysphasic	10	7.4	3.34
Autistic	15	5.8	2.86

facial affective cues. The impairment seemed to be independent of the gross level of language retardation. The deaf group performed normally on the SCT even though they showed the greatest degree of language retardation, and the normal group performed significantly better than the autistic group although their language age was the same. The results suggest that both the autistic and the dysphasic groups have a specific disorder in social comprehension as well as being language-delayed. Another interpretation is that there is a central disorder in these children that affects understanding of all kinds, not just verbal comprehension. The results give some indication that the autistic children were most impaired. However, the lack of a significant difference between the autistic and dysphasic groups on the SCT makes this conclusion tentative, and fails to provide clear support for the earlier study described above, which was carried out in the United Kingdom (Bartak, Rutter, and Cox, 1975, 1977) and in which very clear demarcation between these groups was shown. Further work with larger groups of well-defined dysphasic children might help to clarify the findings. The small sample used for this research covered a large age range and showed the most variability in SCT scores.

Other chapters in this volume point out the importance of nonlinguistic factors in communication. The deficit found here may rest upon some ill-defined cognitive ability on which language development may depend. Certainly, in the case of autistic children who *do* learn to speak, it is found that they often lack the ability to make use of verbal skills socially (Bartak, Rutter, and Cox, 1975).

It might be argued that autistic children are suffering from a specific cognitive impairment that affects both language and social development. Such an impairment might affect analytic ability. However, if this were so, it is difficult to see why autistic children perform well on tasks requiring analytic ability such as WISC Block Design or Raven's Colored Progressive Matrices. In addition, there is little evidence to suggest that the SCT task is a test of analytic ability. It may be that there is a general cognitive deficit that affects ability to extract significant information from situations. In a linguistic context, this would result in the non-use of cues for given versus new information, for example, and could result in the non-use of stress in speech or other aberrations of intonation, and this is observed in speaking, autistic children. Systematic teaching in both linguistic and nonlinguistic areas may help autistic children to improve in social and communicative development.

REFERENCES

Baker, L., Cantwell, D. P., Rutter, M., and Bartak, L. 1976. Language and autism. In: E. R. Ritvo (ed.), Autism, Diagnosis, Current Research and Management. Spectrum Pubns., Inc., New York.

Bartak, L., Rutter, M., and Cox, A. 1975. A comparative study of infantile autism and specific developmental receptive language disorder: I. The children. Br. J. Psychiatry 126:127–145.

Bartak, L., Rutter, M., and Cox, A. 1977. A comparative study of infantile autism and specific developmental receptive language disorder: III. Discriminant function analysis. J. Autism Child. Schizophr. 7:383–396.

Churchill, D. W. 1972. The relation of infantile autism and early childhood schizophrenia to developmental language disorders of childhood. J. Autism Child. Schizophr. 2:182–197.

Cohen, D. J., Caparulo, B. K., and Shaywitz, B. A. 1976. Primary childhood aphasia and childhood autism: Clinical, biological, and conceptual observations. J. Am. Acad. Child Psychiatry 15:604–645.

Cox, A., Rutter, M., Newman, S., and Bartak, L. 1975. A comparative study of infantile autism and specific developmental receptive language disorder: II. Parental characteristics. Br. J. Psychiatry 126:146–159.

De Hirsch, K. 1967. Differential diagnosis between aphasic and schizophrenic language in children. J. Speech Hear. Disord. 32:3–10.

Eisenson, J. 1971. Speech defects: Nature, causes and psychological concommitants. In: W. Cruickshank (ed.), Psychology of Exceptional Children and Youths. 3rd Ed. Prentice-Hall, Englewood Cliffs, N.J.

Ekman, P., Friesen, W. V. 1975. Unmasking the Face: A Guide to Recognizing Emotions from Facial Clues. Prentice-Hall, Englewood Cliffs, N.J.

Ekman, P., Friesen, W. V., and Ellsworth, P. 1972. Emotion in the Human Face: Guidelines for Research and in Integration of Findings. Pergamon Press, Inc., New York.

Goode, M., Bartak, L., and James, M. Measurement of an aspect of social comprehension. In preparation.

Hermelin, B., and O'Connor, N. 1970. Psychological Experiments with Autistic Children. Pergamon Press, Inc., New York.

Lockyer, L., and Rutter, M. 1970. A five-to-fifteen-year follow-up study of infantile psychosis - IV. Patterns of cognitive ability. Br. J. Social Clin. Psychol. 9:152–163.

Reynell, J. 1969. Reynell Developmental Language Scales. N.F.E.R., Slough, Bucks.

Rutter, M. 1974. The development of infantile autism. Psychol. Med. 4:147–163.

Sahlmann, L. 1969. Autism or aphasia? Dev. Child Neurol. 11:443–448.

Schonell, F. J., and Schonell, F. E. 1960. Diagnostic and Attainment Testing. Oliver and Boyd, Edinburgh.

Wechsler, D. 1949. Wechsler Intelligence Scale for Children. Psychological Corporation, New York.

Language Processing and Its Disorders

Katharine G. Butler

There has been increasing interest in the last few years in the early identification of language-processing disorders in young children. In the United States, this interest stems, at least partially, from the efforts during the 1970s to isolate specific factors that contribute to language-processing disorders in language- and learning-disordered children. As defined by Massaro (1975), language processing is "the abstraction of meaning from an acoustic signal or from printed text," and can be viewed as a sequence of operations or stages that occur between stimulus and meaning.

Attentional, perceptual, and linguistic behaviors of young children interact in a complex fashion within language processing thus creating design and interpretation problems in research efforts. Recent studies have attempted to measure such behaviors in children as well as in adults. As Geffen and Sexton (1978) reported, one way of examining the role of attention in language processing is to ask children to divide attention between two stimuli or to focus attention on one stimulus while rejecting others (Broadbent, 1971; Kahneman, 1973; Triesman, 1969). Hagen and Hale (1973) reviewed a number of studies and reported that in the auditory modality, it is not yet clear whether the ability to ignore irrelevant information or to resist distraction improves with age. Sexton and Geffen (1979) concluded that attention should be viewed as a multiprocess construct. They also reported that voluntary selective attention was age dependent, but that perceptual factors such as dichotic interaction and hemispheric asymmetry were not age dependent, at least in the three strategies of attention studied in dichotic monitoring tasks.

Research conducted by Butler (1977) indicates that young children, and even more so, high-risk children, are significantly less able than their age-mates to resist auditory distraction or to ignore irrelevant information under competing message tasks. Doyle (1973) demonstrated that normal children at ages 8 and above could inhibit intrusion from distracting stimuli. Geffen and Sexton's (1978) study also indicted that there was marked improvement in children who were between the ages of 7 and 10 in a perceptual monitoring task that required focused attention. Geffen and Sexton interpreted the results in terms of improved selective perception rather than improvement in storage or retrieval, and they concluded that strategies of focusing and dividing attention can be identified in children as young as age 7. Paris (1978) also considered strategies of attention and recall but noted that children at ages 5 to 8 "usually fail to notice important dimensions of the stimuli and fail to apply mnemonic strategies spontaneously." Others also reported that young children are unaware of a number of their own memory monitoring processes (Flavell and Wellman, 1977).

Over the past decade, much of the research on attention has centered on one of two general models—the first model favoring early selection of incoming information with attention being selected and restricted early in the sequence, and the second model favoring selection of incoming information later in the sequence. As Norman (1975) indicated, there is research evidence that supports both models, and there is also evidence that supports neither. Because there are still unanswered questions in the realm of attention and language processing, and because selective attention in young children is difficult to measure, interpretation of selective attention assessment procedures and outcomes with young high-risk children must be approached with caution. Craik and Levy (1977) pointed out the dangers of trying to separate into stages or mechanisms the cognitive processes involved in language processing. For example, they noted that meaning and long-term memory are involved from the beginning, that attention involves sensory analysis, pattern analysis, meaning, and long-term memory, and finally, that each stage of a process, although functionally distinct, need not necessarily be completed prior to the next stage or level.

In this research, it was found clinically that children with language-processing disorders frequently reveal signs of information overloading earlier than do normal children. The analysis and determination of meaning is perhaps more difficult, and the overload is more apparent for these children. Studies that include an observation of a relationship between language processing and a variety of selective attention tasks within an auditory figure-ground or within a competing message paradigm include: Anderson and Novina (1973), Friedlander and DeLara (1973), and Marston and Larkin (1979).

PRESCHOOL LANGUAGE PROCESSING PERFORMANCE

For a study by Shigezumi (1976), preschool children were given three test instruments: The Butler Kindergarten Auditory Figure-Ground Test (B-KAFGT), Experimental Form B, and the Pre-Primary Auditory Screening Test (Pre-PAST), Experimental Edition (both brief audiotaped tests measuring several aspects of language processing), and the Preschool Language Scale (PLS).

Subjects

Sixty children, from three preschools in Solano County California, were assessed on two measures of auditory language processing and one measure of language, as noted above. The sample was composed of 29 males and 31 females, with a mean age of 4 years, 2 months (4;2). The range of the subjects' ages was 3;0–4;11. Sixty-five percent of the children were Caucasian, 13.3% were Black, 6.7% were Asian-American, and 1% were Mexican-American.

Instruments

The B-KAFGT, Experimental Form B, consists of five subtests and a preliminary training segment. The subtests include: 1) following directions against variable background noise; 2) following directions against stable background noise; 3) following directions against a verbal background; 4) responding to a foreground nonlinguistic signal against a verbal background; and 5) following more complex directions against variable background noise. The test was individually administered by means of audiotaped presentation, except for the pretraining segment. The response mode includes the child's moving a block to specified locations on the testing table and pointing to body parts.

The Pre-PAST was developed under a Title VI-B Elementary and Secondary Education Act project through the Office of the Solano, California, County Superintendent of Schools in 1973–1976. It consists of four subtests that include: 1) auditory discrimination; 2) auditory figure-ground; 3) auditory memory; and 4) auditory sequencing. The test was individually administered by means of audiotaped presentation. In response to a verbal stimulus, the child pointed to a target picture from among three or four foils. Table 1 presents further information about the processing measure.

The PLS (Zimmerman, Steiner, and Evatt, 1974) is an informal inventory that attempts to measure auditory comprehension and verbal ability. Its primary use is as a preliminary screening instrument. The Auditory Comprehension Scale (AC) measures the child's ability to receive

Table 1.   Examples of Pre-PAST and B-KAFGT (Form B) Subtests

Test	Subtests	Number of items	Brief description	Examples
Pre-PAST	I	6	Auditory discrimination	S points to picture of stimulus word. Example: *thread* from among bed, bread, head
	II	5	Auditory figure-ground	S points to picture of stimulus phrase: "Boy fishing" with background noise
	III	4	Auditory memory	S points to pictures of a number of objects after time delay
	IV	4	Auditory sequencing	S points to pictures of objects in sequence
B-KAFGT (Form B)	Pretraining	3	Response mode trained	S places block in box as directed by E
	I	10	Directions against variable background noise	S places block in box or removes block, under variable classroom noise
	II	5	Directions against stable background noise	S gives or removes blocks from E, under music condition
	III	10	Directions against verbal background	S puts blocks "on the paper" or "on the plate" under linguistic background condition
	IV	8	Foreground nonlinguistic signal against verbal background	S gives block to E in response to intermittent signal (dog bark)
	V	10	Directions against variable background noise	S points to body parts: Example: "Point to your ear"

auditory information and does not require a verbal response, and the Verbal Ability Scale (VA) measures the child's ability to verbalize, as measured by his response to a series of graded tasks. The test is administered live-voice, with no time limitations.

Procedure

All three instruments were administered to the students in a free-field setting. A tape recorder was used for the Pre-PAST and the B-KAFGT. Assessments were conducted individually in a quiet setting (Shigezumi, 1976). Three sessions were required for the administration of the three instruments.

Results

Table 2 provides the means and standard deviations of the two language-processing tests (Pre-PAST and B-KAFGT) for the preschool population by age groups. There was a significant difference between the means for the 3-year-olds and those for the 4-year-olds in the areas of auditory memory and auditory sequencing, as well as for the total test scores on the Pre-PAST. There was, however, no significant difference found for auditory discrimination and auditory figure-ground. In particular, the performance of 3- and 4-year-olds was very similar in the area of auditory discrimination.

One might speculate that children in both age groups were unable to make semantic differentiations that were based on perceptually derived features. As Clark (1979) noted, although children may begin by using a single general feature, as more meanings must be differentiated the child must eventually encode information from a combination of features. On minimally differentiated items in terms of acoustic cues, such as those found in subtest I of the Pre-PAST, both age groups responded at approximately the same level. Wood (1974) noted that 3-year-olds, in a "signal matching" task, found such a task beyond their perceptual capabilities, but she noted that the low rate of success might relate to a lack of understanding of the task requirements rather than to a problem in processing. As Pisoni (1975) reported, interpretation of a speech stimulus is not determined exclusively by the properties of the physical signal. Rather, what is perceived depends upon the child's knowledge of his language and other factors that determine what the child expects to hear. He hypothesized that in the speech perception system, phonological, syntactic, and semantic operations occur simultaneously. Thus, whether the inability to differentiate at the semantic level relates to perceptual factors, or to phonological, syntactical, or semantic factors, is difficult to determine. In addition, auditory discrimination is the first subtest in the Pre-PAST

Table 2.   Performance of 3-year-olds and 4-year-olds on two tests of language
processing (Pre-PAST and B-KAFGT, Form B)

Test	Subtests	Subjects 3;0 to 4;0 mean age 3;6 (N = 21)		Subjects 4;0 to 5;0 mean age 4;5 t (N = 39)		
Pre-PAST		Mean	SD	Mean	SD	
	I	3.24	1.38	3.54	1.34	0.81
	II	2.43	1.05	2.97	1.23	1.79
	III	0.71	0.98	1.36	1.35	2.50*
	IV	0.43	0.58	0.85	1.00	2.05*
Total		6.81	2.87	8.80	3.45	2.38*
B-KAFGT						
	I	6.05	1.85	7.05	1.47	3.13**
	II	2.62	1.09	2.82	1.30	1.27
	III	4.14	2.63	5.85	2.69	2.38*
	IV	2.80	2.48	2.97	2.52	0.25
	V	3.95	1.65	4.18	2.92	0.39
Total		19.57	6.55	23.00	5.65	2.03*
df = 20, 38						

*$p < 0.05$
**$p < 0.01$

and by its very position in the testing sequence, may contribute to the non-significant findings. It should be noted that the Pre-Past does not provide for cuing (pretest training of the task), as does, for example, the B-KAFGT. Perhaps factors such as task-understanding and task-expectancy were not present in sufficient degree during the initial stages of the Pre-PAST test administration. Clinically, it has been noted that 3-year olds in particular, and also a significant number of 4-year-olds require a pretraining or pretesting opportunity to focus upon the task at hand over a number of trials. With the B-KAFGT, for example, it was found that 3-and 4-year-olds required approximately 50% more opportunities to deal with the practice items than did the 5-year old children in the kindergarten normative populations.

On the B-KAFGT, significant differences were noted on two of the subtests and on the total score. As noted in Table 2, the B-KAFGT does provide pretraining (three trials over a 30-second period). Performance on both subtest I and subtest III was significantly better in 4-year-olds. These two subtests measure the ability of the subjects to follow directions ("Put a block in the box/Take a block out of the box") against background noise and to follow directions ("Place a block on the paper/Place a block on the plate") against background linguistic conditions. The remaining three subtests (II, IV, V) did not reveal significant differences in performance between the 3- and the 4-year-olds. Subtest IV requires a response to an auditory vigilance task and utilizes a foreground nonlinguistic signal against a linguistic background. Subtest V requires a more complex response such as "Point to your shoe" or "Point to your chin," against a variable background noise. It is interesting to note that subtest V of the B-KAFGT and Pre-PAST subtest II both involve a "pointing" response to directions given against the variable background noise of a classroom and both tasks reveal similar performances between 3- and 4-year-olds. However, B-KAFGT IV is the only subtest of either instrument that utilizes a foreground nonlinguistic signal against a linguistic background and it is a task that is subject to highly variable performance on the part of the 3- and 4-year-old subjects. The ability of children in this age range to resist linguistic auditory distraction and to focus attention on a foreground nonlinguistic stimulus in the presence of highly interesting background linguistic stimuli seems to be limited.

Comparison of Preschool and School-Age Performance

The performance of the 56 preschool subjects was then compared with a sample of 329 kindergarten children who had previously been tested. Significant differences again were found between the two groups, not only on the total test scores, but on all of the four subtests of the Pre-PAST (discrimination, memory, and sequencing, $p < 0.01$; auditory figure-ground, $p < 0.05$). Thus, the significant differences noted between 3- and 4-year-olds on the parameters of auditory memory and sequencing and following directions against a noise background (a selective attention task), and the significant differences found between these two groups and a large sample of kindergarten children (mean age 5;1) provide additional evidence that some language-processing tasks develop incrementally in normal children.

Pearson-Product correlations between the two assessment measures of language processing, the Pre-PAST and the B-KAFGT, and the PLS revealed some interesting differences, which are noted in Table 3. The PLS, as noted earlier, has two subtests, auditory comprehension and verbal ability, as well as a language score. Shigezumi (1976) reported that 4-year-olds scored significantly higher than 3-year-olds on both the subtests and the total score of the PLS.

Although there are a number of significant, albeit modest, correlations among the subtests of the two language-processing instruments and the PLS, one of the subtests of the Pre-PAST and four of the B-KAFGT subtests did not correlate significantly with the PLS Language score. All of these subtests have a figure-ground or competing message format. In addition, none of the auditory figure-ground tasks on either instrument were significantly correlated with auditory comprehension on the PLS. When considering the relationship of auditory figure-ground tasks utilizing linguistic stimuli with "language," one must ask what constitutes the

Table 3.   Pearson-Product Correlations between two measures of language processing and the PLS in preschool children

Tests		Subtests	PLS Auditory comp.	PLS Verbal ability	PLS Language score
Pre-PAST					
	I	discrimination	0.38**	0.37**	0.37**
	II	figure-ground	0.20	0.37**	0.25
	III	memory	0.37**	0.49**	0.45**
	IV	sequencing	0.41**	0.41**	0.38**
Total score			0.47**	0.57**	0.51**
B-KAFGT					
	I	linguistic information against variable background noise	0.13	0.20	0.17
	II	linguistic information against stable background noise	0.05	0.09	0.06
	III	linguistic information against verbal background	0.19	0.28*	0.19
	IV	foreground non-linguistic information against verbal background	−0.03	0.04	0.08
	V	linguistic information against variable background noise	0.27	0.42**	0.36**
Total score			0.23	0.34**	0.29

*p < 0.05
**p < 0.01

exact nature of the figure and of the ground; the degree of linguistic complexity and of intrinsic interest of both the figure and the ground; the degree to which selective attention and the ability to resist distractions of an auditory nature are being measured; and finally, the degree to which attention is divided between the two sets of information. As noted by Geffen and Sexton (1978), it is not yet clear whether the ability to ignore irrelevant information or to resist distraction improves with age, nor is it yet clear whether the processes involved in the selection of the wanted items and the attention to irrelevant information operates during the perceptual processing stage or during recall from memory.

Overall, correlations were higher between the two language-processing instruments and the verbal ability scale of the PLS. All of the subtests of the Pre-PAST and two of the B-KAFGT's reveal positive correlations, a rather unexpected finding because none of the language-processing tasks required verbal expression.

The results of the Shigezumi (1976) study are of particular interest when compared to earlier normative studies with the B-KAFGT. Channon (1976), in a normative study of the instrument (Experimental Form A), had as subjects 84 kindergarten children whose mean age was 5;7. She reported that the subtest dealing with the foreground nonlinguistic information against a linguistic background was most difficult for normal 5-year-olds. The ability to resist the distraction of an interesting linguistic background was significantly lower than in other subtests of the B-KAFGT, but was well above the performance of high-risk children. An analysis of variance indicated that all auditory figure-ground tasks measured were impervious to socioeconomic differences.

In a separate study (Butler, 1978), the B-KAFGT was administered to 115 kindergarten children who were identified as high-risk for learning difficulties, and to 846 normal kindergarten children from the same population. It was found that not only was the performance of such high-risk subjects significantly reduced on the total test score, but high-risk children, like the children tested by Channon, did particularly poorly on the subtest that deals with a foreground nonlinguistic signal against a linguistic background (subtest IV on B-KAFGT, Experimental Form B).

CONCLUSION

Although young children demonstrate an increasing ability to focus attention on one stimulus while rejecting others, the type of stimulus and background noise conditions contribute to variable performance. The ability to resist distraction and to maintain auditory vigilance is limited in 3- and 4-year-olds and reveals modest increases in 5-year-olds. High-risk children, at age 5, perform more poorly than normal 5-year-olds on some, but not all, auditory figure-ground tasks. In general, high-risk children demonstrate significantly lower scores and a concomitantly greater degree of vulnerability to language-processing tasks that require selective attention. The degree to which information overloading occurs, or the degree to which auditory distractibility and auditory fatigue play a part is open to speculation.

As Wiig and Semel (1976) commented, the relationships between cognitive-semantic processing, linguistic processing, and perceptual processing are relevant to the determination of language-processing disorders and each must be assessed differentially. Such assessment requires careful attention to factors such as selective attention and resistance to distraction. The instruments reported here have been designated as screening instruments and as such, they provide information within the identified scope of such brief procedures. Sophisticated instruments have not yet been devised.

REFERENCES

Anderson, A. H., and Novina, J. 1973. A study of the relationship of the tests of central auditory abilities and the ITPA. J. Learn. Disabil. 6(3):46048

Broadbent, D. E. 1971. Decision and Stress. Academic Press, Inc., London.

Butler, K. 1978. Educational and social implications of auditory processing deficits. In: Proceedings of the 17th International Congress of Logopedics and Phoniatrics, Copenhagen, Denmark, pp. 371–382, Vol. 2. S. Karger, Basel, Switzerland.

Butler, K. 1978. Kindergarten Auditory Figure-Ground Test (B-KAFGT), Experimental Test Form A. O. G. Johnson (ed.), Tests and Measurements in Child Development, pp. 899–900. Jossey-Bass Inc., Pubs., San Francisco.

Channon, R. R. 1976. A normative study of an experimental auditory figure ground test for kindergarten children. Unpublished master's thesis, San Jose State Univ., San Jose, Cal.

Clark E. 1979. What's in a word? On the child's acquisition of semantics in his first language. In: V. Lee (ed.), Language Development, pp. 186–234. John Wiley & Sons, Inc., New York.

Craik, I. M., and Levy, B. A. 1977. The concept of primary memory. In: W. K. Estes (ed.), Handbook of Learning and Cognitive Processes, pp. 133–175, Vol. 4. Lawrence Erlbaum Associates, Hillsdale, N.J.

Doyle, A. 1973. Listening to distraction: A developmental study of selective attention. J. Exp. Child Psychol. 15:100–115.

Flavell, J. H., and Wellman, H. M. 1977. Metamemory. In: W. K. Estes (ed.), Handbook of Learning and Cognitive Processes, Vol. 4. Lawrence Erlbaum Associates, Hillsdale, N.J.

Friedlander, B. A., and DeLara, H. C. 1973. Receptive language anomaly and language/reading distinction in "normal" primary-grade school children. Psychol. in Schools 10(1):12–18.

Geffen, G., and Sexton, M. A. 1978. The development of auditory strategies of attention. Dev. Psychol. 14(1):11–17.

Hagen, H., and Hale, G. 1973. The development of attention in children. In: A. D. Pick (ed.), Minnesota Symposium on Child Psychology. Vol. 7. Univ. of Minnesota Press, Minneapolis.

Kahneman, D. 1973. Attention and Effort. Prentice-Hall, Englewood Cliffs, N.J.

Marston, L. E., and Larkin, M. 1979. Auditory assessment of reading underachieving children. Lang. Speech Hearing Services in Schools. 10(4):212–220.

Massaro, D. (ed.).1975. Understanding Language. Academic Press, New York.

Norman, D. A. 1975. Memory and Attention. John Wiley & Sons, Inc., New York.

Paris, S. G. 1978. Memory organization during children's reported recall. Dev. Psychol. 14(1):94–106.

Pisoni, D. B. 1975. Mechanisms for auditory discrimination and coding of linguistic information. Acta Symbolica 6(2):65–112.

Pre-Primary Auditory Screening Test (Pre-PAST), Experimental Edition, 1978. Office of the Solano County Superintendent of Schools, Fairfield, Cal. Title VI-B Project.

Sexton, M. A., and Geffen, G. 1979. Development of three strategies of attention and dichotic monitoring. Dev. Psychol. 15(3):299–310

Shigezumi, K. 1976. Auditory processing and language development in pre-school children. Unpublished master's thesis, San Jose State Univ., San Jose, Cal.

Triesman, A. M. 1969. Strategies and models of selective attention. Psychol. Review 76:282–299.

Wiig, E., and Semel, E. M. 1976. Language Disabilities in Children and Adolescents. Charles E. Merrill Publishing Company, Columbus, Ohio.

Wood, N. 1974. Auditory closure and auditory discrimination in young children. Acta Symbolica 5(2):68–74.

Zimmerman, I. L., Steiner, V. G., and Evatt, R. L. 1974. Preschool Language Scale. Charles E. Merrill Publishing Company, Columbus, Ohio.

Hierarchical Ordering Disability and Aphasic Children

Richard F. Cromer

Research on particular problems often reflects the theoretical presuppositions of those working in that field and the study of language disorders is no exception. However, in the case of language studies, this truism is particularly important because theories of the structure of language have undergone such drastic revision over the past 20 years. Earlier behavioral theories focused on the temporal order of the elements in sentential word strings. Principles of sequential association were used to explain most language processes, and even theorists of information processing viewed the information content of words in a sentence primarily in terms of sequence. Research on language disorders has continued to reflect a primary concern with the serial order of words in strings and has been paid less attention to the possible programming mechanisms that may underlie such output.

For example, some researchers believe that a sequencing or temporal order deficit is either the cause of the language difficulty found in various groups of aphasic patients, or that it at least is an important associated condition (Critchley, 1953; Efron, 1963; Hirsh, 1959; Jackson, 1888; Lowe and Campbell, 1965; Monsees, 1961; Sheehan, Aseltine, and Edwards, 1973; Tallal and Piercy, 1973a, 1973b, 1974, 1975). It has also been argued, however (Cromer, 1978a), that sequential or temporal order deficit theories do not seem to be adequate to account for the problems of aphasic children.

As early as 1951, psychologists began to question the validity of explanations of serially ordered behavior that were based only on the assumption that the processes themselves were serially ordered. In his classic paper, Lashley (1951) claimed that associative chain explanations were

319

inadequate to account for the real structure of such sequences of actions as rhythmic activity, motor movements, piano playing, typing, speech, and language. He claimed, for example, that theories that attempted to describe grammatical form in terms of the associative linkages of words in a sentence would overlook the essential structure of sentences. Such theories also would be unable to account adequately for the processes by which sentences are produced or understood. Since Chomsky (1965), most linguistic analyses, regardless of the specific details of competing theories, have noted the importance of processes of embedding and interruption—processes that are difficult to account for in terms of simple temporal sequences. By redirecting attention to mechanisms or processes that underlie sequential output but are not themselves sequential, it may be possible to explain more adequately some language disorders.

EVIDENCE THAT APHASIC CHILDREN
MAY SUFFER FROM A HIERARCHICAL ORDERING DEFICIT

Rhythm

One type of behavior that often was believed to be structured as a sequential concatenation of stimuli is rhythm. This view was challenged, however, by Martin (1972) in his careful analysis of rhythmic activity. The notion that rhythm comprises only periodic, repetitive behavior is a misconception, he claimed. A series of sequential elements cannot have a structured internal organization. The alternative viewpoint, for which Martin presented a strong case, is that rhythms are composed of hierarchically structured units. In such a structured ensemble, the change of any one element alters the interrelations of all the elements. Altering one rhythmic element does not merely change its relationship to the beats that immediately precede and follow it; rather, the perceived overall structure is changed. Martin claimed that this view has important implications for both the production and the perception of language. For example, a hierarchical structure allows sounds to be temporally patterned with trajectories that in time allow them to be tracked without continuous monitoring; that is, the perception of early elements in a pattern allows for the anticipation of elements that occur later. In contrast, a mechanism capable only of processing incoming sounds successively would require continuous attention. Even on tasks such as digit span capacity, normal individuals group the elements that occur at constant intervals into rhythmic units.

It has often been reported that developmentally aphasic children have an almost uniformly poor sense of rhythm (Griffiths, 1972). Lea (1975) developed and administered three auditory tests of rhythms to children with various speech and language disorders. He found high significant correlations between rhythmic ability and language ability. Furthermore, it was the receptive aphasic children who scored the poorest on all three rhythm tests. Kracke (1975) found that aphasic children performed significantly more poorly on tasks of identifying rhythmic sequences than did either normal or profoundly deaf children. This was true whether the rhythms were presented in an auditory mode or by a tactile method. Kracke reported that the aphasic children used an "element-by-element" strategy to retain the rhythms they were required to identify, even going so far, in some cases, as attempting to remember the bursts with verbal labeling such as "long-long-short." This is a purely sequential strategy for dealing with the task. By contrast, the normal and the profoundly deaf children tried to perceive the rhythmic patterns as a whole, in a direct unreflective way. Kracke characterized this as a Gestalt strategy. Because temporal Gestalts would seem to depend on the same hierarchical abilities discussed here, the poor performance of the aphasic children on simple rhythmic matching tasks may be evidence of an impairment that involves more general consequences than merely an inability to handle rhythmic patterns.

Hierarchical Disability in the Writing of Aphasic Children

Further evidence of a possible hierarchical ordering disability in aphasic children comes from an analysis of the children's writing. In order to learn about the nature of the deficit in some aphasic children, this author has studied a small, very special subgroup of such children (Cromer, 1978a, 1978b). These children, either from birth or from a very early age, have neither comprehended nor produced language. They met the criteria proposed in Griffiths' (1972) definition of developmentally aphasic children: failure of the normal growth of language function when deafness, mental deficiency, motor disability, and severe personality disorder can be excluded. The children seemed to be normal in most respects. They were of normal intelligence, as assessed by nonverbal tests. Furthermore, they did not have hearing loss or emotional problems that could have had causal bearing on their aphasic condition. It must be emphasized that these children were rather different from those usually designated aphasic. Most children who are labeled *aphasic* are children with language disorders that vary in nature and extent. In contrast, although the children studied were not alike in all of their abilities, they had a critical disability in common—they totally lacked the comprehension and production of structured language, at least in the auditory modality. They were, however, capable of comprehending and producing single words that were semantically correct in that they were appropriate to the situation. They were bright and interested, and seemed to be frustrated by their lack of communicative ability. This description may imply that their problem was purely an auditory one, and indeed, some researchers have proposed that the deficit in developmental aphasia is specifically auditory (Eisenson, 1968; Mark and Hardy, 1958; Rosenthal, 1972; Tallal and Piercy, 1975; Worster-Drought and Allen, 1929). The children in this group attended a special residential school, and some of the children also were studied by Kracke (1975) and Lea (1975) for rhythmic disabilities. They had been taught to read and to write. Because writing was their only form of language production, it was interesting to study the grammatical structures they produced to see if any light could be shed on their disorder.

The rationale for the study was that if their problem was primarily an auditory one, there should be basic similarities between their writings and the writings of congenitally profoundly deaf children. If, however, their deficit was of a different nature, their writings should differ from those of the deaf children and perhaps give some clues as to the nature of their disorder. It had alredy been noted that grammatical structures used in their spontaneous writing were not normal, but deaf children also evidence many problems in written syntax. Therefore, the grammatical structures of these two groups of children were compared.

There were ten aphasic children of the type described. Four of them were developmentally aphasic in that they had never possessed language skills; the remaining six had had some language before a deterioration, for unknown reasons, occurred. The ages of onset of language loss in these six children were 2;6, 2;9, 4;0, 4;6, 5;0, and 7;0. The ages of the ten children at the time of data collection ranged from 7;6 to 16;0 with a median age of 13;6. The overall median IQ of the group was 99.5. In the task described below, two children wrote only lists of words or they drew pictures. Two children produced writings that were so grammatically bizarre that an analysis of their writings has not yet been attempted. The writings of the other six children were compared to those of six congenitally profoundly deaf children (hearing loss between 90 db and 120 db). Their age range was 9;11 to 10;8, with a median age of 10;5. This is some three years younger than the median age of the aphasic group. The median IQ of the deaf group was 101.5, and was, therefore, essentially identical to that of the aphasic children.

The samples of writing were collected in a standarized situation. Small groups of children viewed a short (approximately 2-minute) non-verbal story that was enacted with puppets.[1] The puppet shows were designed to elicit a number of varied grammatical forms. For example, two

---

[1]Maria Black, a linguistics student at University College, London, helped with the presentation of the stories.

characters of the same type were used to encourage the use of plurality (e.g., "two ducks") in later descriptions. Differing motivations were included to force differentiation of the two animals by using adjectives and other descriptive devices, as in "the duck with the little eyes/the duck with the big eyes." Events in the story were repeated to elicit adverbial expressions such as "at first" and "again." At the end of each puppet show, the children wrote a description of what they had just seen. They were allowed as much time to write as they desired. This was usually about 30 to 45 minutes.

A partial grammatical analysis of the writings by the aphasic children and by the deaf children is in Cromer (1978b), and is only summarized here. The mean number of words per sentence was essentially identical for the two groups (7.76 words per sentence for the deaf and 7.61 words per sentence for the aphasic children). In spite of this overall similarity, the writings were found to be significantly different when these sentences were anlayzed into phrase structure categories such as noun phrases, verb phrases, prepositional phrases, and adverbial phrases. The sentences of the deaf children had a mean of 4.51 categories per sentence while the sentences of the aphasic children had only 3.73 ($p < 0.01$). The number of different types of verb forms used was similarly restricted in the writings of the aphasic children. Each aphasic child attempted, on average, only 2.16 different verb types in his story, while the mean different verb types used by each deaf child was 3.33 ($p < 0.02$). The interesting finding, however, concerns the types of sentences used by the two groups. The sentences of the deaf children were more complex in that the children attempted to combine various elements by such devices as embedding some units within others, and in general by processes involving the interruption of an ongoing sequence. A count was therefore made of the total number of sentences that included one or more embedded or conjoined structures as opposed to simple sentences without these. The deaf children produced sentences 35.9% of which had one or more embedded and conjoined structures. This contrasted with only 12% of the sentences of the aphasic group ($p < 0.001$). In the writings by the deaf children, 10.9% of the sentences contained two or more embeddings and conjoinings. None of the sentences of the aphasic children could be so classified ($p < 0.01$). It should be noted that a child was credited with attempting such forms even if he made grammatical errors in doing so. Thus, the writings by the deaf were not correct by adult standards. In fact, their grasp of grammatical devices was inconsistent and limited. But when the structures they attempted were compared to those of the aphasic children, these differences emerged. The aphasic children never used relative clauses or complement verb structures, but again, these were found in the writings of the deaf children.

The lack of complexity in the aphasic children's writings was not attributable merely to the lack of complex sentences. It was also reflected in the lack of certain structural properties within simple sentences. The aphasic children never linked two adjectives (as in "the big, tall one"), never produced adverb-adjective strings (as in "the very big ball"), and rarely used conjunctions, even internally, as in linking two noun phrases and they virtually never used a conjuction to link two independent clauses. All of these forms were attempted by the deaf children.

The writings of the aphasic children seem to reflect an inability to deal with hierarchical structuring in a planning or programming sense. Such an ability involves the analysis of complex behavior into its component parts in which the performance of some parts is postponed during the performance of other parts. This ability is crucial to the comprehension and production of linguistic structure.

AN EXPERIMENT INVESTIGATING
HIERARCHICAL STRUCTURING DISABILITY

Aphasic children seem to have a problem with hierarchical ordering, which is evidenced both in their inability to deal with rhythmic stimuli and in their failure to use certain types of linguistic structures in their writing. Furthermore, their deficit does not seem to be primarily auditory in nature, although it might be reflected in a variety of auditory tasks. The aphasic children performed poorly with rhythmic structure whether the structure was presented in an auditory or tactile mode. Their writing differed significantly from that of profoundly deaf children even though both groups were primarily learning language "by eye." How might it be possible to test more directly for a hierarchical structuring deficit? A child may fail to perform appropriately on a particular task for a variety of reasons. What is needed is a task which may be performed sequentially *or* in a hierarchical manner. Such a task has been designed by Greenfield and Schneider (1977) for studying development in normal children. Subjects are required to build a mobile or tree structure from construction straws to match a model that is placed in front of them. The child is allowed to construct the model by whatever method he chooses. When he has finished, an alternative method is required by the experimenter. In this task, Greenfield and Schneider found that the youngest children (of those who could build the structure at all) used what they called a chain strategy that consisted of starting their construction at the bottom of one side and working sequentially up the figure, across the midline and down the other side. When instructed to construct the model by another method, requiring interruption and thus hierarchical planning, 6-year-olds were unable to do so. By contrast, older children (7-, 9-, and 11-year-olds) usually began their construction with the superordinate connecting level. Although many of these children also used a chain strategy to complete the construction of the figure, the scores for interrupting the chain increased with age. And, older children were able to construct the mobile with the hierarchical strategy when asked to do so.

The task used in this experiment was similar but not identical to that used by Greenfield and Schneider. Furthermore, the rationale was not the same. Greenfield and Schneider claimed that their task represents a direct relationship between hierarchical actions and heirarchical language structures. It is not possible to make so strong a claim. The rationale for this experiment differs in that nothing was assumed about the direct relationship of language and action. Language relies on a number of cognitive processes, some of which may even be specific to it. If any of these processes is impaired, language will be affected. Thus, children with a particular type of hypothesized impairment should show deficits on any tasks, including language tasks, that require the use of these underlying processes. The prediction in this experiment, then, is that aphasic children, although said to perform normally on most nonverbal tasks, will perform more poorly at constructing a mobile-type figure hierarchically than would a control group of deaf children. They should, however, be able to perform the task sequentially.

The group of aphasic children consisted of five developmentally receptive aphasic children selected from the ten children who had taken part in the written language study. In addition, seven expressive aphasic children from the same residential school were included. The range of ages of the 12 children was 8;5 to 16;4 with a median age of 12;6. As a preliminary comparison, eight congenitally profoundly deaf children were tested. The age range of the deaf group was 9;3 to 12;3 with a median age of 10;0. Thus, the deaf children were about 2½ years younger than the aphasic children.

There were two main tasks. First, the child was shown a drawing of a tree structure. (See Figure 1.) He was given a pencil and paper and merely was instructed to copy it. The order in which he drew the elements was observed and noted by two judges. When the child completed his drawing, he was given a clean piece of paper and instructed to draw it again. On this second trial, the experimenter indicated that he should make his drawing using a method that was the opposite of the one he had spontaneously used in his first drawing. This was done by pointing to the parts of the figure in the order that they should be drawn before the child attempted his copy.

After some interpolated tasks, the second experimental task was introduced. The child was shown a completed mobile built with plastic straws. This was hung on a hook in front of him and he was instructed to

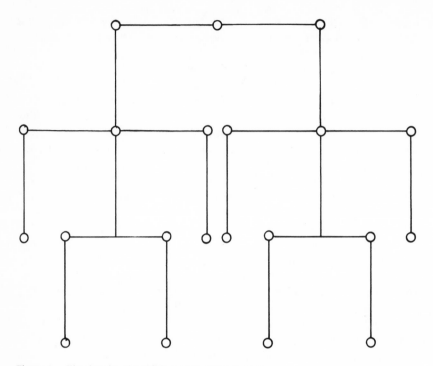

Figure 1.   The drawing the children were asked to copy.

build one exactly like it with straws and connecting links, which were provided on the table. The Greenfield and Schneider mobile, while constructed of the same type of straws, was, nevertheless, two dimensional. In this experiment, however, a three-dimensional figure was used, with the middle elements oriented at 90° from the upper and lower parts. (See Figure 2.) The child was thus more easily able to reverse his construction constantly, as he built it. This ensured that no part was consistently on the left or right and thus possibly in a field of visual neglect as is found in brain damaged patients. When the child completed his spontaneous construction, he was instructed to build it again, and the strategy opposite to the strategy he basically used in his first construction was demonstrated. Once again, two judges observed the child as he made his construction and noted the order in which each straw was placed.

Both tasks were scored using Greenfield and Schneider's method. The figure has seven subparts. Shifts in construction from one part to another received a score of one. Shifts that involved crossing from one side of the figure to the other were given double weight. The center segment was not counted as being left or right and was therefore excluded from any double-weighted shift. Because there are seven parts to the figure, the minimum shift score is six. Therefore, a constant of six was

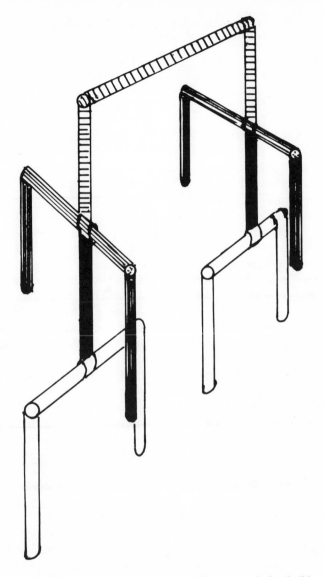

Figure 2.   An illustration of the straw model the children were asked to build.

substracted from the totals. Using this method, a chain or sequential strategy would result in a zero score. The most interrupted strategy—shifting every time across the figure for the drawing or placing of each segment—would result in a score of 25. The mean scores for the two groups are shown in Table 1. These means are based on the highest score obtained by the child in his two attempts on each task. The mean score on the task requiring the child merely to copy the drawing in front of him was

Table 1.   Mean shift scores of the two groups on the drawing and construction tasks, based on the child's highest score for each

	Aphasic children (N = 12)	Deaf children (N = 8)
Drawing task	4.42	7.38
Construction task	7.00	10.00

4.42 by the aphasic group. This was significantly lower than deaf children's mean of 7.38 (Mann-Whitney $U = 18$, $p < 0.025$). In the construction task, although the aphasic mean of 7 was lower than the deaf mean of 10, this difference did not reach statistical significance.

There seems to be some evidence, then, that the aphasic children find the drawing and construction tasks difficult when required to use a hierarchically planned rather than a sequential strategy. Their shift scores were significantly lower on the drawing task than the scores of the deaf children on the same task. Although the difference between the aphasic group and the deaf group was not significant for the construction task, qualitative evaluation indicates they had a much more difficult time with the hierarchical task. Three aphasic children who attempted to build the structure hierarchically when asked to do so were unable to complete the structure or to build the mobile correctly. They had, however, been able to build the same figure sequentially. Other children completed the structure but mainly fell back into using a chaining method to do so.

The difference between group means was diminished by the performance of one of the receptive aphasic children who scored 17, the second highest shift score of all 20 children. It is interesting to note that in the language sample, on the basis of which a hierarchical disability for this group has been postulated, his writing had not been analyzed because it was different from the other children and was so bizarre that an analysis of its patterns has not been carried out.

Greenfield and Schneider, using their version of this task, found a developmental trend continuing at least through 11 years of age. In this experiment, the median age of the aphasic children was 12;5, but the median age of the deaf group was only 10;0. It is expected that a wider divergence of scores will be found when a deaf group matched for age with the aphasic group is tested.

In this experiment, it seems that the aphasic children had difficulties with tasks requiring hierarchical structuring. Some of the aphasic children were able to draw or build the model when they used a sequential strategy, but failed completely to do so when forced to use a method requiring interruption and hierarchical planning. It may of course be that a hierarchical structuring disability is not the underlying cause of their language difficulties, but merely an associated condition. But the notion of a hierarchical disability fits in better with what is known about the essential structure of the tasks on which they evidenced poor performances—rhythm and language. Neither the structure of these tasks (and the ones studied in this experiment), nor the manner of performance of these children on them, seems to indicate a problem merely of sequential order. It seems that some aphasic children suffer from a hierarchical planning or programming deficit.

REFERENCES

Chomsky, N. 1965. Aspects of the Theory of Syntax. M.I.T. Press, Cambridge, Mass.

Critchley, M. 1953. The Parietal Lobes. Edward Arnold & Co., London

Cromer, R. F. 1978a. The basis of childhood dysphasia: A linguistic approach. In: Maria Wyke (ed.), Developmental Dysphasia, pp. 85–134. Academic Press, Inc., New York.

Cromer, R. F. 1978b. Hierarchical disability in the syntax of aphasic children. Int. J. Behav. Dev. 1:391–402.

Efron, R. 1963. Temporal perception, aphasia and déjà vu. Brain 86:403–424.

Eisenson, J. 1968. Developmental aphasia: A speculative view with therapeutic implications. J. Speech Hear. Disord. 33:3–13.

Greenfield, P.M., and Schneider, L. 1977. Building a tree structure: The development of hierarchical complexity and interrupted strategies in children's construction activity. Dev. Psychol. 13:299–313.

Griffiths, P. 1972. Developmental Aphasia: An Introduction. Invalid Children's Aid Association. London.

Hirsh, I. J. 1959. Auditory perception of temporal order. J. Acoust. Soc. Am. 31:759–767.

Jackson, J. H. 1888. On a particular variety of epilepsy ("intellectual aura"), one case with symptoms of organic brain disease. Brain 11:179–207.

Kracke, I. 1975. Perception of rhythmic sequences by receptive aphasic and deaf children. Br. J. Disord. Commun. 10:43–51.

Lashley, K. S. 1951. The problem of serial order in behaviour. In: L. A. Jeffress (ed.), Cerebral Mechanisms in Behaviour, pp. 112–136. John Wiley & Sons, Inc., New York.

Lea, J. 1975. An investigation into the association between rhythmic ability and language ability in a group of children with severe speech and language disorders. Unpublished masters thesis, University of London, Guy's Hospital Medical School.

Lowe, A. D., and Campbell, R. A. 1965. Temporal discrimination in aphasoid and normal children. J. Speech Hear. Res. 8:313–314.

Mark, H. J., and Hardy, W. G. 1958. Orienting reflex disturbances in central auditory or language handicapped children. J. Speech Hear. Disord. 23:237–242.

Martin, J. G. 1972. Rhythmic (hierarchical) versus serial structure in speech and other behaviour. Psychol. Rev. 79:487–509.

Monsees, E. K. 1961. Aphasia in children. J. Speech Hear. Disord. 26:83–86.

Rosenthal, W. S. 1972. Auditory and linguistic interaction in developmental aphasia: Evidence from two studies of auditory processing. In: D. Ingram (ed.),

Papers and Reports on Child Language Development. Special Issue: Language Disorders in Children, no. 4, pp.19–34. Stanford University.

Sheehan, J. G., Aseltine, S., and Edwards, A. E. 1973. Aphasic comprehension of time spacing. J. Speech Hear. Res. 16:650–657.

Tallal, P., and Piercy, M. 1973a. Defects of non-verbal auditory perception in children with developmental aphasia. Nature, 241:468–469.

Tallal, P., and Piercy, M. 1973b. Developmental aphasia: Impaired rate of non-verbal processing as a function of sensory modality. Neuropsychologia 11:389–398.

Tallal, P., and Piercy, M. 1974. Developmental aphasia: Rate of auditory processing and selective impairment of consonant perception. Neuropsychologia 12:83–93.

Tallal, P., and Piercy, M. 1975. Developmental aphasia: The perception of brief vowels and extended stop consonants. Neuropsychologia 13:69–74.

Worster-Drought, C., and Allen, I. M. 1929. Congenital auditory imperception. J. Neurolo. Psychopath. 9:193–208.

A Syntactic Analysis
of Language Delay and
Language Impairment

Lyn R. Haber

The literature on linguistic deviance, or non-normal language, in children is a scholarly morass of conflicting opinion and data. There is a summary of the literature on the language of mentally retarded children in Cromer (1974), and on children of normal intelligence in Bloom and Lahey (1978), and an overall review is provided by deVilliers and deVilliers (1978). The main point of contention is whether the acquisition process, and/or language of linguistically deviant children differs from that of normal children only in that it is slow, or delayed, or whether it differs substantially in more basic ways.

The plethora of terms in the literature, such as language disorder, language disability, dyslexia, and delayed language, has further confused the issue.

Some researchers found differences only in rate of acquisition (for example, Lackner, 1968; Johnston and Schery, 1976; and Morehead and Ingram, 1973); others found qualitative differences (for example, Menyuk, 1964; Leonard, 1972; and Lee, 1966). There are at least four general difficulties in interpreting previous research. First, researchers use entirely different techniques for gathering data, including collecting spontaneous speech and using tightly controlled elicitation techniques such as a Berko (1958) type morphology task. Second, many different aspects of language for example, phonological rules, different parts of speech, and syntactic patterns are evaluated and tabulated. Third, in most of the studies, the subject N is very small (an N of one in Menyuk, 1964, for example). Fourth, where multiple Ns are involved, researchers often ask whether the subject's language is delayed or qualitatively different, and they assume that subjects are homogeneous in this respect. By tabulating across subjects, it is difficult to determine whether the language acquisition of some children is delayed or whether it is qualitatively different in relation to that of normal children. Crystal, Fletcher, and Garman (1976), who analyzed more than 200 subjects individually, found delay in some children and qualitative differences in others.

For clarity, three specific terms are used in this chapter: language deviance, language delay, and language impairment. *Language deviance* is a cover term for any atypical language behavior. *Language delay* refers to slow but normal acquisition, so that the language of a delayed child is indistinguishable linguistically from that of a younger child. *Language impairment* refers to a qualitative difference in linguistic behavior. This distinction between language impairment and language delay was suggested by Ingram (1976), Haber (1977), and Bloom and Lahey (1978).

The purpose of the research reported here is to operationalize the distinction between language impairment and language delay, and to demonstrate that not only during the acquisition period, but at any later point in life, language impairment in the output or expressive system can be diagnosed and distinguished from other forms of linguistic deviance.

This research documents the same distinction in the language behavior of three different subject populations. In each group some children control linguistic structure, whereas others do not. Furthermore, this research demonstrates the usefulness of a syntactically based test to discriminate between impaired and non-impaired children.

If language is viewed as systematic and if language impairment is defined as the inability to use the system, then a test that distinguishes between impairment and delay must determine whether the child can use this system. Systematicity in language use can now be tested best in aspects of syntax, because some rules of syntax—in contrast to those of semantics or pragmatics—have been worked out to a considerable extent; they have met with general agreement; and the requisite data can be collected quite simply.

THE TEST INSTRUMENT

The Kypriotaki Aux Test, or KAT (1974), is a test of syntactic use. The KAT is designed to test the acquisition of the auxiliary verb phrase in English, and it probes six transformations as well. It is based on Chomsky's (1957, 1965) analysis of Aux, which allows eight possible Aux configurations in a kernel sentence. Table 1 shows the eight Aux strings, realized in statement and passive:

1.   Aux → Tense (Modal) (Have + en) (Be + ing).

In the KAT, each of these eight configurations is embedded in a seven-word sentence and appears in one of six transformations: active

Table 1.   The eight Aux strings, with sample sentences in the active and passive transformations

Aux	Active/Passive
1. Tense	Mommy cooks me dinner in the evening. Julie was caught by a green monster.
2. T Modal	You can see me on the floor. Shoes should be tied with double knots.
3. T Have	Tim has caught a big, slippery fish. Cookie Monster has been painted upside down.
4. T Be	The man is driving a new car. Songs are being sung in the classroom.
5. T M H	He could have hit the hard ball. Balls could have been hit by Jeff.
6. T M B	The teacher can be singing you songs. Chris should be being driven to school.
7. T H B	He has been riding a new bicycle. The bicycle has been being ridden fast.
8. T M H B	She should have been holding the rabbit. You should have been being held tightly.

statements, questions, and negative questions, and in passive statements, questions, and negative questions. The 48 resulting sentences are divided into three sets of 16 sentences. The child is interviewed individually on three different days and asked to repeat 16 sentences each time.

As a repetition task, it may be argued that the KAT does not accurately reflect the child's comprehension, or his or her spontaneous use of language (Kemp and Dale, 1973; Bloom, Hood, and Lightbrown, 1974; and see Hood and Lightbrown, 1978, for a review). The intention here is not to describe what the child does say, or how well he or she understands what the experimenter says, but to represent the system by which he or she organizes the elements of the Aux, and their contribution to transformations. A comparison between the child's adultlike and non-adultlike responses reveals the child's co-occurrence rules, where he has them, and also permits a view of variable behavior when fixed rules are absent. The relation between the various behaviors found (stable rules, variable responses, etc.) and comprehension and/or production could be explored, but the issue here is whether the child uses syntactic systematicity, which is easily determined with a repetition task.

Procedure

The testing procedure for the KAT is fully described in Kypriotaki (1974) and Haber (1977). Practice sentences are given until the child successfully repeats a negative question. Sentences are presented in random order. Responses are scored on a preprinted sheet and also are tape-recorded.

The data reported here were collected by two testers: this author and an assistant, Celia Maloney. To ensure reliability in recording responses, the testers conducted several hours of the testing together and later, they checked approximately one-third of the tapes against the on-the-spot transcriptions. The transcriptions failed to match on less than 1% of the responses.

Children were tested mainly in school corridors, or in a classroom corner. Both the experimenter and the subjects were impeded by the noise and commotion of the changing of classes, record-playing, singing, and piano-playing. This undoubtedly contributed to measurement error.

Subjects

Subjects for this study were from four populations, and all were pupils in public schools in the Rochester, New York area.

From all four samples, children whose native language was not English were excluded as were children with uncorrected visual deficits, and children with known hearing or neurological impairment. Records on the children were not always complete or consistent, so the purity of these samples is approximate.

The first group, or referred Group, was formed by asking all K-3 teachers in a large school district to identify those children they suspected of having language problems. More than 200 children were selected by the 80 teachers.

A large proportion of these children were native speakers of either a non-English language or a nonstandard dialect of English, or had articulation problems. A total of 68 children were actually tested.

The second group, called the high-risk group, was composed of 43 learning disabled children who were attending special classes provided by the New York State Board of Cooperative Education (BOCES).

The third group consisted of 85 mentally retarded children, ages 5;0 to 19;1, who were attending special classes at the same facilities as those attended by children in the high risk and the referred groups. This sample included 32 children classified as trainable (IQs of about 20–50), and 53 children classified as educable (IQs of 50–80). The mentally retarded children were included in order to provide a population that was known to have language deviance.

The fourth group was composed of 36 presumably normal 4-year-olds. These children were from two nursery schools in Rochester, and their performance on the KAT was reported in Kypriotaki (1974).

Scoring

Each response was scored for the rendition of the Aux elements and, independently of the Aux response, for the transformation. Data are reported on four measures: two that were derived from analyses of Aux configurations, and two from the transformation response. Aux configurations were scored for correct Aux repetitions and for nongrammatical Aux strings. In response to the stimulus:

2. My daddy has met all my friends

the following responses were both scored as correct:

3. My daddy has met my friends
4. Your daddy has met all my friends.

Nongrammatical Aux strings are Aux utterances that cannot be derived from formula 1. For example:

5. Are songs been sung in the classroom?
6. Songs is singing in the classroom

Transformations are scored for nonstatements (an utterance lacking either a subject NP or a main verb) and for the correctness of the repetition of the transformation. (For a detailed discussion of the scoring, see Haber, in press.) The following are examples of nonstatements:

7. Grandma pretty clothes to me
8. Songs in the classroom
9. The man new car?

Correct transformations are defined according to Chomsky's (1965) formulae for statement, question, negative question, and for their combinations with passive, and they are scored without regard to whether the Aux is grammatically correct. Thus, the following responses were scored as transformationally correct:

10. Q: Is Mark been holding the rabbit?
11. NQP: Hasn't the bicycle being ridden fast?
12. P: Bills be paid by a father

In the following discussions, nonstatements are presented first because they represent the most basic lack of structure; next are nongrammatical Auxes, which refer to structure specifically within the Aux string; and number of correct Aux repetitions and correct transformations are presented and analyzed last.

Nonstatements   Nonstatements are a special kind of anomalous response in that they violate not only semantics, but also fundamental structure. Regardless of the linguistic model used to describe English sentences, a full simple sentence must contain a subject and a verb, an agent and an action. Nonstatements violate this structure. They are, therefore, theoretically the single most important criterion for distinguishing language impairment from language delay.

Nongrammatical Aux   Like nonstatements, this is a criterion based on the theoretical prediction that the language-impaired child lacks structure. Here, the systematicity of a specific structure, the Aux, is probed. The younger child who cannot produce a complex Aux string frequently and systematically reduces it to a lawful string within his grammatical system. Or, a child may hypothesize an Aux segmentation or movement incorrectly (as noted in Kypriotaki, 1974; and Mayer, Erreich, and Valian, 1978), in which case, a number of the child's Auxes may fail to correspond to the adult model, depending on which Aux configurations he has re-analyzed. Whether the child is simplifying the Aux lawfully, where his alterations are systematic they can be described in terms of structural linguistic strategies—strategies the language-impaired child is predicted to lack. Therefore, the nongrammatical Aux score is computed to exclude those strategic, but non-adult, responses described by Kypriotaki (1974) and Mayer et al. (1978), and also to exclude lawfully simplified Aux. Because the normal or delayed child may experiment with several non-adult hypotheses at once, which would make some of his responses seem both ungrammatical and asystematic, or because he might occasionally give simply a muddled response, the presence of a number of ungrammatical Auxes need not implicate impairment. Development is expected to progress toward adultlike performance, and the cutoff point must be found empirically.

Correct Repetition of the Aux   This measure is intended to assess the degree of delay. However, as is shown below, the number of Aux repeated correctly can also be used as an indicator of impairment. Correct Aux is based on a tabulation of only those Aux strings repeated in full and within grammatical frames. The correct Aux score reflects the fact that as the child learns more Aux elements and they become familiar to him, he makes fewer errors in repetition. In contrast, the very young child, as he begins to acquire the Aux system, makes mistakes and reduces complex Aux strings to ones familiar to him. This means that a non-impaired child who rarely repeats an Aux correctly, and who receives a very low correct Aux score, could nonetheless alter those Auxes lawfully or systematically, and receive a low nongrammatical Aux score.

Incorrect Transformation   Because impairment is defined as the inability to use the langauge system, it is predicted that language-impaired children are unable to manipulate transformations. Therefore, in the scoring of transformations, a response was accepted if it corresponded to the transformation of the stimulus, irrespective of the grammatical correctness of the Aux string. Although most 4-, and even 3-year-old children command statements, questions, and negative questions, they do not control the passive. Passive, particularly in combination with the other transformations and especially with complex Aux configurations, continues to produce erroneous repetitions until the fourth grade (Haber, 1977). Therefore, the prediction was that the non-impaired child would rarely err in repeating a transformation, and, that when he did, his errors would be concentrated on the passive.

To summarize the scoring, four different measures are reported here from the KAT. Each measure is predicted to distinguish children who are impaired from those who are acquiring language normally, regardless of the rate. Thus, each of these measures should yield the same classification of children into the same two groups—impaired and non-impaired. It cannot be predicted what the cutoff score dividing the two groups will be before examining the data, except for nonstatements—the presence of which, it is predicted, indicates impairment. However, it is expected that the magnitude of the score below the cutoff will be indicative of the rate of normal acquisition, with scores near the impairment cutoff signifying substantial delay in normal acquisition. Of course, delay must be measured with respect to what is normal or typical at each chronological age. Measuring the degree of delay is discussed by Haber (1977, in press).

Results

Nonstatements   Theoretically, the non-impaired child should never produce a nonstatement, and the one or two that occurred in the responses of a non-impaired child most likely resulted from measurement errors in this data. Measurement error here includes performance errors on the child's part, as well as experimenter's errors such as blurred presentation of the stimulus or inaccurate recording of the response. Another kind of measurement error arose from experimenter differences. One experimenter accepted nonstatements unquestioningly; the other frequently had the child try the sentence again at some random point during the testing. There were no instances in the data where a nonimpaired child persevered in using a nonstatement. In this study, several obviously nonimpaired children produced one or two nonstatements, which clearly were a result of measurement error. Therefore, after examining the distribution of the responses, the theoretical stipulation of zero nonstatements was modified and the cutoff point for impairment was set at more than two.

Table 2 classifies the children as impaired or non-impaired, by group, based on the number of nonstatements given. Table 2 shows that there is a large class of children in all four groups who virtually never produced a nonstatement. The three experimental groups also contained some children (over half, for the retarded population) who produced many nonstatements.

Nongrammatical Aux   Because normal children also were expected to produce nongrammatical Auxes, no theoretical prediction of the cutoff

Table 2.   Classification based on the number of nonstatements produced by the four groups

| | | Number of nonstatements | |
		Non-impaired	Impaired
Group	N	0–2	3–48
Normal 4's	35	35	0
Referred	68	55	13
High-risk	43	32	11
Retarded	85	33	52
Total	231	155	76

value separating impaired from non-impaired was made. Therefore, the cutoff was determined empirically by classifying children simultaneously according to the number of nonstatements and the number of nongrammatical Auxes they gave. Table 3 shows that when the nongrammatical Aux score is divided about in half (0–25 and 26–48), the cross classification is virtually identical, in fact, only six of the 231 children (less than 3%) are classified differently by the two criteria. It should be noted that this virtually perfect correlation is not attributable to an artificial statistical restriction. Although a nonstatement is also a nongrammatical Aux by definition (because the cutoff for nonstatement is 2 or less), the full range of variation is possible. Therefore, the finding that the two different linguistic criteria produce the identical classification supports the theoretical model of language impairment that is developed in this research.

Correct Aux   The third criterion scored was the number of Auxes repeated exactly and within a grammatical frame. On this criterion, unlike the others, a very low score indicates impairment, and a high score, non-impairment. When the children are simultaneously classified according to the number of nonstatements and the number of correct Auxes they produced (see Table 4), a cutoff of 0–11 and 12–48 classifies all but nine of the 231 children similarly—more than 96% agreement.

Thus, although normal children can and do fail to repeat correctly many Aux configurations, if they miss more than three-fourths of them,

Table 3.   Contingency relation between nonstatements and nongrammatical Aux across all groups

| | Nonstatements | | |
	Non-impaired	Impaired	Total
Nongrammatical Auxes	0–2	3–48	
0–25	154	5	159
36–48	1	71	72
Total	155	76	231

Table 4.   Contingency relation between correct Aux repetions and nonstatements across all groups

| | Nonstatements | | |
	Non-impaired	Impaired	Total
Correct Aux	0–2	3–48	
12–48	153	5	158
0–11	2	71	73
Total	155	76	

they fall into the impaired category, and are not just very slow in their language acquisition.

Table 5 presents the median scores, or the central tendency, for the four groups, each as a whole and then broken down into impaired and non-impaired. In the referred group (second row), when the group is considered as a whole, the 34th child produced only eight nongrammatical Auxes. When the referred children are divided into non-impaired and impaired, the median non-impaired child still produced only eight nongrammatical Auxes, but the median impaired child produced 33 of them. Table 5 confirms that non-impaired children, regardless of IQ or suspected learning disability (the high risk group), perform alike, and the same is true of impaired children.

Incorrect Transformation   In this case also, there is no theoretical basis for choosing a cutoff, so all children were simultaneously classified according to the number of wrong transformations and the number of nonstatements they produced. (See Table 6.) The empirically determined cutoff is again in the middle of the range (0–24 and 25–48). At that division point, the minimum number of children are classified differently—10 out of 231, or less than 5%. Again, because this relationship could have been zero, the virtually perfect cross-classification supports the theoretical notion of language impairment.

Fifteen children from the entire sample of 231, or less than 7% are inconsistently classified in Tables 3, 4, and 6. Table 7 shows their scores on nonstatements, nongrammatical Auxes, correct Aux, and incorrect transformations.

For each subject, the score that fails to conform to the predicted bimodal pattern has been asterisked. Subjects number H22 and 44 received low scores (nonimpaired) on all criteria but Nonstatements. Therefore, the Nonstatement score, which falls within the impaired range, is asterisked. Because these utterances were not retested, these two children were classified as nonimpaired.

Subjects 107, A12 and 80, test as delayed on all but correct Aux, where they fall just within the impaired range. Correct Aux is designed as

Table 5. Median scores for nongrammatical Aux and correct Aux

	Sum over both groups		Non-impaired		Impaired	
	Nongrammatical	Correct	Nongrammatical	Correct	Nongrammatical	Correct
Normal four-year-olds (N = 35)	13	26	13	26		
Referred (N = 68)	8	28	8 (N = 58)	29	33 (N = 10)	6
High-risk (N = 43)	12	26	8 (N = 33)	29	38 (N = 10)	1
Retarded (N = 85)	30	6	11 (N = 33)	23	42 (N = 52)	1

Table 6.   Contingency relation between nonstatements and incorrect transformations, across groups

		Nonstatements		
		Non-impaired	Impaired	Total
Incorrect transformations		0–24	3–48	
Non-impaired	0–25	155	10	165
Impaired	25–48	0	66	66
Total		155	76	231

an indicator of delay, and these low scores suggest severe delay, but not impairment.

For children whose scores fail to fall within a predicted pattern, the following procedures should be followed. First, check the school records and talk with the teacher: the child may be bilingual or hard of hearing (if possible, actually have the child's ears checked). If either of these is true, ignore the test results, they do not apply. Second, turn back to the raw data and see whether the ambiguous classification resulted from a measurement error. If it does, classify the child as non-impaired. Third, if a child gives no nonstatements and is near threshold otherwise, he is non-impaired. Fourth, if the child gives even one nonstatement and the other scores are high (especially nongrammatical Aux and incorrect transformation, which both measure structure), he is impaired. Finally, any child is classified as impaired who gives more than two nonstatements (and with an improved testing procedure this step should apply for any child who gives a nonstatement).

On the basis of Tables 3, 4, and 6, and on the discussion of the 15 subjects who appeared in wrong cells in those tables, 74 children in this sample can be classified as impaired and 157 as non-impaired.

The results in Table 5 indicate that the impaired/non-impaired distinction cuts across the subject populations used. The consistency and the power of the syntactically based distinction between impairment and non-impairment can be further demonstrated by means of error analyses.

Error Analysis 1: Altered Auxes   It is beneficial to analyze in more detail the kinds of errors made by a child when he or she did not repeat an Aux correctly. If a nonstatement or a nongrammatical repetition of the Aux was produced, no further breakdown was made, but many times when an Aux was not repeated correctly, it was altered to another lawful Aux configuration. This usually involved simplifying the Aux string by omitting one or more elements. In this example, the element *have* is omitted in the response:

13.   Stimulus, T M H B: Should you have been holding the rabbit?
14.   Response T M B: Should you be holding the rabbit?

Table 7. Scores on all criteria for the 15 children out of the 231 who were ambiguously classified

Subject number	Chronological age	Nonstatement	Nongrammatical Aux	Correct Aux repetition	Incorrect transformation	Final classification
		0–2	0–25	0–11	0–24	
H22	6;7	3	20	14	9	Non-impaired
44	9;9	3	18	23	11	,,
107	4;4	0	23	10*	8	,,
A12	10;6	1	18	10*	15	,,
80	9;9	0	24	10*	12	,,
F211	7;1	2*	27	9	29	Impaired
H21	6;6	4	27	10	13*	,,
65	9;6	6	33	8	23*	,,
15	10;9	8	26	8	19*	,,
20	12;7	6	27	11	14*	,,
H29	6;9	3	29	12*	9*	,,
D5	6;9	4*	24	12	19	,,
A3	6;11	5	22*	6	35	,,
H25	6;7	5*	19	17	20	,,
F210	5;11	9*	22	18	21	,,

*This score accounted for the inconsistent classification.

When 2 or more Aux segments appeared in the surface string, as in Example 13, non-impaired children responded 50% of the time by deleting a single element, as in 14.

Language impairment is defined here as the inability to systematically manipulate the regularities in language. Therefore, impaired children should not systematically delete single elements, but, in contrast, they are expected to rely heavily on minimal strings (main verb). Over one-third of the responses of the impaired children were of this type. Thus, given the stimulus 13 above, a typical impaired child's response is

T(?)   I hold my rabbit

In repetitions such as these, in which the Aux has been reduced to main verb only, it is unclear whether Aux (here in the form of tense) is present. Consider the following examples:

16.   Stimulus T M P: Dinner should be cooked in the evening.
17.   Response T(?):   Dinner cooked in the evening.
18.   Stimulus T M H: You could have eaten a chocolate sundae.
19.   Response T(?):   You eat a [klɔk] sundae.
20.   Stimulus T H P: Have I been watched all day long?
21.   Response T(?):   I watch all day long?

The presence of even the Aux element, tense, in these responses, is a question of interpretation.

Impaired children produced these minimal string responses more than one-third of the time, but non-impaired children virtually never gave them: only 6% of their responses were of this type. Furthermore, in nearly all of the instances in which non-impaired children altered Auxes to tense plus main verb only, they did so by the alteration of a particular Aux string, *tense + have*, as in:

22.   Stimulus T H: Has Keith caught a big, slippery fish?
23.   Response T: Did Keith catch a big, slippery fish?

In contrast to this regular pattern of simplification in non-impaired children, alterations of the Aux string to this simplest configuration occur randomly, from all strings, in the repetitions of the impaired children.

The finding that when non-impaired children alter Aux strings, they do so consistently, in relation to the elements contained in the stimulus, whereas the alterations of the impaired children are unrelated to the elements in the stimulus string, confirms the hypothesis that impaired children lack linguistically based strategies.

Error Analysis II: Altered Transformations   A more detailed analysis of what the child does when he fails to repeat a transformation correctly reveals the same contrast between language impairment and non-impairment. Non-impaired children rarely fail to repeat a transformation, and when they do, their misrepetitions are directly related to the difficulty of the stimulus. Their manipulations consist of the systematic deletion of a specific transformation, most commonly the passive. Thus, QP is altered to Q, and NQP to NQ.

About 75% of the responses of the impaired children were either statements or nonstatements, and the children responded with these strings regardless of the transformation of the stimulus. This finding exactly parallels that reported for altered Auxes.

Not an Analysis   The following comparison between responses of impaired and non-impaired children provides a "feel" for the language of these children. Table 8 presents a subset of the responses from impaired and non-impaired children, in which passive statement transformations were altered to active statements. This alteration of Aux was selected because passive statement is the only transformation which non-impaired children, as well as impaired children, alter to statements. In general, the non-impaired children give longer responses. When functors are present in the stimulus, they nearly always occur in the responses of the non-impaired children. And the majority of the responses are altered rather than ungrammatical Auxes, showing that the normal child restructures overly complex forms to conform with his own system.

The responses of the impaired children fall into two general categories. First, the majority of them are shorter overall, frequently lacking functors. These responses generally include the semantically most salient words in the original sequence of the stimulus. Thus, these responses are frequently nongrammatical, but coherent.

A second group of impaired children's responses seem to indicate that the child has no idea what he is saying. Examples are the responses of subjects 23, 63, and 26:

24.   Dinner cooked in eating
25.   Shoes should tie with doubles,
26.   Bayings paying to fa.

Table 8.   Active statements altered from passive statements—sample responses from impaired and non-impaired children

Stimulus:		He was caught by a green monster.
Non-impaired		No exs
Impaired	23:*	He caught green monster.
Stimulus:		Dinner should be cooked in the evening.
Non-impaired	70:	Dinner should be cooking in the evening.
	17:	Dinner must be cooking in the evening.
	22:	Dinner should cook by the evening.

Impaired	60:	Dinner cook evening.
	23:	Dinner cooked in eating.
Stimulus:		Shoes should be tied with double knots.
Non-impaired	59:	Shoes should tied with double knots.
	44:	Shoes should be tying with double knots.
Impaired	69, 87:	Shoes tied double knots.
	57:	Shoes tied.
	60:	Shoes tied double.
	67:	David [ə] tied in knots.
	63:	Shoes should tie with doubles.
	64:	Shoe [toy] knotten.
Stimulus:		Cookie Monster has been painted upside down.
Non-impaired	H28, H44, 77, 9, 35:	Cookie Monster has been painting upside down.
	78, 41:	Cookie Monster been painting upside down.
	79:	Cookie Monster had painted upside down.
Impaired	67, 69, 49:	Cookie Monster painted upside down.
	63:	Cookie Monster coulda paint them.
Stimulus:		Bills have been being paid by father.
Non-impaired	H4:	Bills be paying by father.
	F211, A20:	Bills [ə] been paying by father.
Impaired	60:	Bill paiden.
	68:	Bill paying father.
	66:	Bills paying by father.
	49:	Bills paid by father.
	26:	Babies paying to fa.
Stimulus:		The bicycle has been being ridden fast.
Non-impaired	H9, 17, 11:	The bicycle has been riding fast.
	A5:	The bicycle been [ridiŋ] fast.
	29:	The bicycle has been being [ridiŋ] fast.
	18:	The bicycle has been [ridiŋ] fast.
Impaired	47:	The bicycle ridden fast.
	88:	Bicycle go ride.
Stimulus:		Dogs should have been being given food.
Non-impaired	H32:	Dogs should been being given food.
	H54:	Dogs should have been giving food.
	D11:	Dogs should of have been giving food.
	A15:	Dogs should been giving food.
	A20:	Dogs have been giving food.
	66:	Dogs should be giving food.
Impaired	84, 60:	Dogs given food.
	69:	Dogs giving food.
	66:	Dogs given a bone.
	67:	Dogs [ə ə] given [ə].
	57:	Dogs have food.
	16:	Dogs been eating food.

*Subject identification number.

Such aberrant responses were never given by normal children, but were repeatedly offered by only a few—not all—of the impaired children.

The Relation Between Language Impairment And Intelligence

A major finding in this study is that language impairment is independent of intelligence. Intelligence was not measured; however, as a group, the retarded children had low IQs (20–80), whereas children from each of the other three samples were drawn from regular elementary schools, in which the IQ range is assumed to be 90 and above. In each of the analyses of impairment presented—nonstatements in Table 2, nongrammatical Aux in Table 3, correct Aux repetitions in Table 4, incorrectly repeated transformations in Table 6, and the discussion of altered Auxes and altered transformations in the error analyses—the impaired children pattern alike regardless of their IQ, and the non-impaired children also pattern alike, again, regardless of their group. Although not reported here, it has been shown (Haber, 1978) that even within the retarded group, impaired children in the 20–50 IQ range performed more like impaired children in the 50–80 range than like non-impaired children in the low range.

Thus, in spite of the obvious testing bias that an impaired child suffers when tested with a verbal IQ measure, the presence or absence of language impairment can neither be predicted by IQ, nor be considered to be a result of low IQ.

Linguistic Deviance

Two very different kinds of linguistic deviance occur in spoken language. The first, language impairment, refers to an output system lacking organized linguistic structure. The language-impaired child does not systematically manipulate linguistic structures, such as transformations or Aux. His language differs from that of a normal child at any stage of acquisition. An additional claim, not tested here (but demonstrated in Haber, 1978) is that the impaired child never achieves normal or adultlike verbal performance.

The second kind of linguistic deviance involves the rate, but not the manner, of acquisition of expressive language. Language delay, and also advanced language, represent typical patterns of acquisition, but at atypical rates. A language-delayed child falls somewhere on a continuum of development, and his speech resembles that of a normal but younger child. Degree of delay has not been analyzed in this paper, but in fact, the non-impaired children in these samples range from delayed to typical.

A troubling question has arisen from the results of the KAT. Although the focus here is on the distinction between impairment and non-impairment, the KAT also identifies degrees of delay. (See Haber,

1977). The scoring criteria for delay have not yet been standardized, but it is already clear that some of the "old" retarded population (age 14 and above) who tested as delayed rather than impaired were performing at a level below that of the normal 4-year-olds. When these "old" delayed retardates were compared with younger ones (age 5-9), the older ones performed better on every criterion scored, therefore, they are clearly continuing to acquire language. Yet their incredibly slow rates of acquisition suggest that they may never catch up within a normal life span. The delay of the severe retardate may represent a form of impairment, or a borderline territory where linguistic structure is acquired and used, but at a very low level. If the world were an orderly place, this kind of impairment would occur only in conjuction with a very low IQ.

The Kypriotaki Aux Text uses spoken language, or output, to explore linguistic competence. Such a probe is theoretically accurate only if output mirrors competence. As with the highly skilled mathematics professor who invariably makes addition errors, performance need not mirror competence. However, just as that mathematics professor would not last long behind a cash register in everyday life, so the language-impaired child cannot survive in a regular school system. This is primarily because a teacher cannot rely on the child's verbal output as a measure of his skill or comprehension. Therefore, for the purposes of the schools, the caveat between competence and performance is irrelevant. Whether or not he has in fact acquired the linguistic system of his native language the language-impaired child cannot survive in a normal school system as such systems are presently structured.

Language-impaired children are not a homogeneous group (any more than linguistically deviant children are). This fact is both theoretically and empirically evident. Theoretically, given the complexity of the language system, it is clear that impairment can occur at various points, from decoding to encoding. Empirically, it can easily and quickly be shown that a large number of language-impaired children cannot use linguistic structure verbally, but have nevertheless acquired it. These impaired children understand the language system, including the most complex Aux strings and transformations. Their impairment is restricted to the verbal output system. They perform flawlessly on tests of receptive language, and they can learn to read, write, type, and sign. Other language-impaired children are far more variable in their receptive ability.

When a child gives an atypical response, there is no way to tell whether this arose from difficulty he had with the stimulus (the input) or with producing the response (the output). However, it is expected that responses based on input impairment differ dramatically from those based on output impairment. Within the impaired population, some children were found whose responses in the repetition task were lengthy and

Table 9. Responses from six children—fluent anomolies

Stimulus:		Was _____ treated to a chocolate sundae?
Response	H21:	Wasn't Heidi treated at a chocolate sundae?
Response	H29:	Was Tammy treated in a chocolate sundae?
Response	15:	Michelle treated a chocolate sundae.
Stimulus:		He was treated to a chocolate sundae.
Response	20:	He treated chocolate sundae.
Stimulus:		Should dogs have been being given food?
Response	H21:	Should dogs be feeding for good?
Stimulus:		Could Big Bird have been met yesterday?
Response	H21:	Can Big Bird be happy yesterday?
Stimulus:		Couldn't Big Bird have been met yesterday?
Response	H21:	Couldn't Big Bird say yesterday?
Stimulus:		Big Bird could have been met yesterday.
Response	D5:	Big Bird had bird yesterday.
Stimulus:		Bills have been being paid by father.
Response	D5:	Bills have buying with fathers.
Stimulus:		Have bills been being paid by father?
Response	65:	Bills should be having by father.
Stimulus:		Will Mommy buy presents for Cindy's birthday?
Response	D5:	Could Mommy buy your presents for birthday?
Stimulus:		Won't Mommy buy presents for Kathy's birthday?
Response	65:	Won't Mommy was being presents for Kathy's birthday?
Stimulus:		Tammy paints funny pictures in art class.
Response	H29:	Tammy makes funny places in art class.
Stimulus:		I have been watched all day long.
Response	H29:	I am being watched by all day long.
Stimulus:		The bicycle has been being ridden fast.
Response 1	H29:	The bicycle will be [ridiŋ] by the class.
Response 2	H29:	The bicycle will be ridden by the fast.
Stimulus:		Should shoes be tied with double knots?
Response	15:	Shoes with tied double knots.
Stimulus:		Has Cookie Monster been painted upside down?
Response	15:	Has Cookie Monster cook upside down?

fluent, but semantically anomolous; others gave two- or three-word answers, typically containing only content words, with noticeable pauses between each word. Examples of fluent, anomolous responses are given in Table 9. These responses characterize the six children in Table 7 who tested as impaired on all criteria except their use of transformations.

These responses look like "slips of the tongue," but two facts make this an unlikely explanation. First, these children gave a number of these anomolous responses. Second, while non-impaired children, including normal 4-year-olds, occasionally gave such responses, they either asked to try again, or they made a comment such as "I gummed up that one." The fluency and ability to manipulate transformations but not finer sentence structure, which is seen in these six children, may characterize one type of language impairment.

The KAT was not designed to distinguish among different types of language impairment. There is a very broad distinction within the impairment group, expressive and receptive. A modification for children of the Goodglass-Kaplan (1976) adult aphasia test should verify this distinction easily. It is likely that the distinction is too crude and that, in fact, testing with the Goodglass will show greater complexities.

Differentiating among types of language impairment is of critical importance both for linguistic theory and for schools. For the purpose of linguistic theory, the language-impaired child provides a key to understanding the language acquisition device. The differences among these children should provide researchers with important insights into how the language acquisition process works—as well as into the processes of encoding and decoding speech—by indicating where and how these processes break down. Schools recommending placement and specialists developing therapy for these impaired children both need to be responsive to the nature of the children's impairment. The child who has normal or above normal intelligence and an expressive impairment would benefit enormously from learning nonspoken forms of communication such as sign, reading, writing, and typing. For a child with receptive impairment, a different approach should be tried (but this is a much more complicated problem).

SUMMARY

In this paper, a theoretical distinction was made between language impairment and language delay, in which the former was said to present qualitative differences from normal language development and the latter only quantitative ones. This distinction was operationalized into a set of four testable predictions about the ability to manipulate language systematically. These four criteria, as predicted, separately, yet similarly, classified the 231 children in this sample.

Furthermore, the power of a test of linguistic systematicity (in contrast to analyses of vocabulary breadth or MLU, or a count of different parts of speech) has been shown.

The findings spotlight the critical need for further research on the multifaceted nature of language impairment.

Finally, it has been shown that the KAT provides a usable and practical test for application in educational settings.

REFERENCES

Bates, E. 1976. Language and Context: The Acquisition of Pragmatics. Academic Press, Inc., New York.

Berko, J. 1958. The child's learning of English morphology. Word 14:150–177.

Bloom, L., Hood, L., and Lightbrown, P. 1974. Imitation in language development: If, when and why. Cognitive Psychol. 6:380–420.

Bloom, L., and Lahey, M. 1978. Language Development and Language Disorders. John Wiley & Sons, Inc., New York.

Chomsky, N. 1957. Syntactic Structures. Mouton, The Hague.

Chomsky, N. 1965. Aspects of the Theory of Syntax. M.I.T. Press, Cambridge, Mass.

Chomsky, N., and Halle, H. 1968. The Sound Pattern of English. Harper & Row Pubs., Inc., New York.

Clark, H., and Clark, E. 1977. Psychology and Language. Harcourt Brace Jovanovich, Inc., New York.

Cromer, R. F. 1974. Receptive language in the mentally retarded: Processes and diagnostic distinctions. In: R. Schiefelbusch and L. Lloyd (eds.), Language Perspectives—Acquisition, Retardation and Intervention, pp. 237–268. University Park Press, Baltimore.

Crystal, D., Fletcher, P., and Garman, M. 1976. The Grammatical Analysis of Language Disability. Edward Arnold Ltd., London.

deVilliers, J. G., and deVilliers, P. A. 1978. Language Acquisition. Harvard University Press, Cambridge, Mass.

Goodglass, H., and Kaplan, E. 1976. The Assessment of Aphasia and Related Disorders. Lea & Febiger, Philadelphia.

Haber, L. 1977. A linguistic definition of language delay: evidence from the acquisition of Aux. Paper presented at the Summer Linguistic Society of American Meeting, Honolulu, Hawaii.

Haber, L. An analysis of linguistic deviance. In: K. Nelson (ed.), Child Language Acquisition, Volume 3, Gardner Press, New York. In press.

Ingram, D. 1976. Phonological Disability in Children. Elsevier-North Holland Publishing Company, New York.

Johnston, J. R., and Schery, T. K. 1976. The use of grammatical morphemes by children with communication disorders: In: D. M. Morehead and A. E. Morehead (eds.), Normal and Deficient Child Language. University Park Press, Baltimore.

Kemp, J., and Dale, P. 1973. Spontaneous imitation and free speech: A developmental comparison. Paper presented at the Biennial Conference of the Society for Research in Child Development, March, Philadelphia.

Kypriotaki, L. 1974. The acquisition of Aux. In: Papers and Reprints on Child Languages Development. No. 8, pp. 87–103. Stanford University, Stanford, Cal.

Labov, W. 1972. Negative attraction and negative concord. In: Language in the Inner City: Studies in the Black English Vernacular, pp. 130–200. University of Pennsylvania Press, Philadelphia.

Lackner, J. R. 1968. A developmental study of language behavior in retarded children. Neuropsychologia 6:301–320.

Lee, L. 1966. Developmental sentence types: A method for comparing normal and deviant syntactic development. J. Speech Hear. Disord. 31:311–330.

Leonard, L. 1972. What is deviant language? J. Speech Hear. Disord. 37:427–447.

Mayer, J. W., Erreich, A., and Valian, V. 1978. Transformations, basic operations and language acquisition. Cognition 6:1–13.

Menyuk, P. 1964. Comparison of grammar of children with functionally deviant and normal speech. J. Speech Hear. Res. 7:109–121.

Miller, G. 1956. The magical number seven, plus or minus two: Some limits on our capacity for processing information. Psychol. Rev. 63:81–97.

Morehead, D., and Ingram, D. 1973. The development of base syntax in normal and linguistically deviant children. J. Speech Hear. Res. 16:330–352.

Pike, K. 1964. Beyond the sentence. In: R. Brend (ed.), Selected Writings, 1972, pp. 192–199, Mouton, The Hague.

Venezky, R. 1974. Theoretical and experimental bases for teaching reading. In: T. Sebeok (ed.), Current Trends in Linguistics, Volume 12, pp. 2057–2100. Mouton, The Hague.

Children with Abnormal Speech Development Loss of Early Speech

Sagako Usuda and Takeshi Koizumi

It has been observed by many investigators that some autistic children regress in speech and/or behavior in the course of their development. In this study, children with delayed speech, including autistic children, were examined for this type of regression. Regression of behavior, in this study, means the deviation from the relatively normal development, for example, the exhibition of disturbed interpersonal relationship, difficulty in social adaptation, and deterioration in the areas of self-help. It was not difficult to obtain a precise history of children with delayed speech, especially concerning the phenomenon of regression in speech and/or behavior. The history of the loss of early speech, one of the phenomena of regression, was relatively impressive to the mothers and precisely reported by them. For this reason, children with loss of early speech were selected for study.

PROCEDURE

In this study, information is summarized on 100 children with delayed speech who visited the Department of Psychiatry, Niigata University School of Medicine and the Niigata Prefectural Child Guidance Clinic, Niigata, Japan, from September 1975 to June 1977.

The term delayed speech is used as a broad classification that refers only to the fact that a child has not acquired speech at the expected time nor with the expected accuracy (Wood, 1964). At the first visit, some of these children spoke no words, some spoke a few words but were unable to gain more words, and the others spoke many isolated words but could not use such words for communicative purposes. Their ages at the first visit were from 3 years (3;0) to 4 years 11 months (4;11).

The abnormal speech development of these 100 children was diagnosed as being associated with mental retardation, lack of adequate models and/or stimulation, autistic syndrome, and developmental speech disorder syndrome. Children with abnormal speech development associated with deafness, impaired vision, Down's syndrome, cerebral palsy, and abnormalities of articulatory organs were excluded from the study.

The following were obtained: 1) the child's history, 2) information through a questionnaire, and 3) psychiatric and physical examination. Some of the children also underwent X-ray examination of the head and/or electroencephalography. Hearing tests were administered by ear specialists if the child was suspected of having decreased hearing.

Observations were repeated on more than half of the children and efforts were made to treat them with their mothers, who were trained as co-therapists.

RESULTS

Examination of Abnormal Speech Development

According to the histories of the 100 children, 28 of them had completely lost their early speech words such as *papa, mama, nenne* 'going to sleep,' *Bubu* 'automobile,' and *Wanwan* 'dog.' It was reported that the words had been uttered at the appropriate situation but it was uncertain whether these words had been spoken of the child's own accord or as mere echolalias.

The 100 children with abnormal speech development were compared with 50 children who had normal speech development. (See Table 1.) The 100 children were divided into two groups: children with the loss of early speech (28) and children (72) who had not lost their early speech but had not spoken a single word.

There were approximately five times more boys than girls among the 100 children with abnormal speech development, and about eight times more boys than girls among the 28 children with loss of early speech.

There was a significantly lower incidence of retarded initial walking ($p < 0.05$) and retarded initial speaking ($p < 0.01$) among the 28 children with loss of early speech than among the other 72 children.

There was a higher incidence of prenatal and perinatal troubles ($p < 0.01$) among children with the abnormal speech development in comparison with children with normal speech development. Prenatal and perinatal troubles included asphyxia, moderate or severe jaundice of the newborn, full term immaturity of infants, prematurity of infants, forceps delivery, vacuum extraction, abdominal cesarean section, weak pains, and prolonged labor.

Table 1. Comparison of 100 children with abnormal speech development with those who have normal speech development[a]

	Children with abnormal speech development			Children with normal speech (control)
Items examined	Total	Children with loss of early speech	Others	
Number of children	100	28	72	50
Male:female	4.9:1	8.3:1	4.1:1	1.2:1
Age of initial walking 1;5 and over	25% (25)	7.1% (2)	31.9% (23)	0
Less than 1;5	75% (75)	92.9% (26)	68.1% (49)	100% (50)
Age of speaking first word 2;5 and over	28% (27)	3.6% (1)	38.2% (26)	0
Less than 2;5	72% (69)	94.4% (27)	61.8% (42)	100% (50)
Unknown	(4)	(0)	(4)	(0)
Prenatal and perinatal troubles +	51% (51)	39.3% (11)	55.6% (40)	24% (12)
−	49% (49)	60.7% (17)	44.4% (32)	76% (38)
Mother Employed	47% (49)	39.3% (11)	50.0% (32)	16% (8)
Housewife	53% (53)	60.7% (17)	50.0% (32)	84% (42)
Maternal deprivation[b] +	40% (40)	42.9% (12)	38.9% (28)	
−	60% (60)	57.1% (16)	61.1% (44)	

[a]The number of cases is indicated in parentheses.
[b]Including both definite and masked maternal deprivations.

More mothers of the children with abnormal speech development had jobs than those of the children with normal speech development, although the geographical distribution of the children with normal speech development may be insufficient for comparison.

There was a similarly high incidence of maternal deprivation (Bowlby, 1966) and masked maternal deprivation (Prugh and Harlow, 1966; Shimada, 1976) among both groups. Maternal deprivation and masked maternal deprivation are defined as separation from mothering, and insufficiency of mothering due to various causes, respectively. In this study, maternal deprivation did not include institutionalization, but it included children under the care of others for more than a few weeks.

Development and Loss of Early Speech

The history of speech development of the 28 children with the loss of early speech is summarized here. Eleven children spoke their first word before age 1;5, eight children between 1;5 and 2;0, eight children between 2;0, and 2;5, and one child at 2;5.

Regarding age in the loss of early speech: 12 children lost early speech before 2;0, seven children between 2;0 and 2;5, six children between 2;5 and 3;0, and three children at 3;0 and older.

The time-period from the speaking of the first word to the loss of early speech was within 6 months in 20 children, and more than 6 months in eight children. The time period from the loss of early speech to the regaining of speech was within 1 year in six children, from 1 to 2 years in seven children, and 15 children had not yet regained speech by the first visit. Some of the children with loss of early speech repeatedly lost and regained their speech, which was not recognized as regained speech.

History of First Year

Table 2 summarizes the history of the first year for the 100 children with abnormal speech development, and for 50 children with normal speech development.

The first two items in Table 2, lack of cheer, and weak sucking while nursing, may be considered as congenital difficulties, and/or as a result of a complicated delivery. There was a higher incidence of these two items among the 100 children with abnormal speech development than among the 50 children with the normal speech development; however, the difference was not statistically significant. The incidence of the first two items was higher among the 28 children than among the other 72 children, but was not significant.

The other five items may be considered as congenital, as a result of complicated delivery, and/or as failure in the establishment of the mother-child attachment. There was a higher incidence of these symp-

Table 2. History of first year

Symptoms	Children with abnormal speech development			Children with normal speech (Control) (%) (50 cases)
	Total (%) (100 cases)	Children with loss of early speech (%)* (28 cases)	Others (%)* (72 cases)	
Lack of cheer	13	21.4 **	9.7	2
Weak sucking while nursing	18	25.0	15.3	10
Failure to cry	59	71.4 ***	54.2 ***	4
Trouble free	77	78.6 ***	76.4 ***	12
Lack of babbling	25	28.6 ***	23.6 ***	0
Failure to smile	22	14.3 **	25.0 ***	0
Not afraid of strangers	58	50.0 **	61.1 ***	10

* X^2 comparison of group with control group.

**$p < 0.01$.

***$p < 0.001$.

toms among the 28 children with the loss of early speech, as well as among the 100 children with abnormal speech development, than among the 50 children with normal speech development, with statistically significant differences in all of the five items. It seemed likely that early in life, perhaps within the first year, many of the 100 children with abnormal speech development exhibited weak responses to environmental stimuli. It was considered that their physiological and social responses were so weak that they discouraged the affection of their mothers and that the discouragement failed to promote the social responses of the children afterward.

Follow-up Study of Abnormal Speech Development

Follow-up studies of 74 out of the 100 children with abnormal speech development were conducted in May and June, 1978 (see Table 3). Thirty-one of these 74 children had no history of any regression in speech and/or imitative action in the course of development (Group A). Seventeen of the 74 children had a history of various types of regression in speech and/or imitative action without the loss of early speech (Group B), and 26 of the 74 children had a history of loss of early speech (Group C). These 26 children were among the 28 children with the loss of early speech previously mentioned. Most of the children in Groups A and B underwent psychiatric examination and their mothers answered questionnaires, while in some cases only the mothers responded to questionnaires. All in Group C underwent psychiatric examination and responded to questionnaires.

At the time of follow-up, 43 children (Groups B and C), or 58% of the total sample, manifested some type of regression in speech and/or imitative action including loss of early speech. Boys were markedly predominant in both Groups B and C.

Table 3.   Follow-up study of children with abnormal speech development and speech development of 3 groups

Items examined	Group (Number of children)*					
	A (31)		B (17)		C (26)	
Mean age at first visit	3 yrs., 10 mos.		3 yrs., 7 mos.		3 yrs., 9 mos.	
Mean age at follow-up	6 yrs		5 yrs., 8 mos.		5 yrs., 6 mos.	
Male:female	2.9:1		7.5:1		7.7:1	
Stage Speech development						
I No single word	12.9%	(4)	17.6%	(3)	42.3%	(11)
II Individual words	6.4%	(2)	11.8%	(2)	19.2%	(5)
III Phrase of two words	6.4%	(2)	11.8%	(2)	23.1%	(6)
IV Phrase of three words	25.8%	(8)	11.8%	(2)	7.7%	(2)
V Complete sentence	41.9%	(13)	29.4%	(5)	7.7%	(2)
VI Almost normal	6.4%	(2)	17.6%	(3)		(0)

*Total number—74 (out of 100). Group A—children without regression in speech and/or imitative action; Group B—children with regression in speech and/or imitative action; Group C—children with loss of early speech.

Speech development was divided into 6 stages: children in Stage I can speak no single word; in Stage II, individual words; in Stage III, phrases of two words; in Stage IV, phrases of three words; in Stage V, children can speak complete sentences but cannot communicate normally; and in Stage VI, almost normal speech. Many children in Group A belonged to Stage V, whereas many children in Group C belonged to Stage I. Because of the difference in the mean age at the follow-up study between Group A and Group C, differences between them are hard to interpret, therefore, sub-samples of 24 children were drawn from Groups A and C, matched by age. The adjusted results of the speech development are rearranged and shown in Figure 1. From these results, it is clear that the loss of early speech is a sign of great disadvantage to speech development. Many children with the loss of early speech developed incomplete speech afterward.

Comparison Among Children with Loss of Early Speech

The speech development of the children who lost early speech was so insufficient at the follow-up study that these 26 children were examined in detail. These children were divided into 3 groups: the children speaking no single word (Group 1), the children speaking individual words (Group 2), and the children speaking phrases of two words or more (Group 3). (See Table 4.)

No girls were included in Groups 1 and 2. The children in Groups 1 and 2 spoke their first word at a younger age and lost their early speech also at a younger age than the children in Group 3. Speaking first word and losing early speech at a younger age did not, however, lead to a better prognosis. This result may be comprehensible when related to the diagnoses of the children in the three groups, which is discussed below.

These 26 children with the loss of early speech were further studied by means of the questionnaires that their mothers answered. Because the results of the questionnaries to a mother as a retrospective study may not be accurate, efforts were made to check up on the history of the child's first year in detail. Some cases were further examined through photographs and/or a diary of child care. The results are shown in Table 5.

Table 4.   26 children with loss of early speech (I)

Items examined	Group (Number of children)*		
	1 (11)	2 (5)	3 (10)
Mean age at first visit	4 yrs.	3 yrs., 8 mos.	3 yrs., 5 mos.
Mean age at follow-up	5 yrs., 11 mos.	5 yrs., 8 mos.	5 yrs.
Male:female	11:0	5:0	7:3
Mean age of speaking first word	1 yr., 5 mos.	1 yr., 5 mos.	1 yr., 9 mos.
Mean age in loss of early speech	1 yr., 11 mos.	1 yr., 11 mos.	2 yrs., 5 mos.

*Group 1—children speaking no single word; Group 2—children speaking individual words; Group 3—children speaking phrases of two words and/or more.

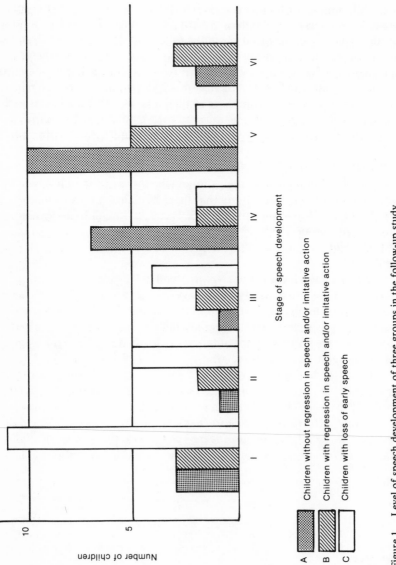

Figure 1.   Level of speech development of three groups in the follow-up study.

Table 5.   26 children with loss of early speech (II) studied by the questionnaires to mothers

Question	Answer	Group 1	Group 2	Group 3	Total
1. Did your child wave bye-bye and/or play peek-a-boo before losing early speech?	Yes	10	5	7	22
	No	0	0	3	3
	Uncertain	1	0	0	1
2. Did your child wave bye-bye and/or play peek-a-boo during the loss of early speech?	Yes	1	2	2	5
	No	9	3	7	19
3. Did you think that your child had normally developed until your child lost early speech?	Yes	8	3	4	15
	No	3	2	6	11
4. Do you think there was any direct cause to the loss of early speech by your child?	Yes	2	2	2	6
	No	9	3	8	20
5. Do you think there were any factors which may have caused abnormal speech development?	Yes	9	5	8	22
	No	2	0	2	4

Question 1 is *Did your child wave bye-bye and/or play peek-a-boo before losing early speech?* Almost all mothers answered yes, but many of them added "The bye-bye and peek-a-boo were scanty and feeble." Only two mothers said "my child pointed before losing early speech." Based on the results of Question 1, mother–child interaction would not develop sufficiently from the first year.

Question 2 is *Did your child wave bye-bye and/or play peek-a-boo during the loss of early speech?* Nineteen of 26 mothers answered no. This result indicates that many children with the loss of early speech also lost imitative action as well as speech, at almost the same time.

Question 3 is *Did you think that your child had normally developed until your child lost early speech?* More than half of the mothers answered yes. The loss of early speech was not always the indicator of onset of deviant speech development but it was often the first sign a mother noticed.

Question 4, *Do you think there was any direct cause to the loss of early speech by your child?* mostly was answered, no.

Question 5 is *Do you think there were any factors which may have caused the abnormal speech development?* Most of the mothers answered yes. The factors noted by the mothers were, for example, "I could not take care of my child sufficiently because of my employment," "I was too busy bringing up his siblings to always be his companion," or "Because of my illness, my child was placed under the care of others." It is uncertain to what degree factors such as these really affected the deviant speech development in each case, but they might have helped to manifest the problem. There was no distinct difference among the three groups in the results of these five questions.

Improvement of Behavior of Children with Loss of Early Speech

The deviant behaviors of the children in Group 1 were compared with those of the children in Group 3 in order to find a method to improve the children's speech. Fourteen symptoms concerning relationships with people were examined first (Table 6). The children in Group 1 had exhibited an average of 13 symptoms prior to the follow-up study. The children in Group 1 exhibited several of these symptoms at the time of follow-up study, while the children in Group 3 presented only a few symptoms. Children with the worst speech development (Group 1) improved in relationships with people, but not satisfactorily.

The frequency of ritualistic and compulsive phenomena (items 15 to 23), sterotyped repetitive movements and self-injury (items 24 to 26), and difficulty in social adaptation (items 27 to 33) are shown in Table 7. Hand-flapping in front of the eyes and self-injury were not observed in Group 3. The children in Group 1 did not also satisfactorily improve in the social adaptation.

Table 6. Improvement of behavior in Group 1 and Group 3 of children with loss of early speech (I)

Symptoms	Group (Number of children)			
	Group 1 (11)		Group 3 (10)	
	X*	Y	X	Y
Relationship to people				
1. Lack of eye contact	11	1	8	1
2. Expressionless face	9	2	6	0
3. Failure to cry or weep even at tumbling	11	4	6	0
4. Unwilling to be touched	9	4	3	1
5. Exhibits neither need for nor want of mother's affection	7	2	7	0
6. Does not turn when called	10	1	7	1
7. Goes astray when released	11	3	8	0
8. Hyperactivity	11	8	8	0
9. Failure to follow mother	11	1	7	2
10. Failure to scramble for toys with others	11	5	7	1
11. Uses others as physical extension of self (does not point)	11	9	9	1
12. Often isolates oneself in corner of room	9	3	4	1
13. Often climbs on shelves or window sills	11	8	6	0
14. Indifferent to others and plays alone	11	11	10	6
Mean number of symptoms exhibited by a child	13.0	5.8	9.8	1.7

*X—number of children who had presented the symptoms prior to the follow-up; Y—number of children who presented the symptoms at the time of follow-up.

Table 7. Improvement of behavior in Group 1 and Group 3 of children with loss of early speech (II)

Symptoms	Group (Number of children)			
	Group 1 (11)		Group 3 (10)	
	X	Y	X	Y
Ritualistic and Compulsive Phenomena				
15. Insists on aligning objects	4	2	4	0
16. Insists on taking the same route	5	0	3	1
17. Takes only few kinds of food	8	6	6	3
18. Insists on handling same objects	6	5	2	1
19. Watches only self-selected television commercial	9	3	4	2
20. Preoccupied with spinning objects	5	3	4	3
21. Manipulates unfamiliar apparatus	2	1	4	4
22. Preoccupied with unfamiliar letters and/or numerals	1	1	4	4
23. Often recites TV commercial phrases without apparent cause	0	0	7	7
Stereotyped Repetitive Movements and Self-injury				
24. Hand-flapping in front of eyes	5	4	0	0
25. Jumping and/or self-spinning	7	4	5	1
26. Self-injury	6	4	0	0
Difficulty in Social Adaptation				
27. Difficulty in training	11	5	10	4
28. Lack of response or answer	11	9	8	2
29. Difficulty in playing in a group	11	11	9	5
30. Frequently raises a queer voice	9	5	7	3
31. Smiles for no apparent reason	8	7	4	1
32. Raises temper or panics when inhibited	6	3	9	4
33. Abnormal sleeping habits	8	2	4	0

In conclusion, the children who showed better speech development afterward had had fewer impaired behaviors prior to the follow-up than the children who did not regain their words.

Comparison of Abnormal Speech and Psychiatric Diagnosis

A diagnosis of each child who lost early speech was made by two psychiatrists at the follow-up study (Table 8). Autistic syndrome was further classified into three subcategories following the DeMyer's method (DeMyer, 1973). In Group 1, nine children were diagnosed as low autistic, and two children as mentally retarded. In Group 2, one child was diagnosed as low autistic, two as middle autistic, and two as mentally retarded. In Group 3, one as middle autistic, three as high autistic, five as mentally retarded and one as moderately severely affected in developmental speech disorder syndrome (Ingram, 1959, 1972). Only two children with mental retardation in Group 3 could use words suitably for communicative purposes and had a normal manner of speaking, although they could not speak complete sentences. The rest of the children in Group 3 had a variety of difficulties for example, too high a pitch, a monotone pitch, echolalia, and/or speaking unrelated to the situation.

In order to compare with the diagnosis of these children, a diagnosis was made of each child in Groups A and B (Refer to Table 3). The results are shown in Table 9. Most of the children in Groups A and B were diagnosed as mentally retarded or as having developmental speech disorder syndrome. Among the 24 children diagnosed as having autistic syndrome in all groups, 16 children (67%) were in Group C.

DISCUSSION

The regression of speech and/or behavior in infancy has been reported as a symptom of autism and early childhood psychosis by many researchers (Creak, 1963; Ishii et al., 1966; Rutter and Lockyer, 1967; Ornitz and Ritvo, 1968; Marui et al., 1972; Wakabayashi, 1974). Rutter and Lockyer

Table 8. Diagnosis at follow-up in children with loss of early speech

Diagnosis	Group 1	Group 2	Group 3	Total
Low autistic*	9	1	0	10
Middle autistic*	0	2	1	3
High autistic*	0	0	3	3
Mental retardation	2	2	5	9
Developmental speech disorder syndrome**	0	0	1	1
Total	11	5	10	26

* by M. K. DeMyer (1973).
** by T. T. S. Ingram (1959).

Table 9.   Diagnosis at follow-up in children with abnormal speech development

Diagnosis	Group A	Group B	Group C	Total
Low autistic	0	3	10	13
Middle autistic	1	0	3	4
High autistic	3	1	3	7
Mental retardation	14	7	9	30
Developmental speech disorder syndrome	13	6	1	20
Total	31	17	26	74

(1967) reported that in one-fifth of the children with infantile psychosis, there was a fairly convincing history of normal development before the occurrence of any signs of psychosis. Additionally, it was observed by Wing (1976) that the parents reported a period of apparently normal development before a setback occurred and autistic behavior began some time before the age of 3 in approximately one-third of the children with early childhood autism. Wakabayashi (1974) showed that 26 out of 116 autistic children (22.4%) had refracted course and regressive changes in their histories.

The features of speech development in mental retardation have been explained as simple delay with the same sequence as normal speech development by Donovan (1957). Molloy (1961) pointed out, however, that there are some mentally retarded children who spoke words for a while and lost them for 2 or 3 years.

In this study, the loss of early speech, a phenomenon of regression, was investigated. Twenty-eight out of 100 children with abnormal speech development completely lost their early speech. The phenomena of the regression were represented not only as symptoms of autistic syndrome but also as symptoms of mental retardation and developmental speech disorder syndrome. It seems likely, however, that the majority of the children were more or less autistic during the regression, regardless of the diagnoses, because they showed variously deviant behaviors.

Among the 24 children with diagnosed autistic syndrome, 16 children (67%) had lost their early speech and 20 children (83%) had various types of regression in speech and/or behavior including the loss of early speech. These high incidences may come from the method used for the follow-up study and/or from the fact that the children with slight or short-time regression were included. Furthermore, the children investigated in this study had not always shown normal development before the regression or the loss of early speech.

Many of the children with loss of early speech, as well as other children with abnormal speech development, had exhibited some abnormal features even within the first year. Wing (1971, 1976) mentioned that it is difficult to say exactly what proportion of autistic children really have an early period of normality before becoming autistic because careful questioning of the parents often reveals some developmental abnormalities even before the noticeable setback.

Many researchers have noticed the high proportion of boys among the children with delayed speech. In this study, there was a significantly large number of boys among the children with abnormal speech development; the male/female ratio was 4.9:1, and among the children with the loss of early speech it was even higher, 8.3:1. One of the causes for the predominance of boys, it is presumed, is that boys are more interested in objects and less interested in other persons than girls are at the age of about 1;5 years.

In order to clarify the cause of the loss of early speech, several biological and environmental factors were examined in this study. Concerning the retarded initial walking and speaking first word, the children with the loss of early speech showed significantly lower incidence than that of other children with abnormal speech development, and concerning prenatal and perinatal troubles, employment of mothers, and maternal deprivation, there was no difference among them. Regarding the histories of the first year, the children with the loss of early speech showed higher incidence in two items—lack of cheer and weak sucking while nursing—than other children with abnormal speech development, but not significantly so (Table 2).

The follow-up study revealed that the loss of early speech was a sign of great disadvantage to speech development, as described by other investigators (Ishii et al., 1966; Marui et al., 1972; Wakabayashi, 1974). Perhaps whatever caused the loss of early speech also affected the speech development severely afterward.

A model for the appearance of symptoms in delayed speech with deviant behaviors is schematically illustrated in Figure 2. In this model, the deviant behaviors, called autistic symptoms, are considered to be directly caused neither by biological factors alone nor by the psychological environment alone. In each case, two or more factors inside the child and many factors within the environment continue to interact variously from the child's birth onward.

The factors inside the child are primary retardation, organic brain dysfunction, a certain inherited personality, and others that are probably induced by genetic inheritance and prenatal and perinatal troubles. EEG abnormalities and epileptic fits, which are often observed in autistic children, according to the investigators (Schain and Yannet, 1960; Brown, 1963; Rutter et al., 1967; Lobascher, Kingerlee, and Gubbay, 1970;

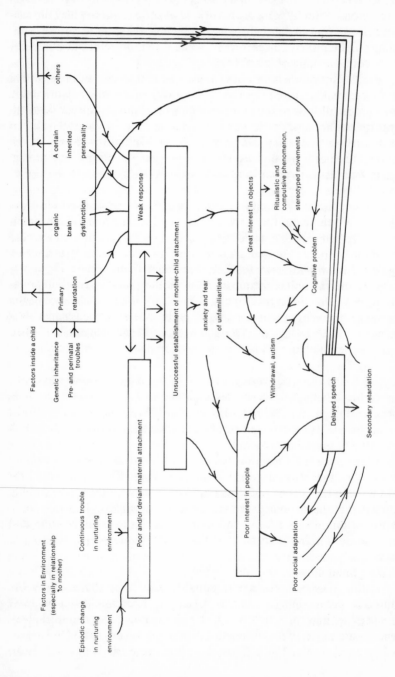

Figure 2.   Delayed speech with deviant behaviors—a hypothesis for the mechanism of symptoms.

Kanner, 1971; Ando, 1971), may be the manifestation of organic brain dysfunction. With regard to a certain inherited personality, it was assumed, for example, that there was an inclination to be interested in objects more intensively than in other persons. These factors would affect the child's development at each stage afterward.

Factors inside the child may cause the abnormal responses of the child, i.e., weak in most cases (Table 2) and hypersensitive in a few cases. This abnormality in physiological and social responses discourages the mother from her mothering effort. Even if each factor inside the child is not so strong, the child's interest in other persons, especially in his mother, may not grow well when there are episodic changes and/or continuous troubles in the nurturing environment. Thus, the mother-child interaction cycle is not activated sufficiently, and attachment (Bowlby, 1969; Taguchi, 1974) cannot be established well. Schopler (1976) proposed the interaction model—with an autistic infant who has biologically impaired reflexes and social responses, the mother is negatively reinforced for her mothering efforts and the interaction cycle is directed more by biological factors than it is with the normal child.

Most of the so-called autistic behaviors are secondary symptoms derived from the unsuccessful establishment of mother-child attachment during the first year. The unsuccessful establishment of the mother-child attachment is probably induced mainly by the child's biological factors, as mentioned above.

Children with the loss of early speech were selected for subjects in order to study the phenomenon of regression, but the results indicated that the loss of early speech did not occur at the onset of the impaired condition, as shown in Table 2. The loss of early speech also may be one of the symptoms derived from the unsuccessful establishment of mother-child attachment in many cases. The prognosis of the children with the loss of early speech was worse than that of other children with delayed speech. This fact may suggest that the establishing of attachment in the children with the loss of early speech is more difficult than in other children and that the difficulty is related to severe organic brain dysfunction. In case of an unsuccessful establishment of attachment during the first year, the child may be inclined to have great interest in objects and may lose his early speech from the age at which he can independently move and progress in intelligence.

It was sometimes observed that the children who had developed normally and spoken phrases of two words or more, regressed and exhibited the autistic pattern of behavior without any distinctly proven psychological and physical disorders. In addition, the regression to autistic behaviors has been reported to be associated with various conditions of overt organic brain damage (Creak, 1963; Rutter and Lockyer, 1967). The assumption about the delayed speech with deviant behavior, shown in Figure 2, is not applicable to all autistic symptoms, including such regression.

Wood (1964) referred to "vocalizations with pointing" at age 1;3 and "questions" between the second and third years as the milestones in the language development of normal children. Vocalizations with pointing and questions are also based on the mother-child attachment.

In order to improve the speech of children suffering from delayed speech accompanied by deviant behavior, the establishment of the mother-child attachment may be vital as the first step. Therefore, it is necessary to improve the factors in the child's environment, particularly in his relationship to the mother, because the factors inside a child can hardly be changed radically. It is possible to conclude that the later the improvement in relationship to the mother occurs, the more difficult the speech development will be. On the basis of this assumption, mothers are always advised to try to improve their relationship with their children as soon as possible.

When a child fails to establish mother-child attachment and to gain communicative skills at the appropriate period of development because of severe biological and environmental factors, it may be very difficult to make up the time later. Once the mother-child attachment is established, even if delayed, it seems likely that the subsequent speech development will be relatively satisfactory.

SUMMARY

Some of the 100 children had no words, some had a few words but were unable to gain more words, and others had many isolated words but could not use such words for communicative purposes. It was observed that 28 of 100 children had regressed from almost normal or slightly delayed speech to the complete loss of early speech. Most of the children who lost their early speech developed incomplete speech afterward. It was clear at the follow-up study that the loss of early speech was a predictor of slow speech development later. In addition, many deviant behaviors were observed during the abnormal speech period, such as the lack of eye contact, the failure to point, the spinning of objects, hyperactivity, and abnormal sleeping habits. Most of the children who did not regain communicative ability and continued to show deviant development during relatively long observation periods were more appropriately diagnosed as suffering from an autistic syndrome. The children who regained words for communicative skills within relatively short time and did not show such deviant behavior so long, were more often diagnosed as suffering from mental retardation.

REFERENCES

Ando, M. 1971. [Autistic syndrome and EEG]. Clinical Electroencephalography (Japanese) 13:402-405.

Bowlby, J. 1966. Maternal Care and Mental Health. Schocken Books, New York. (originally published in the Bulletin of W.H.O., 1951, 3, 355-534.)

Bowlby, J. 1969. Attachment and Loss. Vol.1. The Hogarth Press, London.

Brown, J. L. 1963. Follow-up of children with atypical development (infantile autism). Am. J. Orthopsychiatry 33:855-861.

Creak, E. M. 1963. Childhood psychosis—A review of 100 cases. Br. J. Psychiatry 109:84-89.

DeMyer, M. K. et al. 1973. Prognosis in autism—A follow-up study. J. Autism Child Schizophr. 3:199-246.

Donovan, H. 1957. Organization and development of a speech program for the mentally retarded children in New York City Public Schools. Am. J. Ment. Defic. 62:455-459.

Ingram, T. T. S. 1959. Specific developmental disorders of speech in childhood. Brain 82:450-467.

Ingram, T. T. S. 1972. The classification of speech and language disorders in young children. In: M. Rutter and J. A. M. Martin (eds.), The Child with Delayed Speech, pp. 13-32. Spastics International Medical Publications, London.

Ishii, T. et al. 1966. [The study of autistic child (No. 3)]. Psychiatria et neurologia Japonica (Japanese) 68:178-179.

Kanner, L. 1971. Follow-up study of eleven autistic children originally reported in 1943. J. Autism Child. Schizophr. 1:119-145.

Lobascher, M. E., Kingerlee, P. E., and Gubbay, S. S. 1970. Childhood autism—An investigation of aetiological factors in twenty-five cases. Br. J. Psychiatry 117:525-529.

Marui, F. et al. 1972. A research for typifying the language development of autistic children. The Bulletin of Nagoya University School of Pedagogy. 19:185-197.

Molloy, J. S. 1978. Teaching the retarded child to talk, translated by T. Matsuoka and I. Sasaki. Nipponbunkakagakusha, Tokyo. (originally published by The John Day Company, New York, 1961)

Ornitz, E. M., and Ritvo, E. R. 1968. Perceptual inconstancy in early infantile autism—The syndrome of early infant autism and its variants including certain cases of childhood schizophrenia. Arch. Gen. Psychiatry 18:76-98.

Prugh, D. G., and Harlow, R. G. 1966. "Masked deprivation" in infants and young children. In: M. D. Ainsworth et al. (eds.), Deprivation of Maternal Care, pp. 201-221. Schocken Books, New York. (originally published as No. 14 in the series Public Health Papers issued by W. H. O., 1962.)

Rutter, M., and Lockyer, L. 1967. A five to fifteen year follow-up study of infantile psychosis—I. Description of sample. Br. J. Psychiatry 113:1169-1182.

Rutter, M., Greenfeld, D., and Lockyer, L. 1967. A five to fifteen year follow-up study of infantile psychosis—II. Social and behavioural outcome. Br. J. Psychiatry 113:1183-1199.

Schain, R. J., and Yannet, H. 1960. Infantile autism—An analysis of 50 cases and a consideration of certain relevant neurophysiologic concepts. J. Pediatr. 57:560-567.

Shimada, S. 1976. A clinical study on masked maternal deprivation. Jap. J. Child Psychiatry 17:261-275.

Taguchi, T. 1974. [Clinical study of speech development]. Kohseikan, Tokyo. (Japanese)

Wakabayashi, S. 1974. A study on the refracted course of infantile autism. Jap. J. Child Psychiatry 15:215–230.

Wing, L. 1971. Perceptual and language development in autistic children—A comparative study. In: M. Rutter (ed.), Infantile Autism—Concepts, Characteristics and Treatment. Churchill, London.

Wing, L. 1976. Diagnosis, clinical description and prognosis. In: L. Wing (ed.), Early Childhood Autism—Clinical, Educational and Social Aspects (2nd ed.), pp. 15–64. Pergamon Press, London.

Wood, N. E. 1964. Delayed Speech and Language Development. Prentice-Hall, Englewood Cliffs, N. J.

Teaching Swedish Deaf Preschool Children To Read

Ragnhild Söderbergh

THE PROJECT AND ITS BACKGROUND

This reading project for deaf preschool children was carried out in the county of Malmöhus in southern Sweden from September 1976 to June 1977. Forty deaf and severely hearing-impaired children were involved. When the project started, the children were 3–6 years old. Twenty-seven of the children were 5–6 years old and they were instructed in groups in preschool with four or five children in each group: two groups in Helsingborg, two in Lund and one in Vellinge. The other 13 children, ages 3–4, were taught individually, at home.

In Sweden, children normally start school at age 7. At age 6 (sometimes 5), they may attend preschool, which is not compulsory. In preschool, children draw, paint, cook, bake, grow plants, play indoor and outdoor games, go for excursions, etc.

Deaf children, who are admitted into preschool at age 4, are integrated with the hearing children for part of the time, but they also receive special training individually and as a group with other deaf children. Before the age of 4, deaf children are visited once a week in their homes by training teachers.

Although reading is not usually taught in preschool (children are not supposed to start reading before age 7) in Sweden, attempts at reading instruction have been included in the training of deaf preschool children for several years. This instruction has been restricted primarily to teaching the children their own names, the names of family members and peers, and a few nouns.

The county of Malmöhus' project was designed to emphasize more reading. A program was set up in the spring of 1976 by a group consisting of the children's teachers, two psychologists, the deaf care administrator of the county and this author, who was asked to act as a linguistic adviser because of her previous research on reading with normal and deaf preschool children.

Guidelines of the Project

Certain theoretical guidelines and practical techniques were decided upon but teachers generally were free to work according to their own temperment, pedagogic experience, and knowledge of the children.

Theoretical Guidelines   It was decided that reading and writing would be integrated into the normal preschool activities. Reading and writing, as far as possible, would be *functional*, that is, it would fill a need in the children's daily life that was not filled by other means of communication or other linguistic media. It also was decided that the lessons would not be, in any way, traditional. The training and rehearsal necessary to ensure that written words would be remembered by the children were always to take the form of *play*.

Practical Arrangements   The teacher was to write on big sheets of paper instead of the blackboard so that written texts could be saved and referred to later. Cards with separate words written on them and alphabet cards were also used. Capitals and small letters were written in the manner recommended by the National Swedish Board of Education (SÖ).

Collaboration Between Teachers and Parents   Teachers and parents met regularly for informal discussions. The teachers met and informed one another about the progress of their work. Through this collaboration between teachers and between parents and teachers, there was a constant exchange of ideas, which enriched the program as the work went on.

IMPLEMENTATION OF THE PROGRAM

According to the theoretical guidelines, reading and writing were to be functional, and at the same time, tied to the child's everyday activities. These principles were best carried out by instructing the preschool children in groups. Following are a few examples of the activities used.

Functional Reading Activities

If cooking was on the day's schedule, the group would sit down with the teacher and plan what to buy, talking it over in sign language and/or speech. (According to the grade of deafness, sign language and speech were used in different proportions. The totally deaf children predominately used sign language and their teacher used sign language and simultaneous speech. The severely hearing-impaired children understood more speech, and their sign language was merely a visual aid). Then, the teacher wrote down what had been decided upon, using the children's own words and phrases and expanding upon them when necessary:

We are going shopping
We shall buy butter, sausages, and potatoes
Then we shall peel the potatoes
We shall cook the potatoes and fry the sausages
Then we shall eat the sausages and the potatoes

All the children read the text, first in chorus (using sign language), and then individually. The essential, or key, words—*buy, butter, sausages, potatoes, peel, cook, fry,* and *eat*—were underlined in the text and the children were given separate cards on which those words were printed. Next, the children wrote individual shopping lists and the group went to the store. When they returned, each child was assigned a task. Everybody's part of the job was written down and hung on the wall above the place where each child was working:

I am peeling potatoes
I am cutting the sausages
I am frying the sausages
I am cooking the potatoes

Finally, the children ate the meal.

On the following day, the rest of the food was taken out of the refrigerator. The children tasted it, talked about what they had done on the previous day, looked at the texts and read them again, and looked at the cards. The children then compared the words on the cards with the same words written on a sheet of paper.

One day the children were going to the public baths. Planning for the visit, they cut out pictures of towels, soap, bathing costumes, etc., taped them to a sheet of paper, and wrote in the words, towel, soap, etc. The teacher and the children talked about the coming event, and instructions were written on a big sheet of paper:

We are going to the baths
We are going by car
We shall bring bathing costumes
We shall bring towels
We shall bring soap

The essential words were underlined and the children were given the corresponding word cards. Finally, the children were helped to copy the instruction into their notebooks to take home to their parents. At home, the children read the instructions with the parents and packed their things.

Another day, a group of children who had been painting, had splattered wet paint all over themselves. In the preschool's big bathroom, everybody was allowed to undress and bathe. The children had a great afternoon shampooing, showering, and splashing water at one another. On the following day, the group talked about their adventures and made a story out of them. The teacher wrote on the big sheet in front of the children, and the children wrote and drew in their own books, which they took home to show to their parents.

In the activities described above, reading and writing are functional: shopping lists, packing lists, working instructions, messages from school to home, notes codifying the common decisions of the group, and diaries of interesting events.

The children were especially fond of the diaries in their working books, and read them over and over again. Such diaries were the starting points of new conversations in the groups about similar topics. When the children were reading in the diary about a visit they had paid to one of the parents at his job, they immediately began to talk about their own parents' jobs. Part of this conversation was written down and read, and on a later occasion, the children read it again, adding what they themselves planned to do when they grew up.

Matching the Words with Things   During the first weeks of reading, all the new words were matched with real things. It was considered necessary to tie written words directly to the nonverbal reality, thus making the children understand that written words are language. This is essential to the deaf child, who often does not have a spoken word or sign attached to the thing or event that teachers try to represent with a written symbol. By tying the written symbol to reality, and at the same time talking about this reality in signs and in spoken language, the teacher gave the child a multiple set of symbols. The child learned the sign, the spoken word (through speech-reading), and the written word, all on the same occasion.

Rehearsal and Key Words   Part of the written material could be rehearsed in a natural way because the children wanted to read it again, and thus learn it. But to make sure that the children really learned and also remembered the words that were not repeated in the reading, repetitions had to be arranged. To that end, different sorts of games were invented. The words repeated in games were mostly the so-called key words. These key words were written down on cards. The rehearsal of written words, during the first weeks, very often took the form of games in which the children matched written words to things—toys, fruit, clothes, etc. Little by little, as the children matured, real things were replaced by pictures.

Several card games that could be played in groups were very popular with the older children (6-7 years old). The younger children were more fond of role play. For example, one child played the postman, delivering letters to all the children. The envelops would carry the names of the children and contain words or sentences to be read. The children also pretended to be picking mushrooms in the wood and putting the mushrooms into baskets. The "mushrooms" were cut out in outline, and had words written on them.

A special group activity was very popular with the younger children—"singing songs". The songs were written down on the sheet in front of the children, and "sung" rhythmically in sign language. The teachers both sang and signed while the kids signed and made whatever sounds they could. Such "songs" eventually were learned by heart, both in written and sign form.

Analysis of Words   To help the children analyze the words, alphabet cards were used. First, the children were asked to put a card with a word on it in front of them (e.g., *apelsin,*) and, looking at the card, try to put the corresponding lettercards (*a, e, i, l, n, p,* and *s*) together to form the word. When they had practiced this, they were allowed to have a look at the wordcard, then it was taken away and they had to put the corresponding letters together from memory. The last and most difficult stage was to take a wordcard, read it, put it away, pick the corresponding letters out of a box, mix the letters, and then put them together to form the word.

EVALUATION OF RESULTS

To enable teachers to evaluate the results of the reading project, diaries were kept, videotapes were taken, and interviews were made.

The diaries recorded the words and sentences that were read every week, and included observations on the reading of individual children.

Videotapes of the children making up stories, reading them together with their teacher, and playing reading games were made.[1]

The teachers, parents, and psychologists were asked to give their views on the reading project and on the achievements of the children. The nine oldest children were 7 years old in autumn, 1977, when they started obligatory school—the school for deaf children, in Lund. When the autumn term ended, their teachers were asked what their opinions were of these children, especially as compared with deaf children beginning school without previous knowledge of reading and writing.

What the Interviews Revealed

The following section summarizes the opinions of the teachers, psychologists, and parents about the children and their achievements. Judgments were made on the general, social and linguistic development of the children and on their achievements in reading and writing.

---

[1]The videotapes used for this study were taken by professor Kerstin Nordén, School of Education, Malmö, Sweden, as part of her own project dealing with the cognitive, social, and emotional development of deaf children.

General   The children were considered to be more inquisitive and more eager to know about things and the names of things than they were previously. This eagerness to know was especially observed by the parents. The teachers who taught the seven children beginning the deaf school in the autumn of 1977, observed that these children generally were very active and eager to work. The psychologists observed that language-made-visible (sign language and written language) seemed to make the children more sure of themselves.

Socially   The children benefited from starting to read in preschool. In comparison with their hearing peers, they were not deprived children but children with a specific ability: they were deaf but nevertheless could read and write at an age when hearing children normally could not.

Linguistically   The children's sign language improved. At the start of the project, they used only strongly context-bound one- or two-word phrases. By the end of the project, however, they were also able to use multiword phrases and talk about the present, the past and the future. They learned auxiliaries, pronouns, prepositions, conjunctions, and articles, and they also used these in their sign language. Their speech improved; they produced more speech, and it became better articulated.

The teachers at the school for deaf children were rather impressed by the children's general linguistic ability. They were surprised to find that the children had a functioning language, and that it was possible to communicate with them. The children understood what was said to them, and they could argue and solve everyday practical problems by means of language.

Reading and Writing Abilities

The children taking part in the reading project learned how to *use* reading and writing. They try to read whatever printed material they come across, and they frequently ask about written messages (e.g., notices, advertisements, newspapers, books). They ask adults to write down words for them, and they try to write by themselves whenever there is a need for it. At the end of the spring of 1977, a boy in one of the Lund groups was hospitalized. His classmates and their teacher wrote an illustrated letter to him, which he read and answered. This meant very much both to the boy and to his peers. In short, the children like to read and are highly motivated both to read and write. They do not passively sit down to receive instruction, but add to their knowledge by actively applying what they have already learned and by seeking new knowledge.

An analysis of the diaries and the videotapes revealed additional information that supported the general statements made above. The result of this analysis is totally in accordance with the results obtained in earlier studies of normal hearing and deaf-reading children, ages 2-6 (Jocić and

Savić, 1973; Past, A. W., 1976; Past, K. E. C., 1975; Söderbergh 1975a, 1976a, 1976b, 1977). Learning to read is learning a written language. To a 7-year-old hearing-child, it normally means learning a language that has a counterpart in an already known spoken language. Because of that knowledge, it is possible to teach reading to 7-year-olds by simply transforming spoken language to written language—a purely formal instruction. This is what is normally done in schools. Deaf children and very young hearing-children (1 ½ to 3 years old), however, have little knowledge of spoken language. Thus, reading instructions of this kind is unsuccessful with them. For them, reading must be taught in a manner such as that described above, that is, a way in which language is tied directly to reality, to a concrete experience. This kind of "natural" instruction also makes it possible to study the children's acquisition of spoken language, how they learn the semantics, syntax, morphology, and graphonomy of written language (graphonomy is the counterpart of the phonology of spoken language).

Semantics: Understanding, Learning, and Using Written Words

The reading instruction started with the presentation of separate words and of short, easy phrases, in an active, real context, accompanied by speech and sign language. Then, the children discovered that what you do when you write on a paper is something similar to what you do when you make signs in the air and what you do when you move your tongue and lips—you convey a message. The signs, the lip and tongue movements, and the scribble on the paper refer to something in the outer reality, they mean something. It is the same discovery that the baby makes when he starts to understand his first language; what you say is meaningful, words are symbols. And, exactly as the baby first learns what is meaningful to him, what has a purpose to him, the children learning to read remember best such words that have a personal touch, that are closely tied to their most intimate reality, to their immediate experience. The parallel to the baby's learning of his first vocabulary is all the more striking the younger the children learning to read.

Children learn best their own names, the names of the other children, the names of family members, and the words for their own clothes and personal belongings. One 4-year-old boy was instructed at home. The teacher started by showing him fruit and trying to teach him the names of different fruits. He was completely uninterested, did not want to read that "the lemon is sour," but became very interested as soon as the teacher changed the subject to the names of family members. Another small boy (also instructed in his home) did not understand what reading was until he had shown the teacher his new cap, which he was very proud of, and had been allowed to read the word, cap. The youngest boy in one of the preschool groups was particularly interested in the names of clothes, and he started to learn written words by being allowed to dress and undress a paper doll. He was directed by the teacher, who showed him wordcards for the different clothes he was going to put on the doll. Food also seemed to be a good subject to most children, and words like sausages and potatoes were learned immediately. One group of children who had just gotten bicycles, wanted very much to compare their bikes, to talk, and to write and read about them: *Lotta has a blue bike, Martin has a red bike,* etc.

Not only was the "personal touch" important for the learning of words, but certain linguistic factors also played a role. In the beginning of the reading instruction, nouns seemed easier to learn than verbs and adjectives. This tendency to remember nouns is also characteristic of children's first-language learning. The functional aspect mattered, as well. *Och* 'and', a very popular word, was easily learned probably because it could be used for chaining nice words together, e.g., *Mattias and Martin and Camilla and Jojo.* One girl learned *vi* 'we' immediately because it was so easy for her to write.

Immediate Experience   Immediate experiences were very important for deaf children, who often do not have knowledge of certain symbols, either in sign language or in spoken language, when they see them for the first time in writing. Thus, a deaf child may be confronted with three new symbols at the same time: the written symbol, the sign, and the spoken word—all denoting a certain object or event. This must be a very frustrating experience. It is well illustrated by two children in one of the Helsingborg groups. When they first saw *slowly* and *quickly*, the children were unfamiliar with them as written words, as spoken words, and as sign language words. The teacher had to tie the symbols directly to reality by letting the children experience slowness and quickness to help them acquire the concepts. This was a very slow process. The children eventually succeeded by being allowed to play a game. All the children were running in a row, the first child having a signboard with *slowly* written on one side, *quickly* on the other. When the first child showed the *slowly* side, all children would walk slowly, when he turned the *quickly* side toward them, they would start to run.

Group Experience   When playing different games with wordcards, the children were extremely observant of what was happening. If a child received the same wordcard that another child had received on an earlier occasion, this was immediately attended to by all of them. Such reactions were observed carefully by studying the videotapes, from which the gestures and facial expressions of all the children can be checked. The contextual memory of children is often amazing. At a game of cards, one girl got the word *kastar* 'throws'. A boy sitting beside her then violently signed the word many times and pointed to another boy, indicating that some days earlier they had written that this other boy "*threw* stones."

The mistakes made by different children in the group were noted very carefully and were talked about long afterward: "Do you remember when Mattias could not write 'jag' but wrote 'jga' instead?"

The importance of the "personal touch" for learning also applies to the character and personality of the individual child. One very clever boy, who was instructed at home, refused to collaborate until he himself was allowed to decide what to read and about what to write. On the whole, it is most important to follow the initiatives of the children, to listen to them and to consider their ideas, rather than insisting on sticking to a general plan.

Written language, like other language, should not only be understood and learned, it also should be used and practiced. Because of the functional approach used in this project, the children very quickly grasped the use of written language and they themselves tried very early to write. Unfortunately, learning to write may be very difficult for some children, but many of the children in this project discovered that they could use the prefabricated wordcards to communicate. For example, Jo-jo, during a videotaped session when the children were eating sausages, found the wordcard for *korv* 'sausages' and *gott* 'good', held them up to the camera and with a big smile said "korv gott" 'sausages good.'

Graphonomy, Morphology, and Syntax: Analyzing and Learning the Structure of Language

Linguistic items called graphemes in written language, and phonemes in spoken language, combine into units called morphemes, and these units can be combined in different ways to form syntactical units. All these combinations follow strict rules. When learning the written language, the child also discovers and learns this structure, and learns the structural rules. He does so not through formal instruction, but by carefully observing and analyzing the written material presented to him.

The child's observations on and analysis of written material can be followed by a careful study of his own reading. Here, what are called reading errors can be detected. There are two kinds of reading errors made by both hearing and deaf children: graphematic reading errors and semantic reading errors.

Graphematic errors occur when, for example, *baka* 'bake' is mistaken for *bada* 'bathe' or when words like *halsduk* 'scarf' and *handduk* 'towel' are mixed up. As shown by Söderbergh (1977), this kind of reading error is dependent on the degree of similarity between the two words. Graphematic reading errors occur from the very beginning of reading instruction, and they show that the children at once pay great attention to the graphematic characteristics of words, even in detail. Graphematic reading errors also occur occasionally with advanced readers.

An example of a semantic error is when *ledsen* 'sad' is read as *gråter* 'is weeping'. This type is rather common when the child starts to read, but it disappears before he has attained full reading ability. The error is a semantic one, that is, a word is read as a semantically more or less similar word. Examples from this project include *springer* 'runs' read as *hoppar* 'jumps,' and *stövlar* 'boots' read as *vantar* 'gloves' (clothes for feet/ hands, respectively). This error seems to be more common with hearing children who have a greater vocabulary with more synonyms to choose from than have deaf children. The explanation of this kind of error is that the child starting to read English or Swedish at first does not know that the writing system is alphabetical, that the letters of written language correspond to the sounds of words in the spoken language. When reading a word as its synonym or as a semantically similar word, the child treats the writing system as ideographical. A written word symbol in that case may formally be read in many different ways, the important thing is only that the meaning remains the same. This is well illustrated in the reading experiment conducted by Kay and Al Past, who taught their 2-year-old daughter Mariana to read in both English and Spanish. During her first reading months, Mariana very often read a Spanish word as its English counterpart, or vice versa. (Past, K. E. C., 1975).

Semantic reading errors disappear shortly before the child attains full reading ability, that is, when the child is about to break the code to discover the correspondence between letters and sounds. This is something that is done automatically by the early reading child through his own comparisons among and analyses of the written words he encounters. (Söderbergh, 1977).

The deaf child faces a formidable task in breaking the code (Söderbergh, 1976b). In this project, the children seemed to break it because the teachers allowed them to spell the key words with the finger alphabet, read them on the teacher's lips, and to try to pronounce them by themselves. It was observed that when reading difficult words, the deaf children sometimes stopped, fingerspelled the words, and in this way, identified them. Afterward, the children could make the right signs for the words in sign language. This may mean that the deaf children break the code visually—kinesthetically instead of auditorally, or orally.

Through reading, the child not only breaks the code but also discovers the morphology of the written language. By contrasting such words as *boll, bollar* 'ball,' 'balls,' the child discovers the plural ending *-ar*. By contrasting *leker, lekte* 'plays,' 'played,' he discovers the formal opposition between present and past tense. For the hearing child, this discovery means simply that his implicit knowledge of spoken language is brought to the surface by appearing before his eyes in the corresponding written form. However, for the deaf child, whose spontaneous language, sign language, does not have the morphology of spoken language, new knowledge must be acquired. The deaf child learns about the morphological system only through reading.

The reading deaf children in this project were very observant of the morphological variations of written language. This fact is well illustrated by Martin, who was reading a text about the children's cooking. The text on the sheet said *steka* 'fry,' but he himself had received a reading card saying *steker* 'fries.' The teacher said that the two words were the same, but Martin protested, saying they were not the same. He asked for an explanation, and the teacher had to put the two forms of the word into context to show the difference.

The same critical judgment was shown by two children asked to identify key words in a text. The text showed the word *åkte* 'went.' The teacher asked a girl to find a card with the same word on it, but the only one available read *åka* 'go.' The teacher asked her to pick it up. The videotape shows that the girl did so, but that she refused to read the word, and that a boy watching the scene shook his head energetically and made the sign for *no* several times.

Very early in their training the children observed and talked about letters and combinations of letters. A girl tells the teacher that *ska* 'shall' is at the end of *väska* 'bag,' Mattias noticed that his name and the word *mössa* 'cap' both begin with an *m*. The children spontaneously compared different words, counted the letters and noted similarities and differences. In this way, they discovered the graphemes and the distribution of graphemes, the graphotactic structure of words in Swedish. Knowledge of this structure, together with their expanding knowledge of morphology, made it easier for them to take in and remember new written words. Their knowledge of graphotax made such spellings as *jga* for *jag* impossible—an error made at first that was subsequently laughed at by the children. Their knowledge of morphology enabled them to read many new words containing combinations of already known morphemes. Knowing the four ending morphemes *-s, -or, -n,* and *-na,* and the two base morphemes *klocka* and *flicka,* the child was also able to read 14 different words that are combinations of these morphemes: *klockas, flickas, klockan, flickan,* etc.

The small child learning language, first acquires words with a reference, deictic words like *there*, which refer directly to reality, and nouns and verbs denoting concrete things and visible events. The functors, which help to build up syntactic structure by tying these words together in the sentence and indicating relations between them, are learned much later.

The deaf child's sign language has few functors—auxiliaries, prepositions, conjunctions, articles, etc.—and these are used rarely. The reading deaf children in this study acquired functors through the written language and began using them also in their sign language. In the conversation preceding or paralleling the writing of stories, the teachers expanded the short sentences of the children by adding functors. They then wrote these expanded versions of the children's phrases on the paper, and read these completed phrases together with the children. The videotapes clearly show the children's growing syntactic ability in mastering prepositions. A videotape from the autumn of 1976 shows children and teacher talking about going by car *to* the public baths. The children were then unable to use the preposition *till* 'to.' Nevertheless, the teacher added it, and they read it together. In the spring of 1977, Martin dictated to his teacher "*Martin har ont benet*" (i.e. 'Martin has ache leg' or 'Martin's leg aches',) the correct Swedish construction should have a preposition: ont *i* benet 'in the leg.' The teacher wrote and said "*i* benet" and Martin immediately corrected himself and signed "i benet." The girl sitting on his right asked, in sign language, "*i*?" Martin noded energetically and added the sign for "benet" 'the leg.'

There is a marked interest in functors among the reading deaf children, an interest often not noticed or understood by the teachers because they are not linguists. The children want to find out about functors and they often ask for explanations, which are very hard to give indeed. One of the videotapes showed the children being asked to underline key words, but they insisted on underlining the two functors: *en* 'a,' 'an' and *och* 'and.' The teacher did not agree, however, and instead, underlined a noun and a verb.

Reading is Reconstruction

Traditional reading instruction builds on the assumption that reading is just mapping sounds onto letters and blending them, or, if the whole word method is used, to match written words with spoken ones and add them together. Reading is seen as addition from left to right, and every deviation from this left to right running path is looked upon as a sign that the child does not know, has not understood, has not been able to follow the instructions, etc. Research has shown that reading is not addition but reconstruction, creation, and hypothesis testing. When a child reading an alphabetic language says a synonym instead of the word actually written, this is hypothesis-testing, not just guessing. Many examples of reading errors of this type made by deaf children have already been presented in this chapter.

Reading is reconstruction for hearing people, both adults and children. People take in only as much of the written text as will enable them to reconstruct that text on the basis of knowledge of language. Children's knowledge of spoken language also allows them to read words that are new to them in the written language, if these words belong to their spoken language. The context helps them to put it in the right words.

Deaf children's poor knowledge of language might lead to the belief that reconstruction in reading is not possible for them. Nevertheless, many instances of reconstruction in the reading of the deaf children in this project were found.

One boy tended to mix up the verbs *äter* 'eats' and *åker* 'goes by' because of their graphical similarity. After being shown the sentence *Mattias och Karin åker buss* 'Mattias and Karin go by bus,' he started reading *Mattias och Karin äter*... but interrupted himself and changed his reading to *åker* under the influence of the following word, *buss*. The semantics of the sentence helped him to solve the problem. Another boy, having read many sentences beginning "Mattias mother/father etc. works," was going to read a sentence containing the word *mends*; he first read *works* but changed his reading to *mends* when he found that the object was the noun *cars*. Another videotape showed the teacher writing the sentence, *Vi ska gå till affären och köpa korv, potatis, mjölk* 'We are going to the supermarket to buy sausages, potatoes, milk.' When reading this text, the children changed it to *och mjölk* 'and milk,' in accordance with their knowledge of Swedish syntactic rules.

REFERENCES

Doman, G. 1964. How to Teach Your Baby to Read: The Gentle Revolution. Random House, New York.

Goodman, K. S., and Goodman, Y. M. 1976. Learning to Read is Natural. Paper presented at Conference on Theory and Practice of Beginning Reading Instruction, Pittsburgh.

Jocić, M., and Savić, S. 1973. Acquisition of Reading Ability in Early Childhood. Several Question of Theory and Practice. Paper read at the 3rd Congress of Yugoslav Pedagogues, Ohrid.

Leimar, U. 1974. Läsning på talets grund (Reading on the base of speech). Liber Läromedel, Lund.

Nordén, K., Preisler, G., and Heiling, K. 1979. Inlärningsprocesser och personlighetsutveckling has döva barn. [Learning processes and personality development in deaf children.] Notiser och rapporter fran Pedagogisk-Psykologiska Institutionen, Lärarhögskolan i Malmö, Lunds Universitet, nr 356.

Past, A. W. 1976. Preschool Reading in Two Languages as a Factor in Bilingualism. Unpublished doctoral dissertation, The University of Texas at Austin.

Past, K. E. C. 1975. Reading in Two Languages from Age Two: A Case Study. Unpublished masters thesis, The University of Texas at Austin.

Söderbergh, R. 1973. Project Child Language and Project Early Reading: A Theoretical Investigation and its Practical Application. Stockholm University, Child Language Research Institute.

Söderbergh, R. 1975a. Reading and stages of language acquisition. In: W. C. McCormack and S. A. Wurm (eds.), Language and Man: Anthropological Issues, pp. 149–164 Mouton, The Hague.

Söderbergh, R. 1975b. Language Acquisition and Reading. Paper presented at the Third International Child Language Symposium, May, London.

Söderbergh, R. 1975c. Review of: Language by Ear and by Eye (eds. Kavanagh, J. F., and Mattingly, J. G.). J. Child Lang. Vol. 2, 1:153–168.

Söderbergh, R. 1976a. Learning to read between two and five: Some observations on normal hearing and deaf children. In: Clea Rameh (ed.), Semantics: Theory and Application, pp. 257–279. Georgetown University Round Table on Languages and Linguistics, 1976.

Söderbergh, R. 1976b. Learning to Read: Breaking the Code or Acquiring Functional Literacy? Paper presented at the Georgetown University Round Table on Languages and Linguistics, 1976. Child Language Research Institute, Stockholm University.

Söderbergh, R. 1977. Reading in Early Childhood: A Linguistic Study of a Preschool Child's Gradual Acquisition of Reading Ability. Georgetown University Press, Washington, D. C.

Wolff, J. G. 1973. Language, Brain and Hearing. Methuen & Co., London.

Index

Abnormal speech development
  autistic chilren, 366–377
    early period of normality, 367
    symptoms in delayed speech with
      deviant behaviors, 367
  biological and environmental fac-
    tors, 367
  compared with normal speech
    development, 354–355
  examination of, 354–356
  follow-up study, 358–359
  genetic inheritance, 367–368
  history of first year, 356–358
  improvement of behavior, 362–365
  infantile psychosis, 366
  loss of early speech, 353–372
    comparison among children with,
      359–362
  maternal deprivation, 356, 367
  mental retardation, 366–368
  organic brain syndrome, 367–370
  prenatal and perinatal problems,
    354
  preponderance of boys, 354, 367
  procedure, 353–354
  prognosis, 369
  psychiatric diagnosis, 365–367
  regression of speech and/or
    behavior, 365–366
  symptoms, 356–358, 367
  unsuccessful establishment of
    mother-child attachment,
    369–370
Accentuation, 7–27
  accentual rules, 8
  accentual variation, 12–22
    child-child interaction, 14
    linguistic features and style,

14–16
    mother-child interaction, 14–22
    "parents' code," 19
    "peers' code," 16, 19
    reading, 14
  acquisition of, 9–12
  basic accentual patterns, 7–8
    accented and unaccented, 7–8
  dialectal variation, 7–27
    interdialectal variation and in-
      tradialectal variation, 22–26
    Tokyo and Kyoto dialects, 7–27
    two regional diets, 7–27
Adolescents, speed of second
    languague acquisition,
    209–210
Adult language, cognitive develop-
    ment and, 104
American Anthropologist, 241
Aphasic children
  hierarchical ordering disability,
    319–330
    embedded or conjoined struc-
      tures, 323–324
    grammatical analysis, 323
    hierarchical structuring deficit,
      295,324–329
  hierarchical structuring disability,
    295
    drawing tree structure, 324–329
  language development, 293–297
  maternal speech, 218
  poor sense of rhythm, 320–321
  writing of, 321–324
    grammatical analysis, 323
Asphyxia, 354
Assertions, 135
Assessment instruments, design of,
    293, 294